P9-CNB-184

THE DECAMERON

A NEW TRANSLATION

21 NOVELLE
CONTEMPORARY REACTIONS
MODERN CRITICISM

W. W. NORTON & COMPANY, INC.
also publishes

THE NORTON ANTHOLOGY OF AMERICAN LITERATURE
edited by Nina Baym et al.

THE NORTON ANTHOLOGY OF CONTEMPORARY FICTION
edited by R. V. Cassill

THE NORTON ANTHOLOGY OF ENGLISH LITERATURE
edited by M. H. Abrams et al.

THE NORTON ANTHOLOGY OF LITERATURE BY WOMEN
edited by Sandra M. Gilbert and Susan Gubar

THE NORTON ANTHOLOGY OF MODERN POETRY
edited by Richard Ellmann and Robert O'Clair

THE NORTON ANTHOLOGY OF POETRY
edited by Alexander W. Allison et al.

THE NORTON ANTHOLOGY OF SHORT FICTION
edited by R. V. Cassill

THE NORTON ANTHOLOGY OF WORLD MASTERPIECES
edited by Maynard Mack et al.

THE NORTON FACSIMILE OF
THE FIRST FOLIO OF SHAKESPEARE
prepared by Charlton Hinman

THE NORTON INTRODUCTION TO LITERATURE
edited by Carl E. Bain, Jerome Beaty, and J. Paul Hunter

THE NORTON INTRODUCTION TO THE SHORT NOVEL
edited by Jerome Beaty

THE NORTON READER
edited by Arthur M. Eastman et al.

THE NORTON SAMPLER
edited by Thomas Cooley

GIOVANNI BOCCACCIO

THE DECAMERON

A NEW TRANSLATION

21 NOVELLE
CONTEMPORARY REACTIONS
MODERN CRITICISM

Selected, Translated, and Edited by

MARK MUSA *and* PETER BONDANELLA

INDIANA UNIVERSITY

W · W · NORTON & COMPANY

New York · London

AUSTIN COMMUNITY COLLEGE
LEARNING RESOURCE SERVICES

Copyright © 1977 by W. W. Norton & Company, Inc.

Printed in the United States of America.
All Rights Reserved

W. W. Norton & Company, Inc., 500 Fifth Avenue, New York, NY 10110
W. W. Norton & Company Ltd., 10 Coptic Street London WC1A 1PU

Library of Congress Cataloging in Publication Data
Boccaccio, Giovanni, 1313–1375.
    The Decameron.
    (A Norton critical edition)
Translation of Decamerone.
    Bibliography: p.
    1. Musa, Mark, 1934.   II. Bondanella, Peter E., 1943–
III. Title.
PQ4272.E5A357 1977   853'.1   77–5664

4 5 6 7 8 9 0

ISBN 0-393-04458-0
ISBN 0-393-09132-5 pbk.

For
Chandler B. Beall
and
Charles S. Singleton

Contents

viii · *Contents*

Preface

The present edition of selections from Boccaccio's *Decameron* contains new translations of twenty-one tales, including representative *novelle* from each of the ten days of storytelling, as well as the Author's Introduction, the Prologue to the Fourth Day, and the Author's Conclusion, all in their entirety. The selection represents, we feel, the most important tales Boccaccio wrote, viewed from the standpoint of literary history and subsequent influence upon other European writers. In addition, these stories represent, in our opinion, the most interesting and innovative of the author's themes and are most representative of his narrative techniques. Any abridged translation of *The Decameron* which does not present all of Boccaccio's one hundred *novelle* cannot, of necessity, also include all the comments of the storytellers, since they often run from the end of one tale into the beginning of the next. It is our conviction that the stories the storytellers narrate, together with the major frame elements, provide sufficient information to the reader who is either reading the work in translation rather than the original Italian or studying only a part of this massive work in a literature or humanities class.

The critical material is of two kinds—contemporary reactions and modern criticism. The first includes important letters from Francesco Petrarca to Boccaccio, establishing the fact that Boccaccio experienced a religious crisis after *The Decameron* was completed; furthermore, Petrarca's letters reflect a typical early humanist reaction to any work written in the vulgar tongue, which other scholarly readers of Boccaccio's works—Leonardo Bruni, Filippo Villani, Giannozzo Manetti—continued in the fourteenth and fifteenth centuries. The last selection, by Ludovico Dolce, shows the changing critical perspective on *The Decameron* in the sixteenth century, as the early humanist preference for Boccaccio's Latin works was replaced by a new enthusiasm for *The Decameron* which led to its eventual elevation to the status of a classic and a model for much of later Italian prose.

The modern criticism includes a representative selection of past and current critical approaches to Boccaccio's *Decameron*. Some essays reflect important historical interpretations (Ugo Foscolo and Francesco De Sanctis). Others illustrate particular critical methods—the philological (Auerbach), the philosophical (Scaglione), the formalist (Clements), the structuralist (Todorov), the rhetorical (Booth), the archetypal (Cottino-Jones), and the historical (Bergin). Because of the growing interest in the relationship of film, literature, and narrative technique, a study of the most recent artistic reinterpretation of *The Decameron*, the film by Pier Paolo Pasolini, is included in this edition.

An abridged version of *The Decameron*, as this is, will no doubt disappoint some readers, for they may find their favorite stories have been omitted. These gentle readers are invited by the editors to turn to the bibliography of the present work for a complete translation in English of *The Decameron*, or, if they be so kind, let them wait as the editors bring to a close their task of a complete translation of *The Decameron.*, with a separate volume of aesthetic and historical notes.

Our very special thanks to Thomas G. Bergin, Sterling Professor (Emeritus), Yale University, and to John C. McGalliard, Professor of Comparative Medieval Literatures (Emeritus), University of Iowa.

MARK MUSA
PETER BONDANELLA

Indiana University

The Text of
The Decameron

Translators' Note

Fu, secondo che io già intesi, in Perugia un giovane il cui nome era Andreuccio di Pietro, cozzone di cavalli, il quale, avendo inteso che a Napoli era buon mercato di cavalli, mesisi in borsa cinquecento fiorin d'oro, non essendo mai più fuori di casa stato, con altri mercatanti là se n'andò; dove giunto una domenica sera in sul vespro, dall'oste suo informato, la seguente mattina fu in sul mercato, e molti ne vide ed assai ne gli piacquero e di più e più mercato tenne; né di niuno potendosi accordare, per mostrare che per comperar fosse, sí come rozzo e poco cauto, più volte in presenza di chi andava e di chi veniva trasse fuori questa sua borsa de' fiorini che aveva.

There once was in Perugia, according to what I have been told, a young man whose name was Andreuccio di Pietro, a dealer in horses, who, when he heard that in Naples horses were being sold at a low price, put five hundred gold florins in his purse, and, though he had never been outside of his town before, set out for Naples with some other merchants and arrived there on Sunday evening around vespers, and at the advice of his landlord, the following morning he went to the market place, where he saw many horses, a good number of which he liked, but he was not able to strike a bargain no matter how hard he tried; in fact, to show that he was really ready to do business, being the crass and incautious fool that he was, more than once, in the presence of whoever came and went by, he would pull out his purse full of florins.

Above is the opening sentence of the well-known *novella* of Andreuccio from Perugia (II, 5). We have cited both the original Italian text and our own version to illustrate the method we have generally followed in our translation of *The Decameron*. We have found that most translators will break this long, opening sentence into as many as four shorter ones. Boccaccio's prose, however, is a Ciceronian prose style full of ample and complicated periods where subordinate clauses abound and a conscious effort is made to use these complex elements for artistic effects. The transformation of this unique prose into a series of short, terse sentences reminiscent of the style of Ernest Hemingway destroys, in the case above, one of Boccaccio's main objectives: he is obviously attempting to suggest, through the syntax of the sentence, the entire complicated plot of the *novella* which follows. Furthermore, in terms of the story's content, Boccaccio has skillfully drawn our attention to the importance of the purse of florins (soon to be lost and eventually to be transformed into a ruby) by ending this lengthy sentence with a reference to "his purse full of florins." The reader cannot hope to appreciate fully this opening sentence until he has read the entire *novella*, but it is the duty of the faithful translator, we feel, to have the entire *novella* in mind before a single sentence is rendered into English. Besides remaining true to the syntax and the diction of Boccaccio's original, we have at all times tried to render this fourteenth-century masterpiece into an English which avoids the use of archaisms as a means of reproducing what is assumed to be a medieval "flavor" in a translation. Furthermore, the format of a critical edition with sufficient notes to the text has enabled us to avoid another common translator's temptation, that of expanding the original to include information needed to clarify a difficult or obscure meaning.

M. M., P. B.

The Structure of *The Decameron*

Author's Preface and Introduction: The narrator addresses his reader directly, explains the origins of his *novelle*, introduces his ten storytellers (Pampinea, Filomena, Neifile, Filostrato, Fiammetta, Elisa, Dioneo, Lauretta, Emilia, and Panfilo), and describes the Black Plague of 1348 in Florence. Each of the storytellers will tell a story on each of ten days of storytelling, and each storyteller (except Dioneo) must tell a story which follows a topic determined by the king or queen of the previous day. The entire collection contains 100 *novelle*.

Day I: Subjects freely chosen (the reign of Pampinea).

Day II: Stories about those who attain a state of unexpected happiness after a period of misfortune (the reign of Filomena).

Day III: Stories about people who have attained difficult goals or who have recovered something previously lost (the reign of Neifile).

Day IV, Prologue: The narrator defends himself from the criticism that greeted the stories of the first three days of storytelling.

Day IV: Love stories with unhappy endings (the reign of Filostrato).

Day V: Love stories which end happily after a period of misfortune (the reign of Fiammetta).

Day VI: Stories about how intelligence helps to avoid danger, ridicule, or discomfort (the reign of Elisa).

Day VII: Stories about tricks played by wives on their husbands (the reign of Dioneo).

Day VIII: Stories about tricks played by both men and women on each other (the reign of Lauretta).

Day IX: Subjects freely chosen (the reign of Emilia).

Day X: Stories about those who have performed generous deeds and who have acquired fame in so doing (the reign of Panfilo).

Author's Conclusion: The narrator defends the tone of his work against those critics who view it as obscene or others who claim the stories are sometimes too long, as well as against those who accuse him of slandering churchmen or betraying his scholarly inclinations by composing such a frivolous work as *The Decameron*.

Contents of *The Decameron*

Here begins the book called Decameron, *also known as Prince Gale-*
otto,[1] *in which one hundred tales are contained, told in ten days*
by seven women and three young men.

The Author's Preface

Human it is to have compassion for the unhappy, and a great deal
is required of those who are happy, especially if they required comfort in the past, and managed to find it in others. Now, if any man
ever had need of compassion or found it dear to him, or received
comfort from it, I am that man; for, from my earliest youth until
the present time, I have been inflamed beyond all measure with a
most exalted and noble love, perhaps too exalted and noble for my
lowly station. Although I was praised and more highly esteemed by
those who were discreet and who had some knowledge of this love,
nevertheless it was extremely difficult to bear: certainly not because
of the cruelty of the lady I loved but rather because of the over-
whelming fire kindled in my mind by my poorly restrained desire
which, since it would not allow me to rest content with any acceptable goal, often caused me to suffer more pain than was necessary.
In my suffering, the pleasing conversation and consolation of a
friend often gave me much relief, and I am firmly convinced I
should now be dead if it had not been for that. But since He who
is infinite has been pleased to decree by immutable law that all
earthly things should have an end, my love, more fervent than any
other, a love which no resolution or counsel or evident shame or
danger that might result from it could break or bend, in the course
of time diminished by itself, and at present it has left in my mind
only that pleasure which it usually retains for those who do not
venture too far out on its dark seas; and thus where there once used
to be a source of suffering, there now remains a sense of delight, for
every torment has been removed.

But while the pain has ceased, I have not lost the memory of
favors already received from those who were touched by my heavy
burdens; nor, I believe, will this memory ever pass, except with my
death. And because it is my feeling that gratitude, among the other
virtues, should be praised the most and its opposite condemned,
in order not to appear ungrateful, I have promised myself to employ my limited talents in doing what I can (now that I am able to

1. According to Arthurian legend and
medieval literary tradition, Galeotto
(Gallehault) acted as a go-between in
the love affair of Lancelot and Queen
Guinevere. Here, Boccaccio refers specifically to a line in Dante's *Inferno*
(Canto V, line 137) where a book described as the instigator of the fatal
love affair between Paolo and Francesca
(now damned to eternal punishment in
the realm of the lustful) is compared
to Galeotto's role in bringing Lancelot
and Guinevere together.

say that I am free of love) in exchange for what I received—if not to repay those who helped me (since their intelligence and their good fortune will perhaps make this unnecessary), then, at least, to assist those who may be in need of it. And however slight my support or comfort (if you wish) may be to those in need, nevertheless it seems to me that it should still be offered to those who are in most need of it, for it will be most useful and valuable to them.

And who will deny that such comfort, no matter how insufficient, is more fittingly bestowed on gracious ladies than on men? For they, in fear and shame, conceal the hidden flames of love within their delicate breasts, a love far stronger than one which is openly expressed, as those who have felt and suffered know; and besides this, restricted by the wishes, the pleasures, and the commands of fathers, mothers, brothers, and husbands, they remain most of the time enclosed in the confines of their bedrooms where they sit in almost complete idleness, now wishing one thing and now wishing another, turning over in their minds various thoughts which cannot always be pleasant ones. And because of these thoughts, if melancholy brought on by burning desire should arise in their minds, they will be forced to suffer this serious pain unless it be replaced by other thoughts. What's more, they are less able than men to bear these discomforts; this does not happen with men in love, as we can plainly see. If men are afflicted by melancholy or heavy thoughts, they have many ways of alleviating or forgetting them, for if they wish, they can go out and hear and see many things; they can go hawking, hunting, or fishing; they can ride, gamble, or attend to their trades. Each of these pursuits has the power, either completely or in part, to occupy a man's mind and to remove from it a painful thought, even if only for a brief moment; and so, in one way or another, either consolation follows or the pain becomes less. Therefore, I wish to make up in part for the wrong done by Fortune, who is less generous with her support where there is less strength, as we witness in the case of our delicate ladies. As support and comfort for those ladies in love (to those others who are not I leave the needle, spindle, and wool winder), I intend to tell one hundred stories, or fables, or parables, or histories, or whatever you wish to call them, as they were told in ten days (as will become quite evident), by a gracious band of seven ladies and three young men who came together during the time of the plague (which just recently took so many lives) and I shall also include several songs sung for their delight by these same ladies. In these stories will be seen delightful as well as sad examples of love and other adventures, of both modern and ancient times. The ladies, just mentioned, will read them and perhaps derive from the delightful things that happen in these tales both pleasure and useful counsel, inasmuch as they will recognize what should be avoided and what should be sought after. This, I believe, can only end in the soothing of their melancholy. And if this happens (and may God grant that it does), let them thank Love for it, who, in freeing me from his bonds, has given me the power to attend to their pleasure.

The Author's Introduction

Here begins the first day of The Decameron, *in which, after the author has explained why certain people (soon to be introduced) have gathered together to tell stories, they speak on any subject that pleases them most, under the direction of Pampinea.*

Whenever, gracious ladies, I consider how compassionate you are by nature, I realize that in your judgment the present work will seem to have had a serious and painful beginning, for it recalls in its opening the unhappy memory of the deadly plague just passed, dreadful and pitiful to all those who saw or heard about it. But I do not wish this to frighten you away from reading any further, as if you were going to pass all of your time sighing and weeping as you read. This horrible beginning will be like the ascent of a steep and rough mountainside, beyond which there lies a most beautiful and delightful plain, which seems more pleasurable to the climbers in proportion to the difficulty of their climb and their descent. And just as pain is the extreme limit of pleasure, so misery ends by unanticipated happiness. This brief pain (I say brief since it contains few words) will be quickly followed by the sweetness and the delight, which I promised you before, and which, had I not promised, might not be expected from such a beginning. To tell the truth, if I could have conveniently led you by any other way than this, which I know is a bitter one, I would have gladly done so; but since it is otherwise impossible to demonstrate how the stories you are about to read came to be told, I am almost obliged by necessity to write about it this way.

Let me say, then, that thirteen hundred and forty-eight years had already passed after the fruitful Incarnation of the Son of God when into the distinguished city of Florence, more noble than any other Italian city, there came the deadly pestilence. It started in the East, either because of the influence of heavenly bodies or because of God's just wrath as a punishment to mortals for our wicked deeds, and it killed an infinite number of people. Without pause it spread from one place and it stretched its miserable length over the West. And against this pestilence no human wisdom or foresight was of any avail; quantities of filth were removed from the city by officials charged with this task; the entry of any sick person into the city was prohibited; and many directives were issued concerning the maintenance of good health. Nor were the humble supplications, rendered not once but many times to God by pious people, through public processions or by other means, efficacious; for almost at the beginning of springtime of the year in question the plague began to show its sorrowful effects in an extraordinary manner. It did not act as it had done in the East, where bleeding from the nose was a manifest sign of inevitable death, but it began in both men and women with certain swellings either in the groin or under the armpits, some of which grew to the size of a normal apple and others to the size of an egg (more or less), and the people called them *gavoccioli*.[2] And from the two parts of the body already mentioned, within a brief space of time, the said deadly *gavoccioli* began to spread indiscriminately over every part of the body; and after this, the symptoms of the illness changed to black or livid spots appearing on the arms and thighs, and on every part of the body, some large ones and sometimes many little ones scattered all around. And just as the *gavoccioli* were originally, and still are, a very certain indication of impending death, in like manner these spots came to mean the same thing for whoever had them. Neither a doctor's advice nor the strength of medicine could do anything to cure this illness; on the contrary, either the nature of the illness was such that it afforded no cure, or else the doctors were so ignorant that they did not recognize its cause and, as a result, could not prescribe the proper remedy (in fact, the number of doctors, other than the well-trained, was increased by a large number of men and women who had never had any medical training); at any rate, few of the sick were ever cured, and almost all died after the third day of the appearance of the previously described symptoms (some sooner, others later), and most of them died without fever or any other side effects.

This pestilence was so powerful that it was communicated to the healthy by contact with the sick, the way a fire close to dry or oily things will set them aflame. And the evil of the plague went even further: not only did talking to or being around the sick bring infection and a common death, but also touching the clothes of the sick or anything touched or used by them seemed to communicate this very disease to the person involved. What I am about to say

2. *Gavoccioli*—or *bubboni*, in modern Italian—are called "buboes" in English, the source of the phrase "bubonic plague." The plague of 1348 is often known as the Black Plague because of the black spots Boccaccio describes. One of the most important casualties of this plague in literature was Laura, the woman who inspired the many sonnets and songs in the *Canzoniere* ("Songbook") by Boccaccio's friend and contemporary, Francesco Petrarca (1304–74). Both *The Decameron* and the *Canzoniere* deal with the experience of human love, and both are set against a stark background of plague, death, and earthly mutability.

is incredible to hear, and if I and others had not witnessed it with our own eyes, I should not dare believe it (let alone write about it), no matter how trustworthy a person I might have heard it from. Let me say, then, that the power of the plague described here was of such virulence in spreading from one person to another that not only did it pass from one man to the next, but, what's more, it was often transmitted from the garments of a sick or dead man to animals that not only became contaminated by the disease, but also died within a brief period of time. My own eyes, as I said earlier, witnessed such a thing one day: when the rags of a poor man who died of this disease were thrown into the public street, two pigs came upon them, as they are wont to do, and first with their snouts and then with their teeth they took the rags and shook them around; and within a short time, after a number of convulsions, both pigs fell dead upon the ill-fated rags, as if they had been poisoned. From these and many similar or worse occurrences there came about such fear and such fantastic notions among those who remained alive that almost all of them took a very cruel attitude in the matter; that is, they completely avoided the sick and their possessions; and in so doing, each one believed that he was protecting his good health.

There were some people who thought that living moderately and avoiding all superfluity might help a great deal in resisting this disease, and so, they gathered in small groups and lived entirely apart from everyone else. They shut themselves up in those houses where there were no sick people and where one could live well by eating the most delicate of foods and drinking the finest of wines (doing so always in moderation), allowing no one to speak about or listen to anything said about the sick and the dead outside; these people lived, spending their time with music and other pleasures that they could arrange. Others thought the opposite: they believed that drinking too much, enjoying life, going about singing and celebrating, satisfying in every way the appetites as best one could, laughing, and making light of everything that happened was the best medicine for such a disease; so they practiced to the fullest what they believed by going from one tavern to another all day and night, drinking to excess; and often they would make merry in private homes, doing everything that pleased or amused them the most. This they were able to do easily, for everyone felt he was doomed to die and, as a result, abandoned his property, so that most of the houses had become common property, and any stranger who came upon them used them as if he were their rightful owner. In addition to this bestial behavior, they always managed to avoid the sick as best they could. And in this great affliction and misery of our city the revered authority of the laws, both divine and human, had fallen and almost completely disappeared, for, like other men, the ministers and executors of the laws were either dead or sick or so short of help that it was impossible for them to fulfill their duties; as a result, everybody was free to do as he pleased.

Many others adopted a middle course between the two attitudes just described: neither did they restrict their food or drink so much as the first group nor did they fall into such dissoluteness and drunkenness as the second; rather, they satisfied their appetites to a moderate degree. They did not shut themselves up, but went around carrying in their hands flowers, or sweet-smelling herbs, or various kinds of spices; and often they would put these things to their noses, believing that such smells were a wonderful means of purifying the brain, for all the air seemed infected with the stench of dead bodies, sickness, and medicines.

Others were of a crueler opinion (though it was, perhaps, a safer one): they maintained that there was no better medicine against the plague than to flee from it; and convinced of this reasoning, not caring about anything but themselves, men and women in great numbers abandoned their city, their houses, their farms, their relatives, and their possessions and sought other places, and they went at least as far away as the Florentine countryside—as if the wrath of God could not pursue them with this pestilence wherever they went but would only strike those it found within the walls of the city! Or perhaps they thought that Florence's last hour had come and that no one in the city would remain alive.

And not all those who adopted these diverse opinions died, nor did they all escape with their lives; on the contrary, many of those who thought this way were falling sick everywhere, and since they had given, when they were healthy, the bad example of avoiding the sick, they, in turn, were abandoned and left to languish away without care. The fact was that one citizen avoided another, that almost no one cared for his neighbor, and that relatives rarely or hardly ever visited each other—they stayed far apart. This disaster had struck such fear into the hearts of men and women that brother abandoned brother, uncle abandoned nephew, sister left brother, and very often wife abandoned husband, and—even worse, almost unbelievable—fathers and mothers neglected to tend and care for their children, as if they were not their own.

Thus, for the countless multitude of men and women who fell sick, there remained no support except the charity of their friends (and these were few) or the avarice of servants, who worked for inflated salaries and indecent periods of time and who, in spite of this, were few and far between; and those few were men or women of little wit (most of them not trained for such service) who did little else but hand different things to the sick when requested to do so or watch over them while they died, and in this service, they very often lost their own lives and their profits. And since the sick were abandoned by their neighbors, their parents, and their friends and there was a scarcity of servants, a practice that was almost unheard of before spread through the city: when a woman fell sick, no matter how attractive or beautiful or noble she might be, she did not mind having a manservant (whoever he might be, no matter how young or old he was), and she had no shame whatsoever in revealing any part of her body to him—the way she would have done to a woman—when the necessity of her sickness required her to do so. This practice was, perhaps, in the days that followed the pestilence, the cause of looser morals in the women who survived the plague. And so, many people died who, by chance, might have survived if they had been attended to. Between the lack of competent attendants, which the sick were unable to obtain, and the violence of the pestilence, there were so many, many people who died in the city both day and night that it was incredible just to hear this described, not to mention seeing it! Therefore, out of sheer necessity, there arose among those who remained alive customs which were contrary to the established practices of the time.

It was the custom, as it is again today, for the women, relatives, and neighbors to gather together in the house of a dead person and there to mourn with the women who had been dearest to him; on the other hand, in front of the deceased's home, his male relatives would gather together with his male neighbors and other citizens, and the clergy also came (many of them, or sometimes just a few) depending upon the social class of the dead man. Then, upon the shoulders of his equals, he was carried to the church chosen by him before death with the funeral pomp of candles and chants. With the fury of the pestilence increasing, this custom, for the most part, died out and other practices took its place. And so, not only did people die without having a number of women around them, but there were many who passed away without even having a single witness present, and very few were granted the piteous laments and bitter tears of their relatives; on the contrary, most relatives were somewhere else, laughing, joking, and amusing themselves; even the women learned this practice too well, having put aside, for the most part, their womanly compassion for their own safety. Very few were the dead whose bodies were accompanied to the church by more than ten or twelve of their neighbors, and these dead bodies were not even carried on the shoulders of honored and reputable citizens but rather by gravediggers from the lower classes that were called *becchini*. Working for pay, they would pick up the bier and hurry it off, not to the church the dead man had chosen before his death but, in most cases, to the church closest by, accompanied by four or six churchmen with just a few candles, and often none at all. With the help of these *becchini*, the churchmen would place the body as fast as they could in whatever unoccupied grave they could find, without going to the trouble of saying long or solemn burial services.

The plight of the lower class and, perhaps, a large part of the middle class, was even more pathetic: most of them stayed in their homes or neighborhoods either because of their poverty or their hopes for remaining safe, and every day they fell sick by the thousands; and not having servants or attendants of any kind, they almost always died. Many ended their lives in the public streets, during the day or at night, while many others who died in their homes were discovered dead by their neighbors only by the smell of their decomposing bodies. The city was full of corpses. The dead were usually given the same treatment by their neighbors, who were moved more by the fear that the decomposing corpses would contaminate them than by any charity they might have felt towards the deceased: either by themselves or with the assistance of porters (when they were available), they would drag the corpse out of the home and place it in front of the doorstep where, usually in the morning, quantities of dead bodies could be seen by any passerby; then, they were laid out on biers, or for lack of biers, on a plank. Nor did a bier carry only one corpse; sometimes it was used for two or three at a time. More than once, a single bier would serve for a wife and husband, two or three brothers, a father or son, or other relatives, all at the same time. And countless times it happened that two priests, each with a cross, would be on their way to bury someone, when porters carrying three or four biers would just follow along behind them; and where these priests thought they had just one dead man to bury, they had, in fact, six or eight and sometimes more. Moreover, the dead were honored with no tears or candles or funeral mourners but worse: things had reached such a point that the people who died were cared for as we care for goats today. Thus, it became quite obvious that what the wise had not been able to endure with patience through the few calamities of everyday life now became a matter of indifference to even the most simple-minded people as a result of this colossal misfortune.

So many corpses would arrive in front of a church every day and at every hour that the amount of holy ground for burials was certainly insufficient for the ancient custom of giving each body its individual place; when all the graves were full, huge trenches were dug in all of the cemeteries of the churches and into them the new arrivals were dumped by the hundreds; and they were packed in there with dirt, one on top of another, like a ship's cargo, until the trench was filled.

But instead of going over every detail of the past miseries which befell our city, let me say that the same unfriendly weather there did not, because of this, spare the surrounding countryside any evil; there, not to speak of the towns which, on a smaller scale, were like the city, in the scattered villages and in the fields the poor, miserable peasants and their families, without any medical assistance or aid of servants, died on the roads and in their fields and in their homes, as many by day as by night, and they died not like men but more like wild animals. Because of this they, like the city dwellers, became careless in their ways and did not look after their possessions or their businesses; furthermore, when they saw that death was upon them, completely neglecting the future fruits of their past labors, their livestock, their property, they did their best to consume what they already had at hand. So, it came about that oxen, donkeys, sheep, pigs, chickens and even dogs, man's most faithful companion, were driven from their homes into the fields, where the wheat was left not only unharvested but also unreaped, and they were allowed to roam where they wished; and many of these animals, almost as if they were rational beings, returned at night to their homes without any guidance from a shepherd, satiated after a good day's meal.

Leaving the countryside and returning to the city, what more can one say, except that so great was the cruelty of Heaven, and, perhaps, also that of man, that from March to July of the same year, between the fury of the pestiferous sickness and the fact that many of the sick were badly treated or abandoned in need because of the fear that the healthy had, more than one hundred thousand human beings are believed to have lost their lives for certain inside the walls of the city of Florence whereas, before the deadly plague, one would not have estimated that there were actually that many people dwelling in that city.

Oh, how many great palaces, beautiful homes, and noble dwellings, once filled with families, gentlemen, and ladies, were now emptied, down to the last servant! How many notable families, vast domains, and famous fortunes remained without legitimate heir! How many valiant men, beautiful women, and charming young men, who might have been pronounced very healthy by Galen,[3] Hippocrates,[4] and Aesculapius [5] (not to mention lesser physicians), dined in the morning with their relatives, companions, and friends and then in the evening took supper with their ancestors in the other world!

Reflecting upon so many miseries makes me very sad; therefore, since I wish to pass over as many as I can, let me say that as our city was in this condition, almost emptied of inhabitants, it happened (as I heard it later from a person worthy of trust) that one Tuesday

3. Greek anatomist and physician (A.D. 130?–201?).

4. Greek physician (460?–377? B.C.), to whom the Hippocratic oath, administered to new physicians, is attributed.

5. The Roman god of medicine and healing, often identified with Asclepius, Apollo's son, who was the Greek god of medicine.

morning in the venerable church of Santa Maria Novella [6] there was hardly any congregation there to hear the holy services except for seven young women, all dressed in garments of mourning as the times demanded, each of whom was a friend, neighbor, or relative of the other, and none of whom had passed her twenty-eighth year, nor was any of them younger than eighteen; all were educated and of noble birth and beautiful to look at, well-mannered and gracefully modest. I would tell you their real names, if I did not have a good reason for not doing so, which is this: I do not wish any of them to be embarrassed in the future because of the things that they said to each other and what they listened to—all of which I shall later recount. Today the laws regarding pleasure are again strict, more so than at that time (for the reasons mentioned above when they were very lax), not only for women of their age but even for those who were older; nor would I wish to give an opportunity to the envious, who are always ready to attack every praiseworthy life, to diminish in any way with their indecent talk the dignity of these worthy ladies. But, so that you may understand clearly what each of them had to say, I intend to call them by names which are either completely or in part appropriate to their personalities. We shall call the first and the oldest Pampinea and the second Fiammetta, the third Filomena, and the fourth Emilia, and we shall name the fifth Lauretta and the sixth Neifile, and the last, not without reason, we shall call Elissa. [7] Not by prior agreement, but purely by chance, they gathered together in one part of the church and were seated almost in a circle, saying their rosaries; after many sighs, they began to discuss among themselves various matters concerning the nature of the times, and after a while, as the others fell silent, Pampinea began to speak in this manner:

"My dear ladies, you have often heard, as I have, how a proper use of one's reason does harm to no one. It is only natural for everyone born on this earth to aid, preserve, and defend his own life to the best of his ability; this is a right so taken for granted that it has, at times, permitted men to kill each other without blame in order to defend their own lives. And if the laws dealing with the welfare of every human being permit such a thing, how much more lawful, and with no harm to anyone, is it for us, or anyone else, to take all possible precautions to preserve our own

6. This church, called "novella" or "new" because it replaced a preexisting structure, was begun in 1279 and was completed by Jacopo Talenti in 1348. An excellent example of Italian Gothic style, it is also noted for the Renaissance façade grafted onto its exterior by Leon Battista Alberti in the fifteenth century and for frescoes in its interior chapels done by various artists.

7. The qualities usually associated by critics with these ladies are as follows: Pampinea (a wise and confident lady, often in love and the most mature of the group); Filomena (wise and discreet and full of desire); Elissa (very young and dominated by a violent passion); Neifile (also young but ingenuous); Emilia (in love with herself); Lauretta (a jealous lover); and Fiammetta (happy to love and to be loved but afraid that she will lose her love).

lives! When I consider what we have been doing this morning and in the past days and what we have spoken about, I understand, and you must understand too, that each one of us is afraid for her life; nor does this surprise me in the least—rather I am greatly amazed that since each of us has the natural feelings of a woman, we do not find some remedy for ourselves to cure what each one of us dreads. We live in the city, in my opinion, for no other reason than to bear witness to the number of dead bodies that are carried to burial, or to listen whether the friars (whose number has been reduced to almost nothing) chant their offices at the prescribed hours, or to demonstrate to anyone who comes here the quality and the quantity of our miseries by our garments of mourning. And if we leave the church, either we see dead or sick bodies being carried all about, or we see those who were once condemned to exile for their crimes by the authority of the public laws making sport of these laws, running about wildly through the city, because they know that the executors of these laws are either dead or dying; or we see the scum of our city, avid for our blood, who call themselves *becchini* and who ride about on horseback torturing us by deriding everything, making our losses more bitter with their disgusting songs. Nor do we hear anything but "So-and-so is dead," and "So-and-so is dying"; and if there were anyone left to mourn, we should hear nothing but piteous laments everywhere. I do not know if what happens to me also happens to you in your homes, but when I go home I find no one there except my maid, and I become so afraid that my hair stands on end, and wherever I go or sit in my house, I seem to see the shadows of those who have passed away, not with the faces that I remember, but with horrible expressions that terrify me. For these reasons, I am uncomfortable here, outside, and in my home, and the more so since it appears that no one like ourselves, who is well off and who has some other place to go, has remained here except us. And if there are any who remain, according to what I hear and see, they do whatever their hearts desire, making no distinction between what is proper and what is not, whether they are alone or with others, by day or by night; and not only laymen but also those who are cloistered in convents have broken their vows of obedience and have given themselves over to carnal pleasures, for they have made themselves believe that these things are permissible for them and are improper for others, and thinking that they will escape with their lives in this fashion, they have become wanton and dissolute.

"If this is the case, and plainly it is, what are we doing here? What are we waiting for? What are we dreaming about? Why are we slower to protect our health than all the rest of the citizens? Do we hold ourselves less dear than all the others? Or do we believe that our own lives are tied by stronger chains to our bodies than those of others and, therefore, that we need not worry about anything which might have the power to harm them? We are mistaken and deceived, and we are mad if we believe it. We shall have clear proof of this if we just call to mind how many young men and ladies have been struck down by this cruel pestilence. I do not know if you agree with me, but I think that, in order not to fall prey, out of laziness or presumption, to what we might well avoid, it might be a good idea for all of us to leave this city, just as many others before us have done and are still doing. Let us avoid like death itself the ugly examples of others, and go to live in a more dignified fashion in our country houses (of which we all have several) and there let us take what enjoyment, what happiness, and what pleasure we can, without going beyond the rules of reason in any way. There we can hear the birds sing, and we can see the hills and the pastures turning green, the wheat fields moving like the sea, and a thousand kinds of trees; and we shall be able to see the heavens more clearly which, though they still may be cruel, nonetheless will not deny to us their eternal beauties, which are much more pleasing to look at than the empty walls of our city. Besides all this, there in the country the air is much fresher, and the necessities for living in such times as these are plentiful there, and there are just fewer troubles in general; though the peasants are dying there even as the townspeople here, the displeasure is the less in that there are fewer houses and inhabitants than in the city. Here on the other hand, if I judge correctly, we would not be abandoning anyone; on the contrary, we can honestly say it is we ourselves that have been abandoned, for our loved ones are either dead or have fled and have left us alone in such affliction as though we did not belong to them. No reproach, therefore, can come to us if we follow this course of action, whereas sorrow, worry, and perhaps even death can come if we do not follow this course. So, whenever you like, I think it would be well to take our servants, have all our necessary things sent after us, and go from one place one day to another the next, enjoying what happiness and merriment these times permit; let us live in this manner (unless we are overtaken first by death) until we see what ending Heaven has reserved for these horrible times. And remember that it is no more forbidden for us to go away virtuously than it is for most other women to remain here dishonorably."

When they had listened to what Pampinea had said, the other women not only praised her advice but were so anxious to follow it that they had already begun discussing among themselves the details, as if they were going to leave that very instant. But Filomena, who was most discerning, said:

"Ladies, regardless of how convincing Pampinea's arguments are, that is no reason to rush into things, as you seem to wish to do.

Remember that we are all women, and any young girl can tell you that women do not know how to reason in a group when they are without the guidance of some man who knows how to control them. We are changeable, quarrelsome, suspicious, timid, and fear-ful, because of which I suspect that this company will soon break up without honor to any of us if we do not take a guide other than ourselves. We would do well to resolve this matter before we de-part."

Then Elissa said:

"Men are truly the leaders of women, and without their guid-ance, our actions rarely end successfully. But how are we to find any men? We all know that the majority of our relatives are dead and those who remain alive are scattered here and there in various groups, not knowing where we are (they, too, are fleeing precisely what we seek to avoid), and since taking up with strangers would be unbecoming to us, we must, if we wish to leave for the sake of our health, find a means of arranging it so that while going for our own pleasure and repose, no trouble or scandal follow us."

While the ladies were discussing this, three young men came into the church, none of whom was less than twenty-five years of age. Neither the perversity of the times nor the loss of friends or parents, nor fear for their own lives had been able to cool, much less extinguish, the love those lovers bore in their hearts. One of them was called Panfilo, another Filostrato, and the last Dioneo, each one very charming and well-bred; and in those turbulent times they sought their greatest consolation in the sight of the ladies they loved, all three of whom happened to be among the seven ladies previously mentioned, while the others were close relatives of one or the other of the three men. No sooner had they sighted the ladies than they were seen by them, whereupon Pampinea smiled and said:

"See how Fortune favors our plans and has provided us with these discreet and virtuous young men, who would gladly be our guides and servants if we do not hesitate to accept them for such service."

Then Neifile's face blushed out of embarrassment, for she was one of those who was loved by one of the young men, and she said:

"Pampinea, for the love of God, be careful what you say! I realize very well that nothing but good can be said of any of them, and I believe that they are capable of doing much more than that task and, likewise, that their good and worthy company would be fitting not only for us but for ladies much more beautiful and at-tractive than we are, but it is quite obvious that some of them are in love with some of us who are here present, and I fear that if we take them with us, slander and disapproval will follow, through no fault of ours or of theirs."

Then Filomena said:

"That does not matter at all; as long as I live with dignity and have no remorse of conscience about anything, let anyone who wishes say what he likes to the contrary: God and Truth will take up arms in my defense. Now, if they were just prepared to come with us, as Pampinea says, we could truly say that Fortune was favorable to our departure."

When the others heard her speak in such a manner, the argument was ended, and they all agreed that the young men should be called over, told about their intentions, and asked if they would be so kind as to accompany the ladies on such a journey . Without further discussion, then, Pampinea, who was related to one of the men, rose to her feet and made her way to where they stood gazing at the ladies, and she greeted them with a cheerful expression, outlined their plan to them, and begged them, in everyone's name, to keep them company in the spirit of pure and brotherly affection.

At first the young men thought they were being mocked, but when they saw that the lady was speaking seriously, they gladly consented; and in order to start without delay and put the plan into action, before leaving the church they agreed upon what preparations must be made for their departure. And when everything had been arranged and word had been sent on to the place they intended to go, the following morning (that is, Wednesday) at the break of dawn the ladies with some of their servants and the three young men with three of their servants left the city and set out on their way; they had traveled no further than two short miles when they arrived at the first stop they had agreed upon.

The place was somewhere on a little mountain, at some distance away from our roads, full of various shrubs and plants with rich, green foliage—most pleasant to look at; at the top there was a country mansion with a beautiful large inner courtyard with open collonades, halls, and bedrooms, all of them beautiful in themselves and decorated with cheerful and interesting paintings; it was surrounded by meadows and marvelous gardens, with wells of fresh water and cellars full of the most precious wines, the likes of which were more suitable for expert drinkers than for sober and dignified ladies. And the group discovered, to their delight, that the entire palace had been cleaned and the beds made in the bedchambers, and that fresh flowers and rushes had been strewn everywhere. Soon after they arrived and were resting, Dioneo, who was more attractive and wittier than either of the other young men, said:

"Ladies, more than our preparations, it was your intelligence that guided us here. I do not know what you intend to do with your thoughts, but I left mine inside the city walls when I passed through them in your company a little while ago; and so, you must either make up your minds to enjoy yourselves and laugh and sing with me (as much, let me say, as your dignity permits), or you must give me leave to return to my worries and to remain in our troubled city."

To this Pampinea, who had driven away her sad thoughts in the same way, replied happily:

"Dioneo, you speak very well: let us live happily, for after all it was unhappiness that made us flee the city. But when things are not organized they cannot long endure, and since I began the discussions which brought this fine company together, and since I desire the continuation of our happiness, I think it is necessary that we choose a leader from among us, whom we shall honor and obey as our superior and whose every thought shall be to keep us living happily. And in order that each one of us may feel the weight of this responsibility together with the pleasure of its authority, so that no one of us who has not experienced it can envy the others, let me say that both the weight and the honor should be granted to each one of us in turn for a day; the first will be chosen by election; the others that follow will be whomever he or she that will have the rule for that day chooses as the hour of vespers [8] approaches; this ruler, as long as his reign endures, will organize and arrange the place and the manner in which we will spend our time."

These words greatly pleased everyone, and they unanimously elected Pampinea queen for the first day; Filomena quickly ran to a laurel bush, whose leaves she had always heard were worthy of praise and bestowed great honor upon those crowned with them; she plucked several branches from it and wove them into a handsome garland of honor. And when it would be placed upon the head of any one of them, it was to be to all in the group a clear symbol of royal rule and authority over the rest of them for as long as their company stayed together.[9]

After she had been chosen queen, Pampinea ordered everyone to refrain from talking; then, she sent for the four servants of the ladies and for those of the three young men, and as they stood before her in silence, she said:

"Since I must set the first example for you all in order that it may be bettered and thus allow our company to live in order and

8. According to church practice, special forms of prayers were prescribed by canon law for recitation at specified times during the day. As a result, people often told the time according to these seven canonical hours: matins (dawn); prime (about 6:00 A.M.); tierce (the third hour after sunrise, about 9:00 A.M.); sext (noon); nones (the ninth hour after sunrise, or about 3:00 P.M.); vespers (late afternoon); and compline (in the evening just before retiring).
9. The leaves of the laurel bush were traditionally used in ancient times to fashion crowns or garlands not only for warriors and heroes but also for outstanding poets, musicians, and artists. Laura, the inspiration of Petrarca's *Canzoniere,* was so named because of her association with the laurel and, therefore, with excellence in poetry. Most medieval and Renaissance illustrations of the great Italian poets Dante, Petrarca, and Boccaccio picture them with such laurel crowns, implying that they have equaled and perhaps even excelled the poets of classical antiquity.

in pleasure, and without any shame, and so that it may last as long as we wish, I first appoint Parmeno, Dioneo's servant, as my steward, and I commit to his care and management all our household and everything which pertains to the services of the dining hall. I wish Sirisco, the servant of Panfilo, to act as our buyer and treasurer and follow the orders of Parmeno. Tindaro, who is in the service of Filostrato, shall wait on Filostrato and Dioneo and Panfilo in their bedchambers when the other two are occupied with their other duties and cannot do so. Misia, my servant, and Licisca, Filomena's, will be occupied in the kitchen and will prepare those dishes which are ordered by Parmeno. Chimera, Lauretta's servant, and Stratilia, Fiametta's servant, will take care of the bedchambers of the ladies and the cleaning of those places we use. And in general, we desire and command each of you, if you value our favor and good graces, to be sure—no matter where you go or come from, no matter what you hear or see—to bring us back nothing but pleasant news."

And when these orders, praised by all present, were delivered, Pampinea rose happily to her feet and said:

"Here there are gardens and meadows and many other pleasant places, which all of us can wander about in and enjoy as we like; but at the hour of tierce let everyone be here so that we can eat in the cool of the morning."

After the merry group had been given the new queen's permission, the young men, together with the beautiful ladies, set off slowly through a garden, discussing pleasant matters, making themselves beautiful garlands of various leaves and singing love songs. After the time granted them by the queen had elapsed, they returned home and found Parmeno busy carrying out the duties of his task; for as they entered a hall on the ground floor, they saw the tables set with the whitest of linens and with glasses that shone like silver and everything decorated with broom blossoms; then, they washed their hands and, at the queen's command, they all sat down in the places assigned them by Parmeno. The delicately cooked foods were brought in and very fine wines were served; the three servants in silence served the tables. Everyone was delighted to see everything so beautiful and well arranged, and they ate merrily and with pleasant conversation. Since all the ladies and young men knew how to dance (and some of them even knew how to play and sing very well), when the tables had been cleared, the queen ordered that instruments be brought, and on her command, Dioneo took a lute and Fiammetta a viola, and they began softly playing a dance tune. After the queen had sent the servants off to eat, she began to dance together with the other ladies and two of the young men; and when that was over, they all began to sing carefree and gay songs. In this manner they continued until the queen felt that it was time to retire; therefore, at the queen's request, the three young men went off to their chambers (which were separate from those of the ladies), where they found their beds prepared and the rooms as full of flowers as the halls; the ladies, too, discovered their chambers decorated in like fashion. Then they all undressed and fell asleep.

Not long after the hour of nones, the queen arose and had the other ladies and young men awakened, stating that too much sleep in the daytime was harmful; then they went out onto a lawn of thick, green grass, where no ray of the sun could penetrate; and there, with a gentle breeze caressing them, they all sat in a circle upon the green grass, as was the wish of their queen. Then she spoke to them in this manner:

"As you see, the sun is high, the heat is great, and nothing can be heard except the cicadas in the olive groves; therefore, to wander about at this hour would be, indeed, foolish. Here it is cool and fresh and, as you see, there are games and chessboards with which all of you can amuse yourselves to your liking. But if you take my advice in this matter, I suggest we spend this hot part of the day not in playing games (a pastime which of necessity disturbs the player who loses without providing much pleasure either for his opponents or for those who watch) but rather in telling stories, for this way one person, by telling a story, can provide amusement for the entire company. In the time it takes for the sun to set and the heat to become less oppressive, you will each have told a little story, and then we can go wherever we like to amuse ourselves; so, if what I say pleases you (and in this I am willing to follow your pleasure), then, let us do it; if not, then let everyone do as he pleases until the hour of vespers."

The entire group of men and women liked the idea of telling stories.

"Then," said the queen, "if this is your wish, for this first day I order each of you to tell a story about any subject he likes."

And turning to Panfilo, who sat on her right, she ordered him in a gracious manner to begin with one of his tales; whereupon, hearing her command, Panfilo, while everyone listened, began at once as follows:

First Day,
First Story

Ser Cepparello tricks a holy friar with a false confession and dies; although he was a most evil man during his lifetime, he is after death reputed to be a saint and is called Saint Ciappelletto.

Dearest Ladies, it is fitting that everything done by man should begin with the marvelous and holy name of Him who was the Creator of all things; therefore, since I am to be the first to start our storytelling, I intend to begin with one of his marvelous deeds, so that when we have heard about it, our faith in him will remain as firm as ever and his name be ever praised by us.

It is clear that since earthly things are all transitory and mortal, they are in themselves full of worries, anguish, and toil, and are subject to countless dangers which we, who live with them and are part of them, could neither bear nor defend ourselves from if strength and foresight were not granted to us by God's special grace. Nor should we believe that such special grace descends upon us and within us through any merit of our own, but rather it is sent by his own kindness and by the prayers of those who, like ourselves, were mortal and who have now become eternal and blessed with him, for they followed his will while they were alive. To these saints, as to advocates who from experience are aware of our weakness, we ourselves offer our prayers concerning those matters we deem desirable, because we are not brave enough to offer them to so great a judge directly. And yet in him we discern his generous mercy toward us, and since the human eye cannot gaze into the secrets of the divine mind in any way, it sometimes happens that, fooled by a false judgment, we choose as an advocate before his majesty one who is sentenced by him to eternal exile; nevertheless he, to whom nothing is hidden, pays more attention to the purity of the one who prays than to his ignorance or the damnation of his intercessor and answers those who pray to him just as if these advocates were blessed in his presence. All this will become most evident in the tale I am about to tell: I say evident, in accordance with the judgment of men and not that of God.

Now, there was a very rich man named Musciatto Franzesi; he was a famous merchant in France who had become a knight. He was obliged to come to Tuscany with Messer Charles Landless,[1]

---

1. Charles (1270–1325), count of Valois, Maine, and Anjou, and third son of Philip III, king of France. Upon the request of Pope Boniface VIII, Charles crossed the Alps in 1301 to assist Guelf forces in Italy. When his eldest son ascended the French throne in 1328, he became the founder of the royal house of Valois.

the brother of the King of France, who had been sent for and encouraged to come by Pope Boniface.[2] Musciatto found that his affairs, like those of most merchants, were so entangled in every which way that he could not easily or quickly liquidate them, and he decided to entrust them to various people, and he found a means of disposing of everything. Only one difficult thing remained to be done: to find a person capable of recovering certain loans made to several people in Burgundy. The reason for his hesitation was that he had been informed the Burgundians were a quarrelsome lot, of evil disposition, and disloyal; and he could not think of an equally evil man (in whom he could place his trust) who might be able to match their wickedness with his own. After thinking about this matter for a long time, he remembered a certain Ser Cepparello from Prato, who had often been a guest in his home in Paris. This person was short and he dressed very elegantly; and the French, who did not know the meaning of the word "Cepparello" (believing that it meant "chapelet," in their tongue "garland"), used to call him not Ciappello but Ciappelletto, since he was short; and as Ciappelletto he was known to everyone, and few knew him as Ser Cepparello.[3]

Ciappelletto was, by profession, a notary; he was very much ashamed when any of his legal documents (of which he drew up many) was discovered to be anything but fraudulent. He would have drawn up, free of charge, as many false ones as would have been requested of him, and more willingly than another man might have done for a large sum of money. He gave false testimony with the greatest of pleasure, whether he was asked to give it or not; and since in those days in France great faith was placed in such oaths, and since he did not mind taking a false oath, he won a great many lawsuits by his wickedness every time he was called upon to swear, upon his life, to tell the truth. He took special pleasure and went to a great deal of trouble to stir up scandal, mischief, and enmities between friends, relatives, and anyone else, and the more evil that resulted from it, the happier he was. If he were asked to be present at a murder or at any other evil affair, he went there very gladly, never refusing, and he frequently found himself happily wounding or killing men with his very own hands. He was a great blasphemer of God and the saints, losing his temper on the slightest occasion, as if he were the most irascible man alive. He never went to church, and he made fun of all the church's sacraments,

2. Benedetto Caetani (1235?–1303), elected to the papacy as Boniface VIII on December 24, 1294. Because of his reputation for corruption and simony, Dante provided a place for him in hell (*Inferno*, Canto XIX) even before he passed away.

3. Messer(e) is the equivalent of Sir, Mister, or Master. It is also frequently found in the shortened form of Ser, as in Ser Cepparello. A similar expression commonly used to address women of a certain position is Madonna, meaning "my lady," also found in the shortened form Mona.

using abominable language to revile them; on the other hand, he frequented taverns and other dens of iniquity with great pleasure. He was as fond of women as dogs are of a beating with a stick; he was, in fact, more fond of men, more so than any other degenerate. He could rob and steal with a conscience as clean as a holy man making an offering. He was such a great glutton and big drinker that it would oftentimes produce bad effects on him; he was a gambler who often used loaded dice. But why am I wasting so many words on him? He was probably the worst man that ever lived! His cunning, for a long time, had served the wealth and the authority of Messer Musciatto, on whose behalf he was often spared both by private individuals (against whom he often committed crimes) and by the courts (against whom he always did).

When this Ser Cepparello came to the mind of Messer Musciatto, who was well acquainted with his life, he decided that he was just the man to deal with the evil nature of the Burgundians; and after summoning him, he spoke to him as follows:

"Ser Ciappelletto, as you know, I am about to leave here for good, and since, among others, I have to deal with these tricky Burgundians, I know of no one more qualified than yourself to recover my money from them; and since you are doing nothing else at the moment, if you look after this matter for me, I shall gain the favor of the court for you and I shall give you a just portion of what you manage to recover."

Ser Ciappelletto, then unemployed and in short supply of worldly goods, saw refuge and support about to depart, and without further delay, constrained, as it were, by necessity, made up his mind and announced that he would be happy to go. After they had made their agreement, and Ser Ciappelletto had received the power of attorney and necessary letters of recommendation from the king, Messer Musciatto departed and Ciappelletto went to Burgundy where hardly a soul knew him: and there, in a kind and gentle manner, unlike his nature, he began to collect the debts and to do what he had been sent to do—it was almost as though he were saving all his anger for the conclusion of his visit. And while he was doing this, he was lodged in the home of two Florentine brothers who lent money there at usurious rates and who showed him great respect (out of their love for Messer Musciatto); during this time he fell ill. The two brothers had doctors and nurses brought in immediately to care for him, and they bought everything necessary to restore his health. But all help was useless, for the good man (according to what the doctors said) was already old and had lived a disordered life, and every day his condition went from bad to worse, like someone with a fatal illness. The brothers were very sorry about this, and one day, standing rather close to the bedchamber where Ser Ciappelletto lay ill, they began talking to each other:

"What are we going to do with him?" said one to the other. "We're in a fine fix on his account! Sending him away, as sick as he is, would be a great source of reproach for us and an obvious sign of little sense, since people have seen how we received him at first, and then how we had him cared for and treated so well; and now, what will they say if they see him, at the point of death, being thrown out of our house all of a sudden without having done anything to displease us? On the other hand, he has been such a wicked man that he does not wish to confess himself or to receive any of the church's sacraments; and if he dies without confession, no church will wish to receive his body, and he will be thrown into a ditch just like a dead dog. And suppose he does confess? His sins are so many and so horrible that the same thing will happen, since neither friar nor priest will be willing or able to absolve him, and so, without absolution, he will be thrown into a ditch just the same. And if this happens, the people of this city, who already speak badly of us because of our profession (which they consider iniquitous) and who wish to rob us, will rise up in a mob when they see this and cry out: 'These Lombard dogs are not accepted by the church; we won't put up with them any longer!' They will run to our house and rob us not only of our property but of our lives as well; in any case, we are in trouble if he dies."

Ser Ciappelletto, who as we said was lying near where they were talking, had sharp ears, as is often the case with the sick, and he heard what they said about him. He had them summoned and told them:

"I don't want you to be afraid of receiving any harm on my account; I heard what you said about me, and I am very sure that things would happen as you say they would if everything went as you think it might; but things will turn out differently. Since I have committed so many offenses against God during my lifetime, committing one more against him now will make no difference. So find me the most holy and worthy priest that you can (if such a one exists), and leave everything to me, for I guarantee you that I shall set both your affairs and mine in order in a way that will please you."

Although the two brothers did not feel very hopeful about this, they went, nevertheless, to a monastery of friars and asked for some holy and wise priest to hear the confession of a Lombard who was ill in their home; and they were given an old friar who was a good and holy man, an expert in the Scriptures, and a most venerable man, for whom all the citizens had a very great and special devotion; and they took him with them. When the friar reached the bedchamber where Ser Ciappelletto was lying, he sat down at his side; first, he began to comfort him kindly, and then he asked him how long it had been since his last confession. To this question, Ser

Ciappelletto, who had never in his life made a confession, replied:

"Father, I usually confess myself at least once a week, but there were many weeks that I confessed more often; and the truth is that since I have been ill—almost eight days now—I have not been to confession, so grave has been my illness."

Then the friar said:

"My son, you have done well, and you must continue to do so; and I see that since you have confessed so often, there will be little for me to ask or listen to."

Ser Ciappelletto replied:

"Father, don't say that; I have never confessed so many times or so often that I have not always wished to confess again all the sins I can remember from the day of my birth to the moment I am confessing; therefore, I beg you, my good father, that you ask me point by point about everything, as if I had never confessed before, and do not let my illness stand in your way, for I prefer to mortify this flesh of mine rather than, in treating it gently, to do something which might lead to the perdition of my soul which the Savior has redeemed with his precious blood."

These words pleased the holy man very much, and they seemed to him to be the sign of a well-disposed mind; and after he had commended Ser Ciappelletto highly for his practice, he began by asking him if he had ever sinned in lust with any woman. To this Ser Ciappelletto replied with a sigh:

"Father, on this account I am ashamed to tell you the truth for fear of sinning from pride."

To this the friar answered:

"Speak freely, for the truth was never a sin either in confession or elsewhere."

Then Ser Ciappelletto said:

"Since you assure me that this is the case, I shall tell you: I am as virgin today as when I came from my mother's womb."

"Oh, you are blessed by God!" said the friar, "how well you have done! And in so doing, you merit even more praise, for you have more freedom to do the contrary than we and others who are bound by religious rules have."

After this, he asked if he had displeased God through the sin of gluttony. To this, breathing a heavy sigh, Ser Ciappelletto replied that he had, and many times; for in addition to the periods of fasting which are observed during the year by the devout, he fasted every week for at least three days on bread and water, but he had drunk the water with the same delight and appetite as any great drinker of wine would—especially after he had worn himself out in prayer or in going on a pilgrimage; and he had often longed for those rough salads made of wild herbs such as women make when they are in the country, and on occasion eating had seemed better to him than it should have seemed to someone like himself who fasted out of religious devotion. To this the friar replied:

"My son, these sins are natural ones and are very minor; therefore, I do not want you to burden your conscience with them more than necessary. No matter how very holy he may be, every man thinks that eating after a long fast and drinking after hard work is good."

"Oh, father," said Ser Ciappelletto, "don't say this just to console me; as you well know, things done in God's service should be done completely and without any hesitation; whoever does otherwise, sins."

The friar, who was most pleased to hear this, said:

"I am happy that you feel this way, and your pure and good conscience pleases me very much. But tell me, have you ever committed the sin of avarice by coveting more than was proper or by keeping what you should not have kept?"

To this Ser Ciappelletto answered:

"Father, do not suspect me of this because I am in the home of these usurers. I have nothing whatsoever to do with their profession; on the contrary, I came here to admonish and chastise them and to save them from this abominable kind of profit taking, and I believe that I might have accomplished this if God had not struck me down in this manner. But you should know that my father left me a rich man, and when he died, I gave the larger part of his inheritance to charity; then, to sustain my life and to enable me to aid Christ's poor, I carried on my small business affairs, and in my work I did wish to make a profit, but I always divided these profits with God's poor, giving one half to them and keeping the other half for my own needs; and my creator has aided me so well in this regard that my business affairs have always prospered."

"Well done!" replied the friar, "but have you not often become angry?"

"Oh," said Ser Ciappelletto, "that I have, and often. And who could keep himself from doing so, seeing all around me, every day, men doing evil deeds, disobeying God's commandments, and not fearing his judgments? Many times there have been days I would have rather been dead than to live to see young men chasing after the vanities of this world and to hear them swear and perjure themselves, to see them going to taverns, not visiting the churches, and following the ways of the world rather than those of God."

Then the friar said:

"My son, this is righteous anger, and I can impose no penance upon you for that. But, by any chance, did your wrath ever lead you to commit murder or to vilify anyone or to do any other kind of injury?"

To this Ser Ciappelletto answered:

"Alas, father! How could you say such things and be a man of God? If I had even so much as thought about doing any of those things you mentioned, do you believe that God would have done so much for me? These things are for criminals and evil men, and every time I met such a man, I always said: 'Begone! And may God convert you!' "

Then the friar said:

"May God bless you, my son! Have you ever given false testimony against anyone, or spoken ill of anyone, or taken their property without their permission?"

"Yes, indeed," answered Ser Ciappelletto, "I have spoken ill of others, for I once had a neighbor who did nothing but beat his wife unjustly, and one time I spoke badly about him to his wife's relatives, such was the pity I had for that poor creature; only God can tell you how he beat her every time he had had too much to drink."

Then the friar said:

"Now, you tell me you have been a merchant. Have you ever tricked anyone, as merchants are wont to do?"

"Of course," replied Ser Ciappelletto, "but I do not know who he was; all I know is that he was a man who brought me money which he owed me for some cloth I sold him, and I put it in my strongbox without counting it; a month later I discovered that he had given me four pieces more than he owed me, and since I saved the money for more than a year in order to return it to him but did not see him again, I finally donated it to charity."

"That was a small matter," said the friar, "and you did well in doing what you did with it."

And besides this, the holy friar asked him about many other matters, always receiving from him similar replies. And as he was about to give him absolution, Ser Ciappelletto said:

"Father, there is another sin which I have not mentioned."

The friar asked him what it was, and he answered:

"I recall that one Saturday after the hour of nones, I had my servant sweep the house and did, therefore, not show the proper reverence for the holy sabbath."

"Oh," said the friar, "that is a minor matter, my son."

"No," replied Ser Ciappelletto, "don't call it a minor matter. Sunday can never be honored too much, for on that day our Savior rose from the dead."

Then the friar asked:

"What else have you done?"

"Father," replied Ser Ciappelletto, "one time without thinking I spat in the house of God."

The friar began to smile and said:

"My son, that is nothing to worry about; we priests, who are religious men, spit there all day long."

Then Ser Ciappelletto said:

"Then you do great harm, for no place should be kept as clean as a holy temple in which we give sacrifice to God."

And, in brief, he told the friar many things of this sort; and finally he began to sigh and then to weep loudly, which he was very good at doing whenever he wished. The holy friar asked:

"My son, what's the matter?"

Ser Ciappelletto replied:

"Alas, father, there is one remaining sin which I shall never confess, such is the shame I have of mentioning it, and every time I recall it, I cry as you see me doing now, and I feel sure that God will never have mercy on me for this."

Then the holy man said:

"Now there, my son, what's this you're saying? If all the sins which were ever committed by all men, or which will ever be committed as long as the world lasts, were all in one man, and he was as penitent and as contrite as I see you are, the kindness and mercy of God is so great that if he were to confess, God would freely forgive him of all those sins. Therefore, speak without fear."

Still crying loudly, Ser Ciappelletto said:

"Alas, father, mine is too great a sin, and I can hardly believe that God will forgive me unless your prayers are forthcoming."

To this the friar replied:

"Speak freely, for I promise to pray to God for you."

Ser Ciappelletto continued to cry without speaking, while the friar continued to exhort him to speak. But after Ser Ciappelletto had kept the friar in suspense with his extended weeping, he heaved a great sigh and said:

"Father, since you promise to pray to God on my behalf, I shall tell you: when I was a little boy, I cursed my mother one time."

And having said this, he began crying loudly again. The friar answered:

"Now there, my son, does this seem such a great sin to you? Oh! Men curse God all day, and he gladly forgives those who repent for having blasphemed against him; do you not believe that he will forgive you as well? Do not cry; take comfort, for he will surely forgive you with the contrition I see in you—even if you had been one of those who placed him upon the cross."

Then Ser Ciappelletto said:

"Alas, father! What are you saying? My sweet mother, who carried me in her womb nine months, day and night, and who took me in her arms more than a hundred times! Cursing her was too evil, and the sin was too great; and if you do not pray to God on my behalf, he will not forgive me."

When the friar saw that Ser Ciappelletto had nothing more to say, he absolved him and gave him his blessing, thinking him to be a most holy man, just as he fully believed everything Ser Ciappelletto had told him. And who would not have believed it, seeing a man at the point of death confess in such a way? And then, after all this, he said to him:

"Ser Ciappelletto, with the help of God you will soon be well; but if it happens that God calls your blessed and well-disposed soul to himself, would it please you to have your body buried in our monastery?"

To this Ser Ciappelletto answered:

"Yes, father. Nor would I desire to be anywhere else, since you have promised to pray to God for me; moreover, I have always had a special devotion for your order. Therefore, when you return to your monastery, I beg you to send me that most true body of Christ which you consecrate each morning upon the altar—although I am not worthy of it—so that I may, with your permission, partake of it, and afterwards may I receive Holy Extreme Unction, for if I have lived as a sinner, at least I shall die as a Christian."

The holy man said that he would be pleased to do this and that he had spoken well and that he would arrange it so that the Sacrament should be brought to him immediately, which it was. The two brothers, who had strongly suspected that Ser Ciappelletto would trick them, had placed themselves near a partition which divided the bedchamber where Ser Ciappelletto was lying from another room, and as they listened, they could easily overhear and understand everything Ser Ciappelletto said to the friar; and at times they had such a desire to break out laughing that they would often say to each other:

"What kind of man is this? Neither old age nor illness, nor fear of death (which is so close), nor fear of God (before whose judgment he must soon stand), have been able to turn him from his wickedness, or make him wish to die differently from the manner in which he has lived!"

But when they heard it announced that he would be received for burial in the church, they did not worry about anything else. Shortly afterwards, Ser Ciappelletto took communion, and growing worse, without remedy, he received Extreme Unction; and just after vespers on the same day during which he had made his good confession, he died. Whereupon the two brothers, using his own money, took all the necessary measures to bury him honorably, and they sent word to the friars' monastery for them to watch over the body during the evening, according to custom, and to come for it in the morning. The holy friar that had confessed him, hearing that he had passed away, went with the prior of the monastery and had the assembly bell rung, and to the assembled friars he described what a holy man Ser Ciappelletto had been—according to what he had been able to learn from his confession; and hoping that God might perform many miracles through him, he convinced his brothers that they ought to receive his body with the greatest reverence and devotion. The prior and all the other friars—all of them gullible—agreed to this, and in the evening, when they all went to where the body of Ser Ciappelletto was lying, they held a great and solemn vigil over it, and the following morning, chanting and all dressed in their vestments with their prayer books in hand, and preceded by their crosses, they sought his body out, and with the greatest ceremony and solemnity they carried it to their church, followed by almost all of the people in the city, both men and women; and when they had placed it in the church, the holy friar, who had confessed him, mounted the pulpit and began to preach marvelous things about him and his life, his fastings, his virginity, his simplicity, innocence, and holiness, recounting, among other things, what Ser Ciappelletto had tearfully confessed to him as his greatest sin, and describing to them how he was scarcely able to convince him that God might forgive him for it; from this he turned to reprove the people who were listening, and he said:

"And you, who are cursed by God, blaspheme against him, his Mother, and all the saints in paradise when a little blade of straw is caught under your feet!"

And besides this, he said a good deal more about his loyalty and his purity; in short, with his words, which were taken by the people of the countryside as absolute truth, he fixed Ser Ciappelletto so firmly in the minds and the devotions of all those who were present there that after the service was over, everyone pressed forward to kiss the hands and feet of the deceased, and all his garments were torn off his corpse, since anyone who could get a hold on a piece of them considered himself blessed. And it was necessary to keep his body there the entire day, so that all those who wished were able to look upon him. Then, the following night, he was honorably buried in a chapel within a marble tomb, and immediately, on the following morning, people began going there to light candles and to worship him and to make vows to him and to hang wax images as *ex votos*.[4] And meanwhile, the fame of his sanctity and the devotion in which he was held grew so much that no other saint received as many vows as he did from those poor people who found themselves in difficulty; and they called him and still continue to call him Saint Ciappelletto, and they claim that God has performed many miracles through him and continues to perform them to this day for anyone who seeks his intercession.

It was in this manner, then, that Ser Cepparello from Prato lived and died and became a saint, just as you have heard; nor do I wish to deny that it might be possible for him to be in the blessed

4. A votive offering, usually given or dedicated in fulfillment of a vow or pledge.

presence of God, since although his life was evil and sinful, he could have become so truly sorry at his last breath that God might well have had pity on him and received him into his kingdom; this is hidden from us, but from what is clear to us, I believe that he is, instead, in the hands of the Devil in hell rather than in paradise. And if this is the case, we can recognize the greatness of God's mercy towards us, who pays more attention to the purity of our faith than to our errors by granting our prayers in spite of the fact that we choose his enemy as our intercessor—fulfilling our requests to him just as if we had chosen a true saint as intermediary for his grace. And so, that we may be kept healthy and safe through the present adversity and in this joyful company by his grace, praising the name of Him who began our storytelling, let us hold him in reverence and commend ourselves to him when we are in need, being most certain that we shall be heard.

And here Panfilo fell silent.

First Day,
Second Story

A Jew named Abraham, encouraged by Giannotto di Civignì, goes to the court of Rome, and after observing the wickedness of the clergy, he returns to Paris and becomes a Christian.

Panfilo's story was praised in its entirety by the ladies and parts of it moved them to laughter; after all had listened carefully and it had come to an end, the queen ordered Neifile, who was sitting next to Panfilo, to continue the order of the entertainment thus begun with a story of her own. Neifile, who was endowed no less with courtly manners than with beauty, answered that she would gladly do so, and she began in this manner:

Panfilo has shown us in his storytelling that God's mercy overlooks our errors when they result from matters that we cannot fathom; in my own tale, I intend to show you how this same mercy patiently endures the faults of those who with their words and deeds ought to bear witness to this mercy and yet do the contrary; I shall show how it makes these things an argument of his infallible truth so that with firmer conviction we may practice what we believe.

I have heard it told, gracious ladies, that in Paris there once lived a great merchant and a good man by the name of Giannotto di Civignì, a most honest and upright man, who had a flourishing business in cloth; and he had a very close friend who was a rich

Jew named Abraham, also a merchant and an upright, trustworthy person. Giannotto, recognizing his friend's honesty and upright qualities, began to feel deep regret that the soul of such a valiant, wise, and good man through lack of faith would have to be lost to hell. Because of this he began to plead with him in a friendly fashion to abandon the errors of the Jewish faith and to turn to the Christian truth, which, as he said, his friend could see prospering and increasing continuously, for it was holy and good, while in contrast, he could observe his own Judaism growing weak and coming to nothing. The Jew replied that he believed no faith was holy or good except the Jewish faith and that since he had been born into it, he intended to live and die within it; nor could anything cause him to turn away from it. Giannotto did not, however, abstain on this account from addressing similar words to him some days later and from indicating to him in a clumsy way, as most merchants are wont to do, the reasons why our faith is better than the Jewish one. Although the Jew was a great master of Jewish law he nonetheless, moved by the great friendship he had for Giannotto or perhaps by the words which the Holy Spirit sometimes places in the mouth of an ignorant man, began to enjoy Giannotto's arguments very much; but he still remained fixed in his own beliefs and would not let himself be converted. And the more stubborn he remained, the more Giannotto continued to entreat him until the Jew, won over by such a continuous insistence, declared:

"Now see here, Giannotto, you want me to become a Christian, and I am willing to do so on one condition: first I want to go to Rome to observe the man you say is God's vicar on earth; I want to observe his ways and customs and also those of his brother cardinals; and if they seem to me to be such men that, between your words and their actions, I am able to comprehend that your faith is better than my own, just as you have worked to demonstrate it to me, I shall do what I told you; but if this is not the case, I shall remain the Jew that I am now."

When Giannotto heard this, he was extremely sad and he said to himself:

"I have wasted my time which I thought I had employed so well, believing that I might have converted him, but if he goes to the court of Rome and sees the wicked and filthy lives of the clergy, not only will he not become a Christian from a Jew, but if he were to have become a Christian before, he would, without a doubt, return to being a Jew."

So, turning to Abraham, he said:

"Listen, my friend, why do you want to go to all that trouble and expense to go from here to Rome? Not to mention the fact that for a rich man like yourself the trip is full of dangers both by sea and by land. Don't you believe you can find someone to baptize you right here? And should you have any doubts concerning the faith that I have explained to you, where would you find better teachers and wiser men capable of clarifying whatever you wish to ask about than right here? For these reasons, in my opinion, your journey is unnecessary. Remember that the priests there are just like those we have here, except for the fact that they are better insofar as they are nearer to the chief shepherd; therefore, you can save this journey for another time, for a pilgrimage to forgive your sins, and I may, perhaps, accompany you."

To this the Jew replied:

"I am convinced, Giannotto, that things are as you have told me, but to be brief about it, if you want me to do what you have begged me so often to do, I am determined to go there—otherwise I shall do nothing about the matter."

When Giannotto saw his friend's determination he said: "Go, then, with my blessing!"—and he thought to himself that he would never become a Christian once he saw the court of Rome; but, since it would make little difference one way or the other, he stopped insisting. The Jew mounted his horse and set out as quickly as he could for the court of Rome, and upon his arrival, he was received with honor by his Jewish friends. While he was living there, without telling anyone why he had come, the Jew began carefully to observe the behavior of the Pope, the cardinals, and the other prelates and courtiers; and from what he heard and saw for himself—he was a very perceptive man—from the highest to the lowest of them, they all in general shamelessly participated in the sin of lust, not only the natural kind of lust but also the sodomitic, without the least bit of remorse or shame. And this they did to the extent that the power of whores and young boys was of no little importance in obtaining great favors. Besides this, he observed that all of them were open gluttons, drinkers, and sots, and that after their lechery, just like animals, they were more servants of their bellies than of anything else; the more closely he observed them, the more he saw that they were all avaricious and greedy for money and that they were just as likely to buy and sell human (even Christian) blood as they were to sell religious objects, belonging to the sacraments or to benefices, and in this kind of business, they carried on more trade and had more brokers than there were engaged in the textile or other business in Paris; they called their obvious simony "mediation" and their gluttony "maintenance," as if God did not know the intention of these wicked minds (not to mention the meaning of their words), that he might allow himself to be fooled like men by the names things bear. These, along with many other matters best left unmentioned, so displeased the Jew (for he was a sober and upright man) that he felt he had seen enough and decided to return to Paris, and so he did. When Gian-notto learned that he had returned, the last thing he thought about was his conversion, and he went to his friend and together, they celebrated his return; then, when he had rested for a few days, Giannotto asked his friend what he thought of the Holy Father and the cardinals and the other courtiers. To his question the Jew promptly replied:

"I don't like them a bit, and may God condemn them all; and I tell you this because as far as I was able to determine, I saw there no holiness, no devotion, no good work or exemplary life or any-thing else among the clergy; instead, lust, avarice, gluttony, fraud, envy, pride, and the like and even worse (if worse than this is pos-sible) so totally ruled there that I consider that city more as a forge for diabolic works than for divine ones: in my opinion, that Shep-herd of yours (and as a result, all of the others as well) are attempt-ing with all haste and talent and skill to reduce the Christian religion to nothing and drive it from the face of the earth when they really should act as its support and foundation. And since I have observed that in spite of all this, they do not succeed but, on the contrary, that your religion continuously grows and becomes brighter and more illustrious, I am justly of the opinion that it has the Holy Spirit as its foundation and support, as it is truer and holier than any other religion; therefore, although I once was adamant and unheeding to your pleas and did not want to become a Christian, now I tell you most frankly that I would not allow anything to prevent me from becoming a Christian. So, let us go to church, and there, according to the custom of your holy faith, I will be baptized."

Giannotto, who had expected his friend to say exactly the oppo-site, was the happiest man there ever was when he heard the Jew speak as he did; and then he accompanied him to Notre Dame, and asked the clergy there to baptize Abraham. At his request, they did so immediately, and Giannotto raised him from the baptismal font and renamed him Giovanni, and immediately afterwards he had him thoroughly instructed in our faith by the most distinguished teachers. He learned quickly and became a good and worthy man who lived a holy life.

First Day, Third Story

Melchisedech, a Jew, by means of a short story about three rings, escapes from a trap set for him by Saladin.

Neifile's tale was praised by all, and when she had finished talking, at the queen's command, Filomena began to speak in this fashion.

The tale that Neifile told brings back to my memory a dangerous incident that once happened to a Jew; and since God and the truth of our faith have already been well dealt with by us, we should not be forbidden to descend to the acts of men from now on. Now, I shall tell you this story and when you have heard it, perhaps you will become more cautious when you reply to questions put to you.

You should know, my dear companions, that just as stupidity can often remove one from a state of happiness and place him in the greatest misery, so, too, intelligence can rescue the wise man from the gravest of dangers and restore him to his secure state. The fact that stupidity leads one from a state of happiness to one of misery is shown by many examples which, at present, I do not intend to relate, since thousands of clear illustrations of this appear every day; but, as I promised, I shall demonstrate briefly in a little story how intelligence may be the cause of some consolation.

Saladin, whose worth was such that from humble beginnings he became Sultan of Babylon and won many victories over Christian and Saracen kings, discovered one day that he had consumed, in his various wars and his displays of grandiose magnificence, all his treasury, while the occasion arose in which he needed a large amount of money. Not being able to envision a means of obtaining what he needed in a short time, he happened to recall a rich Jew, whose name was Melchisedech, who loaned money at usurious rates in Alexandria, and he thought that this man might be able to assist him, if only he would agree to. But this Jew was so avaricious that he would not do so of his own free will, and the Sultan did not wish to have recourse to force; therefore, as his need was pressing, he thought of nothing but finding a means of getting the Jew to help him, and he decided to use some colorful pretext to accomplish this. He had him summoned, and after welcoming him in a friendly manner, he had him sit beside him and said to him:

"Worthy man, I have heard from many people that you are very wise and most versed in the affairs of God; because of this, I should like to know from you which of the three Laws you believe to be the true one: the Jewish, the Saracen, or the Christian."

The Jew, who really was a wise man, realized too well that Saladin was trying to catch him with his words in order to accuse him of something, and he understood that he could not praise any of the three Laws more than the other without Saladin achieving his goal; therefore, he sharpened his wits, like one who seems to need an answer in order not to be entrapped, and knew well what he had to say before he had to, and said:

"My Lord, the question which you have put to me is a good one, and in order to give you an answer, I shall have to tell you a little story which you shall now hear. If I am not mistaken, I remember having heard many times that there once was a great and wealthy man who had a most beautiful and precious ring among the many precious jewels in his treasury. Because of its worth and its beauty, he wanted to honor it by bequeathing it to his descendants forever, and he ordered that whichever of his sons would be found in possession of this ring, which he would have left him, should be honored and revered as his true heir and head of the family by all the others. The man to whom he left the ring did the same as his predecessor had, having left behind the same instructions to his descendants; in short, this ring went from hand to hand through many generations, and finally it came into the hands of a man who had three handsome and virtuous sons, all of whom were obedient to their father, and for this reason, all three were equally loved by him. Since the father was growing old and they knew about the tradition of the ring, each of the three men was anxious to be the most honored among his sons, and each one, as best he knew how, begged the father to leave the ring to him when he died. The worthy man, who loved them all equally, did not know himself which of the three he would choose to leave the ring, and since he had promised it to each of them, he decided to try and satisfy all three: he had a good jeweler secretly make two more rings which were so much like the first one that he himself, who had had them made, hardly could tell which was the real one. When the father was dying, he gave a ring to each of his sons in secret, and after he died each son claimed the inheritance and position and one son denied the claims of the other, each bringing forth his ring to prove his case; when they discovered the rings were so much alike that they could not recognize the true one, they put aside the question of who the true heir was and left it undecided as it is to this day.

"And let me say the same thing to you, my lord, concerning the three Laws given to three peoples by God our Father which are the subject of the question you posed to me: each believes itself to be the true heir, to possess the true Law, and to follow the true commandments, but whoever is right, just as in the case of the rings, is still undecided."

Saladin realized how the man had most cleverly avoided the trap which he had set to snare him, and for that reason he decided to make his needs known openly to him and to see if he might wish to help him; and he did so, revealing to him what he had in mind to do if the Jew had not replied to his question as discreetly as he had. The Jew willingly gave Saladin as much money as he desired, and Saladin later repaid him in full; in fact, he more than repaid him: he gave him great gifts and always esteemed him as his friend and kept him near him at court in a grand and honorable fashion.

First Day,
Fourth Story

A monk, having committed a sin deserving of the most severe punishment, saves himself by accusing his abbot of the same sin, and thus escapes punishment.

Having completed her story, Filomena fell silent and Dioneo, who was sitting close to her, without awaiting any further order from the queen (for he realized by the order already begun that he was the next to speak), began to speak in the following manner:

Lovely ladies, if I have understood your intention correctly, we are here in order to amuse ourselves by telling stories, and therefore, as long as we do nothing contrary to this, I think that each one of us ought to be permitted (and just a moment ago our queen said that we might) to tell whatever story he thinks is likely to be the most amusing. Therefore, having heard how the good advice of Giannotto di Civignì saved Abraham's soul and how Melchisedech defended his riches against the schemes of Saladin, without any fear of disapproval from you, I am going to tell you briefly how cleverly a monk saved his body from a most severe punishment.

In Lunigiana, a town not too far from here, there was a monastery (once more saintly and full of monks than it now is), in which there lived a young monk whose virility and youth could not be lessened by fasts or by vigils. One day around noon while the other monks were sleeping, he happened to be taking a solitary walk around the church—which was somewhat isolated—when he spotted a very beautiful young girl (perhaps the daughter of one of the local workers) who was going through the fields gathering various kinds of herbs. The moment he saw her, he was passionately attacked by carnal desire.

He went up to her and began a conversation. One subject led to another, and finally, they came to an understanding; he took the girl to his cell without anyone noticing them. His excessive desire got the better of him while he was playing with the girl, and it happened that the abbot, who had just got up from his nap, was passing quietly by the monk's cell when he heard the commotion the pair were making. So that he might better recognize the voices, he silently edged up to the entrance of the cell to listen—it was clear to him that there was a woman inside. At first he was tempted to have them open the door, but then he thought of using a different tactic; so he returned to his room and waited for the monk to come out.

Although he was, to his great pleasure and delight, quite occupied with this young lady, the monk, nevertheless, did suspect that something was up, for he thought he had heard some footsteps in the corridor; in fact, he had peeked out a small opening and had clearly seen the abbot standing there and listening: he was well aware the abbot must have realized that the young girl was in his cell, and knowing that he would be severely punished, he was extremely troubled; but without revealing his anxiety to the girl, he immediately began to think of a number of alternative plans, in an attempt to come up with one which might save him. He hit upon an original solution which would achieve the exact end he had in mind; and pretending that he felt they had stayed together long enough, he said to the girl:

"I have to go and find a way for you to leave without being seen, so stay here until I come back."

Having left the room and locked it with his key, he went immediately to the abbot's room (as every monk must do before leaving the monastery) and with a straight face he said:

"Sir, this morning I could not get in all of the firewood that I had cut for me; with your permission, I should like to go to the forest to have it brought in."

The abbot, thinking that the monk did not know he had been observed by him, was happy at this turn of events, and since this offered him the opportunity to get more firsthand information on the sin committed by the monk, he gladly took the monk's key and gave him permission to leave. And when he saw him go off, he began to plan what he would do first: either to open the monk's cell in the presence of all the monks in order to have them see what the sin was—and in doing so he would prevent grumbling when he punished the monk—or to hear first from the girl how the affair had started. But then thinking that she might very well be the wife or the daughter of some person of importance and, not wanting to shame such a person in front of all his monks, he decided first to see who the girl was and then to make his decision. And so he quietly went to the cell, opened it, entered the room, and closed the door.

When the young girl saw the abbot come in, she became frightened and began to cry out of shame. Master Abbot gave her a quick look and found her to be beautiful and fresh, and although he was old, he immediately felt the warm desires of the flesh, which were no less demanding than those the young monk had felt, and he thought to himself:

"Well, now! Why shouldn't I have a little fun when I can get it? Troubles and worries I can get every day! This is a pretty young girl, and no one knows she's here. If I can persuade her to fulfill my desires, I don't see any reason why I shouldn't. Who will be the wiser? No one will ever know, and a sin that's hidden is half forgiven! This opportunity may never present itself again. I believe it is a sign of great intelligence for a man to profit from what God sends others."

Having thought all this and having completely changed the purpose of his visit, he drew nearer to the girl and gently began to comfort her, begging her not to cry; and, as one thing will lead to another, he eventually explained to her what he desired.

The young girl, who was by no means as hard as iron or diamond, most willingly agreed to the abbot's wishes. He took her in his arms and kissed her many times, then lay down on the monk's bed. And perhaps out of concern for the heavy weight of his dignified person and the tender age of the young girl (or perhaps just because he was afraid to lay too much weight on her) he did not lie on top of her but rather placed her on top of him, and there he amused himself with her for quite a while.

Meanwhile, pretending to have gone into the woods, the monk had concealed himself in the dormitory; when he saw the abbot enter his cell alone, he was reassured that his plan would be successful. And when he saw the abbot lock himself inside, he knew it for certain. Leaving his hiding place, he quietly crept up to an opening through which he could see and hear everything the abbot did and said.

When the abbot decided that he had stayed long enough with the girl, he locked her in the cell and returned to his own room. And after a while, hearing the monk returning and believing that he had come back from the woods, he decided that it was time for him to reprimand him severely—he would have him locked up in prison in order to enjoy by himself the spoils they had both gained. He had him summoned, and he reproached him very severely, and with a stern face he ordered that he be put into prison.

The monk promptly replied:

"But messer, I have not been a member of the Order of Saint Benedict long enough to have had the opportunity to learn every detail of the order's rules. And up until just a moment ago, you never showed me how monks were supposed to support the weight of women as well as fasts and vigils. But now that you have shown me how, I promise you that if you forgive me this time, I shall sin no more in this respect; on the contrary, I shall always behave as I have seen you behave."

The abbot, who was a clever man, realized immediately that the monk had outsmarted him: he had been witness to what he had done; because of this, and feeling remorse for his own sin, he was ashamed of inflicting upon the monk the same punishment that he himself deserved. And so he pardoned him and made him promise never to reveal what he had seen. They quickly got the young girl out of the monastery, and as one might well imagine, they often had her brought back in again.

* * *

Second Day, Fifth Story

Andreuccio from Perugia, having gone to Naples to buy horses, is caught up in three unfortunate adventures in one night; escaping from them all, he returns home with a ruby.

* * *

There once was in Perugia, according to what I have been told, a young man whose name was Andreuccio di Pietro, a dealer in horses, who, when he heard that in Naples horses were being sold at a low price, put five hundred gold florins in his purse, and, though he had never been outside of his town before, set out for Naples with some other merchants and arrived there on Sunday evening around vespers, and at the advice of his landlord, the following morning he went to the market place, where he saw many horses, a good number of which he liked, but he was not able to strike a bargain no matter how hard he tried; in fact, to show that he was really ready to do business, being the crass and incautious fool that he was, more than once, in the presence of whoever came and went by, he would pull out his purse full of florins. While he was in the midst of these dealings, with his purse on full display, a young and very beautiful Sicilian lady—one who, for a small price, would be happy to please any man—passed close to him, and without being seen by him, she caught a glimpse of his purse and immediately said to herself:

"Who would be better off than I if that money were mine?"— and she walked on.

There was with this young lady an old woman, also Sicilian, who, when she saw Andreuccio, let her young companion walk ahead while she ran up to him and embraced him affectionately; when the young girl saw this, she said nothing, and waited nearby for her companion. Andreuccio turned around, recognized the old woman and greeted her with a great deal of pleasure, and after she had promised to visit him at his inn, they parted company without further conversation, and Andreuccio returned to his bargaining; but he bought nothing that morning.

The young woman, who had first seen Andreuccio's purse and then his familiarity with her older companion, cautiously began to ask who that man was and where he came from and what he was doing there and how her friend knew him, in order to try and see if she could find a way of getting that money of his—if not all of it, at least some of it. The old woman told her everything about Andreuccio almost as well as he himself might have done, for she had lived a long time in Sicily and then in Perugia with Andreuccio's father; she also told her where he was staying and why he had come. Once the young woman was completely informed about his relatives and their names, she devised a cunning trick, based on what she had learned, to satisfy her desires. As soon as she returned home, she sent the old woman on errands for the entire day so that she would not be able to return to Andreuccio; then, around vespers, she sent one of her young servant girls, whom she had well trained for such missions, to the inn where Andreuccio was staying. Arriving there, the servant girl found Andreuccio by chance alone at the door, and she asked him about Andreuccio's whereabouts; when he told her he was standing before her, drawing him aside, she said:

"Sir, a gentle lady who lives in this city would like to speak to you at your leisure."

When Andreuccio heard this, he immediately assumed, for he considered himself a handsome young man, that such a woman as that must be in love with him (as if no man as handsome as he could be found in all of Naples), and he replied immediately that he was ready and asked her where and when this lady wished to speak to him. To this, the young servant girl answered:

"Sir, whenever you wish to come, she awaits you at her home."

Quickly, and without mentioning anything to anyone at the inn, Andreuccio replied:

"Let's go, then, you lead the way; I'll follow you."

Whereupon the servant girl led him to her house which was in a district called the Malpertugio, which was as respectable a district as its own name implies.[5] But Andreuccio knew or suspected nothing, believing he was going to a most respectable place and to the house of a respectable woman, and so he calmly followed the servant girl into the house. Climbing up the stairs, the servant girl called to her mistress: "Here's Andreuccio!" and he saw her appear at the head of the stairs to greet him.

5. This ill-famed district of Naples actually existed in Boccaccio's day, and its name might best be rendered into English as "Evilhole."

She was still very young, tall, with a very beautiful face, and elegantly dressed and adorned. Andreuccio started toward her, and she descended three steps to greet him with open arms, and throwing her arms around his neck, she remained in that position for a while without saying a word—as if some overpowering emotion had stolen her words—then she started crying and kissing his forehead, and with a broken voice she said:

"Oh my Andreuccio, what a pleasure to welcome you!"

Andreuccio, amazed at such tender greetings, and completely astonished, replied:

"My lady, the pleasure is mine!"

Then, she took his hand and led him through her sitting room, and from there, without saying a word, into her bedchamber, which was all scented with roses, orange blossoms, and other fragrances; and he saw there a most beautiful curtained bed, and many dresses hanging on pegs (as was the custom there), and other very beautiful and expensive things. And, since all those lovely things were new to him, Andreuccio was convinced that she had to be nothing less than a great lady. They sat together on a chest at the foot of her bed, and she began speaking to him:

"Andreuccio, I am quite sure that you are amazed at my tears and caresses, for perhaps you do not know me or do not remember hearing of me; but you are about to hear something that will amaze you even more: I am your sister! And, now that God has granted me the favor of seeing one of my brothers before I die (Oh, how I wish I could see them all!), I assure you I shall pass away content. Since you know nothing about this, I shall tell you. Pietro, your father and mine, as I think you probably know, resided for a long time in Palermo, and because of his kindness and friendliness, he was dearly loved and still is loved by those who knew him; but among those who loved him very much, my mother, who was a lady of noble birth and then a widow, was the one who loved him the most, so much so that she put aside the fear of her father and brothers and her own honor and lived with him in so intimate a way that I was born, and here I am as you see me. Then when Pietro had to leave Palermo and return to Perugia, he left me, a tiny child, with my mother, and as far as I know, he never thought of me or my mother again: if he were not my father, I would criticize him severely for his ingratitude towards my mother (to say nothing of the love he owed me, his daughter, not born from any servant girl or from some woman of low birth), who had put herself, as well as her possessions, into his hands, moved by a true love for a man she did not really know.

"But what does it matter? Things done badly in the past are more easily criticized than amended—that's how it all ended. He abandoned me as a little girl in Palermo where, grown up almost as much as I am now, my mother, who was a rich lady, gave me as a wife to a rich man of noble birth from Agrigento who, out of his love for me and my mother, came to live in Palermo: and there, as he was an avid supporter of the Guelfs, he began to carry on some kind of intrigue with our King Charles.[6] But King Frederick [7] discovered the plot before it could be put into effect, and this was the cause of our fleeing from Sicily—and just when I was about to become the greatest lady ever to be on that island. Taking with us those few things we could (I say "few" as compared to the many things we owned), we abandoned our lands and palaces and took refuge in this land, where we found King Charles so grateful to us that he restored in part the losses which we had suffered on his account, and he gave us property and houses, and he continues to provide my husband, who is your brother-in-law, with a good salary, as you can see for yourself; and so, my sweet brother, here I am, and with no thanks to you but rather through the mercy of God I have come to meet you."

And when she had said all this, she embraced him once more, and continuing to weep tenderly, she kissed his forehead. Hearing this fable so carefully and skillfully told by the young lady who never hesitated over a word or fumbled in any way, Andreuccio recalled that it was indeed true that his father had been in Palermo, and since he himself knew the ways of young men who easily fall in love when they are young and since he had just witnessed the piteous tears, the embraces, and the pure kisses of this young lady, he took everything she said to be the absolute truth; and, when she had finished speaking, he said:

"My lady, it should not be surprising to you if I am amazed; for to tell the truth, either my father never spoke of you and your mother, or, if he did, I never heard a word about it, for I had no more knowledge of you than if you never existed; but I am all the more delighted to have found a sister, for I am completely alone here, and I never hoped for such a thing, and, truly, I don't know of any man of whatever rank or station to whom you would not be very dear, not to mention an insignificant merchant like me. But I beg you to clarify one thing for me: how did you know I was here?"

To this she answered:

"I was told about it this morning by a poor woman whom I often see, and according to her story, she was with our father for a

6. A reference to Charles of Anjou, King of Naples from 1285 until 1309. The ruling family to which he belonged lost Sicily during the popular uprising known as the Sicilian Vespers, in 1282.
7. King Frederick II of Aragon, king of Sicily from 1296 until 1337.

long time both in Palermo and in Perugia; and if it were not for the fact that it seemed to me more proper for you to come to my house than for me to visit you in a stranger's house, I would have come to see you much sooner."

Then, she began to ask about all his relatives individually by name, and Andreuccio replied to all her questions about them; and her questions made him believe even more of what he should not have believed at all. They talked for a long time and it was a hot day, so she had Greek wine and sweets served to Andreuccio; then it was supper time, and Andreuccio got up to leave, but the lady would not hear of this, and pretending to get angry, she said as she embraced him:

"Alas, poor me! How clearly I see that you care very little for me! How is it possible? Here you are with a sister of yours that you have never seen before, and she is in her own house, where you ought to be lodging, and you want to leave her, to eat at some inn? You shall certainly dine with me, and though my husband is not here (a fact which displeases me a great deal) I shall honor you as best a woman can."

Not knowing what to say to this, Andreuccio replied:

"I hold you as dear as one can hold a sister, but if I don't leave, they'll wait all evening for me to come to supper and I'll make a bad impression."

And she said:

"God be praised! As if I did not have anyone to send to tell them not to wait for you! But you would do me an even greater courtesy by inviting all of your companions to have supper here and then, if you still wished to leave, you could all leave together."

Andreuccio replied that he did not want to be with his companions that evening, and that he would stay as she wished. Then, she pretended to send someone to notify the inn that he should not be expected for supper; and, after much conversation, they finally sat down to supper and were served a number of splendid courses, and she cleverly prolonged the supper until night came; and when they got up from the table and Andreuccio decided to leave, she said that she would not permit it under any circumstances, for Naples was not the kind of town to wander around in at night, especially if you are a stranger, and furthermore, she said that when she sent the message telling them not to expect him for supper, she also told them not to expect him back that night. Since he believed everything she said and enjoyed being with her, because of his false belief, he decided to stay with her. After supper, and not without her reasons, she kept him engaged in a lengthy conversation; and when a good part of the night had passed, she left Andreuccio in her bedchamber in the company of a young boy who would assist him if he wanted anything, and she withdrew into another bed-room with her women servants.

The heat of the night was intense, and because of this and since he was alone, Andreuccio quickly stripped to his waist and took off his pants and placed them at the head of the bed; and then the natural need of having to deposit the superfluous load in his stom-ach beckoned him, so he asked the boy-servant where he should do it, and the boy pointed to a place in one corner of the bedroom and said: "Go in there."

Andreuccio entered without suspecting anything, and, by chance, he happened to place his foot upon a plank which was not nailed to the beam it rested on; this overturned the plank, and he, to-gether with the plank, plunged down. But God loved him so much that He saved him from hurting himself in the fall, in spite of the height from which he fell; he was, however, completely covered by the filth that filled the place. In order for you to understand better what just took place and what is going to take place, I shall now describe to you the kind of place it was. Andreuccio was in a narrow alley like the kind we often see between two houses; some planks had been nailed on two beams placed between one house and the other, and there was a place to sit; and one of the planks which plunged with him to the bottom was precisely one of these two sup-porting planks.

Andreuccio, finding himself down there in the alley, to his great discomfort, began calling the boy, but as soon as the boy heard Andreuccio fall, he ran to tell the lady, and she rushed to Andre-uccio's bedchamber and quickly checked to see if his clothes were still there. She found his clothes and with them his money, which he stupidly always carried with him, for he did not trust anyone; and when this woman of Palermo, pretending to be the sister of a Perugian, had gotten what she had set her trap for, she quickly locked the exit he had gone through when he fell, and she no longer was concerned about him.

When the boy did not answer, Andreuccio began to call him more loudly but that didn't help either; then he became suspi-cious, and began to realize (only too late) that he had been tricked. He climbed over a small wall which closed that alley from the street and ran to the door of the house which he recognized all too well, and there he shouted and shook and pounded on the door for a long time, but all in vain. Then, as one who sees clearly his mis-fortune, he began to sob, saying:

"Alas, poor me! I have lost five hundred florins and a sister and in so short a time!"

And after many such laments, he began all over again to beat on the door and to scream; and he kept this up for so long that many of the neighbors were awakened and forced out of bed by the disturbance; one of the lady's servants, appearing to be sleepy, came to the window and said in a complaining tone of voice: "Who's knocking down there?"

"Oh," said Andreuccio, "don't you recognize me? I am Andreuccio, brother of Madame Fiordaliso." [8]

To this the servant replied:

"My good man, if you've drunk too much, go sleep it off and come back in the morning; I don't know what Andreuccio you are talking about or any other nonsense: off with you, and let us sleep, if you please!"

"What," said Andreuccio, "you don't know what I'm talking about? You've got to know; but if this is what it is like to be related in Sicily—that you forget your ties so quickly—then at least give me back the clothes I left up there, and in God's name I'll gladly be off!"

To this, in a laughing voice the woman replied:

"You must be dreaming, my good man!"

No sooner had she said this than she shut the window. Andreuccio, now most certain of his loss, was so vexed that his anger was turning to rage, and he decided to get back by force what he could not get back with words: he picked up a large stone and began all over again, but with harder blows than before, to beat furiously at the door, and many of the neighbors who had been aroused from their beds not long before thought that he was some sort of pest who had invented all this to bother that good lady, and so, they took offense at the racket he was making; they appeared at their windows, and began to shout in a way not unlike all the dogs in a neighborhood who bark at a stray:

"It's an outrage to come at this hour to a decent lady's house and shout such foul things. In God's name leave, good man; let us sleep, if you don't mind; if you have any business with her, come back tomorrow and don't bother us any more tonight."

The good woman's pimp, who was inside the house and whom Andreuccio had neither seen nor heard, taking courage from his neighbor's words, exclaimed in a horrible, ferocious, roaring voice: "Who's down there?"

Andreuccio raised his head at the sound of that voice and saw someone who seemed, as far as he could tell, to be some big shot; he had a thick black beard and was yawning and rubbing his eyes as if he had just been awakened from a sound sleep. Andreuccio, not without fear, replied:

"I am the brother of the lady who lives here . . ."

But the man did not wait for Andreuccio to finish what he had

8. The irony of this shrewd prostitute's name, "Lily of the Valley," should not be overlooked, as it is a traditional symbol for nobility and chastity, both of which Andreuccio's "sister" lacked. The story, of course, abounds in such irony.

to say; with a voice more menacing than the first time, he exclaimed:

"I don't know what's keeping me from coming down there and beating the shit out of you, you dumb ass, you drunk—you're not going to let anybody get any sleep tonight, are ya?"

He turned inside and banged the window shut. Some of the neighbors, who knew this man for what he was, said to Andreuccio in a kindly way:

"For God's sake, man, get out of here quick unless you want to stick around for your own murder tonight! For your own good, leave!"

Frightened by the voice and face of the man at the window and persuaded by the advice of the neighbors, who seemed kindly disposed toward him, Andreuccio, as sorrowful as anyone ever could be and despairing over the loss of his money, and not knowing which way to go, started moving in the direction that the servant girl had led him that day, as he tried to find his way back to the inn. Even *he* found the stench he was giving off disgusting; so, turning to the left, he took a street called Catalan Street and headed for the sea in order to wash himself off; but he was heading towards the upper part of town, and in so doing, he happened to see two men with lanterns in their hands coming in his direction, and fearing that they might be the police or other men who could do him harm, he cautiously took shelter in a hut he saw nearby. But the two men were headed for the very same spot and they, too, entered the hut; once inside, one of them put down the iron tools he was carrying and began examining them and discussing them with the other. All of a sudden, one of them remarked:

"What's going on here? That's the worst stink I've ever smelled!"

As he said this, he tilted his lantern up a bit and saw Andreuccio, the poor devil. Amazed, he asked:

"Who's there?"

Andreuccio did not utter a word; the two men drew closer with the light, and one of them asked him how he had become so filthy; Andreuccio told them every detail of what had happened to him. Having guessed where all this must have taken place, they said to each other:

"This guy really knows the head of the Mafia—he's been to Buttafuoco's place!" [9]

Turning to Andreuccio, one of them said:

"My good man, you might have lost your money, but you still have God to thank for not going back into the house after you fell; if you had not fallen, you can be sure that before you fell

9. Buttafuoco's name underlines his evil nature, since it means "fire belcher"; furthermore, he is called a "scarabone" by the two men in the original Italian, meaning an important figure in the local criminal underworld, what is known today as the Camorra, a Neapolitan equivalent of the Sicilian Mafia.

asleep, you would have been murdered and, along with your money, you would have lost your life.[1] You have as fat a chance of getting a penny of your money back as you do of getting a snowball out of hell! You could even get killed if that guy finds out you ever said a word about it!"

After telling him this, he consulted with his companion for a while, then said:

"Look, we've taken pity on you, so, if you want to come with us and do what we plan to do, we're sure that your share of what we all get will be more than what you've lost."

Andreuccio was so desperate that he said he was willing to go along. That day an archbishop of Naples named Messer Filippo Minutolo[2] had been buried and with him, the richest of vestments and a ruby on his finger which was worth more than five hundred gold florins; this is what they were out to get, and they let Andreuccio in on their plan. More avaricious than wise, he set off with them, and as they made their way towards the cathedral, Andreuccio stank so badly that one of them said:

"Can't we find some way for this guy to wash up a little, so that he doesn't stink so bad?"

The other answered:

"O.K. We're near a well that should have a pulley and a large bucket; let's go give him a quick washing."

When they reached the well, they discovered that the rope was there but the bucket had been removed; so they decided between themselves that they would tie Andreuccio to the rope and lower him into the well, and he could wash himself down there; then, when he was washed, he could tug on the rope and they would pull him up. And this is what they did. It happened that no sooner had they lowered him into the well than some police watchmen, who had been chasing someone else and were thirsty because of the heat, came to the well for a drink; when the two men saw the police heading for the well, they immediately fled without being seen.

Andreuccio, who had just cleaned himself up at the bottom of the well, gave a pull on the rope. The thirsty night watchmen had just laid down their shields, arms, and other gear and were begin-

---

1. Here, Boccaccio seems to be using Andreuccio's mishap to poke fun at a central tenet of Christian doctrine, the theory of the *felix culpa* or the "fortunate fall." In its proper context, the idea refers to the happy consequences of Adam's fall from grace and his expulsion from Paradise, for this original sin made possible Christ's salvation of the human race from sin. In Andreuccio's case, however, a man is supposed to thank God for having literally fallen into a cesspool, thereby avoiding an even greater evil—his murder. The agent of his salvation is no heaven-sent savior, but rather his natural need to relieve himself!

2. As various scholars have demonstrated, much of this story refers both to real locations in Naples and to actual historical figures. The archbishop in question died on October 24, 1301, thus setting the tale in a period immediately preceding Boccaccio's birth.

ning to pull up the rope, thinking that a bucket full of water was at the other end. When Andreuccio saw himself nearing the rim of the well, he dropped the rope and grabbed the edge with his two hands; when the night watchmen saw him, they were terrified and dropped the rope without saying a word and began to run as fast as they could. Andreuccio was very surprised at all this, and if he had not held on tightly, he would have fallen back to the bottom of the well and perhaps have hurt himself seriously or even killed himself; when he climbed out and discovered these weapons which he knew his companions had not brought with them, he became even more puzzled. Afraid, not understanding a thing, lamenting his misfortune, he decided to leave that spot without touching a thing; and off he went, not knowing where he was going.

But on his way, he ran into his two companions who were on their way back to pull him out of the well, and when they saw him, they were amazed and asked him who had pulled him out of the well. Andreuccio replied that he did not know, and then he told them exactly what had happened and what he had discovered near the well. They then realized what had actually taken place and laughing, they told him why they had run away and who the people were who had pulled him up. And without any further conversation (for it was already midnight), they went to the cathedral and managed to get in without any trouble at all; they went up to the tomb which was very large and made of marble; with their iron bars, they raised up the heavy cover as far as was necessary for a man to get inside, and then they propped it up. And when this was done, one of them said:

"Who'll go inside?"

To this, the other replied:

"Not me!"

"Not me either," answered the other. "You go, Andreuccio."

"Not me," said Andreuccio.

Both of them turned toward Andreuccio and said:

"What do you mean, you won't go in? By God, if you don't, we'll beat your head in with one of these iron bars till you drop dead!"

This frightened Andreuccio, so he climbed in, and as he entered the tomb, he thought to himself:

"These guys are making me go into the tomb to cheat me: as soon as I give them everything that's inside and I am trying to get out of the tomb, they will take off with the goods and leave me with nothing!"

And so, he thought about protecting his own share from the start: he emembered the two men had talked about an expensive ring, so as soon as he had climbed into the tomb, he took the ring from the archbishop's finger and placed it on his own; then, he handed out the bishop's staff, his miter, his gloves, and stripping him down to his shirt, he handed over everything to them, announcing, finally, that there was nothing left, but they insisted that the ring must be there and told him to look all over for it; but Andreuccio answered that he could not find it, and he kept them waiting there for some time while he pretended to search for it. The other two, on the other hand, were just as tricky as Andreuccio was trying to be, and at the right moment they pulled away the prop that held the cover up and fled, leaving Andreuccio trapped inside the tomb.

When Andreuccio heard this, you can imagine how he felt. He tried time and again, both with his head and his shoulders to raise the cover, but he labored in vain; overcome with despair, he fainted and fell upon the dead body of the archbishop (and anyone seeing the two of them there together would have had a hard time telling which one of them was really dead: he or the archbishop). Regaining consciousness, he began to sob bitterly, realizing that he being where he was, without any doubt one of two kinds of death awaited him: either he would die in the tomb from hunger and from the stench of the maggots on the dead body (that is, if no one came to open the tomb) or, if someone were to come and find him in the tomb, he would be hanged as a thief.

With this terrible thought in his head, and filled with grief, he heard people walking and talking in the church; they were people, it seemed to him, who had come to do what he and his companions had already done—this terrified him all the more! As soon as these people raised the cover of the tomb and propped it up, they began arguing about who should go in, and no one wanted to do so; then, after a long discussion, a priest said:

"Why are you afraid? Do you think he is going to eat you? The dead don't eat the living! I'll go inside myself."

After saying this, he leaned his chest against the rim of the tomb, then swung around and put his legs inside, and he was about to climb down when Andreuccio saw him and rose to his feet, grabbing the priest by one of his legs and pretending to pull him down. When the priest felt this, he let out a terrible scream and instantly jumped out of the tomb. This terrified all the others who, leaving the tomb open, began to flee as if a hundred thousand devils were chasing them.

Andreuccio, happy beyond all his hopes, jumped out of the tomb and left the church by the street from which he had come in. It was almost dawn, and he started wandering about with that ring on his finger until finally he reached the water front and stumbled upon his inn where he found that the innkeeper and his companions had been up all night worried about him.

He told them the story of what had happened to him, and the

innkeeper advised him to leave Naples immediately; he did so at once and returned to Perugia, having invested his money in a ring when he had set out to buy horses.

* * *

Second Day, Seventh Story

The sultan of Babylon sends one of his daughters as a wife for the king of Algarve; [3] *in a series of misadventures, she passes through the hands of nine men in different lands in the space of four years; finally, she is returned to her father, who believes she is still a virgin and then continues on her way, as she had before, to the king of Algarve to marry him.*

* * *

Quite a long time ago, there was a sultan of Babylon whose name was Beminedab and during his reign he was fortunate in all he did. Among his many children, both male and female, this man had a daughter named Alatiel who was, according to everyone who saw her, the most beautiful woman ever seen in the world in those times; now, the sultan had been attacked by a great army of Arabs, but with the timely assistance of the king of Algarve, he managed to rout them; in return, as a special favor to the king, who had asked for his daughter's hand, he promised her to him as his wife; and he put her on a well-armed and well-furnished vessel with an honorable escort of men and women and with many noble and rich gifts, and sent her on her way, commending her to God's protection.

The sailors saw that the weather was good, and setting their sails to the winds they left the port of Alexandria and sailed happily for many days; once they passed Sardinia, they felt their voyage was nearing its end, but one day there arose contrary winds which were so unusually strong that they buffeted the lady's ship, causing the sailors, more than once, to consider themselves lost. But, as the brave men that they were, they tried with all their strength and skill to withstand the beating of the heavy seas, and they did so for two days; the storm got progressively worse, and on the third night the tempest was at its peak; the sailors did not know where they were, and they could not determine their position by calculations or by sight, for the heavens were pitch-black from the clouds and

3. Italians of Boccaccio's day called the Moorish kingdom, including most of North Africa and a large section of Spain, by this name.

the night itself, and they were drifting not far from the coast of Majorca when they realized their boat had sprung a leak.

Seeing no other means of escape and everyone thinking only of himself, the officers launched a lifeboat and got into it, deciding to trust it more than the foundering ship; although the men already in the lifeboat tried with knives to fight off the others and prevent them from joining them, every last sailor on board managed to jump into the lifeboat, and thinking in this way to avoid death, they all met it: in such weather the lifeboat could not support so many passengers; it went under and everyone in it perished. Even though the ship was leaking and nearly full of water, it was swept by a gust of wind and driven swiftly onto the shore of the island of Majorca—and on board the vessel there were, by this time, no other passengers except the king's daughter and her ladies in waiting, all of whom were half-dead from fear and the tempest. The shock of the crash was so great that the ship lodged itself tightly in the sand about a stone's throw from the beach, and there it remained all night, battered by the sea, but resistant to the force of the wind.

By daybreak the tempest had calmed down a good deal, and the lady, half-dead and weak as she was, raised her head, and began calling now to one of her servants, now to another, but to no avail—all were too far away. Receiving no reply and seeing there was no one on board, she was greatly amazed and soon she began to feel frightened; as best she could, she got up and saw the other ladies lying all around her, and as she called to one and then another, she soon realized that most of them had died from seasickness and fear—this further increased the lady's terror. Finding herself completely alone there and not knowing where she was, she felt the need of advice and so she started shaking those who were still alive until she got them on their feet; and when she found out that none of her ladies knew where the men had gone and that the ship had struck land and was full of water, she began to weep bitterly with them.

It was already past the hour of nones before they saw anyone on the beach or anywhere else whom they might hope would help them. Around that time, returning from his estates, a gentleman whose name was Pericone da Visalgo happened to be passing by there on horseback with some of his servants; he spotted the ship and, immediately realizing what had occurred, he ordered one of his servants to try to climb aboard as quickly as possible and to report to him what he found there. The servant climbed aboard with much difficulty and found the young lady hiding in fear under the bowsprit with the few companions she had left. When they saw the man, they broke into tears and begged his mercy, but when they realized that they could not understand each other's language, they tried to explain their misadventure to him with sign language.

The servant checked over everything on board as best he could, and then told Pericone what he had found; Pericone immediately had the women brought down, along with their most precious belongings (those which were not waterlogged), and he had them taken to one of his castles where they were properly provided for with food and rest, and from Alatiel's elegant clothes and the honor paid her by the other women he concluded that she was of very noble birth. Although the lady was pale and disheveled as a result of her harrowing experience at sea, she nevertheless seemed most beautiful to Pericone; and because of this he immediately decided to take her for his wife, if she had no husband, or to have her as his mistress, if he could not have her as his wife.

Pericone was a very robust, bold-looking man. He saw to it that the lady was served in the best of fashions until, after several days, she was completely recovered; then he saw that she was even more beautiful than he had imagined, and he was most unhappy that they could not understand each other's language, for he was unable to learn who she was. But he remained moved beyond measure by her beauty, and with gracious and amorous deeds he kept trying to induce her to fulfill his desires without resistance. But all this was to no avail: she rejected all of his advances, and in so doing she increased all the more Pericone's passion for her—and the lady perceived this. After a few days, she guessed by the clothing worn by those around her that she was among Christians and approximately where she was; she realized that identifying herself was of little value and that sooner or later she would have to give in to Pericone's desires either by force or love; therefore, she proudly decided to rise above the misery of her fortune and ordered her three servants (for no more than three remained alive) never to tell anyone who they were unless they found themselves in a situation where revealing their identity offered a clear opportunity for obtaining their freedom; besides this, she advised them, above all else, to protect their chastity, declaring that she herself had decided never to let anyone but her husband enjoy her. Her women commended her for this and said they would do everything they could to obey her.

Burning with desire day by day, and burning even more when he saw the thing he craved so close and yet denied him, Pericone realized that his flattery was of no avail and turned to cunning and deceit, reserving force as a last resort. He had noticed on several occasions that the lady liked wine—as happens with those who are not accustomed to drinking it because their religion prohibits it—so he decided that he might be able to possess her by using wine as an assistant to Venus; and pretending not to care that she rejected him, one evening for a festive occasion he gave a sumptuous dinner to which the lady came; and, since the dinner provided many good things to eat, Pericone ordered the man serving her to give her various mixed wines to drink. He did this very skillfully; and since she was not on her guard and was rather attracted by the pleasure of drinking, she had more than her decorum might have required; and forgetting her past misfortunes, she became happy, and seeing some women dancing in the fashion of Majorca, she began to dance in the Alexandrian style.

When Pericone saw this, he felt he was nearing his goal, and he prolonged the supper for much of the night by providing an abundance of food and drink. Finally, when the guests had left, he went to the lady's bedchamber where he was alone with her; she, being hotter with wine than tempered by chastity, stripped off her clothes without any hesitation of shame in his presence—almost as if Pericone were one of her servants—and got into bed. Pericone was not long following her; he put out all the lights and quickly lay down beside her, and taking her in his arms, with no resistance from her, he began to enjoy her amorously. When she felt what it was like, never before having felt the horn men use to butt, she repented of having rejected Pericone's previous advances; and without waiting to be beckoned to such sweet nights again, she often invited herself not with words, since she did not know how to make herself understood, but with actions.

While she and Pericone enjoyed each other, Fortune, not content to have made the wife of a king the mistress of a lord, prepared an even crueler love for the lady. Pericone had a brother named Marato who was twenty-five years old, handsome, and as fresh as a rose; when he saw the lady, he was immensely attracted to her, and judging from the signs he got from her, he saw that he was in her good graces. He decided that nothing stood in his way except the strict watch Pericone kept over her and he devised a cruel plan whose evil effects followed quickly its inception.

There was at that time, by chance, in the harbor of the city a ship which was loaded with merchandise to be taken to Chiarenza in the Morea [4] and which was owned by two young men from Genoa; it had already hoisted its sails in preparation to depart with the first favorable winds; Marato came to an agreement with its owners, arranging for them to take him aboard along with the lady the following night. When this was done, as soon as night fell, he decided how he would proceed: he went secretly to the home of Pericone, who was not at all suspicious of his brother, and he hid in the house according to the plan which he had made with some of his most trusted companions, to whom he had revealed what he intended to do. And in the middle of the night, he let his compan-

4. The Italian is *Romania,* a term which Italians of Boccaccio's day used for the Morea or the Greek Peloponnesus, the peninsula south of the Gulf of Corinth. At the time Boccaccio composed *The Decameron,* this area was being contested by the Venetian republic, the Byzantine empire, and the Turks.

ions into the house and took them to where Pericone was sleeping with the lady; they went into the bedchamber and murdered Pericone in his sleep, and the lady, awake and weeping, they threatened with death if she made any noise as they took her away. With a large part of Pericone's valuable possessions they went quickly to the harbor unobserved, and there without delay Marato and the lady boarded the ship while his companions returned home. The sailors, with a good, fresh wind, set sail on their journey.

The lady grieved bitterly over her second misfortune as she did over her first; but with the assistance of the holy Stiff-in-hand God gave to man, Marato began to console her in such a way that she soon settled down with him, forgetting about Pericone; but she no sooner felt happy than Fortune, as if not content with her past woes, was preparing a new unhappiness for her: the lady, as was mentioned more than once, was extremely beautiful and most gracious, and the two young owners of the ship fell in love with her so passionately that they forgot every other problem on board and thought of nothing but how to serve and please her, always taking care that Marato would not notice anything.

Since each of them knew that the other was in love, they came to a secret agreement, deciding to share the lady's love between them—as if love could be shared like merchandise or money. The fact that she was well guarded by Marato created an obstacle to their plan, so one day, while the ship was sailing along at a good speed and Marato, unsuspecting, stood looking out to sea from the stern, the two men seized him quickly from behind and threw him into the sea; and they sailed over a mile before anyone noticed that Marato had fallen overboard. When the lady heard about this and saw no way of saving him, she began to bewail her new grief on the ship. The two lovers immediately came to comfort her with sweet words and great promises—none of which she really understood— but she was crying far more over her own misfortune than over the loss of Marato. And after they had talked with her on several occasions and tried to console her, they began to argue about who would be the first to sleep with her. Each one wanted to be the first, but neither could come to an agreement with the other, so they began to argue fiercely with strong words, and this grew into a rage, and finally they went at each other furiously with their knives in hand. Before the other men on board could separate them, they had given each other so many blows that one fell dead on the spot and the other, who was seriously wounded, remained alive; this displeased the lady very much, for she saw herself there alone without the aid or counsel of anyone, and she was very much afraid that the anger of the relatives and friends of the two shipowners might turn on her; but the pleas of the wounded man and their swift arrival at Chiarenza rescued her from the danger of death.

She got off the ship with the wounded man and went with him to an inn, and the reputation of her great beauty immediately spread throughout the city and reached the ears of the prince of Morea, who was at that time in Chiarenza; whereupon he wished to see her for himself, and when he did, he thought that her beauty was even greater than what he had heard, and, right then and there, he fell so passionately in love with her that he could think of nothing else; and when he heard how she arrived there, he thought that he ought to be able to have her.

When the relatives of the wounded man heard that the prince was looking for a way of possessing her, they quickly sent her to him; this pleased the prince a great deal as it also did the lady, since she felt that she had avoided one great danger. The prince saw that she had royal manners besides her beauty, and he guessed that she must be of noble birth (even though he was not otherwise able to learn who she was), and his love for her increased and was so great that he treated her more like his own wife than his mistress. The lady thought over her past misfortunes and now she considered herself to be quite well off; as she was consoled she became cheerful again, and her beauty flowered to such an extent that it seemed as if all of the Peloponnesus talked of nothing else. Because of this, the duke of Athens—a handsome and brave young man, and a friend and relative of the prince—desired to see her; and with the excuse that he had come to visit the prince, as he was accustomed to do on occasion, he arrived at Chiarenza with a numerous and honorable retinue, and he was received nobly and most cheerfully.

After a few days passed, the two men started discussing the charms of this lady, and the duke asked if she was as marvelous as people claimed; to this the prince replied:

"Far more so, but I want you to judge for yourself with your own eyes and not by my words."

On the prince's invitation, the two men went to where the lady was staying; their coming was announced previously, and the lady received them most respectfully and with a smile. She sat down between the two men, but they were not able to enjoy the pleasure of her conversation, for they understood little or nothing of her language; therefore, each of them stared at this marvelous creature, especially the duke, who could hardly believe that she was a mortal; and as he gazed at her, he did not realize that with his eyes he was drinking the poison of love, and thinking that he was merely satisfying his curiosity by looking at her, he found himself totally ensnared by her charms and fell deeply in love with her. After he left the lady with the prince and had time to think things over, he came to the conclusion that the prince was happier than any other man, having such a beautiful lady at his pleasure; and after many and various thoughts, his burning love weighing upon him more than his sense of honor, he decided that no matter what, he had to deprive the prince of this happiness and to do what he could to make it his own.

Wishing to speed up matters, he put aside all reason and justice and turned all his thoughts to treachery: one day, in accordance with the evil plan he devised, together with a most trusted servant of the prince, whose name was Ciuriaci, he prepared all his horses and his belongings for departure, and that night, together with an armed accomplice, he was let quietly into the prince's bedchamber by the aforementioned Ciuriaci. It was a very hot night, and he found the lady asleep and the prince standing naked at a window facing the sea, enjoying a breeze blowing from that direction; his accomplice, who had been told earlier what he was to do, quietly crossed the bedchamber towards the window and stabbed the prince in the back with a knife that went all the way through his body, then he quickly grabbed him and threw him out the window.

The palace stood very high above the ocean, and the window where the prince had been standing looked over a group of houses which had been destroyed by the sea, and thus people rarely or never went there; therefore it happened, as the duke had foreseen earlier, that the fall of the prince's body was never heard by anyone. As soon as the duke's accomplice saw that the deed was done successfully, he quickly drew out a rope which he had secretly carried with him and, pretending to embrace Ciuriaci, he threw it around his neck and pulled hard enough to keep him from making a sound, and when the duke came in, they strangled Ciuriaci and threw his body down to join the prince's. When this was done, certain that they had not been heard by either the lady or anyone else, the duke took a light in his hand and carried it over to the bed and, silently uncovering the lady, who was deep in sleep, he examined all her body, praising it most highly; as she had pleased him clothed, naked she pleased him beyond all measure. Burning now with even more desire and unconcerned with the crime he had just committed, with his hands still bloody, he lay down beside the lady, and made love to her while she, half-asleep, mistook him for the prince.

After he had lain with her for some time, with the greatest of pleasure, he got up and had several of his attendants come in and take the lady quietly out through a secret door—the same one by which he entered—and put her on horseback as quietly as possible; then the duke, with all his men, set out for Athens. But since he already had a wife, the grieving lady was not taken to Athens but rather to one of his most beautiful villas situated just outside the city and above the sea, and there in secret he kept her and had her honorably served, satisfying her every need.

The following morning, the prince's courtiers waited until the hour of nones for him to awaken, but hearing nothing, they opened the door of the bedchamber (which was only half-closed), and finding no one inside, they thought that he had gone somewhere in secret to spend a few pleasurable days with that beautiful lady of his, and they worried about it no more. The following day a madman happened to be wandering through the ruins where the bodies of the prince and Ciuriaci were lying, and he pulled Ciuriaci out by the rope around his neck, and went around dragging the dead man behind him. Many people recognized the body and were amazed; they managed to coax the madman into leading them back to where he had found the body and there, to the very great sorrow of the entire city, they discovered the body of the prince, which they buried most honorably. In attempting to find out who might be responsible for such a heinous crime, they found that the duke of Athens was no longer there but had departed in secret, and they judged, and rightly so, that he must have committed this crime and taken the lady away with him. They immediately took as their new ruler the brother of the dead man, and they strongly urged him to take revenge; when more evidence was found establishing as true what they had guessed to be correct, the prince called together his friends and relatives and vassals from various regions and quickly formed a very large and powerful army to wage war on the duke of Athens.

When the duke heard of this, he, too, made ready all his forces for his defense, and many noblemen came to his aid, and among them was the emperor's son Costanzo and Emanuel his nephew, sent by the emperor of Constantinople, together with a large body of men. These men were most honorably received by the duke and even more so by the duchess, who was Costanzo's sister. As the day of war came closer and closer, the duchess, at an appropriate moment, had both relatives brought to her bedchamber, and there with many tears and words she told them the whole story, explaining to them the reasons for the war and how offended she was by the duke, who thought she did not know that he was keeping that woman of his secretly; and complaining of all this most bitterly, she begged them, for the sake of the duke's honor and for her own consolation, to make amends as best they could. The young men already knew all about the matter and so, without asking too many questions, they comforted the duchess to the best of their ability, and renewing her hope, they departed, having learned from her where the lady was. And having often heard praised the marvelous beauty of the lady, wishing to see her, they begged the duke to show her to them; remembering very little of what had happened to the prince for allowing him to see her, he promised to do so: he had a magnificent banquet prepared in a beautiful garden where the lady lived, and he took them and a few other companions there the following morning to dine with her.

Costanzo sat beside her, and looking at her in amazement, he told himself that he had never seen anything as beautiful as she and that one must certainly excuse the duke, or anyone else, for using any treacherous means possible in order to possess such a beautiful creature; and as he looked at her time and again, praising her more each time, something not unlike what happened to the duke happened to him: he was madly in love with her, and by the time he left her, he had completely abandoned all thought of war and gave himself over to thinking only about how he could take her from the duke, carefully concealing his love from anyone.

And while he was burning with this desire, the time came to march against the prince, who was already nearing the duke's territories; therefore the duke, Costanzo, and all the others marched from Athens, according to a previously established plan, to the border territories so that the prince might be prevented from advancing further. And all the time he was there, Costanzo's heart and thoughts were fixed upon that lady. Since the duke was away, he thought he could easily lead her to fulfill his desire; so, in order to have the chance to return to Athens, he pretended to be very ill; with the permission of the duke, he turned his command over to Emanuel, and returned to his sister in Athens. After he was there for several days, he brought up the topic of the insult which she felt she had received from the duke on account of the lady he kept, and he told her that he would gladly assist her in this matter, if she wished, by taking Alatiel away.

Thinking that Costanzo was doing this out of love for her and not for that lady, the duchess said that this would please her very much, if it could be done in such a way that the duke would never know she had consented to it. Costanzo gave his promise, and the duchess agreed that he should proceed in the manner which seemed best to him.

Costanzo secretly had a swift ship fitted out, and one evening he sent it to a place near the garden where the lady was living. The sailors aboard were given their instructions, and the duke with some friends went to the palace where the lady stayed, and there he was received cheerfully by those in her service and then by the lady herself; and then accompanied by her servants and by the companions of Costanzo, they all, at her request, went into the garden. And pretending to wish to speak to the lady privately on the duke's behalf, he walked with her alone toward a gate which opened out onto the sea; it had already been opened by one of his friends, and the ship signaled to come to that spot, when Costanzo quickly had the lady taken aboard. Then he turned to her servants and said:

"Let nobody move or make a sound unless he wants to die! I am not stealing the duke's mistress; I am removing the shame he has inflicted upon my sister!"

No one dared reply to this, and Costanzo boarded the ship with his companions and sat beside the lady, who was weeping; then he gave orders for the oars to be placed in the water and the ship to set sail, and the oars were more like wings, for they arrived at Aegina [5] close to dawn the following day. There, they left the ship to rest on land, and Costanzo consoled the lady, who wept over her unfortunate beauty; then, they boarded the ship again and within a few days reached Chios.[6] Fearing his father's reprimands and that the lady might be taken away from him, he decided to remain there in a safe place; the beautiful lady continued to weep over her misfortune for some days, but as soon as she received the same comfort from Costanzo as she had from the others before him, she began to enjoy what Fortune had prepared for her.

While things were going as they were, Osbech, who at that time was king of the Turks and constantly at war with the emperor, came, by chance, to Smyrna; [7] and when he heard how Costanzo was living such a lascivious life on Chios with some woman he had stolen and how he was taking no precautions to protect himself, he went there one night with some lightly armed ships and men; he quietly landed at Chios with his men, and took by surprise many of Costanzo's men who were in their beds, unaware that the enemy was upon them; the others, those who did awaken, ran for their weapons and were killed; the entire city was burned, plunder and prisoners were placed aboard the ships, and all returned to Smyrna.

Osbech, who was a young man, discovered the beautiful lady while examining his plunder, and when he understood that this was the one who had been taken while asleep in bed with Costanzo, he was most happy to see her; without further delay, he made her his wife, celebrated the wedding, and slept with her happily for a number of months.

Before these events took place, the emperor had been negotiating with Basano, king of Cappadocia,[8] for him to attack Osbech from one side with his forces while he with his men would attack him from the other, but they had not yet completely come to an agreement, for the emperor did not wish to grant some of the demands which Basano was making, believing them to be somewhat excessive. But when he heard what had happened to his son, he was so grieved that without further delay, he granted what the king of Cappadocia had requested and asked him to attack Osbech as soon as he was able, while he would make ready to attack from the opposite side.

5. An island off the southeastern coast of Greece.
6. A Greek island off the western coast of Turkey in the Aegean Sea.
7. A port city now known as Izmir, lo- cated on the Gulf of Izmir, an inlet of the Aegean extending into western Turkey.
8. An ancient part of eastern Asia Minor, now central Turkey.

When Osbech heard about this, he assembled his army in order to avoid being trapped between these two powerful rulers, and he proceeded to attack the king of Cappadocia, leaving his beautiful lady guarded by one of his friends and faithful vassals; after a time he met the king of Cappadocia in combat and his army was defeated and scattered, while he himself was killed. Victorious, Basano began to advance towards Smyrna, meeting little opposition, and as he approached, everyone paid homage to him as the conqueror.

Antioco, Osbech's vassal in whose care the lady had been left, saw how beautiful she was, and although he was an old man, he found himself unable to keep the trust he had pledged his friend and lord, and he fell in love with her. He knew her language (something which pleased her very much, for she had been forced to live many years almost like a deaf-mute, not understanding anyone and unable to make anyone understand her), and urged on by love, Antioco became so intimate with her in just a few days that not long afterwards, forgetting about their lord who was away at war, they made their intimacy more passionate than friendly, enjoying each other most exquisitely between the sheets.

But when they heard that Osbech had been defeated and killed and that Basano was seizing everything in his path, they both decided not to await his arrival there; they gathered up the greatest part of Osbech's most valuable possessions, and together they went secretly to Rhodes,[9] but they were there for but a short time before Antioco fell mortally ill. They had, by chance, gone to live with a Cypriot merchant who was a most beloved friend of Antioco, and when he felt that he was near death, he decided to leave all his belongings as well as his dear lady to his friend. About to die, he called them both to his side and said:

"There is no doubt I am coming to my end, and this grieves me, for living has never pleased me so much as it does now. There is one thing that, in truth, will allow me to die happy: if I must die, let me die in the arms of those two persons whom I love the most, more than any others in the world—in your arms, dear friend, and in those of this lady whom I have loved more than myself from the very day I met her. It truly grieves me to die and to leave her here, a foreigner without aid or counsel; it would be even more grievous if I did not know you were here, for I believe that, out of affection for me, you will care for her just as you would care for me; therefore, should I die, I beg you with all my strength to take charge of my possessions and of her, and do with them whatever you feel will serve as a consolation to my soul. And you, dearest lady, I beg you not to forget me after my death, so that I may boast in the hereafter that I was loved by the most beautiful woman that was ever

9. The capital of the largest of the Dodecanese Islands in the Aegean Sea.

created by Nature. If you will reassure me on these two matters, I shall be able to pass away with no doubts and in peace."

Hearing these words, the merchant friend and the lady began to weep, and when Antioco finished speaking, they comforted him, giving him their word of honor to do what he had asked in the event of his death; not long afterward he passed away and was buried honorably by them. Then, a few days later, the Cypriot merchant, having concluded his business in Rhodes, decided to return to Cyprus on a Catalan merchant ship which was already in port, and he asked the beautiful lady what she wished to do, since he had to go back to Cyprus. The lady replied that if he were willing, she would gladly go with him, and that she hoped she would be treated and regarded by him as a sister because of his love for Antioco. The merchant said that he would be happy to do anything she wished, and to protect her from any harm which might befall her before they reached Cyprus, he suggested that she pose as his wife.

They boarded the ship and were given a small cabin in the stern, and in order to keep up the pretense, the merchant and the lady slept together in a rather small bed; because of this, something happened which was not intended to happen by either one of them when they left Rhodes: the dark, the comfort, and the warmth of the bed (the power of which is by no means small) excited them, and they forgot about their friendship and love for the dead Antioco, and drawn together by mutual passion, they began to stimulate each other, and before they reached Paphos,[1] where the Cypriot lived, they had begun sleeping together as if they were married; after their arrival at Paphos, she stayed for some time with the merchant.

One day it happened by chance that a nobleman named Antigono came to Paphos on business; he was old and very wise but rather poor, and although he had served the king of Cyprus in many matters, Fortune had been unkind to him. One day, after the Cypriot merchant had gone to Armenia on a voyage of business, Antigono by chance happened to be passing the house where the lovely lady lived when he caught sight of her at one of the windows; because she was so beautiful, he stared at her and then remembered that he had seen her on another occasion, but no matter how hard he tried he could not recall where.

The beautiful lady who for so long had been Fortune's toy now saw the end of her misfortunes was approaching; when she saw Antigono, she remembered that he had held a position of no little importance among her father's servants in Alexandria; suddenly she was filled with the hope of returning to her royal position with his help; and since her merchant was not there, she sent for Antigono

1. A city on the island of Cyprus.

as soon as she could. He came and she asked timidly if he might not be Antigono of Famagusta,[2] as she believed he was. Antigono replied that he was and then he said:

"My lady, it seems that I recognize you, but I cannot remember where I saw you; I beg you, if you please, to recall to my memory who you are."

The lady knew from his words who he was, and breaking into tears, she embraced him—all of this amazed him—and then she asked him if he had ever seen her in Alexandria. When Antigono heard this question, he immediately recognized her as Alatiel, the daughter of the sultan, whom he believed to have died at sea; he tried to pay her the customary respect, but she would not hear of it, and asked him to sit with her for a while. Antigono did so, and he respectfully asked her how and when and from where she had come there, for all of Egypt was convinced that she had drowned at sea some years ago. To this the lady replied:

"I would prefer that my life had ended that way rather than to have led the life I have lived, and I think my father would wish the same thing if he ever found out about it."

And saying this, she began to weep profusely again, and Antigono said to her:

"My lady, do not give up hope before there is need to; if you will, tell me what happened to you and what your life has been like, and perhaps the matter can be treated in such a way that we can, with God's help, find a remedy."

"Antigono," said the beautiful lady, "it seems to me that as I see you here, I see my own father, and moved by that love and tenderness which I feel for him, I revealed my identity to you, although I could have kept it hidden, and there are few people whom I would be happier to see than you; therefore, I shall reveal to you, as if to my own father, all of my wretched misfortunes which I have always kept concealed from everyone. After you have heard them, if you see any means of restoring me to my rightful station, I beg you to make use of them; if not, I beseech you never to tell anyone that you have seen me or have heard anything about me."

After she had said this, she told him, continuing to weep, what had happened to her from the day when she was shipwrecked off the coast of Majorca to the present moment, and, out of pity, Antigono began to cry. After thinking for a while about what she had told him, he said:

"My lady, since you have always concealed your identity during your misfortunes, I shall, without a doubt, return you more beloved than ever to your father, and then you will become the wife of the king of Algarve."

When she asked him how, he explained in detail what she had

2. The leading seaport of Cyprus.

to do; and to avoid any more delays, Antigono returned at once to Famagusta and presented himself to the king, saying:

"My lord, if it please you, you can do great honor to yourself and be of inestimable service to me (who have become poor in your service) without great cost to yourself."

The king asked how this might be done, and Antigono answered:

"The beautiful young daughter of the sultan has arrived at Paphos, the one who was long thought to have been drowned at sea, and in preserving her chastity, she has long suffered the greatest of hardships; now she is poverty-stricken and wishes to return to her father. If it would please you to send her back to him in my care, you would do great honor to yourself and be of great help to me, nor do I believe that the sultan would ever forget such a favor."

The king, moved by royal decorum, immediately agreed; he sent for the lady and had her brought to Famagusta where he and the queen received her with great festivity and honor. When she was questioned about her misadventures, she answered, telling all, according to the instructions given to her by Antigono. At her own request a few days later, the king returned her to the sultan, with a handsome and honorable company of ladies and noblemen under the command of Antigono; no one need ask how well she or Antigono and the rest of her party were received. And after she had rested a while, the sultan wished to know how she managed to be still alive and where she had lived for so long a time without ever sending word concerning her condition. The young lady, who had memorized Antigono's instructions very well, began to speak to her father in this fashion:

"Father, about the twentieth day after my departure from you, our ship foundered in a fierce storm one night and was driven onto some western shores not far from a place called Aiguesmortes,[3] and what happened to the sailors who were aboard the ship I could not tell you; I only remember that when it was day and I came to life almost as if from the dead, the wrecked ship had already been spotted by peasants and they had run to plunder it from all over the countryside; I went ashore with two of my women servants, who were immediately seized by young men and taken off in different directions—what ever became of them, I never knew; then two young men seized me and dragged me off by my hair, and while I was resisting and weeping bitterly, it happened that as the men dragging me were crossing a road to get to a great forest, four men were passing by there at that moment on horse-

3. An important medieval town situated in the region of Provence in France, a major port during the Middle Ages. King Louis IX embarked from there for Egypt in 1248 and for Tunis in 1270 to begin the Seventh and Eighth Crusades. Today, the walled city no longer borders upon the ocean because of geographical changes which have left it landlocked.

back, and when my captors saw them, they immediately abandoned me and took to flight.

"When the four men, who seemed to be persons of authority, saw them flee, they galloped over to where I was and asked me many questions, and I answered but neither they nor I understood the other. After a long discussion, they put me on one of their horses and took me to a convent which was organized according to their religious laws, and there, because of whatever it was they said, I was most kindly received and honored by the nuns, and with great devotion I then joined them in serving St. Peter the Big in the Valley, for whom the women of that country had great love. After I had lived for some time with them and learned some of their language, they asked me who I was and where I came from, and since I knew where I was and feared, if I told the truth, that I might be driven away as an enemy of their religion, I replied that I was the daughter of a great nobleman from Cyprus who was sending me to Crete to be married when, unfortunately, we were driven ashore and shipwrecked.

"And many times in many ways, fearing the worst, I followed their customs; and when I was asked by the oldest of those women, whom they call "abbess," if I wanted to return to Cyprus, I answered that I desired no other thing as much; but since she was concerned for my honor, she never wanted to entrust me to anyone who was going towards Cyprus until about two months ago, when several French gentlemen arrived there with their ladies, among whom there was some relative of the abbess; when she heard that they were going to Jerusalem to visit the sepulcher where the man they consider their God was buried after he was murdered by the Jews, she entrusted me to their care and begged them to take me to my father in Cyprus.

"It would be too long a story to recount how much these noblemen honored me and how cheerfully I was received by their ladies. We boarded the ship, and after some days we arrived at Paphos; I did not know anyone there, nor did I know what I should say to the noblemen who wished to return me to my father according to the instructions that the worthy abbess had given them; but God provided a way out for me, perhaps because he took pity on me, for just as we were disembarking at Paphos, there Antigono was on the shore; I called out to him at once, and so that I would not be understood by either the gentlemen or their ladies, I told him in our own language to welcome me as if I were his daughter. He understood me immediately, and after he had greeted me accordingly and had thanked those gentlemen and those ladies as his poverty permitted, he took me with him to the king of Cyprus, who received me and sent me on to you with such honor that I could never describe it. If there is anything else left to tell, let Antigono tell you, for he has often heard me speak of my adventures."

Antigono then turned to the sultan and said:

"My lord, all she has told you here, she has many times told me, and those ladies and noblemen with whom she came have told me the same thing; she has only left out one part of her story, which I think she has omitted because she feels it is not appropriate for her to mention: that these noblemen and ladies with whom she came spoke very highly about the virtuous life she led with the nuns and about her praiseworthy behavior, and both the ladies and the men shed many tears and expressed their regrets when they had to leave her, handing her over to me. If I wished to tell you everything they said to me, not only the present day but the coming night would not be sufficient; let it suffice for me to say that according to their own words and what I was able to witness for myself, you certainly may boast of having the most beautiful, the most virtuous, and the most chaste daughter that any ruler who wears a crown today possesses."

The sultan was extremely pleased to hear these things and many times he prayed God to grant him the grace to be able to reward properly whoever had honored his daughter, and especially the king of Cyprus for having honorably returned her to him; and some days later, he presented Antigono with sumptuous gifts and gave him leave to return to Cyprus, bringing with him to the king by letter and by special ambassadors his deepest gratitude for the great kindness he had shown to his daughter. After this, he decided to carry out what he had originally planned to do, that is, to make his daughter the wife of the king of Algarve; so he wrote to him , telling him everything that had happened to her and said that if he still wished to marry her, he should send for her. This pleased the king of Algarve very much, and he sent an honorable escort for her and received her most happily. And she, who had lain with eight men perhaps ten thousand times, went to bed with the king as if she were a virgin, and she made him believe that she still was one. And from then on she lived happily with him as his queen. This is why it is said: "A mouth which is kissed does not lose its good fortune; on the contrary, it is renewed like the moon." [4]

* * *

4. The narrator's ambiguous conclusion describing the reaction of the seven ladies to this story (found in the opening of the ninth tale of the same day) is well worth considering in analyzing Boccaccio's view of Alatiel: "The ladies breathed many a sigh over the beautiful woman's various adventures; but who knows what was the cause which moved these sighs? Perhaps there were some of them who sighed no less because of their longing for such frequent embraces than because of their compassion for Alatiel."

Third Day,
First Story

Masetto from Lamporecchio pretends to be a deaf-mute and becomes the gardener for a convent of nuns, who all compete to lie with him.

* * *

In this countryside of ours there was, and still is today, a nun's convent which is very famous for its sanctity and which I shall not name in order not to diminish to any degree its fame. Not long ago, there were only eight nuns and an abbess in the convent, all of whom were young women; there was also a good, sturdy man who took care of their very beautiful garden, but since he was not happy with his salary, he settled his accounts with the nun's steward and returned to Lamporecchio, from where he had come. There, among the others who cheerfully welcomed him back, was a young worker, strong and hardy, who was, for a peasant, a handsome man, and his name was Masetto. He asked the good man, whose name was Nuto, where he had been for so long a time, and Nuto told him, and when Masetto asked him what he did at the convent, Nuto answered:

"I worked in one of their beautiful, large gardens, and sometimes I went to the woods for firewood; I also would get the water from the well, and other such services, but the ladies gave me such a small salary that I could just barely buy shoes for myself. What's more, they were all young, and I thought they had the devil in their bodies, for there was nothing you could do to please them; in fact, when I would be in the orchard, sometimes one of them would tell me 'Put this here' and another would say 'Put this there,' and another would take the hoe from my hand and would say 'That's not the way.' They pestered me so much that I stopped working in the garden, and, for one reason or another, I decided I didn't want to work there any longer, and I came back here. When I left, their steward made me promise to send someone from here who knew how to garden, and I promised him, if I knew someone, I would send him. But his kidneys will turn into relics before I'll look for someone or send him anyone."

When Masetto heard what Nuto had to say, he was consumed with desire to be with these nuns, for he understood from Nuto's words that he would be able to do what he wished there; he also realized that things would not work out for him if he told Nuto about his plans, and so he said:

"Well, you did right to come home. What's a man reduced to when he's around women? He's better off around devils; six out of seven times even they don't know what they want!"

But later on after their conversation, Masetto began thinking about how he should act in order to get the job with the nuns. He knew he could do the work Nuto did just as well as Nuto himself, so he was not afraid of being turned away on that account; he was afraid, rather, of not being hired because he was too young and good-looking. After considering a number of plans, he thought to himself:

"The place is far away from here and no one knows me there; if I can pretend to be deaf and dumb, they'll certainly take me in."

With this in mind, he took up his ax and without telling anyone where he was going, he went to the convent dressed as a poor man; he arrived there and when inside the courtyard he found, by chance, the steward, to whom he made gestures as mutes do, asking him in sign language for a bite to eat for the love of God, and offering to chop some wood if they needed any.

The steward gladly gave him something to eat, and then he showed him some logs which Nuto had not been able to split, and he split them in no time at all, for he was very strong. Then the steward had to go to the forest, so he took Masetto with him, and there he had him cut some firewood, then load it on the donkey, and, by means of gestures, made him understand that he should carry it back to the convent. Masetto did this so well that the steward kept him around for several more days to do some important chores; one day the abbess happened to see him and she asked the steward who he was. He replied:

"My lady, he is a poor deaf and dumb man who came by here one day begging for alms, and I helped him out and, in return, made him do many of the chores that had to be done. If he knew how to work an orchard and wanted to remain here, I think we would have a good servant in him. He is just what we need: he's strong, and we can make him do what we wish, and besides this, you wouldn't have to worry about the possibility of his joking with your young ladies."

To this the abbess replied:

"By God's faith, you are speaking the truth; find out if he knows how to garden and try to keep him here; give him a pair of shoes, an old cloak, and praise him, pamper him, give him plenty to eat."

The steward said he would do so. Masetto, who was not far away, was pretending to clean the courtyard while he listened to everything that was said, and he said to himself with much delight:

"If you put me in there, I'll work your garden like it's never been worked before!"

Now, when the steward saw that he knew how to work very well, he asked him with gestures if he would stay on, and Masetto, with gestures, answered that he was willing to do whatever the steward wanted; so the steward told him to work the orchard and showed him what he had to do; then he left him alone and went off to attend to the other chores of the convent. As Masetto worked day after day, the nuns began to pester him and to make fun of him, as often happens to deaf-mutes; they said the most vile words they knew to him, convinced as ever that he could not understand them; and the abbess thought little or nothing about it, perhaps because she thought that he was as much without a tail up front as he was without a tongue in his mouth. Now one day it happened that two young nuns walking through the garden approached him while he was resting after much hard work, and, as he pretended to be asleep, they began to stare at him; and one of them, the boldest of the two, said to the other:

"If I thought that you could keep a secret, I would tell you a thought that has passed through my mind many times, something which you might find profitable too."

The other nun replied:

"You can tell me, for I shall certainly tell no one else."

Then the bolder one began:

"I don't know if you have ever thought about how carefully we are watched here and how no man ever dares enter here except the steward, who is old, and this deaf-mute, and I have often heard it said by many of the women who come here that all the other pleasures of the world are a joke compared to what happens when a woman gets together with a man. Because of this I have been thinking about seeing if this could be true by trying it with this deaf-mute, since no one else is available; and he is the best person in the world for this purpose, since, even if he wanted to, he could not or would not know how to speak about it; as you can see, he is a stupid youth, mature in everything but his wits. I should very much like to hear what you think about the idea."

"Oh," said the other nun, "what are you saying? Don't you know that we have promised our virginity to God?"

"Oh," answered the first, "how many promises do we make him every day which we can't keep? If we have made him promises, let him find others to keep them for us!"

To this her companion said:

"But if we become pregnant, what'll we do?"

"You're beginning to worry about the worst before it ever happens," the bolder replied. "Worry about it when and if it happens; there are a thousand ways to keep it a secret, if we don't tell about it ourselves."

When her companion heard this, she wanted more than the other to find out what kind of beast a man was, and she said:

"Well, all right, how shall we proceed?"

The other answered her:

"As you see, it is almost nones, and I think that all the sisters are asleep except for us; let's look to see if anyone is in the orchard, and if there is no one around, all we have to do is take him by the hand and lead him over to that hut where he goes when it rains, and one of us can stay inside with him while the other keeps watch. He is so stupid that he'll do whatever we wish."

Masetto heard all this and was ready to obey, waiting only for that moment when one of them would lead him off. Both nuns looked around carefully, and when they saw that they could not be seen by anyone from anywhere, the sister who had first made the suggestion approached Masetto and woke him; he rose immediately to his feet. Then, she took him by the hand, while he made ridiculous giggling noises, and with flattering gestures she led him to the hut, where Masetto did what she wished without waiting for an invitation. After she had what she wished, being a loyal friend, she gave her place to the other nun, and Masetto, still playing the fool, did what she wanted. And before they left, both sisters wished to see what it would be like to have the deaf-mute ride them once more; then later on, discussing it with each other, they decided that it really was as pleasant as they had heard, even more so; and so, whenever they found it convenient, from then on they would amuse themselves with the mute.

One day it happened that one of the other nuns saw what was going on from one of the windows of her cell, and she showed two others; at first they decided to denounce the two girls to the abbess, but then they changed their minds and came to an agreement with them instead: they became partners in Masetto's farm; and because of other various incidents, the convent's other remaining three nuns soon joined their company.

Finally the abbess, who still did not know about any of this, was walking in the garden one day all alone in the heat of the day when she came upon Masetto, who tired so easily during the day because of all the time he spent riding at night; he was stretched out in the shade of an almond tree, asleep, and the wind had blown the ends of his shirt up, leaving him quite exposed. Looking at it and realizing she was all alone, the abbess fell victim to the same lustful cravings that had taken her nuns; she woke Masetto and led him to her room where she kept him for several days, provoking much complaining from the nuns, for the gardener had not returned to work their garden, and the abbess over and over again enjoyed that sweetness which before she used to condemn in others. At last, she sent him back to his room, but she called on him very often and she took more than her share, so that eventually Masetto was not able to satisfy so many, and he realized that his being mute might harm him too much if he allowed it to continue any longer; therefore, one night when he was with the abbess, he loosened his tongue and began to speak:

"My lady, I have heard that one cock is enough to satisfy ten hens, but that ten men can poorly, or with difficulty, satisfy one woman, and I have to satisfy nine of them; I can't stand it any longer; I have reached the point from doing what I've done of no longer being able to do anything! So, either let me go, in God's name, or find some solution to this problem."

When the lady heard the deaf-mute speak, she was completely dumbfounded, and she answered:

"What is this? I thought you were a mute."

"My lady," Masetto said, "I really was, not from birth but rather because of an illness that took my speech from me, and tonight, for the first time, it was restored to me, and for this I give all my thanks to God."

She believed him, and asked him what he meant when he said he had nine women to satisfy. Masetto told her everything, and when the abbess heard this, she realized that all of her nuns were wiser than she; but, being a discreet person, she decided to find a way, together with her nuns, to keep Masetto from leaving and prevent the convent from suffering any scandal. With Masetto's consent, they unanimously agreed (now that what everyone had done behind each other's backs was evident) to make the nearby inhabitants believe that by their prayers and the merits of the saint after whom the convent was named, the power of speech had been restored to Masetto, who had for a long time been mute, and, since their steward had passed away a few days earlier, they decided to give him that position; and his labors were shared in such a way that he was able to perform them. In performing them, he generated a large number of little monks and nuns, but the matter was so discreetly handled that no one heard anything about it until after the death of the abbess, when Masetto was nearing old age and was anxious to return home with the money he had made; he easily got what he wanted when his wishes became known.

So Masetto returned home old and rich and a father, without ever having to bear the expense of bringing up his children, for he had been smart enough to make good use of his youth: having left with an ax on his shoulder, he returned affirming that this was the way Christ treated anyone who put a pair of horns upon his head.[5]

* * *

5. The horns referred to here are those popularly linked to a cuckold. Thus, Boccacio makes fun of the traditional belief that nuns are the brides of Christ, implying that whoever makes love with them also makes Christ a cuckold and is, paradoxically, rewarded for his trouble by God.

Third Day, Tenth Story

Alibech becomes a recluse and a monk named Rustico teaches her how to put the Devil back into hell. Then, she is led away from there to become the wife of Neerbal.

* * *

Gracious ladies, perhaps you have never heard how the Devil can be put back into hell, and so, without diverging in the least from the topic that you will all discuss today, I shall tell you how this is possible. Perhaps when you learn how this may be accomplished, you may still be in time to save your souls; and you will also learn that while Love is more at home in delightful palaces and luxurious bedrooms rather than in poor huts, he, nevertheless, sometimes makes himself felt in dense woodlands, on rugged mountains, and in desert caves. It is not difficult to understand the reason for this, for, after all, there is nothing that is not subject to his power.

Getting to the point, then, let me tell you that there once lived in the town of Capsa in Tunisia a very wealthy man who had, in addition to several sons, a beautiful and gracious daughter whose name was Alibech. She was not a Christian, but because she heard so many Christians in her town praising their faith and the service of God, one day she asked one of these Christians how she could best and most quickly serve God. This person answered that those best served God who denied the things of this world, following the example of those who had gone to live in the Egyptian desert. The young girl was rather naive, for she was no more than fourteen years old. Moved by childish impulse rather than deliberate decision, she set out for the Egyptian desert all alone, without a word to anyone, the next morning. Spurred on by her desire and with great difficulty, she reached those solitary parts after several days, and from afar she saw a small hut towards which she went, and there she found a holy man on the threshold. Amazed to see her, the man asked her what she was doing there. The girl replied that she was inspired by God and that she wanted to enter his service, but that she had not yet met anyone who might teach her how to serve God. Seeing how young and beautiful she was and fearing how the Devil might tempt him if he kept her near him, the good man praised her fine intentions and after having given her a quantity of grass roots, wild apples, and dates to eat and some water to drink, he said to her:

"My child, not so far from here there lives a holy man who is far more qualified than I to teach you what you wish to learn; you should go to him." And he showed her the way. And when she arrived, she heard the same words from this other man, and so she went further on until finally she came to the cell of a young hermit, a very devout and good person whose name was Rustico, and of whom she asked the same questions she had asked the previous two. Since Rustico was anxious to test his will power, he did not send her away or tell her to search for someone else—on the contrary, he kept her with him in his cell. And when night came, he made a bed of palm leaves in one corner of the cell, and he asked her to sleep there. No sooner had he made the bed than temptation began to struggle with his will power, and, discovering that he had greatly overestimated his ability to resist, he shrugged his shoulders and surrendered without much of a battle. Setting aside his holy thoughts, his prayers, and his flagellations, he began contemplating the youth and the beauty of the girl, and also how he ought to act with her, so that she would not become aware of his licentiousness as he went about getting what he wanted from her. After testing her out with some questions, he discovered that she had actually never slept with a man before and that she was really just as naive as she appeared. And so, he decided that she might well be the one to satisfy his desires under the pretext of serving God. He began with great eloquence to show her how much of an enemy the Devil was to God, and then he gave her to understand that no service could be more pleasing to God than to put the Devil back into hell, the place to which God had damned him. The young girl asked him how this might be accomplished, to which Rustico replied:

"You will soon find out, but first you must do whatever you see me do." And he began to remove those few garments he possessed until he was stark naked. And the girl did the same. He then sank to his knees as if he wished to pray, and he made her kneel opposite him in the same fashion. Being in this position, and more than ever burning with desire from the sight of her kneeling there so beautiful, the flesh was resurrected. Alibech looked at it in amazement and said:

"Rustico, what is that thing I see sticking out in front of you and which I do not possess?"

"Oh, my child," replied Rustico, "that is the Devil, about whom I told you. Now you can see him for yourself. He is inflicting such pain on me that I can hardly bear it."

"God be praised!" said the girl. "I am better off than you are, for I do not possess this Devil."

"That is very true," Rustico replied, "but you do have something else which I do not have, and you have it in place of this."

"Oh?" answered Alibech. "What is it?"

"You possess hell," said Rustico, "and I firmly believe that God has sent you here for the salvation of my soul. Since this Devil gives me such pain, you could be the one to take pity on me by allowing me to put him back into hell. You would be giving me great comfort, and you will render a great service to God by making him happy, which is what you say was your purpose in coming here."

"Oh, father," replied the girl in good faith, "since I possess hell, let us do as you wish, and as soon as possible."

"May God bless you, my child," Rustico said. "Let's go then and put him back, so that he will at last leave me in peace."

And after saying this, he led the girl over to one of the beds and showed her what position to take in order to incarcerate that cursed Devil. The young girl, who had never before put a single devil into hell, felt a slight pain the first time, and because of this she said to Rustico:

"This demon must certainly be an evil thing and truly God's enemy, father, for he not only hurts others, but he even hurts hell when put back into it."

"My child," Rustico said, "it will not always be like that." And to prove that it would not be, they put him back in hell seven times before getting out of bed; in fact, after the seventh time the Devil found it impossible to rear his arrogant head, and he was content to be at peace for a while. But the Devil's pride was to rise up many a time, and the young girl, who was always obedient and eager to take him in, began to grow fond of this sport. She said to Rustico:

"Now I certainly understand what those good men of Capsa meant when they declared that serving God was so pleasurable; and I cannot really remember anything I have ever done which was more pleasing or satisfying than putting the Devil back into hell. In fact, I believe that anyone who thinks of anything else but serving God is a fool."

For this reason, she often came to Rustico saying to him:

"Father, I have come here to serve God and not to waste my time. Let's go put the Devil back in hell!"

And sometimes, while they were doing this, she would say to him:

"Rustico, I don't understand why the Devil would ever want to escape from hell, especially if he enjoys being there as much as hell enjoys taking him in and holding him. If this were true, he would never leave."

Since she invited Rustico to partake of this sport too often, constantly encouraging him in the service of the Lord, she took so much out of him that he began to feel the cold where another man would have begun to sweat from the heat. And because of this, he tried to tell the young girl that the Devil should only be punished and put back into hell when he had raised his arrogant head:

"But we, by God's grace, have so humiliated him that he begs God to leave him in peace."

With these words, he was able to keep the girl calm for a while, but when she realized that Rustico was no longer asking her to put the Devil back into hell, she said to him one day:

"Rustico, your Devil might well have been chastised, for he no longer causes you any pain, but my hell will not leave me alone. Therefore, you ought to have your Devil assist me in quenching the fires of my hell; after all, I helped you to humble the pride of your Devil with my hell."

Rustico, who lived on nothing but grass roots and spring water, could not respond very well to her requests, so he told her that to quench the fires of her hell would require a hell of a lot of devils, but that he would do what he could for her. Thus, sometimes he was able to satisfy her, but those times were few—it was like tossing a bean into the mouth of a lion. Therefore, feeling that she was not able to serve God to the extent she would have liked, the young girl would constantly complain. During the battle between Rustico's Devil and Alibech's hell, caused by too much desire and too little strength, it happened that a fire broke out in Capsa in which Alibech's father was burned in his house along with his sons and the rest of his family; as a result, Alibech was left sole heir to all his worldly possessions. A young man named Neerbal, who had spent all of his wealth in sumptuous living, having heard that she was alive, set out to look for her and found her before the court had time to confiscate her father's properties on the assumption that there were no heirs. To Rustico's great relief but against Alibech's wishes, he brought her back to Capsa and took her for his wife, inheriting, in the process, part of her large fortune.

But before Neerbal had slept with her, she was asked by some women how she had served God in the desert. The girl replied that she had served him by putting the Devil back into hell and that Neerbal had committed a grave sin in having taken her away from such a service. The ladies asked:

"How do you put the Devil back into hell?"

With words and gestures the girl showed them how it was done; the women laughed so hard (and they are probably still laughing) as they replied:

"Don't be sad, child. People here do the same thing just as well. Neerbal will be extremely helpful to you in serving God in this fashion."

This story was told and retold all over the city until it actually became a popular proverb, stating that the most pleasurable means of serving God was to put the Devil back into hell. This saying, which spread across the seas to all parts, can still be heard today. And so, young ladies, if you seek the blessing of God, learn to put the Devil back into hell, for this is not only pleasing in the sight of God but also to the parties concerned. And much good may rise and come from it!

* * *

Fourth Day, Prologue

Here begins the fourth day of The Decameron, *during which, under the direction of Filostrato, tales are told about those whose love had an unhappy ending.*

Dearest ladies, both from what I heard from wise men and from the things I often saw and read, I used to think that the impetuous and fiery wind of envy would only batter high towers and the topmost part of trees, but I find that I was very much mistaken in my judgment. I flee and have always striven to flee the fiery blast of this angry gale, by trying to proceed quietly and unobtrusively not only through the plains but also through the deepest valleys. This will be clear to whoever reads these short tales which I have written, but not signed, in Florentine vernacular prose, and composed in the most humble and low style possible; yet for all of this, I have not been able to avoid the terrible buffeting of such a wind which has almost uprooted me, and I have been nearly torn to pieces by the fangs of envy. Therefore, I can very easily attest to what wise men say is true: only misery is without envy in this world.

There have been those, discerning ladies, who have read these tales and have said that you please me too much and that it is not fitting for me to take so much pleasure from pleasing and consoling you, and, what seems to be worse, in praising you as I do. Others, speaking more profoundly, have stated that at my age it is not proper to pursue such matters, that is, to discuss women or to try to please them. And many, concerned about my reputation, say that I would be wiser to remain with the Muses [6] on Parnas-

6. In Greek mythology, any of the nine daughters of Zeus and Mnemosyne (the goddess of memory) who presided over a different art or science: Calliope (epic poetry); Clio (history); Erato (lyric poetry and mime); Euterpe (lyric poetry and music); Melpomene (tragedy); Polyhymnia (singing, rhetoric, and mime); Terpsichore (dancing and choral singing); Thalia (comedy and pastoral poetry); and Urania (astronomy).

sus [7] than to get myself involved with you and these trifles. And there are those still who, speaking more spitefully than wisely, have said that it would be more practical if I were to consider where my daily bread was coming from rather than to go about "feeding on wind" with this foolishness. And certain others, in order to diminish my labors, try to demonstrate that the things I have related to you did not take place in the manner in which I told you.

Thus, worthy ladies, while I battle in your service, I am buffeted, troubled, and wounded to the quick by such winds and by such fierce, sharp teeth as these. As God knows, I hear and endure these things with a tranquil mind, and however much my defense depends upon you in all of this, I do not, nevertheless, intend to spare my own forces; on the contrary, without replying as much as might be fitting, I shall put forward some simple answer, hoping in this way to shut my ears to their complaints, and I shall do this without delay, for if I have as yet completed only one third of my task, my enemies are numerous and presumptuous and before I reach the end of my labors, they will have multiplied—unless they receive some sort of reply before that time; and if this is not done, then their least effort will be enough to overcome me; and even your power, no matter how great it is, would be unable to resist them.

Before I make my reply to anyone, I should like to recount not an entire tale (for in doing so it might appear that I wished to mix my own tales with those of such a worthy company as I have described to you) but merely a portion of a tale, so that its very incompleteness will separate it from any of the others in my book.

For the benefit of my critics, then, let me tell you about a man named Filippo Balducci, who lived in our city a long time ago. He was of rather modest birth, but he was rich, well-versed, and expert in those matters which were required by his station in life; and he had a wife whom he dearly loved, and she loved him, and together they lived a tranquil life, always trying to please one another. Now it happened, as it must happen to all of us, that the good woman passed from this life and left nothing of herself to Filippo except an only child, whom she had conceived with him and who was now almost two years old.

No man was ever more disheartened by the loss of the thing he loved than Filippo was by the loss of his wife; and seeing himself deprived of that companionship which he most cherished, he decided to renounce this world completely and to give himself to serving God, and to do the same for his son. After he had given everything he owned to charity, he immediately went to the top of Mount Asinaio, and there he lived in a small hut with his son,

---

7. A mountain in southern Greece, sacred in Greek mythology to Apollo and to the Muses and, therefore, traditionally linked to poets and poetry.

surviving on alms, fasts, and prayers. And with his son, he was careful not to talk about worldly affairs or to expose him to them; with him he would always praise the glory of God and the eternal life, teaching him nothing but holy prayers. They spent many years leading this kind of life, his son restricted to the hut and denied contact with everyone except his father.

The good man was in the habit of coming into Florence from time to time, and he would return to his hut after receiving assistance from the friends of God according to his needs. Now it happened one day, when his son was eighteen years of age, that Filippo told him he was going into the city, and his son replied:

"Father, you are now an old man and can endure hardship very poorly. Why don't you take me with you one time to Florence so that you can introduce me to your friends and to those devoted to God? Since I am young and can endure hardship better than you can, I can, from then on, go to Florence whenever you like for our needs and you can remain here."

This worthy man, realizing that this son of his was now grown up and was already so used to serving God that only with great difficulty could the things of this world have any effect on him, said to himself: "He is right." And since he had to go anyway, he took his son along with him.

When the young man saw the palaces, the houses, the churches, and all the other things that filled the city, he was amazed, for he had never seen such things in his life, and he kept asking his father what many of them were and what they were called. His father told him, and when one question was answered, he would ask about something else. As they went along this way, the son asking and the father explaining, by chance they ran into a group of beautiful and elegantly dressed young women who were returning from a wedding feast; when the young man saw them, he immediately asked his father what they were. To this his father replied:

"My son, lower your eyes and do not look, for they are evil."

Then the son asked: "What are they called?"

In order not to awaken some potential or anything-but-useful desire in the young man's carnal appetite, his father did not want to tell his son their proper name, that is to say "women," so he answered:

"Those are called goslings."

What an amazing thing to behold! The young man, who had never before seen a single gosling, no longer paid any attention to the palaces, oxen, horses, mules, money, or anything else he had seen, and he quickly said:

"Father, I beg you to help me get one of those goslings."

"Alas, my son," said the father, "be silent; they are evil."

To this the young man replied:

"Are evil things put together like that?"

"Yes," his father replied.

And his son answered:

"I do not understand what you are saying or why they are evil. As far as I know, I have never seen anything more beautiful nor more pleasing than they. They are more beautiful than the painted angels which you have pointed out to me so many times. Oh, if you care for me at all, do what you can to take one of these goslings home with us, and I will see to her feeding."

His father replied:

"I will not, for you do not know how to feed them!"

Right then and there the father sensed that Nature had more power than his intelligence, and he was sorry for having brought his son to Florence. But let what I have recounted of this tale up to this point suffice, so that I may return to those for whom it was meant.

Well, young ladies, some of my critics say that I am wrong to try to please you too much, and that I am too fond of you. To these accusations I openly confess, that is, that you do please me and I do try to please you. But why is this so surprising to them? Putting aside the delights of having known your amorous kisses, your pleasurable embraces, and the delicious couplings that one so often enjoys with you, sweet ladies, let us consider merely the pleasure of seeing you constantly: your elegant garments, your enchanting beauty, and the charm with which you adorn yourselves (not to mention your feminine decorum). And so we see that someone who was nourished, raised, and grew up upon a savage and solitary mountain within the confines of a small hut without any other companion but his father, desired only you, asked for only you, gave only you his affection.

Will my critics reproach me, bite and tear me apart if I—whose body heaven made most ready to love you with, and whose soul has been so disposed since my childhood, when I first experienced the power of the light from your eyes, the softness of your honeylike words, and flames kindled by your compassionate sighs—if I strive to please you and if you delight me, when we see how you, more than anything else, pleased a hermit, and what's more, a young man without feeling, much like a wild beast? Of course, those who do not love you and do not desire to be loved by you (people who neither feel nor know the pleasures or the power of natural affection), reprove me for doing this, but I care very little about them. And those who go around talking about my age show that they know nothing about the matter, for though the leek may have a white top, its roots can still be green. But joking aside, I reply by saying to them that I see no reason why I should be ashamed of delighting in these pleasures and in the ladies that give them, before the end of my days, since Guido Cavalcanti [8] and Dante Alighieri [9] (already old men) and Messer Cino da Pistoia [1] (a very old man indeed) considered themselves honored in striving to please the ladies in whose beauty lay their delight. And if it were not a departure from the customary way of arguing, I certainly would cite from history books and show you that they are full of ancient and worthy men who in their most mature years strove with great zeal to please the ladies—if my critics are not familiar with such cases, they should go and look them up! I agree that remaining with the Muses on Parnassus is sound advice, but we cannot always dwell with the Muses any more than they can always dwell with us. If it sometimes happens that a man leaves them, he should not be blamed if he delights in seeing something resembling them: the Muses are women, and although women are not as worthy as the Muses, they do, nevertheless, look like them at first glance; and so for this reason, if for no other, they should please me. What's more, the fact is that women have already been the cause for my composing thousands of verses,[2] while the Muses were in no way the cause of my writing them. They have, of course, assisted me and shown me how to compose these thousands of verses; and it is possible that they have been with me on several occasions while I was writing these tales, no matter how insignificant they be—they came to me perhaps in honor of the likeness that women bear to them. Therefore, if I compose such tales, I am not as far away from Mount Parnassus or the Muses as some people may think.

But what shall we say about those who feel so much compassion for my hunger that they advise me to find myself a bit of bread to eat? I know only this, that if I were to ask myself what their reply would be if I were to ask them for some bread in my need, I imagine that they would tell me—"Go look for it among your fables!" And yet, poets have found more of it in their fables than many rich men have in their treasures, and many more still, by pursuing

---

8. Italian lyric poet (c. 1250–1300) and a friend of Dante Alighieri, best known for his *canzone* "Donna mi prega" ("A lady begs me"), a philosophical poem dealing with the nature of love.

9. The greatest of Italian poets (1265–1321) and the author not only of *The Divine Comedy*, a Christian epic poem, but also of *The New Life, On Monarchy*, and various sonnets and *canzoni*. The prose sections of *The New Life*, along with those of *The Banquet*, represented the furthest development of Italian literary prose until Boccaccio wrote *The Decameron*.

1. Italian lyric poet (1270–1336) from Pistoia, a friend of Dante and a distinguished jurist who taught at several Italian universities.

2. Although Boccaccio's masterpiece is the prose *Decameron*, many of his works are in verse: the *Caccia di Diana* (a hunting poem in *terza rima*); the *Filostrato* (a verse romance in *ottava rima*); the *Teseida* (an epic poem in *ottava rima*); the *Amorosa visione* (an allegorical work in *terza rima*); and the *Ninfale fiesolano* (an idyll in *ottava rima*). Boccaccio thus used the major rhyme scheme of Dante's *Divine Comedy—terza rima*—as well as the *ottava rima* form, which became the standard verse form for the Renaissance epics of Ariosto and Tasso. Moreover, Boccaccio intersperses his prose works with lyric poems of various forms and themes.

their fables, have increased the length of their lives while, on the contrary, others have lost them early in the search for more bread than they needed. What more, then? Let these people drive me away if ever I ask bread of them—thanks be to God, as yet I have no such need. And if ever the need arises, I know how to endure both in abundance as well as in poverty, just as the Apostle says.[3] And let no one lose courage on my account more than I myself do!

And as for those who say that these things did not happen the way I have told them here, I should be very happy if they would bring forward the original versions, and if these should be different from what I have written, I would call their reproach justified and would try to correct myself; but until something more than words appears, I shall leave them with their opinion and follow my own, saying about them what they say about me.

Most gentle ladies, since I wish this to suffice as my reply for the time being, let me say that armed with the aid of God and that of yourselves, in which I place my trust, and with patience, I shall proceed with my task, turning my back on that wind and letting it blow, for I do not see what more can happen to me than what happens to fine dust in a windstorm—either it does not move from the ground, or it does move from the ground; and if the wind sweeps it up high enough, it will often drop on the heads of men, the crowns of kings and emperors, and sometimes on high palaces and lofty towers; if it falls from there, it cannot go any lower than the spot from which it was lifted up. And if I have ever, with all my strength, striven to please you in any way, I shall now do so even more, for I realize that no one who has the use of his faculty of reason could say that I and the others who love you act in any way but according to Nature, whose laws (that is, Nature's) cannot be resisted without exceptional strength, and they are often resisted not only in vain but with very great damage to the strength of the one who attempts to do so. I confess that I do not possess nor wish to possess such strength, and if I did possess it, I would rather lend it to others than employ it myself. So let my detractors be silent, and if they cannot warm up to my work, let them live numbed with the chill of their pleasures, or rather with corrupted desires, while I go on delighting in my own pleasure during this brief lifetime granted to us. But we have strayed a great deal from where we departed, beautiful ladies, so let us return and follow our established path.

The sun had already driven every star from the sky and the damp shadow of night from the earth, when Filostrato arose and made his whole company stand, and they went into the beautiful garden where they began to amuse themselves; and when it was time to

3. A reference to St. Paul's advice in Philippians 4 : 12.

eat, they breakfasted there where they had eaten supper the previous evening. When the sun was at its highest, they took their naps and then arose, and in their usual manner, they sat around the beautiful fountain. Then, Filostrato ordered Fiammetta to tell the first tale of the day; and without waiting to be told again, she began in a graceful fashion as follows:

Fourth Day,
First Story

Tancredi, prince of Salerno, kills the lover of his daughter and sends her his heart in a gold goblet; she pours poisoned water on it, drinks it, and dies.

Today our king has given us a sad topic for discussion, thinking that since we have come here to enjoy ourselves, we might as well tell stories about the sorrows of others which cannot be told without arousing the pity of those who tell them as well as those who listen to them. Perhaps he did this in order to temper somewhat the happiness we have enjoyed during the past few days; but it is not for me to question his motives or try to change his wishes, so I shall tell you a piteous story of a disastrous event, one which is worthy of your tears.

Tancredi, prince of Salerno, was a most humane lord with a kindly spirit, except that in his old age he stained his hands with the blood of lovers. In all his life he had but one daughter, and he would have been more fortunate if he had not had her. This girl was as tenderly loved by her father as any daughter ever was; and this tender love of his prevented her from leaving his side; and she had not yet married, in spite of the fact that she had passed by many years the suitable age for taking a husband. Then, finally, he gave her in marriage to a son of the duke of Capua, who a short time later left her a widow, and she returned to her father. She was as beautiful in body and face as any woman could be, and she was both young and vivacious, and wiser, perhaps, than any woman should be. She lived like a great lady with her loving father in the midst of great luxury, and since she was aware that her father, because of the love he bore her, was not concerned about giving her away in marriage again, and since she felt it would be immodest of her to request this of him, she decided to see if she could secretly find herself a worthy lover.

After observing in her father's court the many men who usually frequent the courts (both noble and otherwise) and after studying the manners and habits of many of them, one more than any of the others attracted her—a young valet of her father's whose name was Guiscardo, a man of very humble birth but one whose virtues and noble bearing pleased her so much that she silently and passionately fell in love with him, and the more she saw him, the more she admired him. The young man, who among other things was not slow of wit, soon noticed her attention towards him, and he took her so deep into his heart that he could hardly think of anything else but his love for her.

Since they secretly loved each other so much, the young girl desired nothing more than to find herself alone with him, and as she was not willing to trust her love to anyone else, she thought of an unusual device for letting him know how this could be done. She wrote him a letter, and in it she told him what he had to do the following day in order to be with her; then, she put it in a hollow piece of wood and, as if in jest, she gave it to Guiscardo saying:

"Make a bellows of this tonight for your serving girl to keep the fire burning."

Guiscardo took it, and realizing that she would not have given it to him and spoken as she did without some reason, he took it home with him, and after examining the stick, he found that it was hollow, and opening it, he found her letter inside; when he read it and learned what he had to do, he was the happiest man that ever lived, and he carefully prepared to meet her in the way she had described to him in her letter. Near the prince's palace was a cave hollowed out of a hill a long time ago, and it was lit by a small opening in the side of the hill; the cave had been abandoned for so long that the opening was almost covered over by brambles and weeds. One could reach this cave by a secret stairway blocked by a strong door which led from one of the rooms on the ground floor of the palace which the young lady occupied. Hardly anyone alive remembered that the stairway existed, for it had not been used for so long a time. But Love, from whose eyes nothing secret can remain concealed, brought back the stairway to this young lady's enamored mind.

For many days, the young lady tried with tools to open that door in such a way that no one might suspect; finally she succeeded, and once the door was open, she was able to walk down the cave and see the outer entrance; then she sent word to Guiscardo to have him try to come there, indicating to him the probable height from the opening to the floor of the cave below. In order to accomplish this, Guiscardo immediately prepared a rope with knots and loops in it so that he would be able to climb up and down with it; then, wrapped in a leather skin to protect himself from the brambles, without anyone knowing about it, the following night he made his way to the cave opening. He tied one of the loops of the rope firmly to a tree stump growing at the mouth of the opening, and with it he lowered himself into the cave and waited for the lady.

The next day, pretending that she wished to rest, the young lady sent her ladies in waiting away and, alone, she closed herself in her bedroom. Then, opening the stairway door, she descended into the cave, where she found Guiscardo, and they greeted each other with great joy; later, they went to her bedroom where they remained most of that day, to their greatest pleasure. After making arrangements to keep their love affair secret, Guiscardo returned to the cave, and the lady locked the door and came out to rejoin her attendants. Then, when night came, Guiscardo climbed up his rope and left the cave through the same opening that he had entered and returned home. Having learned the way, he was to return frequently in the course of time.

But Fortune, jealous of so long and great a pleasure, turned the happiness of the two lovers into a sorrowful event: Tancredi was sometimes in the habit of visiting his daughter's bedroom to talk to her for a while, and then he would leave. One day after eating, while the lady (whose name was Ghismunda) was in her garden with all her attendants, he went there without being observed or heard by anyone and entered her bedroom. Finding the windows closed and the bed curtains drawn back, and not wishing to take her away from her amusement, Tancredi sat down on a small stool at the foot of the bed; he leaned his head back on the bed and drew the bed curtain around him—almost as if he were trying to hide himself on purpose—and there he fell asleep. Ghismunda, who unfortunately that day had sent for Guiscardo, left her ladies in waiting in the garden and quietly entered her bedroom where Tancredi was sleeping; she locked her door without noticing that someone was there and opened the door to Guiscardo who was waiting for her, and they went to bed together, as they had always done, and while they were playing together and enjoying each other, Tancredi happened to awaken, and he heard and saw what Guiscardo and his daughter were doing. It grieved him beyond all measure, and at first he wanted to cry out, but then he decided to be silent and remain hidden, if he could, so that he could carry out with less shame what he had already decided must be done. The two lovers remained together for a long time as they were accustomed to do, without noticing Tancredi; when they felt it was time, they got out of bed and Guiscardo returned to the cave and the lady left her room. Although he was an old man, Tancredi left the room by climbing through a window down to the garden and, unnoticed, he returned, grief-stricken, to his room.

That night while all were asleep, on Tancredi's orders Guiscardo, hindered by his leather skin, was seized by two guards at the cave opening, and he was taken secretly to Tancredi who, almost in tears when he saw him, said:

"Guiscardo, my kindness towards you did not deserve the outrage and the shame which you have given me this day and which I witnessed with my very own eyes!"

To this, Guiscardo offered no other reply but:

"Love is more powerful than either you or I."

Then Tancredi ordered him to be guarded secretly in a nearby room, and this was done. The following day, while Ghismunda was still ignorant of all this, and after Tancredi had considered all sorts of diverse solutions, shortly after eating he went to his daughter's room, as was his custom; he had her summoned, and locking himself inside with her, he said to her in tears:

"Ghismunda, I thought I knew your virtue and honesty so well that no matter what anyone ever told me, I would never have believed that you would submit to any man who was not your husband, or even think of doing so, if I had not witnessed it with my own eyes; and thinking of it, I shall grieve for the duration of that little bit of life my old age still allows me. Since you had to bring yourself to such dishonor, would to God you had chosen a man who was worthy of your nobility. From among all the men that frequent my court you chose Guiscardo, a young man of basest birth, who was raised at our court from the time he was a small child until today almost as an act of charity. You have caused me the greatest of worry, for I do not know what to do: as he left the cave opening I had him arrested last night and now he is in prison; I have already made my decision about what to do with Guiscardo, but with you—God knows what I should do with you! On the one hand, the love I have always felt for you—more love than any father ever had for a daughter—urges me in one direction; on the other hand, my righteous indignation over your great folly urges me in the other; my love tells me to forgive you and my wrath tells me against my own nature to punish you. But before I make a decision, I should like to hear what you have to say about the matter."

Having said this, he lowered his head, and wept like a severely beaten child. Ghismunda, hearing her father's words and realizing not only that her secret affair had been discovered but that Guiscardo had been seized, felt measureless grief, which she was very near to showing with cries and tears, as most women do; but her proud spirit conquered this cowardice, and her face remained the same through her miraculous force of will, and knowing that her Guiscardo was already as good as dead, she decided that rather than offering excuses for her behavior, she preferred not to go on living; therefore, without a trace of feminine sorrow or contrition for her misdeed, she faced her father as a brave and unconcerned young lady, and with a tearless, open, and unperturbed face, she said to him:

"Tancredi, I am disposed neither to deny nor to beg, since the former would not avail me, and I do not wish to avail myself of the latter; moreover, in no way do I intend to appeal to your kindness and your love but, rather, I shall confess the truth to you, first defending my reputation with good reasons, and then, with deeds I shall follow the boldness of my heart. It is true that I loved and still do love Guiscardo, and as long as I shall live, which will not be long, I shall love him; and if there is love after death, then I shall continue loving him. I was moved to act this way not so much by my womanly weakness but by your own lack of interest in marrying me, as well as by Guiscardo's own worth. It is clear, Tancredi, that you are made of flesh and blood and that you have fathered a daughter made of flesh and blood, not one of stone or of iron; and though you are old now, you should have remembered the nature and power of the laws of youth; although, as a man, you spent the best part of your years soldiering in the army, you should, nevertheless, know how idleness and luxurious living can affect the old as well as the young.

"And I was fathered by you and am of flesh and blood, and have not lived so long that I am yet old—for both these reasons I am full of amorous desire, which has also been greatly increased by my marriage which taught me how pleasurable it is to satisfy such desires. Unable to resist their power, and being both young and a woman, I decided to follow where they led me, and I fell in love. And I tried as best I could to avoid shame to you and to myself in doing what natural sin led me to do. Compassionate Love and kindly Fortune revealed to me a secret way to fulfill my desires without anyone knowing. And no matter who told you or how you found out, I make no denial of any of this. I did not choose Guiscardo at random, as many women do, but I chose him over all others with deliberate consideration and careful forethought, and the two of us have enjoyed the satisfaction of our desires for some time now. Besides reproving me for having sinned in loving, you reprove me even more bitterly—following, in so doing, vulgar opinion rather than the truth—in declaring that I consorted with a man of lowly birth, as if to say you would have not been angry had I chosen a man of noble birth as a lover. You fail to see that it is Fortune you should blame and not my sin, for it is Fortune that most frequently raises the unworthy to great heights and casts down the most worthy.

"But let us leave all that aside and look rather to the principles of things: you will observe that we are all made of the same flesh and that we are all created by one and the same Creator with the same strengths, and equal force and virtue. Virtue it was that first distinguished differences among us, even though we were all born and are still being born equal; those who possessed a greater portion of virtue and were devoted to it were called nobles, and the rest remained commoners. And although a custom contrary to this practice has made us forget this natural law, yet it is not discarded or broken by Nature and good habits; and a person who lives virtuously shows himself openly to be noble, and he who calls him other than noble is the one at fault, not the noble man.

"Look at all your noblemen, examine their lives, customs, and manners on the one hand, and those of Guiscardo on the other; if you judge without prejudice, you will declare him most noble and those nobles of yours mere commoners. I do not trust the judgment of any other person concerning the virtue and valor of Guiscardo except your own words and my own eyes. Who has praised him more than you in all those praiseworthy matters worthy of a valiant man? You were certainly not mistaken; and unless my eyes deceive me, you never praised him for anything he did not clearly achieve in a manner more admirable than your words could express. If in this matter I was deceived in any way, then I was deceived by you. Will you say, then, that I consorted with a man of lowly condition? Then you do not speak the truth; you may, by chance, say that he is a poor man, and this is granted—but only to your shame, for that is the condition in which you kept a valiant servant of yours. Poverty does not diminish anyone's nobility, it only diminishes his wealth! Many kings and great rulers were once poor, and many of those who plough the land and watch the sheep were once very rich and remain so.

"As for your last problem—what to do with me—in no way should you hesitate: if in your old age you are inclined to do what you did not do as a young man—that is, to turn to cruelty—then turn your cruelty upon me. I shall not beg for leniency, for I am the true cause of this sin, if it be a sin; and I assure you that if you do not do to me what you have done or plan to do to Guiscardo, my own hands will do it for you. Now go, shed your tears with women, and if you must be cruel, if you feel we deserve death, then kill both of us with one blow!"

The prince recognized his daughter's greatness of soul, but he did not believe that she was as resolute as her words implied; therefore, having left her and given up all thought of punishing her cruelly, he thought he could cool her burning love with other punishment: he ordered the two men who were guarding Guiscardo to strangle him secretly that night and to cut out his heart and bring it to him. They did just as they were ordered to do; and the following day, the prince sent for a large, handsome goblet of gold, and in it he put Guiscardo's heart; he sent it to his daughter by one of his most trusted servants who was instructed to say the following words when he gave it to her:

"Your father sends you this to console you for the loss of that which you loved the most, since you have consoled him for the loss of what he loved the most."

Ghismunda, firm in her desperate resolution, had poisonous herbs and roots brought to her as soon as her father departed, and she distilled and reduced them to a liquid, in order to have them available if what she feared actually did occur. When the servant arrived and delivered the prince's gift and his words, she took the goblet with a determined look, uncovered it, and seeing the heart and hearing the words, she knew for certain that this was Guiscardo's heart. Turning to the servant, she said:

"There is no burial place more worthy for such a heart than one of gold; in this regard, my father has acted wisely."

And saying this, she raised the cup to her lips and kissed it, and then said:

"Even in this extreme moment of my life, I have always found my father's love for me to be most tender in every respect, but here it shows itself to be more so than ever; therefore, as is fitting to do for such a great gift, I render to him my thanks for the last time."

Then, looking into the goblet which she held firmly in her hand, gazing at the heart, she sighed and said:

"Ah! Sweetest abode of all my pleasures, cursed be the cruelty of he who has forced me to look at you with the eyes of my head! It was already too much to gaze upon you constantly with my mind's eye. Your life has run the course that Fortune has bestowed upon you; you have reached the goal towards which all men race; you have abandoned the miseries and trials of the world and have received from your very enemy the burial that your valor deserved. Nothing is lacking in your last rites except the tears of the one who loved you while you were alive. In order that you might have them, God moved my pitiless father to send you to me, and I shall give you those tears, even though I was determined to die without tears and with a serene face; as soon as I have wept for you, I shall act in such a way that my soul will join yours without further delay, and may you, heart, accept my soul which once was so dear to you. In what company could I go more happily or more securely to unknown places than with you? I am sure that your soul is still here and continues to look upon the places where he and I took our pleasure, and as I am certain that your soul loves me still, may it wait for my soul which loves it so deeply."

And when this was said, she bent over the goblet without a womanly outcry and began to weep, pouring forth many tears as if she had a fountain in her head, and kissing the dead heart a countless number of times: it was a marvelous thing to behold.

Her attendants, who stood all around her, did not understand whose heart it was or what her words meant, but overcome with compassion they all cried; they asked her most piteously, but in vain, why she was weeping, and they sought to comfort her as best they knew how. Then, when she felt she had wept enough, she raised her head, dried her eyes, and said:

"Oh, most beloved heart, all my duty to you is fulfilled; nothing more remains for me to do but to come to you and join my soul to yours."

When she had said this, she took the phial she had prepared the day before containing the liquid, and after pouring it into the goblet where the heart was bathed with her many tears, with no trepidation whatsoever, she lifted it to her lips and drank all of it. Having done this, she climbed upon her bed, with the goblet in her hand, and as modestly as possible she arranged her body upon the bed and placed the heart of her dead lover against her own, and without saying another word she awaited death.

Although her ladies in waiting had seen and heard all these things, they did not understand nor did they know that the liquid she had drunk was poison; they sent word to Tancredi about it, and he, fearing what might happen, immediately came down to his daughter's bedchamber. He arrived there just as she was arranging herself on her bed; observing her condition, he tried to comfort her (only too late) with sweet words and began to weep most sorrowfully. And the lady said:

"Tancredi, save those tears for a less fortunate fate than this, and do not shed them on my account, for I do not want them. Whoever saw anyone but you weep over what he himself wished for? But if you still retain anything of that love you once had for me, grant me one last gift: since it displeased you that I once lived silently and secretly with Guiscardo, let my body be buried openly with his wherever you have cast his remains."

The anguish of his weeping did not allow the prince to answer. When the young woman felt her death was approaching, she drew the dead heart to her breast and said:

"God be with you, I leave you."

And closing her eyes, her senses left her, and she departed from this sorrowful existence. Such, as you have heard, was the sad end of the love of Guiscardo and Ghismunda. Tancredi, who wept much and repented of his cruelty too late, amid the grief of all the people of Salerno, had them buried together honorably in one tomb.

Fourth Day,
Second Story

Brother Alberto convinces a lady that the angel Gabriel is in love with her; then, he, disguised as the angel, sleeps with her many times; fearing her relatives, he flees from her house and seeks refuge in the home of a poor man, who, on the following day, leads him into the piazza dressed as a wild man of the forest, and there he is recognized by his brother monks and is put into prison.

The story told by Fiammetta had more than once brought tears to the eyes of her companions; but when it was completed, Filostrato, the day's king, said with a stern face:

"I should consider my life worth very little in comparison with half the pleasure Guiscardo enjoyed with Ghismunda; nor should any of you marvel at this, since I feel as if I am dying a thousand deaths while I am still alive, and yet not a single bit of pleasure is granted to me. But leaving aside my own problems for the moment, I wish for Pampinea to continue with a story that is somewhat similar to my own sad fate; if she will proceed as Fiammetta has begun, I shall, without a doubt, feel some dewdrops fall upon my amorous fire."

Pampinea, hearing the command directed to her, felt the mood of the company more through her own sensitivity than through the king's words; because of this, she was more inclined to entertain the group rather than to please the king, except insofar as his order to begin was concerned—and so, she decided, without straying from his theme, to tell a humorous story. She began in this manner:

"He who is wicked and thought to be good
Can do lots of evil not being understood."

This proverb provides me with ample material for the theme that has been proposed to me, and it also enables me to demonstrate the nature and extent of the hypocrisy of the monks, who go about with their long, flowing robes, their artificially pale faces, their voices humble and sweet when they are begging alms, but shrill and bitter when they are attacking their own vices in others or when they declare how others gain salvation by giving alms while they do so by taking them; and, moreover, rather than men who have to earn paradise like us, they act almost as if they were its very owners and rulers, granting to each person that dies, according to the quantity of money they are left by him, a more or less choice place up there, and in doing this they first deceive themselves (if they really believe in it), and then they deceive those who put faith in their words. If I were permitted to do so, I would quickly reveal to all those simple-minded people what it is they keep hidden beneath their ample habits. But for now, may God grant that all their lies have the same fate as a certain minor friar who, by no means a young man, was considered in Venice to be one of the best men that St. Francis ever attracted to the order; and it pleases me a great deal to be able to tell you this story for, perhaps, it will cheer somewhat your hearts which are now so full of pity for the fate of Ghismunda.

Gracious ladies, there was once in Imola a man of wicked and corrupt ways named Berto della Massa, whose evil deeds were so well known by the people of Imola that nobody there would believe him when he told the truth, not to mention when he lied. Realizing that his tricks would no longer work there, in desperation he moved to Venice, that receptacle of all forms of wickedness, thinking that he would adopt a different style of trickery there from what he had used anywhere else before. And almost as if his conscience were struck with remorse for his evil deeds committed in the past, he gave every sign of a man who had become truly humble and most religious; in fact, he went and turned himself into a minor friar, taking the name of Brother Alberto da Imola; and in this disguise he pretended to lead an ascetic life, praising repentance and abstinence, and never eating meat nor drinking wine unless they were of a quality good enough for him.

Never before had such a thief, pimp, forger, and murderer become so great a preacher without having abandoned these vices, even while he may have been practicing them in secret. And besides this, after he became a priest, whenever he celebrated the mass at the altar, in view of all the congregation, he would weep when it came to the Passion of Our Savior, for he was a man to whom tears cost very little when they were called for. And in short, between his sermons and his tears, he managed to beguile the Venetians to such an extent that he was almost always made the trustee and guardian of every will that was made, the keeper of many people's money, and confessor and advisor to the majority of men and women; and acting in this way, he changed from a wolf into a shepherd, and his reputation for sanctity in those parts was far greater than St. Francis's was in Assisi.[4]

4. Italian religious leader, writer, and poet (1181?–1226), famous for his Christian humility and for the foundation of the Franciscan order. A legend in his own time, St. Francis inspired many popular stories, now collected in *The Little Flowers of St. Francis*. He was canonized in 1228. Besides numerous Latin works, he is remembered for one masterful poem in Italian, the "Canticle of Brother Sun," a hymn praising the majesty of God's creation.

Now it happened that there was a foolish and silly young woman named Madonna Lisetta da Ca' Quirino (the wife of a great merchant who had gone with his galleys to Flanders) who, along with other ladies, went to be confessed by this holy friar. She was kneeling at his feet and, being a Venetian (and, as such, a gossip like all of them), she was asked by Brother Alberto halfway through her confession if she had a lover. To this question she crossly replied:

"What, my dear brother, don't you have eyes in your head? Do my charms appear to you to be like all those of other women? I could have even more lovers than I want, but my beauty is not to be enjoyed by just anyone. How many ladies do you know who possess such charms as mine, charms which would make me beautiful even in paradise?"

And then she kept on saying so many things about her beauty that it became boring to listen to her. Brother Alberto realized immediately that she was a simpleton, and since he thought she was just the right terrain for plowing, he fell passionately in love with her right then and there; but putting aside his flatteries for a more appropriate time, and reassuming his saintly manner, he began to reproach her and to tell her that her attitude was vainglorious and other such things; and so the lady told him that he was a beast and that he did not know one beauty from another; and because he did not want to upset her too much, Brother Alberto, after having confessed her, let her go off with the other women.

After a few days, he went with a trusted companion to Madonna Lisetta's home and taking her into a room where they could be seen by no one, he threw himself on his knees before her and said:

"My lady, I beg you in God's name to forgive me for speaking to you as I did last Sunday about your beauty, for I was so soundly punished the following night that I have not been able to get up until today."

"And who punished you in this way?" asked Lady Halfwit.

"I shall tell you," replied Brother Alberto. "As I was praying that night in my cell, as I always do, I suddenly saw a glowing light, and before I was able to turn around to see what it was, I saw a very beautiful young man with a large stick in his hand who took me by the collar, dragged me to my feet, and gave me so many blows that he broke practically everything in my body. I asked him why he had done this and he replied:

'Because yesterday you presumed to reproach the celestial beauty of Madonna Lisetta whom I love more than anything else except God.'

"And then I asked: 'Who are you?'

"He replied that he was the angel Gabriel.

" 'Oh My Lord,' I said, 'I beg you to forgive me.'

"'I shall forgive you on one condition,' he said, 'that you go to her as soon as you are able and beg her forgiveness; and if she does not pardon you, I shall return here and beat you so soundly that you will be sorry for the rest of your life.'"

Lady Lighthead, who was as smart as salt is sweet, enjoyed hearing all these words and believed them all, and after a moment she said:

"I told you, Brother Alberto, that my charms were heavenly; but, God help me, I feel sorry for you, and from now on, in order to spare you more harm, I forgive you on condition that you tell me what the angel said next."

Brother Alberto said: "My lady, since you have forgiven me, I shall gladly tell you, but I remind you of one thing: you must not tell what I tell you to anyone in the world, otherwise you will spoil everything, you who are the most fortunate woman in the world today. The angel Gabriel told me that I was to tell you that you are so pleasing to him that often he would have come to pass the night with you if he had not thought it might frighten you. Now he sends me here with a message that he would like to come to you one night and spend some time with you; but since he is an angel and you would not be able to touch him in the form of an angel, he says that for your pleasure he would like to come as a human being, and he asks when you would have him come and in whose shape should he come, and he will come; therefore you, more than any other woman alive, should consider yourself blessed."

Lady Silly then said that it pleased her very much that the angel Gabriel was in love with her, for she loved him as well and never failed to light a cheap candle in his honor whenever she found a painting of him in church; and whenever he wished to come to her, he would be very welcome, and he would find her all alone in her room, and he could come on the condition that he would not leave her for the Virgin Mary, whom, it was said, he loved very much, and it was obviously true, because everywhere she saw him, he was always on his knees before her; and besides this, she said that he could appear in whatever shape or form he wished—she would not be afraid.

"My Lady," Brother Alberto then said, "you speak wisely, and I shall arrange everything with him as you have said. And you could do me a great favor which will cost you nothing; and the favor is this: that you allow him to come to you in my body. Let me tell you how you would be doing me a favor: he will take my soul from my body and place it in paradise, and he will enter my body, and as long as he is with you my soul will be in paradise."

Then Lady Dimwit replied: "That pleases me; I wish you to have this consolation for the beating he gave you on my account."

Brother Alberto then said: "Now arrange for him to find the door of your house open tonight so that he can come inside; since he will be arriving in the form of a man, he cannot enter unless he uses the door."

The lady replied that it would be done. Brother Alberto departed, and she was so delighted by the whole affair that, jumping for joy, she could hardly keep her skirts over her ass, and it seemed like a thousand years to her waiting for the angel Gabriel to come. Brother Alberto, who was thinking more about getting in the saddle than of being an angel that evening, began to fortify himself with sweetmeats and other delicacies so that he would not be easily thrown from his horse; and then he got permission to stay out that night and, as soon as it was dark, he went with a trusted companion to the house of a lady friend of his, which on other occasions he had used as his point of departure whenever he went to ride the mares; and from there, when the time seemed ripe to him, he went in disguise to the lady's house, and went inside; and, having changed himself into an angel with the different odds and ends he brought with him, he climbed the stairs, and entered the lady's bedroom.

When she saw this white object approaching, she threw herself on her knees in front of him, and the angel blessed her and raised her to her feet, and made a sign for her to get into bed; and she, most anxious to obey, did so immediately, and the angel lay down alongside his devout worshipper. Brother Alberto was a handsome young man with a robust, well-built body; Lady Lisetta was all fresh and soft, and she discovered that his ride was altogether different from that of her husband. He flew many times that night without his wings, which caused the lady to cry aloud with delight and, in addition, he told her many things about the glory of heaven. Then as day broke, having made another appointment to meet her, he gathered his equipment and returned to his companion, who had struck up a friendly relationship with the good woman of the house so that she would not be afraid of sleeping alone.

When the lady had finished breakfast, she went with one of her attendants to Brother Alberto's and told him the story of the angel Gabriel and of what she had heard from him about the glory of the eternal life and of how he looked, adding all sorts of incredible tales to her story. To this Brother Alberto said:

"My lady, I do not know how you were with him; I only know that last night, when he came to me and I delivered your message to him, in an instant he transported my soul to a place where there were more flowers and roses than I have ever seen before, and he left my soul in this most delightful spot until this morning at the hour of early prayer. What happened to my body I know not."

"But did I not tell you?" replied the lady. "Your body passed the entire night in my arms with the angel Gabriel inside it; and if you do not believe me, look under your left nipple, where I gave the angel such a passionate kiss that he will carry its mark for some days!"

Then Brother Alberto said: "Today I shall perform an act that I have not done for some time—I shall undress myself to see if what you say is true."

And after much more chatter, the lady returned home; and Brother Alberto, without the slightest problem, often went to visit her, disguised as an angel. One day, however, Madonna Lisetta was discussing the nature of beauty with one of her neighbors, and she, showing off and being the silly goose she was, said: "You would not talk about any other women if you knew who it is that loves my beauty."

Her neighbor, anxious to hear more about this and knowing very well the kind of woman Lisetta was, replied: "Madame, you may be right; but as I do not know to whom you are referring, I cannot change my opinion so easily."

"Neighbor," replied Madonna Lisetta, who was easily excited, "he does not want it to be known, but my lover is the angel Gabriel, and he loves me more than himself, and he tells me that this is because I am the most beautiful woman that there is in the world or even in the Maremma." [5]

Her neighbor had the urge to break into laughter right then, but she held herself back in order to make her friend continue talking, and she said: "God's faith, Madame, if the angel Gabriel is your lover and he tells you this, it must really be so; but I did not realize that angels did such things."

"Neighbor," replied the lady, "that is where you are wrong; by God's wounds, he does it better than my husband, and he tells me that they do it up there as well; but since he thinks I am more beautiful than anyone in heaven, he fell in love with me and comes to be with me very often. Now do you see?"

When the neighbor had left Madonna Lisetta, it seemed to her as if a thousand years had passed before she was able to repeat what she had learned; and at a large gathering of women, she told them the whole story. These women told it to their husbands and to other women, who passed it on to others, and thus in less than two days it was the talk of all Venice. But among those whom this story reached were also the woman's in-laws, and they decided, without telling her a word, to find this angel and to see if he knew how to fly; and they kept watch for him for several nights. It just

5. Equating the entire world with this small, marshy region of Tuscany, the lady demonstrates her stupidity both to her neighbor and to the reader.

happened that some hint of this got back to Brother Alberto, so he went there one night to reprove the lady, and no sooner was he undressed than her in-laws, who had seen him arrive, were at the door of the bedroom ready to open it. When Brother Alberto heard this and realized what was going on, he jumped up, and seeing no other means of escape, he flung open a window which looked out on the Grand Canal and threw himself into the water.

The water was deep there, but he knew how to swim well, and so he did not hurt himself; after he swam to the other side of the canal, he immediately entered a home that was opened to him and begged the good man inside, for the love of God, to save his life, as he made up a story to explain why he was there at that hour and in the nude. The good man, moved to pity, gave him his own bed, since he had some affairs of his own to attend to, and he told him to remain there until he returned; and having locked him in, he went about his business.

When the lady's in-laws opened the door to her bedroom and entered, they found that the angel Gabriel had flown away, leaving his wings behind him; they abused the lady no end and finally, leaving her alone, all distressed, they returned to their home with the angel's equipment. In the meanwhile, at daybreak, while the good man was on the Rialto, he heard talk about how the angel Gabriel had gone to bed that night with Madonna Lisetta and had been discovered there by her in-laws, and how he had thrown himself into the canal out of fear, and how no one knew what had happened to him; immediately he realized that the man in his house was the man in question. Returning home and identifying him, after much discussion, he came to an agreement with the friar: he would not give him over to the in-laws if he would pay him fifty ducats; and this was done.

When Brother Alberto wished to leave the place, the good man told him:

"There is only one way out, if you agree to it. Today we are celebrating a festival in which men are led around dressed as bears, others dressed as wild men, and others in one costume or another, and a hunt is put on in St. Mark's Square, and with that the festival is ended; then everyone goes away, with whomever he led there, to wherever they please; and if you wish, so that no one will discover you, I am willing to lead you to wherever you like; otherwise, I don't see any way for you to escape from here without being recognized; and the in-laws of the lady, knowing that you have hidden yourself somewhere around here, have posted guards everywhere to trap you."

Though it seemed rough to Brother Alberto to have to go in such a disguise, his fear of the lady's relatives induced him to agree, and he told the man where he would like to go and that in whatever way he might choose to lead him there, he would be happy. The man smeared him completely with honey, covered him up with feathers, put a chain around his neck and a mask on his head; in one of his hands he put a large club and in the other two great dogs which he had brought from the butcher; at the same time he sent someone to the Rialto to announce that whoever wished to see the angel Gabriel should go to St. Mark's Square. And this is what they call good old Venetian honesty!

And when this was done, he took the friar outside and had him take the lead, holding him by a chain from behind; and many bystanders kept asking: "Who is it? What is it?" Thus he led him up to the piazza where, between those who had followed him and those who had heard the announcement and had come from the Rialto, a huge crowd gathered. When he arrived there, he tied his wild man up to a column in a conspicuous and elevated spot, pretending to wait for the hunt; meanwhile, the flies and horseflies were giving Brother Alberto a great deal of trouble, for he was covered with honey. But when the good man saw that the piazza was full, pretending to unchain his wild man, he tore the mask from his face and announced:

"Ladies and gentlemen, since the pig has not come to the hunt, and since there is no hunt, I would not want you to have come in vain; therefore I should like you to see the angel Gabriel, who descends from heaven to earth to console the Venetian women by night."

When his mask was removed, Brother Alberto was instantly recognized by everybody, and everyone cried out against him and shouted the most insulting words that were ever directed at a scoundrel; besides this, one by one they all started throwing garbage in his face, keeping him occupied this way for a long time until, by chance, the news reached his brother friars; six of them came, and throwing a cloak over him, they unchained him, and in the midst of a great commotion, they led him back to their monastery, where he was locked up, and after a miserable life he is believed to have died there.

Thus a man who was thought to be good and who acted evilly, not recognized for what he really was, dared to turn himself into the angel Gabriel, and instead was converted into a wild man, and, finally, was cursed at as he deserved and made to lament in vain for the sins he had committed. May it please God that the same thing happen to all others like him!

* * *

Fourth Day,
Fifth Story

Isabetta's brothers kill her lover. He appears to her in a dream and tells her where he is buried. She secretly digs up his head and places it in a pot of basil, over which she weeps every day for a long time. Her brothers take it away from her, and, shortly afterwards, she dies of grief.[6]

* * *

In Messina there were three young brothers, all of them merchants, who became very rich after the death of their father (who was from San Gimignano), and they had a sister called Isabetta, a very beautiful and accomplished young girl, who for some reason had not yet married. Besides the three brothers there was a young Pisan named Lorenzo in their shop who saw to all of their business. He being so handsome and charming, Isabetta, after seeing him several times, found that he pleased her immensely; and Lorenzo, too, after seeing her a few times, put aside all his other loves and set his heart on loving her; and, since each found the other equally pleasing, not much time passed before they took courage and did what each of them desired to do the most.

And continuing this way, spending a great deal of time together in their pleasure, they were no longer able to conceal their affair, for one night as Isabetta was going quietly to where Lorenzo slept, the oldest of the brothers noticed her, though she did not see him; since he was a sharp young man, in spite of the fact that his discovery bothered him a great deal, he restrained himself from making a move or uttering a word until the next morning, while he considered and weighed the various solutions to the matter in his mind. Then when day came, he told his brothers what he had seen happen between Isabetta and Lorenzo the previous night, and after long deliberation, so that neither they nor their sister might suffer any loss of reputation, they all decided to pass over the matter quietly and to pretend to have seen or heard nothing until a more suitable time might arise in which they, without damage or dishonor to themselves, might be able to wipe this shame from their faces before it went any further.

Having adopted this proposal, they continued to joke and laugh with Lorenzo as they used to do, and one day, pretending to take

6. This story was used by John Keats as the basis of his well-known poem, "Isabella, or the Pot of Basil."

a trip outside the city, they took Lorenzo with them; and when they came to a very deserted and remote spot, they saw that their chance had come: they killed Lorenzo, who was not on his guard, and they buried him in such a manner that no one would take notice; they returned to Messina and let it be known that they had sent Lorenzo somewhere to do their business—something which was easily believed, since they were in the habit of sending him here and there very often. When Lorenzo did not return, Isabetta anxiously and often asked her brothers where he was, for his absence deeply grieved her. One day, when she had asked about him in a very insistent way, one of her brothers replied:

"What is the meaning of this? What business do you have with Lorenzo that you keep asking about him? If you ask about him again, we shall have to give you the reply you deserve!"

Full of sorrow, grieving, and afraid, for she did not know what could have happened, the young girl stopped asking questions, and many times at night she piteously called out for him and begged him to return; sometimes she would lament his absence with tears, and she remained in this painful state of waiting, without ever cheering up. One night after she had cried so much over Lorenzo's absence that she finally cried herself to sleep, Lorenzo appeared to her in a dream, pale and all unkempt, with his clothes torn and rotting on him, and it seemed to her that he spoke:

"Oh, Isabetta, you do nothing but cry out to me and lament my long absence and bitterly accuse me with your tears; therefore, know that I cannot return here any more, for on the last day you saw me I was killed by your brothers."

He told her the spot where they had buried him and asked her not to call him any longer or to wait for him; then he disappeared. The young woman, having awakened and believing the vision, cried bitterly; after she got up the next morning, not daring to say anything about this to her brothers, she decided to go to the place he had mentioned to see if what had appeared to her in her sleep was the truth. After receiving permission from her brothers to go outside the city for a while to amuse herself in the company of a woman who had on other occasions been with her and Lorenzo and who knew about all her affairs, she set out for that place as soon as she was able. She removed the dry leaves which covered that spot where the ground seemed the softest and she began to dig; she had hardly started when she discovered the corpse of her wretched lover, which was not yet corrupted or decayed, and so she clearly saw the truth of her vision. More sorrowful than any other woman, she realized that this was no place for weeping. If she had been able, she would have willingly carried away his entire body in order to give him a more proper burial; but since she could not do this, with a knife she cut his head from the shoulders as best she could and wrapped it in a cloth; after covering the rest of the body with earth, she gave the head to her servant to carry, and without being seen by anyone, she left that place and returned to her home.

There, with this head, she shut herself in her bedroom, and she cried bitterly and long over it, bathing it with all her tears, giving it a thousand kisses on every side. Then she took a large and handsome vase, the kind in which marjoram or basil is grown, and inside it she placed the head wrapped in a beautiful cloth; then, covering it with earth, she planted above it several sprigs of the finest basil from Salerno, and she watered it only with rose or orange water or with her own tears. She began always to sit near this vase, turning all her desire towards it, for it contained her beloved Lorenzo hidden within; and when she would look at it for a long time, bent over it, she would begin to weep and bathe the basil with her tears.

From the long and continuous care she gave it and because of the richness of the soil which came from the decomposing head within, the basil became most beautiful and very fragrant. And because the young girl followed this practice continuously, she was often observed by her neighbors; they told her brothers, who were also amazed at the fact that her beauty was fading and her eyes appeared to have escaped from her head. They told them what they had seen:

"We have noticed that she does the same thing every day."

When the brothers had heard this and seen it for themselves, after reproving the girl for this several times but without success, they secretly had that vase removed from her room. When she discovered it was missing, she insistently asked for it, and because it was not returned, after incessant weeping, she fell ill, and she asked for nothing in her illness except her vase. The young men were amazed at her insistence and so they wanted to see what was inside it; when they poured the earth out, they saw the cloth and in it the head that was not yet so decomposed that they did not recognize it as Lorenzo's by his curly hair. This amazed them even more, and they feared that the murder might be discovered; they buried the head, without saying anything, and after cautiously concluding their business in Messina they left for Naples.

The young girl wept and wept, continuing to demand that her vase be returned to her; and she died crying; thus her unfortunate love came to an end, but after a time the whole affair became known to many people, one of whom composed that song which is still sung today:

> Who was that wicked man
> who stole my vase from me,
> etc.

* * *

Fifth Day, Fourth Story

Ricciardo Manardi is found by Messer Lizio di Valbona with his daughter; Ricciardo marries her and remains on good terms with her father.

* * *

Not long ago, noble ladies, there lived in Romagna a most wealthy and esteemed knight called Messer Lizio di Valbona, who had the good fortune as he approached old age to have a daughter born to his wife, Madonna Giacomina. His daughter grew up to become the most beautiful and charming girl in those parts; and because she was their only child, they loved and cherished her dearly, and they watched over her with the greatest of care, for they hoped to make quite a match for her.

Now there was a handsome and attractive young man named Ricciardo Manardi da Brettinoro who would often come to Messer Lizio's house, and he was much liked by Messer Lizio; and neither he nor his wife thought any more of keeping an eye on him than they would have done on their own son.

And as Ricciardo noticed more and more how beautiful and graceful the girl was, how accomplished and charming, and that she was of a marriageable age, he fell madly in love with her, and it was only with the greatest of difficulty that he managed to conceal his love. But the young girl was aware of this, and far from rejecting his attentions, she, too, began to fall in love with him, which, of course, pleased Ricciardo very much. Although he often felt the need to speak to her, he kept silent out of timidity, but one day he found the opportunity and courage to say to her:

"Caterina, I beg you not to let me die of love."

"God grant that you do not make me die of it first!" the young girl quickly answered.

This answer greatly increased Ricciardo's ardor and eagerness, and he said to her:

"I shall never refuse to do anything that pleases you. But it is up to you to find a means of saving both your life and my own."

The young girl replied:

"Ricciardo, you see how closely I am watched. I do not see how you can come to me nor I to you; but if you can find a way that will not bring me shame, tell me and I will do it."

Ricciardo thought of several solutions and then said suddenly:

"Caterina, my sweet—I can see no way unless you can manage to be on the balcony overlooking your father's garden, and sleep there. If I knew that you would be there at night, I would find a way to climb up there, no matter how high it might be."

"If you are brave enough to climb up there," Caterina answered, "I believe that I can find a way to sleep there."

Ricciardo agreed; they hastily kissed each other and departed. It was around the end of May, and one day the young girl began to complain to her mother that she had not been able to sleep the night before because of the excessive heat. Her mother replied:

"What heat are you talking about, daughter? It was not at all hot."

To this Caterina answered:

"Mother dear, if you had added 'in my opinion,' then perhaps you would be right. But you ought to remember that young girls get hotter than older women do."

"That is true, my child," said her mother, "but I cannot make it hot and cold whenever I wish, just to please you. You must put up with whatever weather the season brings. Perhaps tonight it will be cooler and you will sleep better."

"God grant that you are right," said Caterina, "but usually the nights do not become cooler as summer approaches."

"Well," said her mother, "what do you want me to do about it?"

"If you and father would not mind," said Caterina, "I should like to have my bed on the balcony which is beside father's bedroom, overlooking his garden, and there I would sleep; and listening to the nightingale sing and being in a cooler place, I should be much better off than in your room."

"Cheer up, my child," said her mother, "I will talk to your father, and we shall do whatever he wishes."

When old Messer Lizio heard this, he became somewhat cross and said:

"What is this nonsense about being serenaded to sleep by a nightingale? I'll make her sleep to the tune of the crickets in broad daylight!"

When Caterina learned of his reply, more out of spite than heat, not only did she refuse to sleep at all the following night, but she also kept her mother from sleeping by constantly complaining about the heat. Next morning, her mother went to Messer Lizio and said:

"Sir, you have little affection for this daughter of yours. What do you care if she sleeps on that balcony? She could not sleep a wink last night because of the heat, and besides that, why does it surprise you to know that she would like to hear the nightingale sing? After all, she is a young girl! Young people like things that are like themselves."

After Messer Lizio heard this argument, he said:

"Very well—make whatever bed you want for her out there and hang a curtain around it; then let her sleep there and listen to the nightingale's song as much as she likes!"

When the young girl learned that her father had given his permission, she immediately had a bed made up on the balcony, and since she was to sleep there that night, she waited until she saw Ricciardo and gave him a prearranged signal by which he understood what he had to do.

When Messer Lizio heard the young girl go to bed, he locked the only door leading from his bedroom to the balcony, and he, too, retired for the night. And when Ricciardo saw that everything was quiet throughout the house, with the help of a ladder he climbed up a wall; then, by climbing up the stones that jutted from the house, he pulled himself, with great difficulty and great danger of falling, up onto the balcony; once there, he was quietly but joyfully received by the young girl. After kissing many times, they lay down together, and for almost the entire night they took delight and pleasure in one another, and as they did, they made the nightingale sing many times.

The night was short and their pleasure was great, and although they were not aware of it, it was almost day when they finally fell asleep without a thing on them and as tired from the hot weather as from their play. Caterina had her right arm under Ricciardo's neck, and her left hand was grasping that thing which you ladies are ashamed to name in the company of gentlemen.

And in this position, they slept, but as day broke it failed to awaken them. Messer Lizio got up, and remembering that his daughter was sleeping on the balcony, he quietly opened the door and said:

"Let us see if the nightingale made Caterina sleep last night."

And walking out on the balcony, he lifted up the curtain around the bed and saw Ricciardo and Caterina sleeping completely naked in each other's arms and in the position just mentioned above. After recognizing Ricciardo, he quietly slipped away and went to his wife's bedroom, and he called to her, saying:

"Hurry, woman, get up and come see how enchanted your daughter is by the nightingale she has caught and is still holding in her hand!"

"How can this be?" asked his wife.

"You'll see," said Messer Lizio, "if you come quickly."

The lady quickly dressed herself and quietly followed Messer Lizio, and when they both reached the bed and lifted the curtain,

Madonna Giacomina saw for herself exactly how her daughter had managed to catch and hold on to the nightingale which she had so longed to hear sing.

Feeling that she had been treacherously deceived by Ricciardo, the lady wanted to scream at him and to insult him, but Messer Lizio told her:

"Madame, if you value my love, do not say a word, for since she has snared him, he shall be hers! Ricciardo is a noble and a rich young man; we have only to gain from such a match. If he wishes to leave this house with my blessing, he will have to marry her first; thus he shall have put his nightingale into his own cage and not into anybody else's!"

This comforted his wife, for she saw that her husband was not angered by what had taken place, and when she considered that her daughter had spent a good night, that she had rested well and caught a nightingale, she kept silent.

Hardly had they spoken these words when Ricciardo woke up; and when he saw that it was day, he thought that he was a dead man for sure, and he called to Caterina and said:

"Alas, my love, what shall we do now that day has come and trapped me here?"

At the sound of these words, Messer Lizio stepped forward, raised the curtain, and said:

"We shall do very well."

When Ricciardo saw him, he felt as if his heart had been ripped from his body, and sitting up straight in the bed, he exclaimed:

"My lord, in God's name have mercy upon me! I realize that as a disloyal and evil man, I deserve death, and, therefore, do with me what you will. But, if possible, I beg you to have pity on me—do not have me killed."

To this Messer Lizio answered:

"Ricciardo, this is not the reward that I should have had from my love and trust in you. But since this is the way things stand, and since it was your youth that made you commit this error, in order that you may save my honor and your own life, before you move from here, take Caterina for your lawful wife. And in so doing, she will be yours for as long as she may live, just as she has been yours this night. And in this manner, you shall have both my pardon and your own safety. But if you do not agree to this, then I suggest you commend your soul to God."

While all of this was being said, Caterina let her hold on the nightingale slip, and covering herself up, she burst into tears, begging her father to forgive Ricciardo; at the same time she implored Ricciardo to do what Messer Lizio wished, so that from then on, they might enjoy without fear other such nights together.

But there was no need for such pleas, since on the one hand, there was the shame of the error committed and the desire for atonement, and on the other the fear of death and the desire to escape it; and above all, there was Ricciardo's burning love and his desire to possess his beloved; freely and without any hesitation whatsoever, Ricciardo therefore agreed to do what Messer Lizio wished.

Messer Lizio then borrowed one of Madonna Giacomina's rings, and right there in their presence, without getting out of bed, Ricciardo took Caterina for his wife. When this was done, Messer Lizio and his wife left them, saying:

"Now go back to sleep, for you probably need sleep more than getting up."

When they had left, the two young people embraced each other, and since they had not traveled more than six miles that night, they went on another two miles before they got up again. And thus they ended their first day.

When they awakened later on, Ricciardo made more conventional arrangements with Messer Lizio; and a few days afterwards, as was proper, in the presence of their friends and relatives he married the young girl all over again, and with great fanfare he took her home to celebrate their marriage at a magnificent wedding feast. And afterwards, he hunted for nightingales both night and day with her in peace and quiet whenever he wished.

* * *

Fifth Day, Ninth Story

Federigo degli Alberighi loves but is not loved. He spends all the money he has in courtship, and he is left with only a falcon which he gives to his lady to eat when she visits his home, for he has nothing else to give her. Learning of this, she changes her mind, takes him for her husband, and makes him rich.[7]

* * *

There was once in Florence a young man named Federigo, the son of Messer Filippo Alberighi, renowned above all other men in Tuscany for his prowess in arms and for his courtliness. As often

---

7. This story forms the basis of Tenny-son's one-act play, *The Falcon*, as well as one of Longfellow's tales in *Tales of a Wayside Inn.*

happens to most gentlemen, he fell in love with a lady named Monna Giovanna, in her day considered to be one of the most beautiful and one of the most charming women that ever there was in Florence; and in order to win her love, he participated in jousts and tournaments, organized and gave feasts, and spent his money without restraint; but she, no less virtuous than beautiful, cared little for these things done on her behalf, nor did she care for him who did them. Now, as Federigo was spending far beyond his means and was taking nothing in, as easily happens he lost his wealth and became poor, with nothing but his little farm to his name (from whose revenues he lived very meagerly) and one falcon which was among the best in the world.

More in love than ever, but knowing that he would never be able to live the way he wished to in the city, he went to live at Campi, where his farm was. There he passed his time hawking whenever he could, asked nothing of anyone, and endured his poverty patiently. Now, during the time that Federigo was reduced to dire need, it happened that the husband of Monna Giovanna fell ill, and realizing death was near, he made his last will: he was very rich, and he made his son, who was growing up, his heir, and, since he had loved Monna Giovanna very much, he made her his heir should his son die without a legitimate heir; and then he died.

Monna Giovanna was now a widow, and as is the custom among our women, she went to the country with her son to spend a year on one of her possessions very close by to Federigo's farm, and it happened that this young boy became friends with Federigo and began to enjoy birds and hunting dogs; and after he had seen Federigo's falcon fly many times, it pleased him so much that he very much wished it were his own, but he did not dare to ask for it, for he could see how dear it was to Federigo. And during this time, it happened that the young boy took ill, and his mother was much grieved, for he was her only child and she loved him enormously; she would spend the entire day by his side, never ceasing to comfort him, and often asking him if there was anything he desired, begging him to tell her what it might be, for if it were possible to obtain it, she would certainly do everything possible to get it. After the young boy had heard her make this offer many times, he said:

"Mother, if you can arrange for me to have Federigo's falcon, I think I would be well very soon."

When the lady heard this, she was taken aback for a moment, and she began to think what she should do. She knew that Federigo had loved her for a long while, in spite of the fact that he never received a single glance from her, and so, she said to herself:

"How can I send or go and ask for this falcon of his which is, as I have heard tell, the best that ever flew, and besides this, his only means of support? And how can I be so insensitive as to wish to take away from this gentleman the only pleasure which is left to him?"

And involved in these thoughts, knowing that she was certain to have the bird if she asked for it, but not knowing what to say to her son, she stood there without answering him. Finally the love she bore her son persuaded her that she should make him happy, and no matter what the consequences might be, she would not send for the bird, but rather go herself for it and bring it back to him; so she answered her son:

"My son, take comfort and think only of getting well, for I promise you that the first thing I shall do tomorrow morning is to go for it and bring it back to you."

The child was so happy that he showed some improvement that very day. The following morning, the lady, accompanied by another woman, as if going for a stroll, went to Federigo's modest house and asked for him. Since it was not the season for it, Federigo had not been hawking for some days and was in his orchard, attending to certain tasks; when he heard that Monna Giovanna was asking for him at the door, he was very surprised and happy to run there; as she saw him coming, she greeted him with feminine charm, and once Federigo had welcomed her courteously, she said:

"Greetings, Federigo!" Then she continued: "I have come to compensate you for the harm you have suffered on my account by loving me more than you needed to; and the compensation is this: I, along with this companion of mine, intend to dine with you—a simple meal—this very day."

To this Federigo humbly replied: "Madonna, I never remember having suffered any harm because of you; on the contrary: so much good have I received from you that if ever I have been worth anything, it has been because of your merit and the love I bore for you; and your generous visit is certainly so dear to me that I would spend all over again that which I spent in the past; but you have come to a poor host."

And having said this, he received her into his home humbly, and from there he led her into his garden, and since he had no one there to keep her company, he said:

"My lady, since there is no one else, this good woman here, the wife of this workman, will keep you company while I go to set the table."

Though he was very poor, Federigo, until now, had never before realized to what extent he had wasted his wealth; but this morning, the fact that he found nothing with which he could honor the lady for the love of whom he had once entertained countless men in the past gave him cause to reflect: in great anguish, he cursed himself and his fortune and, like a man beside himself, he started running here and there, but could find neither money nor a pawnable object. The hour was late and his desire to honor the gracious lady was great, but not wishing to turn for help to others (not even to his own workman), he set his eyes upon his good falcon, perched in a small room; and since he had nowhere else to turn, he took the bird, and finding it plump, he decided that it would be a worthy food for such a lady. So, without further thought, he wrung its neck and quickly gave it to his servant girl to pluck, prepare, and place on a spit to be roasted with care; and when he had set the table with the whitest of tablecloths (a few of which he still had left), he returned, with a cheerful face, to the lady in his garden, saying that the meal he was able to prepare for her was ready.

The lady and her companion rose, went to the table together with Federigo, who waited upon them with the greatest devotion, and they ate the good falcon without knowing what it was they were eating. And having left the table and spent some time in pleasant conversation, the lady thought it time now to say what she had come to say, and so she spoke these kind words to Federigo:

"Federigo, if you recall your past life and my virtue, which you perhaps mistook for harshness and cruelty, I do not doubt at all that you will be amazed by my presumption when you hear what my main reason for coming here is; but if you had children, through whom you might have experienced the power of parental love, it seems certain to me that you would, at least in part, forgive me. But, just as you have no child, I do have one, and I cannot escape the common laws of other mothers; the force of such laws compels me to follow them, against my own will and against good manners and duty, and to ask of you a gift which I know is most precious to you; and it is naturally so, since your extreme condition has left you no other delight, no other pleasure, no other consolation; and this gift is your falcon, which my son is so taken by that if I do not bring it to him, I fear his sickness will grow so much worse that I may lose him. And therefore I beg you, not because of the love that you bear for me, which does not oblige you in the least, but because of your own nobility, which you have shown to be greater than that of all others in practicing courtliness, that you be pleased to give it to me, so that I may say that I have saved the life of my son by means of this gift, and because of it I have placed him in your debt forever."

When he heard what the lady requested and knew that he could not oblige her since he had given her the falcon to eat, Federigo began to weep in her presence, for he could not utter a word in reply. The lady, at first, thought his tears were caused more by the sorrow of having to part with the good falcon than by anything else, and she was on the verge of telling him she no longer wished it, but she held back and waited for Federigo's reply after he stopped weeping. And he said:

"My lady, ever since it pleased God for me to place my love in you, I have felt that Fortune has been hostile to me in many things, and I have complained of her, but all this is nothing compared to what she has just done to me, and I must never be at peace with her again, thinking about how you have come here to my poor home where, while it was rich, you never deigned to come, and you requested a small gift, and Fortune worked to make it impossible for me to give it to you; and why this is so I shall tell you briefly. When I heard that you, out of your kindness, wished to dine with me, I considered it fitting and right, taking into account your excellence and your worthiness, that I should honor you, according to my possibilities, with a more precious food than that which I usually serve to other people; therefore, remembering the falcon that you requested and its value, I judged it a food worthy of you, and this very day you had it roasted and served to you as best I could; but seeing now that you desired it in another way, my sorrow in not being able to serve you is so great that I shall never be able to console myself again."

And after he had said this, he laid the feathers, the feet, and the beak of the bird before her as proof. When the lady heard and saw this, she first reproached him for having killed such a falcon to serve as a meal to a woman; but then to herself she commended the greatness of his spirit, which no poverty was able or would be able to diminish; then, having lost all hope of getting the falcon and, perhaps because of this, of improving the health of her son as well, she thanked Federigo both for the honor paid to her and for his good will, and she left in grief, and returned to her son. To his mother's extreme sorrow, either because of his disappointment that he could not have the falcon, or because his illness must have necessarily led to it, the boy passed from this life only a few days later.

After the period of her mourning and bitterness had passed, the lady was repeatedly urged by her brothers to remarry, since she was very rich and was still young; and although she did not wish to do so, they became so insistent that she remembered the merits of Federigo and his last act of generosity—that is, to have killed such a falcon to do her honor—and she said to her brothers:

"I would prefer to remain a widow, if that would please you; but if you wish me to take a husband, you may rest assured that I shall take no man but Federigo degli Alberighi."

In answer to this, making fun of her, her brothers replied:

"You foolish woman, what are you saying? How can you want him; he hasn't a penny to his name?"

To this she replied: "My brothers, I am well aware of what you say, but I would rather have a man who needs money than money that needs a man."

Her brothers, seeing that she was determined and knowing Federigo to be of noble birth, no matter how poor he was, accepted her wishes and gave her in marriage to him with all her riches; when he found himself the husband of such a great lady, whom he had loved so much and who was so wealthy besides, he managed his financial affairs with more prudence than in the past and lived with her happily the rest of his days.

* * *

Sixth Day,
Fifth Story

Messer Forese da Rabatta [8] *and Maestro Giotto,* [9] *the painter, make fun of each other's poor appearance as they return from the Mugello.*

* * *

Dearest ladies, it often happens that Fortune conceals at times great treasures of virtue in humble artisans, as Pampinea demonstrated a moment ago, and in like manner amazing genius is often found to have been placed in the ugliest of men. This was most evident in two of our citizens of whom I intend to tell you a short tale. One of these men was called Messer Forese da Rabatta. He had a small, deformed body, and a flat, pushed-in face which would have still seemed horrible even when compared to one of the Baronci family; [1] nevertheless, he was so well versed in the law that many worthy men considered him a fountain of knowledge when it came to civil law. The other, whose name was Giotto, was a man of such genius that there was nothing in Nature—the mother and moving force behind all created things with her constant revolution of the heavens—that he could not paint with his stylus, pen, or brush or make so similar to its original in Nature

---

8. Forese da Rabatta was a well-known master of jurisprudence who lived in the first half of the fourteenth century.
9. Giotto di Bondone (1267–1337?), Florentine painter, architect, and sculptor, best known for the magnificent frescoes at the Arena chapel in Padua

and for the design of the bell tower beside the Santa Maria del Fiore cathedral in the center of Florence.
1. The Baronci family was a noble Florentine family famous for its ugliness. Boccaccio refers to them again in another novella (VI, 10).

that it did not appear to be the original rather than a reproduction. Many times, in fact, in observing things painted by this man, the visual sense of men would err, taking what was painted to be the very thing itself.

Now, since it was he who had revived that art of painting which had been buried for many centuries under the errors of various artists who painted more to delight the eyes of the ignorant than to please the intellect of wise men, he may rightly be considered one of the lights of Florentine glory; and even more so, when one considers his great modesty, for he always refused to be called "Maestro," even though he was the master of all living artists and had rightfully acquired the title. Though he refused it, this title suited him all the more because it was eagerly usurped by those who knew far less than he or his pupils did. But regardless of the greatness of his art, neither was he physically more handsome, nor had he a face more pleasing in any respect, than Messer Forese.

But getting to our story, let me say that both Messer Forese and Giotto had land in the Mugello, and Messer Forese had gone to visit his property in the summertime when the courts were closed for holiday; and by chance, as he rode the sorry-looking nag he had rented, he came across the aforementioned Giotto, who was, in like manner, returning to Florence after inspecting his own property. Giotto was no better mounted or dressed than Messer Forese, and these two old men traveled at a leisurely pace, moving along side by side.

It happened, as often happens in the summer, that a sudden rain shower caught them, and quickly they took shelter in the home of a peasant who was a friend and acquaintance of both of them. But after a time, as the rain gave no signs of stopping and because each of them wished to be in Florence that day, they borrowed two old woolen capes from the peasant and two hats, worn with age, for there was nothing better; and they continued on their way.

Now, after they had gone some distance and were soaking wet and covered with mud from the many splashings their nags had given them—something which is not likely to improve a person's appearance—the weather cleared up a bit, and after a long period of silent traveling, they began to talk to each other. And as he rode and listened to Giotto, who was a very fine storyteller, Messer Forese began to look him over from top to bottom; and seeing him so unkempt and wretched, he began to laugh, and without considering his own appearance in the least, he said:

"Giotto, if we met a stranger who had never seen you before, do you think he would believe that you were the best painter in the world, as you really are?"

To this Giotto quickly replied:

"Sir, I think he would believe it if, after looking you over, he were to think you knew your ABCs!"

When Messer Forese heard this, he realized his mistake, and found himself paid back in the same coin for which he had sold the merchandise.

* * *

Sixth Day, Tenth Story

Brother Onion promises some peasants that he will show them a feather from the wings of the angel Gabriel; instead, able to find only some charcoal, he tells them that it is some of the charcoal used to roast Saint Lorenzo.

* * *

Certaldo, as you may have heard, is a fortified city in the Val d'Elsa, within our own territory, which, no matter how small it may be now, was inhabited at one time by noble and well-to-do people. Because it was such good grazing ground, one of the brothers of Saint Anthony used to go there once each year to receive the alms that people were stupid enough to give him. He was called Brother Onion, and he was perhaps received there as warmly for his name as for his piety, since that area of the country produced onions which were famous throughout Tuscany.

Brother Onion was short, redheaded, with a cheerful face, and he was the nicest scoundrel in the world; and besides the fact that he had no education, he was such a skillful and quick talker that whoever did not know him would not only have taken him for a great master of eloquence but would have considered him to be Cicero [2] himself or perhaps Quintilian; [3] and he was a godfather, a friend, or an acquaintance of almost everyone in the district.

Now, as was his custom, he went there for one of his regular

2. Marcus Tullius Cicero (106–43 B.C.), Roman orator and statesman whose works became a model for rhetoric and highly patterned, complex prose. Writers of the early Italian Renaissance (particularly Petrarca, who helped recover surviving manuscripts of Cicero's works, but also Boccaccio) often patterned both their Latin and their Italian prose after his style. Boccaccio's *Decameron* illustrates the extent to which Ciceronian prose became the ancient model upon which much of modern Italian prose was based.

3. Marcus Fabius Quintilianus (35?–97 A.D.), Roman rhetorician whose major treatise on the subject, *Institutio Oratoria,* became a handbook for medieval and Renaissance poets and historians. Quintilian made Cicero and the Ciceronian style one of his chief models for excellent prose.

visits in the month of August; and one Sunday morning, when all the good men and women of the surrounding villages were gathered together in the parish church for mass, Brother Onion stepped forward, when the time seemed right to him, and said:

"Ladies and gentlemen, as you know, it is your practice every year to send some of your grain and crops—some of you more and others less, according to your capacity and your piety—to the poor brothers of our blessed Messer Saint Anthony, so that the blessed Saint Anthony may keep your oxen, your donkeys, your pigs, and your sheep safe from all danger; furthermore, you are used to paying, especially those of you who are enrolled in our order, those small dues which are paid once a year. To collect these contributions, I have been sent by my superior, that is, by Messer Abbot; and so, with God's blessing, after three o'clock this afternoon, when you hear the bells ring, you will come here to the front of the church, where in my usual manner I shall preach my sermon and you will kiss the cross; moreover, since I know you all to be most devoted to my lord Messer Saint Anthony, as a special favor, I shall show you a most holy and beautiful relic which I myself brought back from the Holy Land, overseas: it is one of the feathers of the angel Gabriel, precisely the one which was left in the Virgin Mary's bedchamber when he came to perform the Annuciation before her in Nazareth."

He said this, and then he stopped talking and returned to the mass. When Brother Onion was making this announcement, there happened to be, among the many others in the church, two young men who were most clever: one called Giovanni del Bragoniera and the other Biagio Pizzini, both of whom, after laughing quite a bit over Brother Onion's relic, decided to play a trick on him and his feather—even though they were old and close friends of his. They found out that Brother Onion would be eating that day in the center of town with a friend; when they figured it was around the time for him to be at table, they took to the street and went to the inn where the friar was staying. The plan was this: Biagio would keep Brother Onion's servant occupied by talking to him while Giovanni would look for this feather, or whatever it was, among the friar's possessions and would steal it from him, and then they could see just how he would be able to explain its disappearance to the people later on.

Brother Onion had a servant, whom some called Guccio the Whale, others Guccio the Dauber, and still others Guccio the Pig; he was such a crude individual that even Lippo Topo himself would not have been able to do him justice. Brother Onion would often joke about him with his friends, and say:

"My servant has nine qualities, and if any one of them had

existed in Solomon,[4] Aristotle,[5] or Seneca,[6] it would have sufficed to spoil all of their virtue, their intelligence, and holiness. Just think, then, what kind of man he must be, having nine such qualities, but no virtue, intelligence, or holiness!"

And when he was asked what these nine qualities were, he would answer in rhymes:

"I'll tell you. He's lying, lazy, and dirty; negligent, disobedient, and slanderous; heedless, careless, and mannerless; besides this, he has other various little faults that are best left unmentioned. And what is most amusing about him is that wherever he goes, he wants to take a wife and set up housekeeping; and because he has a long, black, greasy beard, he thinks he is very handsome and attractive— in fact, he imagines that every woman who sees him falls in love with him, and if he were allowed to, he would run after them so fast that he would lose his pants. And it is true that he is of great assistance to me, for he never lets anyone speak in secret to me without wishing to hear his share of the conversation, and if it happens that I am asked a question about something, he is so afraid that I will not know how to reply that he immediately answers 'yes' or 'no' for me as he sees fit."

Brother Onion had left his servant back at the inn and had ordered him to make sure that no one touched his belongings, and especially his saddlebags, for the sacred objects were inside them. But Guccio the Dauber was happier to be in a kitchen than a nightingale was to be on the green branches of a tree, especially if he knew that some servant girl was also there. When he noticed the innkeeper's maid, who was a fat, round, short, and ill-shapen creature with a pair of tits that looked like two pies of cowshit and a face like one of the Baronci family, all sweaty, greasy, and covered with soot, Guccio left Brother Onion's room unlocked and all his possessions unguarded as he swooped down into the kitchen just like a vulture pouncing on some carcass. Although it was still August, he took a seat near the fire and began to talk with the girl, whose name was Nuta, telling her that he was a gentleman by procuration, that he had a fantastic amount of florins (not counting those he had to give away to others), and that he knew how to do and say so many things—more than even his very master ever dreamed of doing and saying. And with absolutely no concern for his cowl, which was covered with so much grease it would have

4. King of Israel in the tenth century B.C., a man noted for his wisdom and reputed to be the author of three of the books of the Old Testament.
5. Greek philosopher (384–322 B.C.), pupil of Plato and tutor of Alexander the Great; author of many philosophical treatises on logic, politics, metaphysics, natural science, and ethics which became especially important for Christian medieval philosophy and theology because of the influence of St. Thomas of Aquinas.
6. Lucius Annaeus Seneca (47? B.C. to A.D. 65), Roman philosopher, political figure, and tragic poet.

seasoned all the soup kettles in Altopascio, or his torn and patched-up doublet, covered with sweat stains all around his collar and under his arms and in more spots and colors than a piece of cloth from India or China ever had, or his shoes, which were all worn out, or his hose, which were rent, he spoke to her as if he were the lord of Châtillon, talking about how he wanted to fit her out in new clothes and take her away from all this drudgery to be in the service of someone else, and how he would give her the hope for a better life (even if he could not give her very much), and he told her many other things in this very amorous manner, but, like most of his undertakings that would blow away with the wind, this one too came to nothing.

And so, when the two young men found Guccio the Pig busy with Nuta (something which made them very happy since this meant that half of their task was done), without anyone to stop them, they entered Brother Onion's bedchamber, which they found open, and the first thing they picked up to search was the saddlebag in which the feather was kept; they opened it, and discovered a little box wrapped in silk, and when they opened it, they found a feather inside, just like the kind that comes from a parrot's tail; and they realized that it had to be the one that Brother Onion promised the people of Certaldo. And it certainly would have been easy for him to make them believe his story, for in those times the luxurious customs of Egypt had not yet penetrated to any great degree into Tuscany, as they were later to do throughout all of Italy, much to its ruin; and if these feathers were known to just a few, those few certainly were not among the inhabitants of that area; on the contrary, as long as the crude customs of their forefathers endured there, not only had they never seen a parrot, but most of the people there had never heard of them.

The young men were happy to have discovered the feather. They took it out, and in order not to leave the little box empty, they filled the box with some charcoal that they found in a corner of the room.

They shut the lid and arranged everything just as they had found it, and unnoticed, they merrily departed with the feather and they waited to hear what Brother Onion would say when he found charcoal in place of the feather. The simple-minded men and women who were in church, having heard that they would be seeing one of the angel Gabriel's feathers after nones, returned home when the mass was finished; one neighbor, one friend spread the news to another, and when everyone had finished eating, so many men and women rushed into town to see this feather that there was hardly enough space for all of them.

After a hearty meal and a short nap, Brother Onion got up a little after nones, and when he heard that a great crowd of peasants was gathering to see the feather, he ordered Guccio the Dauber to come along with him to ring the church bells and to bring the saddlebags with him. With great reluctance, he left Nuta and the kitchen and made his way there very slowly; he arrived there panting, for drinking a good deal of water had bloated his stomach. But on Brother Onion's order, he went to the door of the church and began to ring the bells loudly.

When all of the people were gathered together, Brother Onion began his sermon without noticing that any of his belongings had been tampered with, and he spoke of many things in a way that served his ends, and when he came to the moment of showing the angel Gabriel's feather, he first had the congregation recite the Confiteor and had two candles lighted. First, he drew back his cowl, then he unwound the silk and took out the box; after pronouncing several words of praise about the angel Gabriel and his relic, he opened the box. When he saw it was full of charcoal, he did not suspect that Guccio Whale had done this to him, for he knew him too well to believe he was capable of such tricks, nor did he even blame him for not keeping others from doing this; he merely cursed himself silently for having made him guardian of his belongings when he knew him to be so negligent, disobedient, careless, and absent-minded—nevertheless, without changing expression, he raised his face and hands to heaven, and spoke so that all could hear him:

"O Lord, may thy power be praised forever!" Then, he closed the box and turned to the people, saying:

"Ladies and gentlemen, I will have you know that when I was very young, I was sent by my superior to those parts of the earth of the rising sun, and I was charged by express order to discover the special privileges of Porcelain which, although they cost nothing to seal, are much more useful to others than to ourselves; I set out on my way, leaving from Venice and passing through Greekburg, then riding through the kingdom of Garbo and on through Baldacca, and I came to Parione, whereupon, not without some thirst, I reached, after some time, Sardinia.

"But why do I go on listing all the countries that I visited? After passing the straits of St. George, I came to Truffia and Buffia—lands heavily populated with a great many people—and from there I came to Liarland, where I discovered many of our friars and those of other orders who scorned a life of hardship for the love of God, who cared little about the troubles of others, following their own interests, and who spent no money other than that which had not yet been coined in those countries; and afterwards I came to the land of Abruzzi where men and women walk around on mountaintops in wooden shoes and dress their pigs in their own guts. And further on I discovered people who carry bread twisted around sticks and wine in goatskins; then I arrived at the mountains of Basques, where all the streams run downhill.

"To make a long story short, I traveled so far that I came to Parsnip, India, where I swear by the habit I wear on my back that I saw billhooks fly, an incredible thing to one who has not witnessed it; but Maso del Saggio, whom I found there cracking nuts and selling the husks retail, was witness to the fact that I do not lie about this matter. But, not able to find there what I was seeking, and since to travel further would have meant going by sea, I turned back and came to the Holy Land, where cold bread in the summer costs four cents and you get the heat for nothing; and there I found the venerable father Messer Blamemenot Ifyouplease, the most worthy patriarch of Jerusalem, who, out of respect for the habit of Our Lord Messer Saint Anthony, which I have always worn, wanted me to see all the holy relics he had there with him; and they were so numerous that if I had counted them all, I would have finished up with a list several miles long; but in order not to disappoint you, let me tell you about some of them.

"First he showed me the finger of the Holy Spirit, as whole and as solid as it ever was, and the forelock of the seraphim which appeared to Saint Francis, and one of the nails of the cherubim, and one of the ribs of the True-Word-Made-Fresh-at-the-Windows, and vestments of the holy Catholic faith, and some of the beams from the star which appeared to the three wise men in the East, and a phial of the sweat of Saint Michael when he fought the devil, and the jawbones from the death of Saint Lazarus, and many others.

"And since I freely gave him copies of the *Slopes of Montemorello* in the vernacular and several chapters of the *Caprezio*, which he had been hunting for some time, he gave me in return part of his holy relics, presenting me with one of the teeth of the Holy Cross, and a bit of the sound of the bells of the temple of Solomon, in a little phial, and the feather from the angel Gabriel which I already told you I have, and one of the wooden shoes of Saint Gherardo da Villamagna, which I gave, not long ago in Florence, to Gherardo de' Bonsi, who holds it in the greatest reverence; and he also gave me some of the charcoal upon which the most holy martyr Saint Lorenzo was roasted alive. All these articles I most devoutly brought back with me, and I have them all.

"The truth is that my superior has never permitted me to show them until they were proven to be authentic, but now, because of certain miracles that were performed through them and letters received from the patriarch, he is now sure that they are authentic, and he has allowed me to display them to you. And, since I am afraid to trust them to anyone else, I always carry them with me. As a matter of fact, I carry the feather from the angel Gabriel in one little box, in order not to harm it, and the coals over which

Saint Lorenzo was roasted in another, and both boxes are so much alike that I often mistake the one for the other, and this is what happened to me today; for while I thought that I had brought the box containing the feather here, instead I brought the one with the charcoal. But I do not consider this to be an error; on the contrary, it is the will of God, and he himself placed the box in my hands, reminding me in this way that the Feast of Saint Lorenzo is only two days away; and since God wished me to show you the charcoal in order to rekindle in your hearts the devotion that you owe to Saint Lorenzo, rather than the feather that I had wanted to show you instead, he made me take out these blessed charcoals that were once bathed in the sweat of that most holy body. And so, my blessed children, remove your cowls and come forward devoutly to behold them. But first, I want each of you to know that whoever makes the sign of the cross on himself with this charcoal will live for one year safe in the knowledge that he will not be cooked by fire without his feeling it."

And after he had said those words, he sang a hymn in praise of Saint Lorenzo, opened the box, and displayed the charcoal. The foolish throng gazed upon it in reverent admiration, and they crowded around him and gave him larger offerings than they ever had before, begging him to touch each one of them with the coals. And so, Brother Onion took these charcoals in his hand and on their white shirts and doublets and on the women's veils he made the largest crosses possible, remarking that, as he had proved many times, no matter how much the charcoals were consumed in making those crosses, afterwards they would always return to their former size no sooner than they were placed back in the little box.

And in this manner, and with great profit for himself, Brother Onion turned the entire population of Certaldo into crusaders and, by means of his quick wit, tricked those who had thought they had tricked him by stealing his feather. The two young men had been present during his sermon and had heard the new story he had invented and they laughed so hard that they thought their jaws would break, for they knew how farfetched his story was; and after the crowd broke up, they went up to him and got the greatest joy in the world out of telling him what they had done; then they gave him back his feather, which in the following year raked in for him no less than the charcoal had that day.

* * *

Seventh Day, Second Story

When her husband returns home, Peronella puts her lover inside a barrel which the husband has sold; she says she has already sold it to someone who is inside checking to see if it is sound. When her lover jumps out of the barrel, he has her husband scrape it and then carry it off to his home for him.

* * *

My very dear ladies, the tricks men play on you are so numerous, and especially those that husbands play, that when a woman on occasion does as much to her husband, you should not only rejoice over it and be happy that you heard it talked about, but you should also go around telling it to everyone yourself, so that men may learn that women, for their part, know just as much about these things as they do. This cannot be anything but useful to you, for, when someone knows that others know about such matters, he will not easily wish to deceive you. Who can doubt, therefore, that when men learn what we have to say about this subject today, this will be a very good reason for them to refrain from such deceits, since they will discover that you, too, know how to deceive them, if you wish? It is, therefore, my intention to tell you how a young woman, although she was of low birth, deceived her husband and in a flash managed to save herself.

Not long ago in Naples a poor man took as his wife a beautiful and charming young girl named Peronella; he, with his mason's trade, and she, as a spinster of wool, earned very little, but they managed their lives as best they could. One day a handsome young man saw Peronella and was so charmed by her that he fell in love with her, and he managed to get around her in one way or another so that he soon got on intimate terms with her. And in order to be together, they agreed on a plan between themselves: when her husband would get up early every morning to go to work or to look for a job, the young man would hide until he saw him leave; and as the district in which they lived (which was called Avorio) was not very densely populated, when the husband left, he would enter her house; and this they did many times.

But one morning, out of many mornings, when the good man had left and Giannello Scrignario, the young man, had entered her house and was with Peronella, after a little while the husband returned home (although he usually stayed out all day); and when he discovered the door locked from the inside, he knocked; and after knocking, he began saying to himself:

"O God, may you be praised forever, for although you have made me poor, at least you have consoled me with a good and honest young wife! See how she immediately locked the door from the inside when I left, so that nobody would come in to bother her."

When Peronella heard this and recognized her husband by the way he knocked, she said:

"Alas, Giannello my love, I am done for! It's my husband! He has returned, God damn him, and I don't know what this means, for he never comes back at this hour. Maybe he saw you when you came in! But for the love of God, whatever the reason, get in that barrel over there, and I'll open the door for him and find out what brings him home so early this morning."

Giannello quickly jumped into the barrel, and Peronella went to the door and opened it for her husband, and with a frown on her face she said:

"Now what's the idea of coming home so early this morning? I see you have come back with your tools in hand; it seems to me you don't want to do a thing; and if you keep on this way, how are we going to live? Where will we get our bread? Do you think I'll let you pawn my best gown and my other rags? I do nothing all day but spin wool and work my fingers to the bone just to have at least enough oil to light our lamp. Husband, husband—there's not a neighbor here that isn't amazed and doesn't make fun of me for all the work that I put up with, and you come home with your hands dangling when you should be at work!"

And saying this, she began to cry and to start the whole story over again:

"Alas, poor me, miserable me, what an unhappy hour in which to be born! Under what unlucky star did I come into this world! I could have married a good young man, but I didn't want him, and I settled for this one, who thinks nothing of the woman he took into his home! Other women have a good time with their lovers (and there's not a single one without two or three of them), and they enjoy them and make their husbands think the moon is the sun. And me, poor me! Because I'm good and don't care for such things, I have to suffer with bad luck. I don't know why I don't take a lover like the rest of them do. You listen well, husband mine, if I wanted to sin, I could easily find someone to do it with; there are some handsome young men who love me and wish me well and who have even offered me a good deal of money, clothes, jewelry, if I chose; but since I am not the daughter of a woman of that type, my heart wouldn't allow me to do such a thing. And you come home to me when you should be at work!"

"Hey, for God's sake," said her husband, "don't get so excited; believe me, I know you and what you are like, and this morning I have even seen some evidence of it. True, I was going to work, but what you say shows that you did not realize any more than I that today is the Festival of Saint Galeone, and since there's no work today, I came home early; but I have nevertheless provided for you: I have found a way to keep us in bread for more than a month. I sold the barrel which, as you know, has been taking up room in the house for some time now, to this man you see with me here, and he is giving me five silver coins for it."

Peronella replied:

"And all this is also part of what makes me mad! You are a man, you get around, and you should know how the world is run—you sold a barrel for five silver coins—while I, a woman, when I saw the trouble it was giving us in the house, I, who almost never get out of this house, sold it for seven silver coins to a good man who climbed inside to see if it was sound just as you came in the door."

When the husband heard this, he was more than happy, and he told the man who had come for the barrel:

"My good man, God be with you. You heard my wife; she sold it for seven, and you wanted to give me only five."

"Very well," the good man replied, and he left.

Then Peronella said to her husband:

"Now that you're here, get up here, and see to our business with him."

Giannello, who had his ears cocked to hear whether there was need to fear or to take precautions, heard what Peronella said, and he immediately jumped out of the barrel; and pretending to know nothing of the husband's return he said:

"Where are you, my good woman?"

Her husband came up to him and said:

"Here I am, what can I do for you?"

"Who are you?" asked Giannello. "I should like to speak to the woman with whom I made the bargain for this barrel."

And the good man answered:

"You can deal confidently with me, for I am her husband."

Then Giannello said:

"The barrel seems sound enough to me, but it looks as if you have stored wine dregs in there, for it's completely coated over with some kind of dry stuff that I can't scrape off with my nails, and I will not take it if it isn't cleaned up first."

And Peronella said:

"No, the deal won't be called off for that; my husband will clean the whole thing."

And her husband said, "Of course"; and laying down his tools and rolling up his sleeves, he lit a lamp and picked up a scraper, crawled up into the barrel, and began to scrape it. And Peronella, pretending to be interested in what he was doing, put her head, one shoulder, and an arm into the mouth of the barrel, which was not very large, and began saying to her husband:

"Scrape here, and here, and also over there—and—see there where you left a little."

And while she stood in this position instructing and directing her husband, Giannello, who had hardly satisfied his desire that morning when the husband returned, contrived to satisfy it as best he could, for he could not do it as he really wanted to. He went up behind Peronella who, by standing there, was blocking off the mouth of the barrel, and just as the unbridled stallions of Parthia mount the mares in the open meadows when they are hot with love, so he too satisfied his youthful lust, reaching the climax and getting off at almost the same time as the scraping of the barrel came to an end, and Peronella removed her head from the barrel's mouth, and her husband came out. And so, Peronella said to Giannello:

"Take this light, my good man, and see if it is cleaned to your satisfaction."

Giannello looked inside, replied that everything was fine and that he was satisfied, and paying the seven silver coins to the husband, he had him carry the barrel to his home.

* * *

Seventh Day, Tenth Story

Two Sienese are in love with the same woman, and one of them is the godfather of her child; when he dies and returns to his friend, according to a promise he had made him, he describes how people live in the next world.

* * *

There once lived in the Porta Salaia section of Siena two young men of the lower class, one of whom was called Tingoccio Mini and the other Meuccio di Tura; and they were almost always together and, as far as anyone could tell, they were very fond of each other. Like everyone else, they attended church, and listened to the sermons which often dealt with the rewards and the punishments of souls after death according to the merits of each one. Wishing to have solid proof of this, and not finding a means to have it, they promised each other that whichever of them died first would return to the one who remained alive, if he were able, and would tell him whatever he desired to know; and this promise was sealed with a solemn oath.

After this promise had been made and as they continued to be close friends, it happened that Tingoccio became godfather to the son of one Ambruogio Anselmini of Camporeggi and his wife, Monna Mita. Tingoccio, in the company of Meuccio, would visit his godchild's mother rather frequently, and in spite of his relationship to her, he fell in love with her, for she was a beautiful and attractive woman; and since Meuccio found her pleasing and because he would often hear Tingoccio praise her, he also fell in love with her. And each one avoided speaking about his love to the other, but for different reasons: Tingoccio kept from revealing it to Meuccio because of the wickedness he himself saw in loving his godchild's mother, and he would have been ashamed if anyone had learned of it; Meuccio did not do so because he noticed that she pleased Tingoccio so much, whereupon he said to himself:

"If I reveal this to him, he will become jealous of me, and since he can speak to her whenever he likes, as he is the godfather of her child, he might make her dislike me, and so I may never get what I want from her."

Now these two young men kept on loving in the manner just described, and then it happened that Tingoccio, who was more skillful at demonstrating his desire to the lady, was so clever with his words that he had his pleasure from her; Meuccio noticed this, and although it displeased him very much, he still hoped to fulfill his own desires and pretended not to know anything, so as not to give Tingoccio an excuse or a reason to spoil or to impede any of his plans.

Thus, the two companions were in love, one more happily than the other. The fact was that Tingoccio found himself in possession of the lady's fertile terrain, and he so spaded and ploughed it over that an illness struck him which, after several days, grew worse; and not able to bear it any longer, he passed from this life. On the third day after his death (perhaps because he could not get there any sooner), he came one night, as he had promised, to Meuccio's bedroom and called to him as he slept soundly. When he had awakened, Meuccio said:

"Who are you?"

To this he replied:

"I am Tingoccio, and according to the promise I made you, I have returned to give you news of the other world."

Meuccio was somewhat frightened at the sight of him, but he pulled himself together and said:

"You are welcome, my brother!"

And then he asked him if he were lost, to which Tingoccio replied:

"What is lost cannot be found; and if I am here before you, how could I be lost?"

"That's not what I mean," replied Meuccio, "I'm asking you if you are among the damned souls in the eternal fires of hell."

Tingoccio answered:

"That, no, but I am suffering terrible punishment and am in the greatest of anguish for the sins that I have committed."

Then Meuccio asked Tingoccio which punishments were given in the next life for which sins committed during his life on earth, and Tingoccio explained each of them to him. Then Meuccio asked him if he could do anything for him there in purgatory; Tingoccio replied that he could—he could have masses and prayers said for him and he could give alms, for such things helped them very much. Meuccio said that he would do this gladly; and as Tingoccio was leaving him, Meuccio remembered the woman, and lifting his head a bit, he said:

"I just remembered, Tingoccio: for sleeping with your godchild's mother, what punishment did they give you?"

To this Tingoccio replied:

"Brother, when I arrived there, there was someone who seemed to know every one of my sins by heart, and he ordered me to go to a place in which I lamented my sins in extreme pain and where I found many companions condemned to the same punishment as I was; and standing there among them and recalling what I had done with my godchild's mother, I trembled with fear, for I expected an even greater punishment for that than the one I received, although, in fact, I was then standing in a huge, very hot fire. And as one of those who were suffering at my side noticed this, he asked me:

"Why do you tremble, standing in the fire? Have you done something worse than the others who are here?"

"Oh, my friend," I answered, "I am terrified of the judgment which I expect to be passed on me for a great sin that I have committed."

Then that soul asked me what sin it was, and I replied:

"The sin was this: I slept with the mother of my godchild, and I made love to her so much that I wore it to the bone."

Then, laughing at me, he said:

" 'Go on, you idiot, don't worry, for down here they don't count the mother of a godchild for very much!' And when I heard this, it made me feel much better."

And he said this as the dawn was breaking; then he added:

"Meuccio, God bless you. I can't stay with you any longer."

And quickly he vanished.

When Meuccio heard that in the other world they didn't care whether or not it was with the mother of your godchild, he began to laugh at his stupidity for having already spared a number of such women and, abandoning his ignorance, he became wiser in such matters from that time on.

* * *

Eighth Day, Third Story

Calandrino, Bruno, and Buffalmacco go down to the Mugnone River to look for the magic heliotrope, and Calandrino thinks he has found it; he returns home loaded with stones, and his wife scolds him, and he, in anger, beats her, and tells his companions what they already know better than he.

* * *

Not long ago in our city, which has always abounded in various customs and strange people, there was a painter called Calandrino, a simpleton of bizarre habits who spent most of the time with two other painters called Bruno and Buffalmacco, men who were pleasant enough but also very shrewd and sharp, and they spent their time with Calandrino because they often found his ways and his simple-mindedness very funny.

There was also at that time in Florence a most attractive and charming young man named Maso del Saggio, who was able and fortunate in whatever he wished to do and who, when he heard the many tales about Calandrino's simplicity, decided to amuse himself by playing a trick on him or by making him believe some extraordinary thing; and one day, by chance in the church of San Giovanni, he came upon Calandrino, who was staring at the paintings and the bas-reliefs of the canopy which had been built recently over the altar of that church, and he decided that this was the right time and place to put his plan into action. After informing one of his companions of what he intended to do, Maso walked with him over to where Calandrino was sitting alone, and pretending not to see him, they began to talk to each other about the hidden powers of various stones, about which Maso spoke so convincingly that he might well have been a true and expert jeweler and important lapidary; Calandrino perked up his ears at the sound of this conversation, and when he decided that the secret part of their talk had come to an end, he rose to his feet and went over to join them, much to the delight of Maso, who was asked by Calandrino, picking up their conversation, where such powerful stones might be found.

Maso replied that most of them were found in Berlinzone, the land of the Basques, in a country which is called Bengodi, where they tie up vineyards with sausages and where you can have a goose for a dime and a gosling thrown in with it, and that there was a mountain there made entirely of grated Parmesan cheese upon which there lived people who did nothing but make macaroni and ravioli which they cook in capon broth and which they then cast down upon the ground, and whoever picks up the greater part of it gets the most; and nearby there flowed a stream of sweet white wine, the best that was ever tasted, without a drop of water in it.

"Oh," said Calandrino, "that's a great country; but tell me, what do they do with the capons they cook?"

"The Basques eat them all," answered Maso.

"Were you ever there?" asked Calandrino.

"You ask if I was ever there?" replied Maso. "If I've been there once, I've been there a thousand times!"

Then Calandrino asked: "And how many miles is it from here?"

Maso replied: "More than hundreds, dillions of zillions!"

"Then," concluded Calandrino, "it must be further off than the Abruzzi."

"It certainly is," replied Maso, "more or less."

Since Maso said all this with a straight face, never laughing, the simple-minded Calandrino believed every word of his, and so he said:

"It's too far away for me, but if it were a little closer, I can tell you I'd give it a try once just to see the macaroni come falling down and to stuff myself full of it. But tell me, if you will: aren't any of those powerful stones found in these parts?"

To this Maso replied:

"Yes, two types of stones of great power are found here: there are the sandstones of Settignano and Montisci from which we get our flour when they are made into millstones—that's why they say in these parts that grace comes from God and millstones from Montisci; but there are so many of these sandstones around here that we value them as little as they value their emeralds, of which they have an entire mountain higher than Montemorello, and it shines at night, by God! And did you know that anyone who polishes the millstones and sets them in a ring before a hole is bored in them can have anything he desires, if he takes them to the sultan? The other is a stone which we lapidaries call the heliotrope, a stone of extraordinary powers; for as long as anyone carries it around with him, and as long as he has it on his person, he cannot be seen by anyone.

Then Calandrino said:

"These are great powers, but where is that second stone found?"

To this question, Maso answered that they are usually found in the Mugnone valley.

Then Calandrino asked:

"How large is this stone and what color is it?"

Maso replied:

"There are various sizes, some more and some less large, but they are all a kind of blackish color."

Calandrino took note of all these things to himself, and then pretending to have something else to do, he left Maso, having made up his mind to search for this stone; but he decided not to start looking until he told Bruno and Buffalmacco, who were his special friends. And so, he wasted all the rest of that morning looking for them, in order that they might all go to search for the stones together and without delay and before someone else discovered them. Finally, some time after nones, he remembered that they were working in the convent of the nuns of Faenza, and even though it was a very hot day, he left all his work and ran there to get them; and when he had called them out, he said this to them:

"My friends, if you are willing to trust me, we can become the richest men in Florence, for I have heard from a trustworthy man that in the Mugnone there is found a stone that makes you invisible when you carry it; therefore, I think we should go there and look for it without any delay, before someone else does. We'll find it for sure, for I know what it looks like; and when we have found it, we won't have to do anything but put it in our pockets and go to the bankers, whose tables, as you know, are always full of silver and florins, and take as much as we like. No one will see us, and in this way we can get rich quick and without having to spend the whole day daubing the walls like snails."

When Bruno and Buffalmacco heard this, they began laughing to themselves, and looking at each other, they pretended to be greatly amazed, and they praised Calandrino's suggestion; then, Buffalmacco asked what the name of the stone was. Calandrino, whose brain was soft as pasta, had already forgotten it, and so he answered:

"What do we care about its name when we know its powers? It seems to me that we should go look for it without waiting any longer."

"All right," Bruno said, "but how is it shaped?"

Calandrino answered:

"They come in all shapes and sizes, but all are kind of black; so I think we ought to pick up all the blackish stones we see, until we come across the one; and let's get going and stop losing time!"

To this Bruno said: "Wait a minute." And turning to Buffalmacco he remarked:

"It seems to me that Calandrino has a good idea, but I don't think that this is the best time for it; since the sun is high and blazing down on the Mugnone, it will have dried out all the stones, so that the stones which in the morning before the sun has dried them out look black, now will all look white; and besides this, there are many people around those parts today, since it's a working day in the Mugnone, and if they see us, they might guess what we are doing there and perhaps might do the same thing; and they might uncover the stone before we do, and then the whole thing would have been a waste of time. If you agree, I think that this work should be done in the morning when the black stones can be distinguished better from the white ones, and on a holiday when there won't be anyone to see us."

Buffalmacco praised Bruno's advice, and Calandrino agreed to it, and they also agreed that the following Sunday morning all three of them would go together to look for this stone; but above all else Calandrino begged them not to tell anyone in the world about this, for it had been confided to him in the strictest of confidence. And when they had all agreed, he told them what he had heard about the country of Bengodi, swearing that what he had heard was true. As soon as Calandrino left them, they decided between themselves what they were going to do.

Calandrino waited anxiously for Sunday morning to come and when it came, he got up at daybreak and called his friends, and leaving the city by the San Gallo gate, they went down into the Mugnone, and, moving downstream, they searched for the stone. Calandrino went ahead, since he was the most eager, and darting to this side and to the other, whenever he saw some black stone he pounced upon it, picked it up, and put it inside his shirt. His companions followed behind, gathering a stone here and there, but Calandrino had not gone very far before he found his shirt was full; so, he pulled up the folds of his tunic (which was not cut in the narrow Flemish fashion) and securely fastened them to his waist all around him, forming a large bag which he also filled in a short time; and, again, turning his cloak into a bag, this too was soon filled with stones. Buffalmacco and Bruno saw that Calandrino was loaded with stones and that the meal hour was approaching, so, according to their plan, one said to the other:

"Where's Calandrino?"

Buffalmacco, who saw him right near him, turned in every direction to look for him and replied:

"I don't know, but he was here in front of us just a minute ago."

Bruno answered:

"A minute ago—that's a laugh! By now he's probably home eating for sure, and he's left us with this crazy idea of looking for black stones in the Mugnone."

"Well, then," said Buffalmacco, "he was right to trick us and leave us here, since we were stupid enough to believe him. Who, besides us, could be so dumb as to believe that you can find such a valuable stone in the Mugnone?"

When Calandrino overheard this, he believed he had found the stone and that its powers were now preventing them from seeing him, even though he stood right there in their presence. Overjoyed by his good fortune, without saying a word to them he decided to return home, and turning around, off he went. Seeing this, Buffalmacco said to Bruno:

"What shall we do? Why don't we go home?"

To this Bruno responded:

"Let's go, but I swear to God that Calandrino will never play another trick on me again; and if ever again I get as close to him as I was all morning, I'll give him such a blow on the shins with this stone that he'll remember this trick for at least a month!"

And all at once, saying these words, he drew back his arm and hit Calandrino in the heel with a stone. Calandrino, feeling the pain, raised his foot high as he began to gasp, but he remained silent and kept on going. Then Buffalmacco picked up one of the sharper stones he had collected and said to Bruno:

"Hey, do you see this nice pointed stone? This is how I'd like to toss it at Calandrino!"

And letting it fly, he gave Calandrino a real whack with it right in the kidneys, and to make a long story short, in this manner, now saying one thing and then another, they stoned Calandrino all the way from the Mugnone to San Gallo gate. There, they threw away all the stones they had gathered and stopped to let the customs guards in on the trick, and the guards, pretending not to see Calandrino, let him pass as they broke up with laughter. Without stopping, Calandrino went straight to his home, which was near Canto alla Macina, and Fortune was so favorable to this trick that while Calandrino walked from the river through the city, no one said anything to him, for it was dinnertime and there were few people in the streets. And so Calandrino entered his home with his load. By chance his wife, a beautiful and worthy woman named Monna Tessa, was at the head of the stairs, and somewhat annoyed because he had stayed out so long, as soon as she saw him come in, she began to scold him:

"Where the devil have you been? Everyone has already eaten and you turn up for something to eat now!"

When Calandrino heard this, he realized that he was visible now, and full of anger and grief he screamed:

"Damn you, woman, are you there? Now you've fixed me, but by God, I'll pay you back for it!"

He went upstairs and dumped the stones he had gathered in a room, then ran at his wife like some wild beast, and taking her by the hair, he threw her on the ground at his feet and began kicking and beating her as hard as he could all over, not leaving a hair of her head or bone in her body without a bruise, and the fact that she was begging for mercy with outstretched hands did no good whatsoever.

Buffalmacco and Bruno laughed over the trick with the customs guards for a while and then calmly they began to follow Calandrino at a distance; and when they came to his door, they heard the terrible beating he was giving his wife and they called to him, pretending that they had just returned. Calandrino appeared at the window all sweaty, flushed, and out of breath, and asked them to come up. Pretending to be somewhat angry, they came up the stairs and saw the room full of stones, and his wife in one corner crying in pain, all disheveled, her clothes torn, and her face bruised and beaten; in the other corner of the room they saw Calandrino sitting, his clothes all messed up and all out of breath. After looking at all this for a moment, they said:

"What's this, Calandrino? Have you become a mason with all these stones that we see here?" And besides this, they added: "And what's the matter with Monna Tessa? It looks like you've beaten her. What's going on here?"

Worn out by the weight of the stones he had carried and from the anger with which he had beaten his wife, as well as his grief over the good fortune which he felt he had now lost, Calandrino could not catch enough breath to utter a single word in reply; since he hesitated to answer, Buffalmacco continued:

"Calandrino, if you were angry, you shouldn't have taken it out on us by tricking us the way you did; you talked us into going to look for this precious stone with you, and then without even saying "God be with you" or "Go to hell," you left us like two idiots in the Mugnone and came back here, and we're not happy about it at all! This is the last trick you're ever going to play on us, for sure!"

Gathering up his strength, Calandrino made an effort to reply:

"Friends, don't be angry, for things are not the way they look. Unlucky me, I actually found the stone; do you want to hear the truth? When you first asked each other where I was, I was not more than ten yards from you, and when I noticed that you were coming home but did not see me, I went a bit ahead of you and continued to do so all the way home."

And beginning from the beginning, he told them everything they had done or said until their arrival; he even showed them his back and his heels, how they had been bruised by their stones, and then he continued:

"And I tell you that as I entered the city gate with all these stones on me—these you see here—no one spoke to me, and you know how unpleasant and bothersome those customs guards usually are, wanting to look through everything and all—and besides this, on my way home I met many of my friends and neighbors who would always speak to me and invite me for a drink, but no one even said half a word to me, just like they didn't see me. Finally, when I arrived home, this devil of a damned woman appeared before me and saw me, because, as you know, women cause everything to lose its virtue; so as once I could have called myself the luckiest man in Florence, now I have become the most unlucky, and because of this I beat her as much as my hands could stand, and I don't know what kept me from slitting her throat. Damn the moment I first laid eyes on her and when she first came into this house!"

And flying into a rage once more, he was just about to get up and start beating her again from the beginning. As Buffalmacco and Bruno listened to his story, they pretended to be very much amazed, and from time to time they would confirm what Calandrino said —they wanted to laugh so much that they almost burst! But seeing him so angry that he was about to get up and beat his wife a second time, they rushed over to restrain him, saying to him that it was not her fault but rather his, for he knew that women cause everything to lose its virtue and that he had not told her to stay away from him that day and that this precaution had been denied him by God either because such good luck was not to be his or perhaps because he had in mind to trick his friends, to whom he should have shown his discovery as soon as he had made it.

And after many words and a good deal of trouble, they managed to reconcile the weeping wife with him, leaving him in a melancholy mood with a house full of stones.

* * *

Ninth Day, Second Story

An abbess quickly gets up from her bed in the dark to surprise one of her nuns accused of being in bed with her lover. The abbess herself is with a priest in bed, and she puts his pants on her head, thinking that she is putting on her veil. When the accused nun sees the pants and points them out to the abbess, she is set free and is allowed to be with her lover.

* * *

I would have you know that in Lombardy there is a convent, very famous for its sanctity and religious spirit. Among the nuns there was a young lady of noble blood and endowed with marvelous beauty, whose name was Isabetta. One day she came to the convent's grating to speak to a relative, and she fell in love with a handsome young man who had accompanied him; and the young man likewise fell in love with her, when he saw how beautiful she was and when he saw her love for him in her eyes. And they both sustained this unrequited love for a long time, much to the discomfort of them both.

Finally, since each desired the other, the young man devised a means of being able to visit his nun secretly; this was agreeable to her, and he visited her not once, but many times, to their mutual delight. But as this went on for some time, it happened one night that he was seen by one of the nuns as he was leaving Isabetta's cell, without either of them being aware of this. The nun told the news to several others. At first they wanted to denounce her to the abbess, Madonna Usimbalda, a good and holy woman in the opinion of her nuns and all those who knew her. But after they thought about it, they decided to have the abbess catch her with her young lover so that there would be no way of denying the fact; and so they remained silent and they secretly kept watch over her in turns in order to catch the lovers.

Now Isabetta knew nothing about any of this, and one night she had her lover come to her; this was immediately noted by the nuns who were keeping watch. When it appeared that the time was ripe, a goodly part of the night already having passed, they divided themselves into two groups: one stood guard outside the entrance to Isabetta's cell; the other ran to the bedroom of the abbess. When their knocks were answered with a reply, they said:

"Get up, Mother Superior, get up immediately! We've discovered that Isabetta has a young man in her cell!"

That night the abbess was in the company of a priest whom she often had brought into her bedroom in a chest, and when she heard the noise, fearing that the nuns, in their excessive haste and zeal, might beat down her door, she got up quickly and dressed in the dark as best she could; and thinking that she had picked up her folded nun's veil of the sort which is called "psalters," she picked up the priest's pants instead; and she was in such a hurry that, without realizing it, she threw his pants over her head in place of her "psalters," left her bedroom, and quickly locked it behind her, saying:

"Where is this cursèd woman?"

The other nuns were so anxious and eager to catch Isabetta in the act that they did not notice what the abbess had on her head; she reached the door of the cell and, with the help of the other nuns, forced open the door. They rushed in and found the two lovers in each other's arms; taken by this sudden surprise, not knowing what to do, they lay motionless.

The young girl was immediately led off by the other nuns to the convent's meeting hall. The young man remained there; he dressed, and then waited to see how the affair might end, intending to harm as many of them as he could if anything should happen to his young novice, and to take her away with him.

Having taken her seat in the meeting hall in the presence of all the nuns, who were looking only at the guilty girl, the abbess began to vilify the young nun in terms never before used to a woman, telling her how her indecent, her depraved actions, had they ever become known outside the convent, would ruin the sanctity, the honesty, and the good name of the convent; and to her verbal abuse, she added the most serious of threats.

The young girl, in her timidity and shame, knowing she was guilty, did not know how to reply, hoping with her silence to arouse a feeling of compassion in the others. And as the scolding of the abbess continued, the young girl happened to look up and see what the abbess was wearing on her head, with suspenders dangling on either side. Realizing what the abbess had been doing and regaining her self-confidence, she said:

"God save you, Mother Superior; tie up your bonnet and then tell me what you will."

The abbess, who did not understand what she meant, replied:

"What bonnet, you slut? Even now you have the nerve to be clever? Do you think what you have done is a joking matter?"

Then, a second time, the young girl said:

"Mother Superior, I beg you to tie up your bonnet; then say anything you please to me."

At this, many of the nuns glanced up at the abbess's head, and she put her hands to her veil—then, they all saw why Isabetta had spoken as she had. When she realized that she was equally guilty and that there was no way to cover up her sin from the others, the abbess changed her tone and began to speak in a completely different manner, concluding that it was impossible for anyone to defend oneself from the desires of the flesh. And she said that everyone should enjoy herself as best she could, provided that it be done as discreetly as it had been until that day.

And after Isabetta had been set free, the abbess returned to sleep with her priest, and Isabetta with her lover. And, in spite of all the other nuns that envied her, Isabetta had him come to her many times; the other nuns, without lovers, sought their solace secretly in the best way they knew how.

* * *

Ninth Day,
Tenth Story

At Compare Pietro's request, Father Gianni casts a spell in order to turn his wife into a mare; but when it comes time to stick the tail on, Pietro spoils the spell completely by saying that he doesn't want a tail.

* * *

A year or so ago there was at Barletta a priest called Don Gianni di Barolo who, because his church was a poor one, was obliged to earn his keep by buying and selling and by transporting goods here and there with his mare to the fairs of Apulia. As he went about his business, he became very friendly with a man who was called Pietro da Tresanti, who practiced the same trade with a donkey, and as a sign of his love and friendship, he always addressed him in the Apulian fashion as Compare Pietro.[7] And whenever Pietro came to Barletta, he always invited him to his church, where he gave him lodgings and entertained him as best he could.

Compare Pietro was a very poor man who owned a small house in Tresanti, barely large enough for him, his young and beautiful wife, and his donkey. But whenever Don Gianni happened to be in Tresanti, he always took him to his home and tried to entertain him as best he could in gratitude for the hospitality his friend had shown him in Barletta. But there was the problem of lodgings: since Compare Pietro had only one small bed, in which he and his beautiful wife slept, he could not entertain Don Gianni as he wished. Father Gianni, therefore, was forced to sleep on a pile of straw in the stable with Pietro's donkey and his own mare for company.

Pietro's wife knew how well the priest entertained her husband at Barletta, and often, when the priest came, she suggested that she go sleep with a neighbor of theirs named Zita Carapresa di Giudice Leo, so that the priest could sleep with her husband in their bed. And she suggested this many times to the priest, but he always rejected the idea; in fact, on one occasion he said to her:

"Comare Gemmata, don't bother about me. I'm fine. You see, whenever I want to, I can change this mare of mine into a beautiful young girl and lie with her. Then, whenever I wish, I can turn her back into a mare. And therefore I would never leave her."

---

7. In this context, *compare* and *comare* are friendly terms of address still in use in the south of Italy, and they have no real equivalent in English. Literally, the words mean "godfather" and "godmother."

This story amazed the young woman, who believed it. She told the story to her husband, and then added: "If he is such a good friend of yours, why don't you have him teach you this magic spell so that you can make a mare of me and go about your business with both a donkey and a mare? This way, we'll make twice as much money. And once we're home, you can turn me back into a woman—the way I am now."

Compare Pietro, who was more of a simpleton than not, believed this story and took his wife's advice. As best he knew how, he began urging Don Gianni to teach him the magic spell. Don Gianni tried his best to dissuade him from this foolishness, but he was unsuccessful. He said:

"Very well. Since you will have it no other way, we shall get up early tomorrow morning as usual, before dawn, and I shall show you how it is done. The most difficult part of this task, as you shall soon see, is sticking the tail on."

Compare Pietro and Comare Gemmata, who hardly slept a wink that night so eagerly were they looking forward to the coming event, got out of bed before day was about to break and woke up Don Gianni, who, still in his nightshirt, came into Compare Pietro's little bedroom and said:

"There is no person in the world, other than yourself, for whom I would do this favor, and since it pleases you, I shall do it. But you must do what I tell you to do if you want it to succeed."

The two said that they would do whatever he told them to do. And so, Father Gianni picked up a candle, put it in Compare Pietro's hand, and said to him:

"Watch carefully everything I do and memorize what I say. And no matter what you hear me say or see me do, be sure you do not utter a word; otherwise you will spoil everything. And pray to God that the tail sticks on firmly!"

Compare Pietro took the candle and said that he would do as he was told. Then Don Gianni made Comare Gemmata take off all her clothes and stand with her hands and feet on all fours as if she were a mare, warning her as well not to utter a word no matter what happened. And as his hands caressed her face and her head, he began to say:

"Let this be the beautiful head of a mare."

Then stroking her hair, he said:

"Let this be the beautiful mane of a mare."

And then, fondling her arms, he said:

"And let these be the beautiful front legs and hooves of a mare."

Then, as he fondled her breasts, finding them to be round and firm, a certain something-or-other was awakened and it stood straight up. And he said:

"And let this be the beautiful chest of a mare."

And he did the same thing to her back, her stomach, her buttocks, her thighs, and her legs; and finally, when nothing was left out to make her complete but the tail, he lifted his nightshirt and took out the tool which one uses for planting men, and sticking it into the furrow for which it was made, he said:

"And let this be the beautiful tail for a mare."

When Compare Pietro, who had carefully observed everything up to that point, saw this last maneuver, he said disapprovingly:

"Oh, Don Gianni, no tail! I really don't want a tail there!"

The vital liquid which all plants need to take root had already come when Don Gianni, having pulled it out, replied:

"Alas! Compare Pietro! What have you done? Didn't I warn you not to say a word about what you saw? The mare was just about to be made, but now your babbling has spoiled everything, and there's no way of ever making another one."

Compare Pietro said:

"That's fine with me—I didn't want that kind of tail anyway! Why didn't you ask me to do it? Besides, you stuck it on too low."

Don Gianni replied:

"Because the first time, you wouldn't have known how to stick it on as well as I can."

The young woman, hearing these words, stood up on her feet, and in all seriousness she said to her husband:

"You idiot! Why did you ruin both your business and mine? Have you ever seen a mare that didn't have a tail? So help me God, you are a poor man, but you deserve to be even poorer than you are!"

Now that there was no longer any way to change the young woman into a mare because Compare Pietro had spoken when he had, the woman, sadly and forlornly, put back on her clothes, and Compare Pietro prepared to go about his old trade with just one donkey as he had done before. And with Don Gianni he went off to the fair at Bitonto, but never again did he ask his friend for the same favor.

* * *

Tenth Day, Tenth Story

The marquis of Saluzzo, by the requests of his vassals, is urged to take a wife, and in order to have his own way in the matter, he picks the daughter of a peasant from whom he has two children;

he pretends to her that he has had them killed; then, under the pretense that she has displeased him, he pretends to have taken another wife, and has their own daughter brought into the house as if she were his new wife once he has his real wife driven out in nothing more than her shift; after he discovers that she has patiently endured it all, he brings her back home, more beloved than ever, shows their grown children to her, and honors her, and has others honor her, as the marchioness.[8]

* * *

A long time ago, among the various marquises of Saluzzo, there was the first-born son of the family, a young man named Gualtieri who, having no wife or children, spent his time doing nothing but hawking and hunting, and never thought of taking a wife or of having children—and this was very wise on his part. This did not please his vassals, and they begged him on many an occasion to take a wife so that he would not be without an heir and they left without a master; they offered to find him a wife born of the kind of mother and father that might give him good expectations of her and who would make him happy. To this Gualtieri answered:

"My friends, you are urging me to do something that I was determined never to do, for you know how difficult it is to find a woman with a suitable character, and how plentiful is the opposite kind of woman, and what a wretched life a man would lead married to a wife that is not suitable to him. And to say that you can judge the character of a daughter by examining those of her father and mother is ridiculous (which is the basis of your argument that you can find a wife to please me), for I do not believe that you can come to know all the secrets of the father or mother; and even if you did, a daughter is often unlike her father and mother. But since

---

8. Boccaccio's account of "patient Griselda" had an immediate impact upon the course of English literature. Geoffrey Chaucer read Boccaccio's tale indirectly through a Latin translation of it by Petrarca, and Chaucer used this translation (*De obedientia ac fide uxoria mythologia*) and an anonymous French version as the basis for "The Clerk's Tale" in *The Canterbury Tales*. After two trips to Italy in 1372 and 1378, Chaucer returned to England with many Italian books and a fair knowledge of the works of not only Boccaccio but also Dante and Petrarca. Besides his debt to Boccaccio's tale of Griselda, other important borrowings from Boccaccio occur in Chaucer's *Troilus and Criseyde*, which is based primarily upon Boccaccio's *Filostrato;* "The Knight's Tale" in *The Canterbury Tales*, which employs some of the material in Boc-

caccio's *Teseida;* and "The Franklin's Tale" of *The Canterbury Tales*, which relies upon part of Boccaccio's *Filocolo*. Other superficial similarities between *The Decameron* and *The Canterbury Tales* have been claimed (particularly the use of a frame structure as well as various similar plots), but other popular or literary works that Chaucer could have known have the same characteristics. The fact is that Chaucer seems to have had some direct contact with all or almost all of what we today consider Boccaccio's minor works, but no direct knowledge of *The Decameron*, except through the Latin translaton of Petrarca. Boccaccio's *Decameron* in its entirety was not well known in England until the fifteenth century, and the first complete English translation dates from 1620.

you wish to tie me up with these chains, I will do as you request; and so that I shall have only myself to blame if things turn out badly, I want to be the one who chooses her; and I tell you now that if she is not honored by you as your lady—no matter whom I choose—you will learn to your great displeasure how serious a matter it was to compel me with your requests to take a wife against my will!"

His worthy men replied that they would be happy if he would only choose a wife. For some time Gualtieri had been pleased by the manners of a poor young girl who lived in a village near his home, and since she seemed very beautiful to him, he thought that life with her could be quite pleasant; so, without looking any further, he decided to marry her, and he sent for her father, who was extremely poor, and made arrangements with him to take her as his wife. After this was done, Gualtieri called all his friends in the area together and said to them:

"My friends, you wished and continue to wish that I take a wife, and I am ready to do this, but I do so more to please you than to satisfy any desire of mine to have a wife. You know what you promised me: to honor happily anyone I chose for your lady; therefore, the time has come for me to keep my promise to you, and for you to do the same for me. I have found a young girl after my own heart, very near here, whom I intend to take as my wife and bring home in a few days; so, make sure that the wedding celebrations are splendid and that you receive her honorably, so that I may consider myself as content with your promise as you are with mine."

The good men all happily replied that this pleased them very much and that, whoever she was, they would treat her as their lady and honor her in every way they could; and soon after this, they all set about preparing for a big, beautiful, and happy celebration, and Gualtieri did the same. He had a great and sumptuous wedding feast prepared, and he invited his friends and relatives and the great lords and many others from the surrounding countryside; and besides this, he had beautiful and expensive dresses cut out and tailored to fit a young girl who he felt was about the same size as the young girl he had decided to marry; he also saw to it that girdles and rings were purchased and a rich, handsome crown, and everything else a new bride might require. When the day set for the wedding arrived, Gualtieri mounted his horse at about the middle of tierce, and all those who had come to honor him did the same; when all was arranged, he said:

"My lords, it is time to fetch the new bride."

Setting out on the road with the entire company, they arrived at the little village; they came to the house of the girl's father and found her returning from the well in great haste in order to be able to see the arrival of Gualtieri's bride in time with the other women; when Gualtieri saw her, he called her by name—that is, Griselda—and asked her where her father was; to this she replied bashfully:

"My lord, he is in the house."

Then Gualtieri dismounted and ordered all his men to wait for him; alone, he entered that wretched house, and there he found Griselda's father, who was called Giannucolo, and he said to him:

"I have come to marry Griselda, but before I do, I should like to ask her some things in your presence."

And he asked her, if he were to marry her, would she always try to please him, and would she never become angry over anything he said or did, and if she would always be obedient, and many other similiar questions—to all of these she replied that she would. Then Gualtieri took her by the hand, led her outside, and in the presence of his entire company and all others present, he had her stripped naked and the garments he had had prepared for her brought forward; then he immediately had her dress and put on her shoes, and upon her hair—as disheveled as it was—he had a crown placed; then, while everyone was marveling at the sight, he announced:

"My lords, this is the lady I intend to be my wife, if she will have me as her husband."

And then, turning to Griselda who was standing there blushing and perplexed, he asked her:

"Griselda, do you take me for your husband?"

To this she answered: "Yes, my lord."

And he replied: "And I take you for my wife."

In the presence of them all he married her; then he had her set upon a palfrey and he led her with an honorable company to his home. The wedding feast was great and sumptuous, and the celebration was no different from what it might have been if he had married the daughter of the king of France. The young bride seemed to have changed her soul and ways along with her garments: she was, as we have already said, beautiful in body and face, and as she was beautiful before, she became even more pleasing, attractive, and well-mannered, so that she seemed to be not the shepherdess daughter of Giannucolo but rather the daughter of some noble lord, a fact that amazed everyone who had known her before; moreover, she was so obedient and indulgent to her husband that he considered himself the happiest and the most satisfied man on earth, and she was also so gracious and kind towards her husband's subjects that there was no one who was more beloved or willingly honored than she was; in fact, everyone prayed for her welfare, her prosperity, and her further success. Whereas everyone used to say that Gualtieri had acted unwisely in taking her as his wife, they now declared that he was the wisest and the cleverest man in the world, for none other than he could have ever recognized her noble character hidden under her rude garments and her peasant dress.

In short, she knew how to comport herself in such a manner that before long, not only in her husband's marquisate but everywhere, her virtue and her good deeds became the topic of discussion, and for anything that had been said against her husband when he married her, she now caused the opposite to be said. Not long after she had come to live with Gualtieri, she became pregnant, and in the course of time she gave birth to a daughter, which gave Gualtieri much cause for rejoicing. But shortly afterwards, a new thought entered his mind: he wished to test her patience with a long trial and intolerable proofs. First, he offended her with harsh words, pretending to be angry and saying that his vassals were very unhappy over her because of her low birth and especially now that they saw her bear children; they were most unhappy over the daughter that had been born and did nothing but mutter about it. When the lady heard these words, without changing her expression or her good intentions in any way, she answered:

"My lord, do with me what you believe is best for your honor and your happiness, and I shall be completely happy, for I realize that I am of lower birth than they and am not worthy of this honor which your courtliness has bestowed upon me."

This reply was very gratifying to Gualtieri, for he realized that she had not become in any way haughty because of the respect which he or others had paid her. A short time later, after he had told his wife in vague terms that his subjects could not tolerate the daughter to whom she had given birth, he spoke to one of her servants and sent him to her, and with a very sad expression, he said to her:

"My lady, since I do not wish to die, I must do what my lord commands. He has commanded me to take this daughter of yours and to . . ." And he could say no more.

When the lady heard these words and saw her servant's face, she remembered what her husband had said to her and understood that her servant had been ordered to murder the child; therefore, she quickly took the girl from the cradle, kissed her and blessed her, and although she felt a great pain in her heart, without changing her expression she placed her in her servant's arms and said to him:

"There, do exactly what your lord and mine has ordered you to do; but do not abandon her body to be devoured by the beasts and birds unless he has ordered you to do so."

The servant took the child and told Gualtieri what the lady had said, and he was amazed at her perseverance; then he sent the servant with his daughter to one of his relatives in Bologna, begging her to raise and educate the girl carefully but without ever telling whose daughter she was. Shortly after this, the lady became pregnant again, and in time she gave birth to a male child, which pleased Gualtieri very much; but what he had already done did not satisfy him, and he wounded the lady with even a greater hurt, telling her one day in a fit of feigned anger:

"Lady, since you bore me this male child, I have not been able to live with my vassals, for they bitterly complain about a grandson of Giannucolo's having to be their lord after I am gone; because of this, I am very much afraid that unless I want to be driven out, I must do what I did the other time, and must eventually abandon you and take another wife."

The lady listened to him patiently and made no other reply than this:

"My lord, think only of making yourself happy and of satisfying your desires and do not worry about me at all, for nothing pleases me more than to see you contented."

After a few days, Gualtieri sent for his son in the same way he had sent for his daughter, and he again pretended to have the child killed, actually sending him to be raised in Bologna as he had his daughter; and the lady's face and words were no different from what they were when her daughter had been taken, and Gualtieri was greatly amazed at this and remarked to himself that no other woman could do what she had done: if he had not seen for himself how extremely fond she was of her children as long as they found favor in his sight, he might have believed that she acted as she did in order to be free of them, but he realized that she was doing it out of obedience.

His subjects, believing he had killed his children, criticized him bitterly and regarded him as a cruel man, and they had the greatest of compassion for the lady; but she never said anything to the women with whom she mourned the deaths of her children. Then, not many years after the birth of their daughter, Gualtieri felt it was time to put his wife's patience to the ultimate test: he told many of his vassals that he could no longer bear having Griselda as a wife and that he realized he had acted badly and impetuously when he had taken her for his wife, and that he was going to do everything possible to procure a dispensation from the pope so that he could marry another woman and abandon Griselda; he was reprimanded for this by many of his good men, but to them he answered that it was fitting that this be done.

When the lady heard about these matters and it appeared to her that she would be returning to her father's house (perhaps even to guard the sheep as she had previously done) and that she would have to bear witness to another woman possessing the man she loved, she grieved most bitterly; but yet, as with the other injuries of Fortune which she had suffered, she determined to bear this one too with a stern countenance. Not long afterwards, Gualtieri had forged letters sent from Rome, and he showed them to his subjects, pretending that in these letters the pope had granted him the dispensation to take another wife and to abandon Griselda; and so, having his wife brought before him, in the presence of many people he said to her:

"Lady, because of a dispensation which I have received from the pope, I am able to take another wife and to abandon you; and since my ancestors were great noblemen and lords of these regions while yours have always been peasants, I wish you to be my wife no longer and to return to Giannucolo's home with the dowry that you brought me, and I shall then bring home another more suitable wife, whom I have already found."

When the lady heard these words, she managed to hold back her tears only with the greatest of effort (something quite unnatural for a woman), and she replied:

"My lord, I have always realized that my lowly origins were not suitable to your nobility in any respect, and the position I have held with you, I always recognized as having come from God and yourself; I never made it mine or considered it given to me—I always kept it as if it were a loan; if you wish to have it back again, it must please me (as it does) to return it to you: here is your ring with which you married me—take it. You order me to take back with me the dowry I brought you, and to do this no accounting on your part, nor any purse or beast of burden, will be necessary, for I have not forgotten that you received me naked; and if you judge it proper that this body which bore your children should be seen by everyone, I shall leave naked; but I beg you, in the name of my virginity which I brought here and which I cannot take with me, that you at least allow me to carry away with me a single shift in addition to my dowry."

Gualtieri, who felt closer to tears than anyone else there, stood nevertheless with a stern face and said:

"You may take a shift."

Many of those present begged him to give her a dress, so that this woman who had been his wife for more than thirteen years would not be seen leaving his home so impoverished and in such disgrace as to leave clad only in a shift; but their entreaties were in vain, and in her shift, without shoes or anything on her head, the lady commended him to God, left his house, and returned to her father, accompanied by the tears and the weeping of all those who witnessed her departure.

Giannucolo, who had never believed that Gualtieri would keep his daughter as his wife, and who had been expecting this to happen any day, had kept the clothes that she had taken off that morning when Gualtieri married her; he gave them back to her, and she put them on, and began doing the menial tasks in her father's house as she had once been accustomed to doing, suffering the savage assaults of a hostile fortune with a brave spirit.

After Gualtieri had done this, he led his vassals to believe that he had chosen a daughter of one of the counts of Panago for his new wife; and as he was making great preparations for the wedding, he sent for Griselda to come to him, and when she arrived he said to her:

"I am bringing home the lady I have recently chosen as my wife, and I intend to honor her at her first arrival; you know that I have no women in my home who know how to prepare the bedchambers or to do the many chores that are required by such a grand celebration; you understand these matters better than anyone in the house; therefore, I want you to arrange everything: invite those ladies whom you think should be invited, and receive them as if you were the lady of the house; then when the wedding is over, you can return to your home."

These words were like a dagger in Griselda's heart, for she had not yet been able to extinguish the love that she bore for him (as she had learned to do without her good fortune), and she answered:

"My lord, I am ready and prepared."

And so in a coarse, peasant dress she entered that house which a short time before she had left dressed only in a shift, and she began to clean and arrange the bedchambers, to put out hangings and ornamental tapestries on the walls, to make ready the kitchen, and to put her hands to everything, just as if she were a little servant girl in the house; and she never rested until she had organized and arranged everything as it should be. After this, she had invitations sent in Gualtieri's name to all the ladies of the region and then waited for the celebration; when the day of the wedding came, in the poor clothes she had on and with a pleasant expression on her face and a noble manner, she courageously received all the ladies who arrived for the celebration.

Gualtieri had had her children carefully raised in Bologna by one of his relatives who had married into the family of the counts of Panago; the daughter was already twelve years of age and the most beautiful thing anyone had ever seen, and the boy was already six; he sent a message to his relative in Bologna, requesting him to be so kind as to come to Saluzzo with his daughter and his son, and to organize a handsome and honorable retinue to accompany them, and not to reveal her identity to anyone but to tell them only that he was bringing the girl as Gualtieri's bride.

The nobleman did what the marquis had asked him: he set out, and after several days he arrived at Saluzzo at about suppertime with the young girl, her brother, and a noble company, and there he found all the peasants and many other people from the surrounding area waiting to see Gualtieri's new bride. She was received by the ladies and then taken to the hall where the tables were set, where Griselda, dressed as she was, met her cheerfully and said to her:

"Welcome, my lady!"

Many of the women had begged Gualtieri (but in vain) either to allow Griselda to stay in another room or that she be permitted to wear some of the clothing that had once been hers so that she would not have to meet his guests in such clothing. Everyone sat down at the table and was served, and they all stared at the young girl and agreed that Gualtieri had made a good exchange; but it was Griselda who praised her and her little brother more than any of the others did.

Gualtieri finally felt that he had seen as much evidence as he needed to of his wife's patience; he observed that the new arrangement had not changed Griselda one bit, and since he was certain that her attitude was not due to stupidity, for he knew her to be very wise, he felt that it was time to remove her from the bitterness which he felt she must be concealing under her impassive face; so, he had her brought to him, and in the presence of everyone, he said to her with a smile:

"What do you think of my new bride?"

"My lord," replied Griselda, "she seems very beautiful to me; and if she is as wise as she is beautiful (which I believe to be the case), I have no doubt that you will live with her as the happiest lord in the world; but I beg you as strongly as I can not to inflict those wounds upon her which you inflicted upon the other woman who was once your wife, for I believe that she could scarcely endure them, both because she is younger and because she has been brought up in a more delicate fashion, while the other woman was used to continuous hardships from the time she was a little girl."

When Gualtieri saw that she firmly believed the girl was to be his wife, yet in spite of this said nothing but good about her, he made her sit beside him, and he said:

"Griselda, it is time now for you to reap the fruit of your long patience, and it is time for those who have considered me cruel, unjust, and bestial to realize that what I have done was directed toward a pre-established goal, for I wanted to teach you how to be a wife, to show these people how to know such a wife and how to choose and keep one, and to acquire for myself lasting tranquillity for as long as I was to live with you; when I went to take you for my wife, I greatly feared that this tranquillity I cherished would be lost, and so, to test you, I submitted you to the pains and trials you have known. But since I have never known you to depart from my wishes in either word or deed, and since I now believe I shall receive from you that happiness which I always desired, I intend to return to you now what I took from you for a long time and to soothe with the greatest of delight the wounds that I inflicted upon you; therefore, with a happy heart receive this girl, whom you suppose to be my bride, and her brother as your very own children and mine; they are the ones you and many others have long thought I had brutally murdered; and I am your husband, who loves you more than all else, for I believe I can boast that no other man exists who could be so happy with his wife as I am."

After he said this, he embraced and kissed her, and she was weeping for joy; they arose and together went over to their daughter who was listening in amazement to these new developments; both of them tenderly embraced first the girl and then her brother, thus dispelling their confusion as well as that of many others who were present. The ladies arose from the tables most happily, and they went with Griselda to her bedchamber, and with a more auspicious view of her future, they took off her old clothes and dressed her in one of her noble garments, and then they led her back into the hall as the lady of the house, which she had, nonetheless, appeared to be even in her tattered rags.

Everyone was most delighted about how everything had turned out, and Griselda with her husband and children celebrated in great style, with the joy and feasting increasing over a period of several days; and Gualtieri was judged to be the wisest of men (although the tests to which he had subjected his wife were regarded as harsh and intolerable) and Griselda the wisest of them all.

The count of Panago returned to Bologna several days later, and Gualtieri took Giannucolo away from his work, setting him up as his father-in-law in such a way that he lived the rest of his life honorably and most happily. After giving their daughter in marriage to a nobleman, Gualtieri lived a long and happy life with Griselda, always honoring her as much as he could.

What more can be said here, except that godlike spirits do sometimes rain down from heaven into poor homes, just as those more suited to governing pigs than to ruling over men make their appearances in royal palaces. Who besides Griselda could have endured the severe and unheard-of trials that Gualtieri imposed upon her and remained with a not only tearless but happy face? It might have served Gualtieri right if he had run into the kind of woman who, once driven out of her home in nothing but a shift, would have allowed another man to shake her up to the point of getting herself a nice-looking dress out of the affair!

* * *

The Author's Conclusion

Most noble ladies, for whose happiness I have set myself to this lengthy task, I believe that with the assistance of divine grace and your pious prayers, rather than my own merits, I have completely fulfilled what I promised to do at the beginning of the present work; now, after rendering thanks first of all to God and then to you, it is time for me to rest my pen and my weary hand. But before I rest, I intend to reply briefly to several objections that perhaps some of you and others might have wished to voice, for one thing seems very clear to me: these tales have no more privileged status than any others; and, indeed, I recall having demonstrated this in the Prologue of the Fourth Day. There will, perhaps, be some among you who will say that I have taken too much license in writing these tales; that is, I have sometimes made ladies say things, and more often listen to things, which are not very proper for virtuous ladies to say or hear.[9] I deny this, for nothing is so indecent that it cannot be said to another person if the proper words are used to convey it; and this, I believe, I have done very well.

But let us suppose that you are right (I do not intend to argue with you, for you are certain to win); then, let me say that there are many reasons at hand to explain why I have done as I did. First of all, if there are some liberties taken in any of the tales, the nature of the stories themselves required it, as will be clearly understood by any sensitive person who examines them with a reasonable eye, for I could not have told them otherwise, unless I wished to distort their form completely. And if there should be a few expressions or little words in them that are somewhat freer than a prude might

---

9. In spite of the fact that Boccaccio received some criticism for his tone, his language, and his satire of various Christian practices and the priesthood in general, no attempt was ever made during the day to censor or suppress his work. Laymen and clergymen alike in the Middle Ages had no difficulty in separating a criticism of a particular institution or office holder (which was considered legitimate) from more basic, and therefore heretical, doctrinal disagreements. Dante even condemned popes to hell with impunity. Only when the Protestant Reformation gave rise to serious threats to papal authority and Catholic dogma did the church establish the Index of Prohibited Books, to which list *The Decameron* was added in 1559. A Florentine poet and critic, Lionardo Salviati, was given the task of revising Boccaccio's masterpiece to make it conform to post-Tridentine tastes and moral standards. This revision, known as the "rassettatura" or "tidying up" of the work, was published in Venice in 1582, and what emerged was a completely different book. Sixty stories were "corrected"; all derogatory remarks about the church or clergymen were removed; glosses were added to make the book seem to be a series of moral exempla; even the endings of some tales were distorted to moralize them. In Salviati's defense, one of his primary motivations was the desire to keep the book in circulation, even in its bowdlerized form, since he regarded it as the supreme model of Italian prose, upon which other writers should base their style.

find proper (ladies of the type who weigh words more than deeds and who strive more to seem good than to be so), let me say that it is no more improper for me to have written these words than for other men and women to have filled their everyday conversation with such words as "hole," "peg," "mortar," "pestle," "sausage," "Bologna sausage," and other similar expressions.[1] Moreover, my pen should be granted no less freedom than the brush of a painter, who without any reproach or, at least, any which is justified—not to mention the fact that he will depict Saint Michael wounding the serpent with a sword or a lance and Saint George slaying the dragon wherever he wishes—shows Christ as a man and Eve as a woman, and nails to the cross, sometimes with one nail, sometimes with two, the feet of Him who wished to die there for the salvation of the human race.[2]

What is more, one can see quite clearly that these tales were not told in a church, where things must be spoken of with the proper frame of mind and suitable words (despite the fact that even more outrageous stories are to be found in the church's annals than in my own tales); nor yet in the schools of the philosophers, where a sense of propriety is required no less than in other places; nor in any place among churchmen or philosophers. They were told in gardens, in a place suited for pleasure, in the presence of young people who were, nevertheless, mature and not easily misled by stories, and at a time when going about with your trousers over your head was not considered improper if it served to save your life.

But as they stand, these tales, like all other things, may be harmful or useful, according to whoever listens to them. Who does not recognize wine as a very good thing for the healthy, according to Cinciglione and Scolaio [3] and many others, and yet it is harmful to anyone with a fever? Shall we say because wine harms those with a fever that it is evil? Who does not realize that fire is most useful, and even more, necessary to mankind? Because it destroys homes, villages, and cities, shall we say that it is wicked? In like manner, weapons defend the lives of those who wish to live peacefully, and they also (on many occasions) kill men, not because of any wickedness inherent in them but because those who wield them do so in an evil way.

---

1. The Italian equivalents for these common words were frequently used obscenely. Boccaccio's arguments against critics who viewed his work as improper, immoral, and sometimes obscene have a surprisingly contemporary tone.

2. Boccaccio shrewdly shows his critics how an object, or the word which represents the object, has an unlimited number of connotations. His critics see his use of ambiguous expressions, like those used obscenely in conversation which he himself lists, as a proof of his impropriety. Boccaccio, on the other hand, argues that ambiguity is a fact of life—the same pointed objects or phallic symbols appearing in conversations or bawdy literature may also serve different functions in the most sublime religious art.

3. Boccaccio uses these fictitious characters as representatives of the general class of drunkards and tavern-crawlers, a form of antonomasia similar to using the name "Don Juan" or "Casanova" to refer to a rake or libertine.

No corrupt mind ever understood a word in a healthy way! And just as fitting words are of no use to a corrupt mind, so a healthy mind cannot be contaminated by words which are not so proper, any more than mud can dirty the rays of the sun or earthly filth can mar the beauties of the skies. What books, what words, what letters are more holy, more worthy, and more revered than those of the Holy Scriptures? And yet there are many who have perversely interpreted them and have dragged themselves and others down to eternal damnation because of this. Everything is, in itself, good for some determined goal, but badly used it can also be harmful to many; and I can say the same of my stories.

Whoever wishes to derive wicked counsel from them or use them for bad ends will not be prohibited from doing so by the tales themselves if, by chance, they contain such things and are twisted and distorted in order to achieve this end; and whoever wishes to derive useful advice and profit from them will not be prevented from doing so, nor will these stories ever be described or regarded as anything but useful and proper if they are read at those times and to those people for whom they have been written. Whoever has to say "Our Fathers" and make up spicy tales for her confessor should stay away from these tales. My stories will run after no one asking to be read, although bigots, too, both say and even do such things as are in my stories whenever they can!

There will also be those who will say that there are some stories here which might better have been omitted. This may be true, but I could do nothing but write down the tales as they were told, and if those people who had told them had told them more beautifully, I should have written them more beautifully. But let us suppose that I was both the one who created these stories as well as the one who wrote them down (which I was not)[4]—then, let me say that I would not be ashamed that they were not all beautiful, since no artisan save God himself creates everything perfect and complete; even Charlemagne, who was the first creator of the Paladins,[5] did not know how to create enough of them to make up an army.

4. Boccaccio's claim that he only overheard the tales in *The Decameron* but did not invent them is an example of a literary commonplace which is used by such writers as Cervantes and Manzoni. In the sense that Boccaccio made use of the many oral and written sources at his disposal, he did not create *ex nihil* every aspect of every one of his hundred tales. But he did create literary masterpieces out of these many sources, and he did fashion a literary language with them that remained the model of Italian prose style for centuries to come. His claim, in this instance, allows him to assert that whatever is offensive in his work is not his responsibility but rather that of the teller of the tale; the fiction governing *The Decameron* is therefore that the narrator is only the faithful reporter of what he overheard.

5. Here, Boccaccio makes reference to the legendary knights of Charlemagne's army who were sacrificed in a rear-guard action, recounted first in *The Song of Roland*. In Boccaccio's day, this Old French epic poem was unknown, but the legend of Charlemagne, Roland, and the Twelve Peers (Paladins) of France became part of Italian legend and folklore and was later to inspire a number of Italian epic poems by Ludovico Ariosto, Matteo Boiardo, Luigi Pulci, and Torquato Tasso.

One must be ready to find different characteristics in a multitude of things. No field was ever so well cultivated that it did not contain nettles, brambles, or some other kind of thorny shrub mixed among the better plants. Moreover, in speaking to unassuming young ladies, as most of you are, it would have been foolish to go about trying to find fancy stories and to take great pains speaking in an extremely formal manner. However, whoever goes through these stories can leave aside those he finds offensive and read those he finds pleasing; and in order not to deceive anyone, at the beginning of every story there is a summary of what is contained within.

Also, I suppose there will be people who will say that some of the stories are too long; to them I say once more that for those people who have something better to do with their time, it would be foolish to read any of these tales, no matter how short they might be. And even though much time has passed since I began to write these tales until this moment when my labor is drawing to a close, I have not forgotten that I said I was offering this work of mine to idle ladies and not to others; and for those who read to pass the time of day, no tale can be too long if it serves its purpose. Brevity is much more fitting for the studious who toil not just to pass the time away, but to employ their time to the greatest advantage, but not so for you ladies, who have all that time free which you do not spend on amorous pleasures; besides this, since none of you have been to Athens, Bologna, or Paris to study, it is necessary to speak to you in a more extended fashion than to those who have sharpened their wits with their studies.

There are, without doubt, some others among you who will say that the stories told are too full of nonsense and jokes and that it is not proper for a heavy, serious thinker to have written this way. To them I am obliged to render thanks, and I do so for their zeal and concern for my reputation, but I wish to answer their objections in this way: I confess that I have been heavy (and I have been so many times in my day), so, in speaking to those ladies who have not considered me heavy, let me assure them that I am not heavy—on the contrary, I am so light that I float on water; when you consider that the sermons delivered by friars to reproach men for their sins are, for the most part, full of nonsense, jokes, and foolishness, I felt that these same things would not be out of place in my stories, which are, after all, written to drive away a lady's melancholy. However, should they find themselves laughing too much, they can easily remedy this by reading the Lament of Jeremiah, the Passion of Our Savior, or the Lament of Mary Magdalene.

And who would doubt that there are still others who would say that I have an evil and poisonous tongue, because in some places

I write the truth about the friars? I plan to forgive those who say this, for it is hard to believe that anything but a good motive moves them, since friars are good people and avoid the discomforts of life for the love of God, and do their grinding when there's water to run the lady's mill and say no more about it; and if it were not for the fact that they all smell a little like goats, it would be most pleasant, indeed, to deal with them.

I must confess, however, that the things of this world have no stability whatsoever—they are constantly changing, and this might have happened with my tongue; I do not trust my own judgment (which, in matters concerning myself I avoid as best I can), but a short time ago, a neighbor lady of mine told me that I had the best and the sweetest tongue in the world—to tell the truth, when this was said, only a few of the above stories remained to be written. But now let what I have just said suffice as a reply to those ladies who have argued so spitefully.

I shall leave it to every lady to say and believe as she pleases, for the time has come to end my words and to humbly thank Him who with his assistance has brought me after so much labor to my desired goal, and may his grace and peace be with you always, lovely ladies, and if, perhaps, reading some of these stories has given any of you some little pleasure, please do remember me.

Here ends the tenth and last day of the book called

Decameron, also known as *Prince Galeotto*.

Contemporary
and Modern
Criticism

THOMAS G. BERGIN

An Introduction to Boccaccio †

Italian literature is built firmly and enduringly on the great triangular base of Dante, Petrarca, and Boccaccio. These are figures of such authority and magnetism as not only to have affected the course of Italian letters but to have left as well visible traces of their inspiration and example on the thought and creative fancy of the Western world. Thinking of any one of them, it may sharpen our appreciation of his special talents if we at the same time bear in mind the gifts of the other two. All of the three are of Tuscan stock, all nourished in the same cultural climate; indeed for a few brief years all were sharing this world of the living. Dante, the oldest, died in 1321; Boccaccio, the youngest, was eight years old at the time. There are personal links between the members of the great triumvirate: Petrarca met Dante when the former was still a child and Boccaccio, who ardently admired both of his elders, became a close friend of Petrarca. As not infrequently happens in families where the youngest brother is overshadowed by his talented siblings, Boccaccio is commonly thought of as ranking third, so far as distinction is decent among giants. Yet if he lacks the grandeur of Dante and the grace of Petrarca, it may fairly be claimed for the youngest brother that he is the most versatile and inventive of all of them.

It may even be, in the opinion of today's critics at least, that he invented a good deal of himself, that is to say, much of his own biography. On the authority of a letter from Petrarca (*Sen.* VIII, 1) we can be reasonably sure that Boccaccio was born in 1313, and in his *Amorosa visione* (XIV, 42 ff.) he refers to his legitimization by his father, one Boccaccino di Chelino, a merchant, originally from Certaldo but long associated with the Bardi banking family and domiciled in Florence. As to Giovanni's mother we know nothing at all, unless we are prepared to believe—as nowadays most scholars are not—what her son tells us about her in poetic and veiled fashion in a number of his early romances. He will have us think she was a Frenchwoman and—in one of his accounts—a lady of high degree. It is certainly true that Boccaccino made frequent visits to Paris, some of which coincide very closely in time with what must have been the season of Giovanni's conception. Boccaccio's word was good enough for the French scholar Hauvette, moved

† This introduction to the life and works of Giovanni Boccaccio was originally given as a public lecture in 1975 before the America-Italy Society of New York, and at the New York State University College at Buffalo as part of a symposium on Boccaccio. It is printed with the author's permission.

no doubt by a pardonable chauvinism, to dedicate his study of Boccaccio to the unknown Frenchwoman, but most scholars today, as noted, see her as a creature of pure fiction and opt for a girl either from Florence or Certaldo; she remains, however, when all is said and done, a woman of whom we know nothing. Shortly after legitimizing his love child Boccaccino married, thus forging another casual but interesting link between the members of the great triumvirate: Dante and Petrarca had stepmothers too.

It is also alleged nowadays, such is the uncharitable positivism of twentieth-century scholarship, that Boccaccio invented his adored Fiammetta, to whom he dedicated a number of his works and whose name, with some lingering touch of her magic, survives into *The Decameron*, where she is one of the ten young storytellers. In his own version of the affair, set forth very circumstantially in the *Filocolo*, Boccaccio tells us that he met his charmer on Easter Saturday in the Franciscan church of San Lorenzo in Naples; unlike Petrarca, who chronicles an encounter of such similar circumstance as to arouse in critics the suspicion of plagiarism, literary if not existential, on Boccaccio's part, he does not mention the year. Boccaccio's Fiammetta, according to his account, was a princess of sorts, the illegitimate daughter of Robert, king of Naples and patron of Petrarca. Skeptical historians have been for some time pointing out that there is not a shred of evidence for the existence of any such princess and the unanimous verdict of recent scholars would place the fair Fiammetta beside our hero's French mother, empedestalled in the gallery of fantasy. No doubt they are right, but if they will not let us believe in a princess, yet in view of the outpourings of passion that her name evokes in many works of her admirer, it is hard to believe that there was no Fiammetta at all. Even Vittore Branca, who has done more than most men to demolish Boccaccio's dreamworld, freely concedes that "a generic and total skepticism with regard to the data provided in the romances would be an error as inexcusable as noncritical acceptance of them." [1] And to be sure, even as the doubters must stop short of affirming that young Giovanni had no mother at all, so too the normal pattern of a young man's life, in the Middle Ages as even now, would justify the postulate of some flesh-and-blood inspiration under the seductive Neapolitan sky.

But the allure of Fiammetta has led us to pass over earlier important events in this brief chronicle of the poet's life. He had been brought to Naples by his father, it would appear, in 1327. Boccaccino, in spite of his son's occasional complaints of mistreatment, seems in fact to have dealt very fairly with his love child.

1. *Boccaccio medievale* (Florence: Sansoni, 1970), p. 243. In matters of biographical-bibliographical chronology, I have followed Vittore Branca's *Giovanni Boccaccio: profilo biografico* (Milan: Mondadori, 1967).

He not only legitimized him but gave him a good schooling under the tutelage of Giovanni da Strada, father of the scholar later to receive the laurel wreath and destined to be a lifelong friend of Boccaccio. Boccaccino also saw to it that his boy had instruction in "arismetica," which gave him the elements of accounting. So when the father came to Naples to set up a counting house in association with the Bardi, the boy was prepared to take his place behind the counter, though it is not clear whether he was employed by the Bardi or another house. (It may have been that of the Acciaiuoli, whose scion, Niccola, was to become a prominent figure in the political affairs of the kingdom; he may have opened the doors of many aristocratic palaces to his slightly younger compatriot.) Boccaccio was not happy in the business world, although undoubtedly his experiences as bank clerk, money changer, and occasionally errand boy in the busy port must have been exciting enough. His father indulgently permitted him to leave the counting house and sent him instead to study canon law at the University (1331). This new career was scarcely more appealing than banking to the youth (he tells us in an autobiographical passage in the *Genealogy of the Gods* that he never wanted to be anything but a poet), but it provided him with intellectual stimulation and, one may say, set his path on the road of scholarship. Cino da Pistoia, one of his professors, provided him a living link with the school of the "dolce stil nuovo" and he speaks years later with respect of Paolo da Perugia, the royal librarian who opened for him that rich storehouse of learning and literature. Between banking and schooling Boccaccio spent thirteen years in Naples; they were the truly formative years of his life and the happiest as well. He tells us (*Ep.* XII) that he lived in some elegance and the young bloods of the city were not unwilling to visit his quarters; Naples in fact gave him the triple experience of court life, the business world, and the kingdom of letters. It is not surprising that he left the city reluctantly nor that all his life he longed to return. If like his fellow Tuscans, Dante and Petrarca, Boccaccio too had the experience of exile, he was certainly the happiest of the three expatriates. Dante's exile was not voluntary and the restless Petrarca never lived in any one place for as long a span of time as Boccaccio spent contentedly in the sunny Angevin capital.

Returning to Florence, the young poet found adjustment difficult. The 1340s were not kind to bankers; both the Bardi and the Peruzzi failed, and Boccaccio was obliged to cast around for some means of employment, seeking to establish himself as a kind of secretary, adviser, or ornament to whatever magnate might find him useful. In some such capacity he seems to have served the Polenta of Ravenna (1345–46) and subsequently (1347–48) the Ordelaffi of Forlì. Later he tried—and more than once—to install himself in Naples under the wing of his old friend Acciaiuoli, who became in the course of years the power behind the somewhat unstable throne of Queen Joan. But such appointments as he held were short-lived and unsatisfactory; as the years passed, however, he found recurrent opportunities to serve the Commune of Florence, although on an irregular basis. He was sent as ambassador or emissary on sundry political missions; to various Lords of Romagna, to Louis of Bavaria in the Tyrol, to the powerful Visconti, and on three occasions to the papal court (to Avignon in 1354 and 1365 and to Rome in 1367). In the intervals he was appointed to boards or agencies dealing with such matters as military administration, or remained unemployed, retiring to Certaldo, eking out, according to his own reports, a precarious existence on his onion patch. For our purposes here—and to Boccaccio himself—the most important experience of his later years was his friendship with Petrarca. He first met the singer of Vaucluse in 1350, when he was privileged to entertain the great man in his own house and make him acquainted with an admiring circle. The friendship ripened with the years: visits were exchanged and correspondence flourished. Petrarca had a great influence on his young admirer, sharpening his critical faculties, strengthening his devotion to the cause of poetry, improving his Latin and perhaps his habits. One may perhaps question his master's effect on Boccaccio's purely creative genius; the record seems to show a waning of creative power—or interest—after that memorable encounter of 1350.

The foregoing brief biographical summary is intended merely to indicate the raw experiential material that went into the writings of this versatile author. We may remark on the existential side that the pattern of his life brought him into intimate contact with two very different social cultures. In Naples he lived in a society that was still feudal; the nobility was all-important and the pastimes of the élite, tournaments, pageantry, and love-making, exercised an irresistible attraction on a generous-hearted youth. In Florence the nobility had been barred from office-holding a generation before Boccaccio came on the scene; the recurrent political dissensions were not of dynastic origin as they were in Naples but reflected the class struggle for wealth and power between various levels of the middle class, a state of affairs that the twentieth century can readily understand. Shrewd calculation and opportunism were virtues to be admired in such a culture; business success brought prestige and there was no courtier class to glorify either jousting or flirtation. Equally formative of Boccaccio's achievements was the reading that came his way. Even in his early schooling as a boy he had read Ovid, he tells us; in Naples, among the works available to him in the Royal Library were Provençal and Old French romances, with Italian adaptations thereof, as well as scholarly compilations dealing with mythology, astrology, and history. In Naples, too, he must have encountered the works of Dante Alighieri, whom he was to admire all his life, occasionally imitate and, in his last years, explicate.

Of such experiences, personal or vicarious, are woven the creative works of the omnivorous author, even as his productions of an encyclopedic nature have their genesis in his early researches. Boccaccio is a many-faceted writer, to a greater degree, I think, than either Dante or Petrarca. To categorize his writings, either chronologically or formally, is not especially difficult but a twentieth-century critic attempting to assay them, if he is concerned with being useful to readers approaching Boccaccio for the first time, has a certain problem to face and perhaps a double function to fulfill. As with all writers of the past—at least those of major importance—Boccaccio must be approached with a double standard. There are in his canon works of great interest in the history of Western letters and even Western culture which are properly deserving of the attention of scholars in the field of literary history. They are not always, it is fair to say, works that a reader today seeking aesthetic or emotional satisfaction, and indifferent to their role in history, would find appealing. Among them however, are a few that have retained their freshness over the years and still delight the reader looking simply for enjoyment or catharsis. We shall keep this distinction in mind as we catalogue the artifacts.

Our first category would include four works: the prose *Filocolo* (or *Labor of Love*), the *Caccia di Diana* (*Diana's Hunt*) in *terza rima*, the verse romances *Il filostrato* (*Love's Victim*) and the *Teseida* (or *Emilia's Nuptials*), both in *ottava rima*. All of these were written or at least begun during the author's youthful years in Naples; the order of their composition is not entirely certain. The authoritative critic Vittore Branca assigns the following sequence: *Diana's Hunt* 1334, the *Filostrato* 1335, the *Filocolo* 1336, and would put the composition of the *Teseida*, if not its conception, sometime after the poet's return to Florence in 1340. Branca's arguments are subtle and sophisticated; a critic judging only by proficiency of technique might be inclined to put the *Filostrato* much later in the sequence. It is the most compact and effectively designed of all the works of this period, and it is difficult to believe that it could have preceded such a loosely organized and discursive narrative as the *Filocolo*; it seems indeed to reveal a surer hand than the one that penned the *Teseida*. In any case, all of these works follow the romantic medieval cult of the exaltation of love. Venus triumphs over Diana in the *Hunt*; love motivates the arduous quest of Filocolo for his sweetheart; love bears all before it, including feudal loyalties and the claims of friendship, in the *Teseida*; and love makes a hopeless victim of the young warrior Troilus in the *Filostrato*. Two of these works clearly look back to medieval models: the *Filocolo* is Boccaccio's version of an old love story, perhaps oriental in origin, versified in twelfth-century Old French as *Floire et Blanceflor*; the *Hunt* is an animated version of the catalogues of fair women of which Provençal literature and the lost *sirventese* of Dante provide examples. The remaining two (although also based on earlier models) throw, as it were, their adumbration into the future: Chaucer made use of both of them, and the *ottava rima* in which they are cast as well as the knightly aura that clings to them will characterize in varying degree the chivalrous romances of Boiardo, Ariosto, and Tasso. The student of literary history would find in all of them matters for study; probably, however, only the *Filostrato* could be recommended to a reader of today, accustomed to look for sharp characterization and psychological subtlety in his reading. The obsessed and doomed Troilus, the calculating Cressida, and the mature and tolerant Pandarus have a vitality that transcends their times.

Chronologically the next category would be composed of the works written after the poet's return to Florence and before his masterpiece, *The Decameron*. These include the *Ameto*, sometimes called *The Comedy of the Nymphs of Florence* (1341–42), *L'amorosa visione* (*The Amorous Vision*, 1342), the *Elegy of Lady Fiammetta* (1343–44?), and the *Ninfale Fiesolano* or *Story of the Nymph of Fiesole*, which may be as late as 1346. In this group the differences between the titles are marked, with regard to both form and manner. Like their predecessors, they all exalt the power of love, but the vehicle of the message—save for one exception—depends more on allegory than simple narrative. In the *Ameto* a train of symbolic nymphs teaches virtue and gentility to a crude shepherd, employing a mixture of prose and *terza rima*; to be sure, narrative is not lacking. The lover in the *Amorosa visione* is a kind of immature Dante guided through various circles by a celestial lady; appropriately, *terza rima* is used to describe his progress. The *ottava* returns in the *Ninfale*, in this case not to sing of knights and ladies but, instead, of the nymphs and shepherds of mythology. In the *Elegy*, the abandoned Fiammetta tells the long and sad story of her infatuation and its consequences. Though full of lengthy passages of plaintive repining and saturated with Ovidian echoes, the *Elegy*, by virtue of its realistic detail and psychological authenticity, remains, like the *Filostrato*, a story that can still move a sympathetic reader today.

Another easily classifiable group would be that of the learned compendia: *De claris mulieribus*; *De casibus virorum illustrium*; *De montibus, silvis, fontibus*; and *De genealogia deorum gentilium*. It is difficult to assign a precise date to any of these works, since they were all repeatedly elaborated and revised by their author.

In general one may say that all were begun in the 1350s (the *Genealogia* in 1350, the others somewhat later) and all indicate the new direction—towards Latin and scholarship and away from the vernacular and the creative—pointed out by Petrarca. They proved to be invaluable works of reference for men of letters down through the sixteenth century; they are interesting today, apart from the occasional intrusion of the raconteur into the labors of the compiler, largely for their incidental autobiographical allusions and, in the case of the *Genealogia*, for the definition and defense of poetry passionately put forth by the author. It is interesting to note that in his catalogue of the tribulations of famous men and his parade of noteworthy women Boccaccio cites examples from his own time as well as the familiar cases sanctified by the ancients. These works are monuments of humanism—Boccaccio proudly made use of his recently and painfully acquired acquaintance with Greek—and on them their author labored steadily until the end of his life. They gave him a prestige among his contemporaries that none of his creative works ever won for him. His early biographer, Filippo Villani, cites them with admiration, merely mentioning the compositions in the vernacular.[2] Perhaps, since his *Buccolicum Carmen* (*Rustic Song*) is written in Latin, we might, as Villani does, attach it to this category but it is of different substance, being essentially allegorical autobiography rather than a work of research.

Some works escape easy classification. In the *Trattatello in lode di Dante* (*Treatise in Praise of Dante*) biography, gossip and critical commentary are fused; such a definition might also apply to some extent to the commentary on the early cantos of the *Inferno*. The lyric poems, written at intervals over the course of their author's life, are in the tradition of Dante and Petrarca but have their own character, fresh and spontaneous. The miscellaneous letters have an interest for what they tell us of the writer's opinions and vicissitudes. Also autobiographical in origin, it would seem, is the misogynistic *Corbaccio*, an unsympathetic survey of the physical and moral frailties of womankind, in language and vivacity of style perhaps the closest of all Boccaccio's works to his *Decameron*. In truth, save for its length, it might have provided one of the storytellers of that work with his daily ration, although in spirit it runs counter to the prevailing current of the masterpiece.

All these lesser works are worthy of the attention of the scholar and the historian. There is not one of the creative works without some touch of originality in form or treatment of substance; many of them, as we have indicated, are seminal. If Boccaccio had never written *The Decameron* his name would still loom large in the

---

2. See the translation of Villani's biography reprinted on pp. 188–91 of this edition. [*Editors.*]

chronicles of European literature. Yet it must be said that *The Decameron* is an accomplishment of such scope and vigor as to make the minor creative works seem anemic by comparison and to overshadow the pedantic virtues of the compendia.

Surveying the sequence of youthful compositions enumerated above, a critic might well be at a loss in seeking to explain the genesis of *The Decameron*. From the *Caccia di Diana* to the *Ninfale fiesolano* the substance of Boccaccio's writing had been essentially in the high style; his romances portrayed princes and ladies of high degree; at the very least, as in the case of Fiammetta, people of wealth and prominence. His allegories were, of course, even further removed from the vulgar herd, dealing with lofty quasireligious concepts and clearly intended for an erudite and polished audience. With *The Decameron*, the author takes his readers into a new world—or perhaps for the first time leads them from the cloudland of refined erotic fancy to the land of things as they are, wherein the citizenry is as varied as it is purposeful, where calculation displaces illusion, where the seamy side of things is not concealed and where laughter is not out of place. (There is not so much as a chuckle in any of the chivalrous or allegorical confections.) To some extent it may be surmised that the historical circumstances of the genesis of the masterpiece go far to explain the nature of its substance. The fourteenth century was not the happiest era in the history of Europe and Boccaccio's lifetime spans a period of many miseries. Aside from the dynastic wars of the kingdom of Naples that followed on the death of Robert in 1343, and the recurrent factional brawling in Florence, the early years of the century were marked by famines and financial reverses, and worst of all was the scourge for which the century is best remembered, the Black Death, which came to Florence in the spring of 1348 and moved on to devastate all Europe. *The Decameron* may have been begun in that year and was probably finished in 1351 (its "lascivious" pages would never have been written had he met Petrarca a little sooner). The exuberant vitality of the work may well be seen as a reaction against the horrors of the dreadful scourge; Boccaccio indeed suggests as much in the Introduction to his work, which begins with a description of the stricken city. It is strange that he should have borrowed some of the details from Paulus Diaconus, the chronicler of an earlier pestilence, for it is highly probable that he was an eyewitness himself of the plague's ravages; in any case his portrayal is forceful and no doubt accurate:

> Many ended their lives in the public streets, during the day or at night, while many others who died in their homes were discovered dead by their neighbors only by the smell of their decomposing bodies. The city was full of corpses. The dead were

usually given the same treatment by their neighbors, who were moved more by the fear that the decomposing corpses would contaminate them rather than by any charity they might have felt towards the deceased: either by themselves or with the assistance of porters (when they were available), they would drag the corpse out of the home and place it in front of the doorstep where, usually in the morning, quantities of dead bodies could be seen by any passerby; then they were laid out on biers, or for lack of biers, on a plank. Nor did a bier carry only one corpse; sometimes it was used for two or three at a time. More than once, a single bier would serve for a wife and husband, two or three brothers, a father or son, or other relatives, all at the same time. . . . when all the graves were full, huge trenches were dug in all of the cemeteries of the churches and into them the new arrivals were dumped by the hundreds; and they were packed in there with dirt one on top of another, like a ship's cargo, until the trench was filled.

Petrarca, too, employing the more stately measures of Latin hexameters, remarks on the same scene:

> Funerals meet my terrified eyes, wherever I turn them;
> Horror piles upon horror; the churchyards, crowded
>   with coffins,
> Echo to loud lamentations, while countless bodies unburied,
> Noble and peasant alike, lie in the open, unhonored.

The impersonal impartiality of death, ignoring all social distinctions, may to some extent explain the liberal democracy of *The Decameron*, wherein representatives of all classes are set before us, even as the relaxation of traditional proprieties, also mentioned by the author as characteristic of the time of the plague, may explain its moral permissiveness.

In any event it is on this historical foundation that the structure of *The Decameron* is built. For it was amidst such scenes of horror, Boccaccio tells us, that ten young people met in the church of Santa Maria Novella: seven young women and three young men. The youth of the group is worth stressing—nor should it be forgotten that the author was himself only thirty-four at the time—and in other respects, too, it is a homogeneous company. All are of good family, all are well known to each other, and all are well educated and sophisticated. Several centuries of scholarship have striven in vain to identify them with any actual historical figures or even, in truth, to clarify the teasingly suggestive symbolism of the names they bear—at least as in any way functional in the narrative. At the suggestion of the most mature of the women they decide to leave the city and betake themselves to a country villa and there enjoy themselves as best they may until the plague has run its course—but always, as their leader puts it, "in pure fraternal friendship." To beguile the time they hit upon the notion of story-telling; each member of the house party is to be king or queen for a day and suggest the general topics for the tales to be told. So in the course of their sojourn there are ten days of narration, each with ten stories, totalling a hundred tales and thus equaling, perhaps not by accident, the number of cantos in the *Divine Comedy*. At the end of each day one of the group sings a song celebrating the rapture or the anguish of love, often with covert allusions of a personal nature, puzzling to his hearers and equally so to readers of the work. That the title should be in Greek is in line with Boccaccio's practice, beginning with the *Filocolo*. Its subtitle, "Prince Galeotto," with reference to the legendary friend of Lancelot who carried messages from his lord to Guinevere, signifies a dedication of the work to the service of love.

One may see if one chooses, in the framework of the book, an allegory of the flight from intolerable reality to the solace of art: the creation of one's own world, as it were, as a refuge from the ugly and sordid conditions of the true world of experience. If there is such an allegory it seems only fair to point out that the world into which the young people are subsequently borne from their ivory tower on the wings of their own creative fancy is no utopia or fairyland but a pretty naturalistic cosmos in its own right. So art flees life only to return to it, as it must if it would have meaning.

The design, employing a series of narrators within a fictional frame, is not entirely new. In the fifth book of the *Filocolo* Boccaccio had himself set before us in an idyllic background a group of young aristocrats who tell in turn brief narratives, all of which present questions calling for comment and eventual adjudication by the "queen," who bears the name of Fiammetta. And before Boccaccio's time there had long circulated, in medieval literary circles, versions of the originally oriental compilation of the tales of the Seven Sages. But Boccaccio, setting his scene against a realistic and contemporary background and enlivening his presentation with his own *brio*, makes something new out of the old pattern. One may say much the same of the hundred tales themselves. It is doubtful if any one of them is strictly original with the author; certainly the vast majority are not. The sources are varied. Some, in fact, may be found in the book of the Seven Sages; some have an origin of equivalent venerability. Some have a classical source; on the other hand, many of the livelier ones are from the medieval stock of *fabliaux* (which had been anthologized, as were the lives of the troubadours, also drawn on by our magpie author); some are bits of Florentine gossip or merely current anecdotes. But to all of his tales Boccaccio gave new life and vigor, localizing, characterizing, polishing their plots and performers with shrewd variation and a resourceful and versatile style—and thereby making them truly his own, even as Shakespeare with Macbeth and Hamlet and even Henry V.

Let us grant that not every story is a masterpiece. At one extreme some items are simply witty sayings attributed to well-known figures of the day—and the wit is not always perceptible to twentieth-century tastes. (Some of us may have similar reservations about the drolleries of some of Shakespeare's clowns.) At the other end of the scale, particularly, I think, on the last day, where the author is aiming at indoctrination, some of the characters may seem a little too good to be true. But the great residue is made up of stories memorable for their sharpness of characterization, their skillful construction, and for the indefinable creative magic that enables them to transcend their times and delight a reader of today as much as a contemporary of their creator. Collectively the variety of the work's articulate *dramatis personae* and the authoritative presentation of their milieu compel us to include Boccaccio in that small and select group of writers who may truly be said to have created their own worlds.

The world of *The Decameron* is vast and varied. Even topographically it covers a lot of ground. As if deliberately to suggest the breadth of the author's scope—and incidentally adding an authenticating element to its plots—the settings range from Armenia to Spain and from England to Egypt, although, naturally enough, Italian backgrounds predominate and the tales set in Florence or its environs are more numerous than those of any other group. The social range is no less all-inclusive than the geographical. Vittore Branca calls the book the "epic of the merchant class," but that definition, I think, has reference rather to its ethos than to the status of the characters that are set before us. E. H. Wilkins in his *History of Italian Literature*, calling the roll of the actors who parade before us on this vast stage, notes that among them are "kings, princes, princesses, ministers of state, knights, squires, abbots, abbesses, monks, nuns, priests, soldiers, doctors, lawyers, philosophers, pedants, students, painters, bankers, wine merchants, inn-keepers, millers, bakers, coopers, usurers, troubadours, minstrels, peasants, servants, simpletons, pilgrims, misers, spendthrifts, sharpers, bullies, thieves, pirates, parasites, gluttons, drunkards, gamblers, police—and lovers of all sorts and kinds." [3] To be sure, some of these categories overlap; even so, it is an impressive list and could be enlarged by some refinement: poets, housewives, and hermits come readily to mind. Perhaps a tentative social census of *The Decameron* would be illumi-

---

3. *History of Italian Literature*, 2nd edition (Cambridge: Harvard University Press, 1974), pp. 108–9.

nating; a few random figures may here be cited as evidence of the proportions of the various social levels represented in the tolerant register of Boccaccio's world. My census, admittedly approximate, gives me a total of 338 characters, of which 255 are male and 83 female. Some of these, classical and legendary figures for example, are not appropriate fodder for social classification; of those that are eligible, the middle class comes out ahead, with 140 representatives. It should be said that, especially with regard to the Italian *personae*, the line between the nobility and the *haute bourgeoisie* is not sharply drawn, so that it may be that a few of the 102 characters that I class as "noble" might more properly have gone to swell the middle-class contingent. Twenty-three individuals are specifically defined as "merchants" or wives of merchants; perhaps as many more might be added to that number if we scrutinized them more closely. Some sixty-eight characters, by my tentative count, could fairly be described as belonging to the lower classes: peasants, laborers, and artisans of the humbler callings. This is a sizeable proportion, and it certainly stands out in contrast to the *Divine Comedy*, where, programmatically, as Cacciaguida tells the pilgrim, only people of prominence can serve the didactic ends of the poem. In fact, it is notable that in the *Comedy* even the thieves and highwaymen are of well-known families. Boccaccio too, of course, often used "persons known to fame" to lend authority to some of his tales; what is interesting is the substantial quotient of the obscure. Italians outnumber aliens by about three to one in the world of *The Decameron* and the Florentine colony is by far the largest. The church is not so well represented as one might expect; there are less than a score of clerics clearly identified as such, although their central role in some of the more memorable tales gives them a notable impact, and *The Decameron* would not be the same without them.

More significant than the emergence of the proletariat in the world of *The Decameron* is the proportion and nature of its female element. Here we may remind ourselves of the author's affirmation in his preface to the effect that his compilation was made specifically for the solace of women afflicted by the pangs of love. Lest there be any doubt about his attitude, he breaks off the narrative sequence at the beginning of the fourth day to make explicit avowal of his devotion to ladies and his intention to do everything he can to please them. After all, he says, the Muses are women, and if it does not necessarily follow that women are Muses, still they look like them at first sight. And women have inspired him to write a thousand verses whereas the Muses have not occasioned as much as one.

It is possible to see in this breezy manifesto simply a light-hearted bit of self-mockery. But to most readers it will seem a sincere declaration, supported, as critics have noted, by the record of all the author's preceding works, which are without exception oriented toward love and women. And the statement is authenticated as well by the testimony of *The Decameron* itself.

For confirmation let us again call on statistics. As noted above, a rough count gives us eighty-three women mentioned by name or clearly identified in the course of the hundred tales. This may not seem unduly large if measured against the quotient of over 250 males. Yet it may be said that the ladies have come a long way in less than fifty years, for Dante's *Comedy*, which has a population slightly larger than that of *The Decameron*, contains only a score of women, of which the greater part is composed of *exempla* from antiquity. Of contemporary women, real women, there are but five in the *Comedy*. Further, in Boccaccio's work, the women, like the clergy, make an impression that more than compensates for their numerical inferiority. Indeed, out of the 100 stories there are thirty-two wherein women have a central role and another forty-two in which their part is so significant that there would be no story without them. Of the remaining underprivileged twenty-six, more than half are not stories at all but simply anecdotes or witty sayings. Of the approximately eighty-five items that are truly stories women are either dominant or essential in seventy-nine. *The Decameron* is the nearest thing to a woman's world between Lysistrata and Clare Boothe's celebrated comedy.

A social census of the females of *The Decameron*—one would like to say the "ladies" but the term would not always be appropriate—would show that, as in the case of the other sex, all categories of society are represented. The presence and the ubiquity of women is one of the clearest signs that with *The Decameron* a new culture comes into being, or at least achieves literary recognition.

Scholars of literary history may debate as to whether Boccaccio, traditionalist, fashioner of allegories, disciple of Ovid, should be assigned to the Middle Ages or whether his humanism, his approach to the classics, a certain indifference to transcendental values, may justify us in seeing in him a precursor of the Renaissance. Without venturing a final verdict on this delicate matter, one may certainly affirm that the world of *The Decameron* is no longer the world of the High Middle Ages. In this connection we may appropriately cite the second story of the first day, very early on in the sequence. In this significant *fabula* Melchisedech the Jew, pressed by the sultan to say which of the three great religions, Christianity, Judaism, or Mohammedanism, is the true one, replies with the story of the three rings. He tells the sultan of a great king who let it be known that whichever of his three sons should on his death be given his gold ring should be regarded as the heir to all he possessed. But when death drew near, finding it difficult to choose between them, he had two copies of the ring made, perfect imitations of the original, so that when he died, each son had a gold ring and no man could tell which was the true one. And so it is with the great faiths, concludes Melchisedech; one of us has the true one but we shall not be able to say, in this world at least, which of us has it. This is a far cry from the *Song of Roland*, which had proclaimed with certainty that Christians were right and pagans were wrong; and it was this assurance that had motivated Christian thought and action through the succeeding centuries and which no authoritative spokesman of the West, down to and including Dante, had thought of questioning. In such a society the knight and the priest were supreme: the former, exalting and exemplifying military virtues, fought God's battles, and the latter, in celibate and abstinent meditation, was a constant reminder to the faithful of the transient nature of this world of the living. Undeniably, both knight and cleric have left us precious legacies. They incarnate, however, an idealism of such rigidity as to be beyond the grasp of ordinary mortals. In somber truth, in the High Middle Ages, knightly valor often found its outlet in brigandage and brawling, while the other-worldly posture of the priest, asking too much of frail humanity, was recurrently distorted by venality and corruption. It must be said too that, even at their best, crusading militancy and contempt for this world were hardly likely to build a viable society; neither one was, we might say, "good for business." The business of the chivalrous-ascetic age was in fact carried on by unsung merchants, moneylenders, artisans, and peasants, and it is precisely this sector of society that in *The Decameron* comes into its own, gaining intellectual recognition and winning in some degree pragmatic and even philosophical justification.

So the citizens of the Decameronian commonwealth are less concerned with preparing for the world to come, either by the conscientious slaying of infidels or meditation on the hereafter, than with enjoying what the world of the living has to offer. The achievement of *The Decameron* is in its cheerful and realistic depiction of this *Zeitgeist*. Critics have attacked and conditioned but never refuted the statement of De Sanctis that the moving spirit of the work is "a violent rejection of the mystical and the other-worldly"; and recently Aldo Scaglione has pertinently remarked that the sense of sin is utterly absent from its pages—a striking contrast to the *Divine Comedy*, or the *Rhymes* of Petrarca, for that matter. All of the characters, with the exception of a few pious *exempla*, inserted, one may suspect dutifully, into the carefree procession, accept the world as it is. They realize that they are powerless against the accidents of fortune and they readily—one might say eagerly—yield to the irresistible impulses of their own passions and appetites. Their defense against fate and their ally against the excesses of their instincts is their intelligence. Many readers have seen in the work a programmatic glorification of human ingenuity. (It may be noted that of the seven days that have prescribed topics, no less than four call for tales exemplifying wit or astuteness, and the theme recurs in the other days as well.) Against this assertion the transcendent values of the feudal age pale into insignificance or at least irrelevance. It is possible to schematize the work and see in it a kind of Dantesque progression, as Ferdinando Neri has, and the numerology is faintly suggestive.[4] The numbers 3, 7, 10, and 100, unobtrusively present in *The Decameron*, were also very meaningful for Dante. But such considerations of a quasi-formal nature do not affect the substance, and much less the spirit, of the work. No one is likely to see in *The Decameron* an *Itinerarium mentis in Deum*. If there is a progression from the wickedness of Ciappelletto to the "saintliness" of Griselda, it is a most irregular movement, with much backtracking. And in truth Ciappelletto is not presented to us as exemplifying evil but rather ingenious resourcefulness, and Griselda is less a saint than a pathological case, verging on the monstrous. In the presentation of the gallery of the good on the last day, one may see not so much an echo of Dante's last *cantica* as simply another medieval palinode, such as we find in Andreas Cappellanus, or the troubadour poets, or even in the closing items of Petrarca's *Canzoniere*. Considered objectively, the "virtuous" characters of the last day are not especially saintly. Some of them are decent individuals moved by human compassion and generosity but a few of the more famous examples—the hermit Nathan, the devoted friend Gisippus, and the masochistic Griselda—are simply victims of obsessions, basically egocentric, that take them beyond the pale of normal humanity. Their limitations, in truth, may serve to illustrate the sad state of transcendental values in the culture of the times—or at least as perceived by their creator. Certainly most of the characters in the hundred tales live in this world and are quite content with it; even when luck goes against them they are seldom disposed to forsake it to put their hopes in a dubious hereafter. The case of Ciappelletto, the protagonist of the first story, may be cited as illustrating this hardheaded and, from a religious point of view, disconcerting spiritual disposition. Nothing could be more shocking to the faithful than a false confession made on the point of death. On the face of it, although Panfilo, who tells the tale, piously and correctly points out that a split second of true repentance may have saved him at the last, Ciappelletto has damned his soul for all eternity. But he has saved the good name

4. See "Il disegno ideale del *Decameron*," in *Poesia e storia* (Turin: Casa Editrice Giuseppe Gambino, 1946).

of his business partners in this world, and for this cause he is quite ready to take his chances in the next. If he has not saved his soul, he has certainly saved appearances, thereby setting an example to his fellow citizens in the world of the hundred tales, where the saving of appearances becomes a consistent motif. Suffice it to cite here, as supplementary evidence, the case of the oriental princess Alatiel as told in the seventh story of the second day. Abducted en route to her wedding, the hapless maiden is forced, in the course of her wanderings, to submit to no fewer than nine ravishers, yet in the end, profiting by a turn of fate and following the advice of a wise counselor, she is able to present herself to her unsuspecting fiancé as still *intacta*. And everyone lives happily ever after. So too in the chronicles of these ten lively days there are a score of women so successful in concealing their infidelities that no one thinks any the worse of them, nor does any of them have an uneasy conscience. This is all very cynical but it does betoken a respect for the conventions. The social order is not to be flouted, indeed it is to be honored; it may also be acceptably manipulated —if one is clever enough.

If such a code is ethically questionable, it is fair to say that one of its by-products is tolerance, a quality alien to the medieval rigidity which had characterized the ethos of earlier generations. To this new attitude the fable of Melchisedech may be seen as contributing a quasi-theological support. In this connection, too, a focus on the new feminism of *The Decameron* may prove instructive. For the womenfolk of *The Decameron* exemplify in the sharpest terms the rational-hedonistic, earthbound texture of the work. As we have noted the indulgent democracy which allows scope for the appearance of representatives of various social classes, so we might ponder for a moment the sentimental-psychological categories into which the self-possessed and articulate females of the work might be divided. It should be said at once that for all of the women love is all that matters; there are a few stories in the collection in which men are motivated by purposes unconnected with the sex drive but there is no woman in the course of the hundred tales who is not somehow involved with a man, whether she be predator or prey or (as is most often the case) cheerful accomplice. Which is by no means to say that all the women are alike. One might, fancifully, distinguish two broad categories. The first could be defined as consisting of the inexperienced but eager. Many of these make their appearance in certain stories for years regarded as the naughtiest of the book, precisely because their innocence permits titillating *doubles entendres* and often calls for specific physiological allusion. Perhaps the best examples would be the maiden Alibech, who finds that putting the Devil in hell is an exercise as joyful as it is meritorious, or the ardently experimental Catharine of Romagna who cannot rest until she has captured the nightingale. The most articulate of this group, however, is assuredly the unnamed little nun of the first story of the third day (told, somewhat oddly, by Filostrato, who prescribes tales of tragic import when his turn comes). For this assured young woman, neither her pledge of chastity nor the more practical hazard of pregnancy can avail to alter her purpose: she has heard, on good authority, what it is that brings the greatest joy to a woman and she is determined to experience it for herself. Her confidence sweeps away all objections; indeed not only does she have her way but her example infects her sisters—and to the content of all concerned. Masetto leaves the convent, in due course, with a pleasant sense of mission fulfilled, and if any of the children he has fathered are born of his first discoverer, we may well believe that she has no regrets. This saucy young miss also exemplifies the alert opportunism characteristic of the Decameronian community; when Fortune provides her with an occasion to enrich her experience she takes prompt advantage of it. Indeed, in her practical, earthbound moral attitude and her opportunistic inventiveness she is clearly kin to Ciappelletto.

A larger and perhaps even more characteristic category could be defined as the experienced and aggressive. Examples abound: we may cite the third story of the third day, wherein an unnamed Florentine lady, making an accomplice of a naive priest, conducts, as it were, her own seduction and ingeniously brings her willing lover to her bed. Another case would be that of Lydia (the ninth story of the seventh day) who, bent on making the timid Pyrrhus her lover, makes excellent use of the magic pear-tree, a most extraordinary plant that will later serve Geoffrey Chaucer. Gillette of Narbonne (in the ninth story of the third day) uses her scientific knowledge to win a reluctant husband and, when he abandons her, devises a complicated scheme to recover his person and eventually his affections. Her aggressive ingenuity appealed to Shakespeare who retells her story in *All's Well That Ends Well*. This purposeful and pragmatic brigade includes the most outspoken and clearminded females in *The Decameron*; they know what they want even as the men, who usually want the same thing, and are prepared not only to work for the fulfillment of their desires but to defend them with eloquence. The wife of Ricciardo da Chinzica, in the tenth story of the second day, is very explicit in describing what a woman looks for in her spouse; her language is racy and amusing but her requirements are no different from those of Ghismunda of Salerno who, as befits a princess in a tragic situation, speaks a more elevated—and quotable—language. It is Fiammetta who in the first story of the fourth day tells us how Ghismunda, daughter of Prince Tancredi, having been married and widowed at an early age, secretly and discreetly took a lover, a young man of excellent character but of low social degree. When Tancredi, discovering the affair, reproaches her she impenitently replies: "I was fathered by you and am of flesh and blood, and have not lived so long that I am yet old—for both these reasons I am full of amorous desire, which has also been greatly increased by my marriage which taught me how pleasurable it is to satisfy such desires." She adds that she chose her lover carefully, with regard, however, to his character rather than his social position for, she affirms, "we are all made of the same flesh" and nobility is a matter of conduct and not lineage. It is interesting to note how the defense of love and the woman's right is combined with a democratic social thesis; the pervading dominance of love—even at its lowest level—is an essential element in the egalitarian spirit of *The Decameron*.

Occasionally, it must be admitted, the claims of these self-assured and full-blooded women are pressed a little too far. It is one thing to ignore the artificial barriers of class distinction and quite another to subvert the foundations of society, at least as they have been traditionally understood and accepted. "Doing what comes naturally," however satisfactory to the individual, can threaten the social fabric. Filippa of Prato carries her principles to their extreme. In the seventh story of the sixth day—again from the lips of the versatile Filostrato—we learn how there was once upon a time in Prato a law decreeing death for a woman taken in adultery. A certain Filippa, he tells us, was once caught in the act; brought to court for her sentencing, however, she makes no attempt to deny her guilt but instead boldly attacks the law. Laws, she argues, should be equal for all and should, moreover, be made with the consent of those whom they affect. "Such," she affirms, "is not the case with this statute, which binds only us poor women, who after all have it in our power to give pleasure to many more people than a man ever could. But when the law was drawn up not a single woman gave her consent nor was even consulted." She then, in the presence of the court, asks her husband if she has ever rejected his advances. He admits she has not. And Filippa triumphantly rejoins: "Since he has always had all he wanted of me, what was I to do with what was left over? Isn't it far better to let it give pleasure to some poor fellow that loves me rather than allow it to go to waste?" And so persuasive is her argument that she wins not only her freedom but also abrogation of that unjust law. On reflection one is forced to conclude that although the collection may contain many spicier items, the story of Filippa may well be the most subversive of them all.

It is the prevalence of this type of frank, self-possessed, and sensual womanhood that gives *The Decameron* its particular flavor. Are there no cases of the woman as victim in all the hundred tales? Precious few—and they are not the victims of predatory lovers but rather of circumstance or sheer bad luck. Isabetta of the famous and touching story of the pot of basil (the fifth story of the somber fourth day, told by the tender Filomena) is a victim of her brothers' snobbery and greed. Perhaps Alatiel, whose romantic peregrinations we have mentioned earlier, is a victim of her nine successive ravishers but she seems to enjoy every moment of it— and she comes out all right in the end. Of course the victim, *par excellence*, of the collection is the patient Griselda of the final climactic tale, but she is as much a victim of her own masochism as the perverted sadism of her husband; Petrarca's tears for her to the contrary notwithstanding, a reader of today would consider her a pathological case. The conventional victim of man's lust, exploited, betrayed and abandoned, who has contributed so many pathetic pages to world literature is simply not found in *The Decameron*. Most of Boccaccio's feminine creations are far too intelligent for that sort of destiny. There are to be sure a few silly women in the gallery, of whom the most memorable is the young Venetian matron who was so readily convinced that the Archangel Gabriel was in love with her (in the second story of the fourth day sagaciously chosen by Pampinea to dissipate the gloom occasioned by the sad end of Ghismunda)—but then, Boccaccio remarks, all Venetians are silly, and in any event she turns out to be no more self-deluded than her deceiver. What is perhaps more surprising, and an eloquent token of the new world that emerges in *The Decameron*, is that there is no example of the spiritualized *donna angelica*, the inspirational, untouchable lady of Dante and the troubadours. It is true that the vision of the fair Iphigenia in the forest glade inspires Cymon to give up his boorish style of life and turn to the pursuits of a polished gentleman and courtier, including abduction, violence, and piracy; it does not turn his vision heavenward nor lead him to study St. Thomas Aquinas. And of that love which is the source of chastity, in the words of the Provençal poet, there is hardly a trace at all in Boccaccio's pages. *Au contraire*, one might say.

It is indeed easy to understand, save for the coarse if realistic figures of the *fabliaux*, that the spirit of the Middle Ages could not find room for women of the Decameronian stamp. Knighthood had cast about its ladies an idealistic veil, flattering, no doubt, but hampering natural movement; the medieval monk could see in the female only temptation incarnate. Petrarca's Laura in fact labors under both of these handicaps. Only in a society prepared to appreciate and enjoy the things that this world of the living has to offer can normal women be observed and portrayed without the distortions of sublimations of one kind or another. Boccaccio, to be sure, did not invent normal women. But he may claim to be a pioneer in seeing them with a clear eye and depicting them with an understanding pen. And the woman who moves before us in *The Decameron* is here to stay. We shall find her living on in the Mirandas and the Portias and the Rosalinds of Shakespeare and, indeed, we can recognize her legitimate descendants today, in letters as in life.

The naturalistic character of Boccaccio's women and the racy situations in which they play an emancipated role have given *The Decameron* over the years its well-known reputation for looseness verging on the pornographic. Readers of the late twentieth century will find this hard to understand in view of the kind of literature that floods our permissive bookstalls nowadays. Indeed by contrast *The Decameron* seems quite innocuous. For all its eroticism it is surprisingly limited: there is but one case of homosexuality recorded in the hundred tales and nothing in the least unnatural or perverse. There is no scatological scene nor word—in fact the language, though sometimes suggestive, is never coarse. There are no "four-letter words" in the book. Yet, until recent years *The Decameron* was considered by many to be a "dirty book" and was read rather furtively by all save the emancipated as recently as a generation ago. There is no reason for us to be ashamed of the "Victorianism" of our ancestors in this matter; the author himself came to repent of the creation of his masterpiece. He would have burned it along with his other youthful works had not Petrarca dissuaded him, and in his old age he begs his friend Cavalcanti to keep the book out of reach of his womenfolk. His devotion to the fair sex turned to acrimonious misogynism in the *Corbaccio* (the final version of which is of the early sixties but it probably had a much earlier genesis), and the Boccaccio who scathingly assails the hypocrisy of the friars in the course of the hundred tales has, before 1360, taken minor orders himself. Indeed somewhere in his mid-forties he underwent a "conversion."

Clearly, if we survey panoramically the production of this gifted and versatile artist we can see that his masterpiece must have been the product of a special set of circumstances, a particular and vitalizing moment in his career. His works offer convincing evidence of his ready response to his environment. Under the influence of a feudal and courtly society he wrote chivalrous romances; moving to Tuscany, he turned to allegory. Probably contact with the hardheaded merchants of Florence directed his pen to the creation of the "epic of the merchant class." One may suspect too that *The Decameron* came into being during a time of his own erotic involvement; though he never married he had five illegitimate children, born, it seems likely, during the years immediately following his return to Tuscany. The birth date of Violante (the

"Olympia" of *Buccolicum Carmen* XIV) has been tentatively assigned to 1349–50; she was not the oldest of his children. The cultivation of Petrarca's friendship and the desire to emulate his master provide, as it were, yet another spiritual milieu and he turns to the more scholarly exercises of compilation and theorizing, forsaking the narrative, whether romantic or realistic. It will creep in from time to time, in the *Treatise on Dante* and in the interstices of the *Book of Famous Women* and the other compendia, but it will never again be deliberately cultivated. Villani bears out the artist's own statement when he records that Boccaccio would gladly have recalled his masterpiece but could not. We today who delight in the vigor and honesty as well as the art of the hundred tales may be happy that his efforts to suppress them were in vain. For, as Carducci said many years ago, in the range of Italian letters, at least, and perhaps beyond that range, the Human Comedy of *The Decameron* is the one work worthy to stand beside the *Divine Comedy* of the master whom Boccaccio so deeply revered.

Contemporary

Reactions

FRANCESCO PETRARCA

[Encouragements to Boccaccio, Who Has Been Terrified by a Fanatic into Renouncing Literature] †

From Book I/5

To Boccaccio; from Padua, 28 May 1362.

. . . You write me that a certain Pietro of Siena, recently deceased, a well-known monk, celebrated for his miracles, made a lot of predictions, and among them certain ones about you and me. And you say that an agent came to you to report the predictions. And when you asked how the holy man, whom we had never heard of, happened to know us, the envoy answered: "No doubt he expected to perform a good deed on his own initiative; but when, I presume, he was made aware that imminent death would prevent his performing it, he prayed to Almighty God. And when his prayer reached heaven, he was ordered to appoint suitable deputies, who would fulfill his undertakings. And by the familiar footing that exists between God and the souls of the just, divine power granted that he should recognize that his prayers were heard. And to remove all doubt, Christ himself appeared before him, and on his face the holy man read all things that were and are, and are to come; not like Proteus in Virgil, but more fully, perfectly, clearly; for what, pray, does he not see who has seen him by whom all things are made?"

Well, I grant that to have seen him with mortal eyes is a very

---

† Francesco Petrarca (1304–75) was the most important of Boccaccio's friends. In one of the collections of his many Latin letters—the *Seniles* or *Letters of Riper Years,* a group of approximately 125 letters written between 1361 and 1374—the friendship of these two great poets and humanists can be traced. We owe to Petrarca the account of how Boccaccio experienced a religious crisis some time after the composition of *The* *Decameron* which caused him to have serious doubts about the value of literature in a Christian life. The excerpts reprinted here and on pp. 176–84 were translated and selected by Morris Bishop and originally appeared in Francesco Petrarca, *Letters from Petrarch,* pp. 225–28, 239–48, copyright © 1966 by Indiana University Press. Reprinted by permission of the publisher.

great thing—if it is true. But it is an ancient abuse, that an air of divinity should draw a veil of religion over lies and falsities, that men should pretend to sanctity in order to hide human trickery. But I shan't make any statement about this until the deputy of the dead saint comes to see me. He delivered his message to you first, no doubt because you were nearest; now, you say, he has gone to Naples, and has set sail for France and England, and will eventually visit me. When he gives me my share of the revelation I shall decide how much faith to put in him. I shall form my judgment on his age, face, expression, manners, dress, gestures, walk, way of sitting, voice and speech, and especially on the conclusion of his discourse and on the purpose that is revealed.

But this is what I draw from your words. That holy man, on his deathbed, had a vision of us two and a good many others. He received some very secret revelations to communicate. And he chose as executor of his last will and testament, you might say, that messenger who, you say, is earnest and faithful. This, I suspect, is the whole story. What the others may have heard we don't know; but in your case there are just two revelations (for the other points are minor). This is the first: the end of your life looms; few years remain for you. And the second is that you must renounce the study and practice of poetry. Hence all your consternation and grief, which were communicated to me as I read your letter. But thinking it over I was much relieved, and so will you be if you listen to me, or even to yourself and to the dictates of reason. You will see that the cause of your distress is rather a cause of rejoicing. . . .

He argues that death is not to be dreaded and that the monk's prohibition of poetry is absurd.

Be reasonable. I know of many who have attained the highest saintliness without literary culture; I don't know of any who were excluded from sanctity by culture. I have heard the charge that Paul the Apostle went crazy through reading, but everyone knows how much justice there is in that accusation. Rather, if I may speak of my own observation, the road to virtue through ignorance is level, no doubt, but fit for lazy souls. All good men have the same goal, but there are numberless ways thither, and much variety for the pilgrims. One goes slow, another goes fast; one in darkness, one in the bright light; one takes a low seat, one a higher. Every such journey is a blessed one, but the way of knowledge is certainly more glorious, illumined, and lofty. Hence there is no comparison between the simple piety of a rustic and the intellectual faith of a scholar. Give me an example of a saint who arose from the mass of the unlettered, and I will match him with a greater saint of the other sort.

But I won't detain you longer on this theme. I had to talk at length since I had so much pertinent material. If you cling to your purpose of abandoning literature and of getting rid of your books, the instruments of literature, if your determination is unshakable, then I am indeed grateful that you have offered them to me. You know my passion for books; I can't deny it without disavowing all my writings. And I am happy to be preferred to all others as a purchaser. Though I would seem to be buying something that is already mine, I should not like to see the books of so great a man as you scattered here and there and in profane hands. As we have been one in spirit, though separated physically, I should like to have these adjuncts to our studies go by God's grace integrally and undispersed to some holy house after we are gone, in perpetual memory of us. I had made up my mind to this after the death of him whom I hoped to be the successor of my studies.[1]

You ask me graciously to fix the price of the books. But this I cannot do, for I don't know their titles, number, or value. Send me an itemized list. I shall make this condition, that if ever you should decide to spend with me our few remaining days, as I have always hoped and as indeed you once promised, you will find these books assembled, together with my own, which are yours as well. Thus you will recognize that you have lost nothing, but you will have gained something.

I must finally remark that when you go around telling people that you are in debt to me, you are in error. I am amazed at this excessive, nay absurd, scruple of your conscience. I could object in Terence's words: "You are seeking a knot in a bulrush." You owe me nothing but your love. No, not even that; you have already paid your debt fully and honestly. Perhaps, however, you owe forever what you forever receive; but as you always pay, you never owe. As for your familiar complaints of poverty, I don't want to offer you consolations or examples of illustrious paupers. You know them already. There is just one answer I want to make, clearly and repeatedly. I have offered to share with you the considerable wealth that I have gained late in life; you have preferred liberty of spirit, tranquillity, and actual want; and for this I applaud you. But you have repulsed your friend, who has so often made his appeal to you; and this I do not applaud. I am not able to make you rich from this distance; if I were I should not be employing mere written words, I should reply with tangible goods. But let my resources, more than sufficient for my needs, suffice for us two, in a single house, possessing a single heart. You will offend me if you take umbrage at this; you will offend me more if you doubt me. Farewell.

1. Perhaps his scapegrace son Giovanni.

[Reproof of Boccaccio for Threatening to Burn His Poems; and a Diatribe Against Contemporary Ignoramuses]

From Book V/2

To Boccaccio; from Venice, 28 August 1364.

"I have somewhat to say unto thee," if I, a poor sinner, may quote our Savior. You can already foresee what that "somewhat" is. It will be my usual refrain, so prepare your mind for patience and your ear for reproaches. For although there were never two more harmonious minds than yours and mine, often, to my surprise, our acts and decisions are far different. I often wonder how this comes about, not in your case only, but in that of other friends, in whom the same thing strikes me. I find no better reason than that Mother Nature made us alike, but that habit, which has been called a second nature, makes us unlike. Would that we might have lived together! Thus habit would have made us a single mind in two bodies.

Perhaps you think I am now about to say something important. But no, it is a small matter. It must be a small matter, since what an author belittles is sure to be very little. (Everyone loves his own utterances; hence almost no one is a sound judge of his own work; fondness for our own words beguiles nearly all of us.) You are one in many thousands, since your judgment of your own words is misled not by affection but by hatred and contempt for them. Unless, perhaps, I am deceiving myself, attributing to humility what is really due to pride. I shall explain what I mean by this.

You know that ordinary, numerous lot of men, dealers in words, but not their own, who have multiplied among us to an intolerable degree. They are possessed of no great native wit but of splendid memories, much diligence, and more effrontery. They frequent the halls of kings and potentates. Naked of originality, they deck themselves out with other men's poems. They pick up the best things written by one or another, especially those composed in Italian, and recite them with great expression, thus seeking the applause of the great, and money and fine clothes, and gifts. The material for their support they obtain at second hand, or sometimes from the writers themselves, either by begging or if necessary by paying cash when they find a greedy or poverty-stricken author. This last case was well known to Juvenal: "He will die of hunger unless he can sell his unpublished *Agave* to Paris."

You can readily imagine how insufferable I—and certainly others —find these fellows when they try their cajolements on me. It is true that I am less bothered than I used to be, whether because the character of my work has changed, or because they respect my years, or because they have suffered too many rebuffs in the past. For to discourage them from imposing on me, I often give them a sharp refusal; I won't be swayed by their instances, except occasionally, when I know the petitioner to be needy and humble. Charity sometimes persuades me that I should draw something out of my mind to help feed one of these poor fellows. The product of an hour or so of my labor could long be useful to the receiver. Some of them, who overcame me with their supplications and had their way, were penniless and in rags when they departed; and they returned shortly after dressed in silks, with well-filled bellies and pockets, to thank me that with my aid they had been able to cast off the burden of want. I have sometimes been so moved by such an experience that I resolved never to deny this sort of alms to anyone; but then again I become so annoyed that I renew my original decision.

Incidentally, when I asked some of them why they always applied to me alone and not to others, and especially to you, for these contributions, they answered that they had often asked you, and without success. I was amazed that one so generous as you with things should be judged stingy with his words. I was told that you had burned all the poems you had written in the vulgar tongue! Far from stilling my wonder, this reply added to it. When I asked the reason for your action, all but one were silent, professing ignorance. He offered an opinion—whether his own or something he had heard I don't know—that you had resolved to rewrite all of your juvenilia and maturer works in the light of your ripe—or decrepit—judgment. This amazed him the more, and me too, that you should have such confidence in the prolongation of this precarious life, at your age especially; although I am fully conscious of the vigor and soundness of your mind. "What a strange procedure," I cried, "to burn what you want to correct, so that nothing will be left to correct!"

My bewilderment lasted until I arrived in this city and found here our good friend Donato, who is totally devoted to you. Recently one of our frank and frequent conversations turned on you. He confirmed the story that I had heard, and told me for the first time the reason. He said that from your early years you had delighted in writing only in Italian, and you had devoted to such works most of your time and thought, until you discovered and read through my own youthful efforts of this sort in the vulgar tongue. Then, he said, your urge to write had cooled; and not satisfied to refrain from such writing thereafter, you had conceived a hatred for what you had already published and had burned everything, not with the idea of revising but of destroying. And thus you had deprived yourself and future times of the fruits of your labors in this field, for no other reason than that you judged them unequal to mine. But your self-scorn was unworthy, the burning unjustified; and your motive is more than suspect. I am not sure if this is humility despising itself, or if it is pride, setting itself above all others. You who look into your own spirit must judge of the truth. I lose myself in conjectures, since I am speaking to you, as usual, as if I were talking to myself.

I must praise you, then, for regarding yourself as inferior to men whose superior you are in fact. I much prefer this error to that of putting oneself, in self-esteem, above one's actual superior. I am reminded of Lucan of Cordova, a man of brilliant mind and spirit. But such a character can lead one to great ascents and great downfalls. When still young he found that he had progressed very far in his studies. He reckoned that his early achievements promised so much that, exulting in his success, he dared to compare himself with Virgil. This happened when he was giving a reading of part of his book on the civil war, which his death prevented him from finishing. He said in his introductory remarks: "Isn't this as good as Virgil's *Culex?*" [1] I don't know if his friends made any reply to this insolent question, but as for me, from the time I first read this passage, I have often replied inwardly and angrily to that vain boaster: "My good man, your work may be as good as the *Culex*, but there is an immense difference between it and the *Aeneid*."

In contrast to that vainglorious man, who set himself equal to or above Virgil, you put me in your esteem above yourself. Why then do I not more extol your humility? There is something lurking here that I should like to inquire into. My thought is so baffling that it is hard to dig it out; I shall try, at any rate. I am afraid that this notable humility of yours is a proud humility. Perhaps the phrase, "proud humility," is novel and startling. If it offends you, I shall express myself otherwise. I am afraid, then, that some pride mingles with your excess of humility. I have seen men at banquets or at other gatherings who thought they were not assigned places of sufficient honor; and I have seen them rise suddenly and seek out the lowest place at table. Their pretext was humility, but it was pride that moved them. I have seen another man walk out of the room. Whether this is due to weakness, anger, or pride, they act as if, unless they can have the first place, which after all is bound to be unique, they must be unworthy of any but the lowest seat. But there are degrees of glory as there are of merit.

You do not claim the first place for yourself. That is humility. Some, by no means your equal either in gifts or in style, have dared

---

1. *The Gnat;* a trifle ascribed to Virgil.

to hope for that post and to solicit it, often exciting our laughter and our annoyance as well. They sometimes gain the support of the vulgar; would that it had no more effect in the marketplace than it does on Parnassus! But if you can't bear to be second or third, doesn't that look like pride? Let us suppose that I, who would so proudly be your equal, am your superior; suppose that the master of our vulgar tongue [Dante] takes first place; do not take it ill that one or the other (and especially your great fellow citizen) should precede you. Should you not be proud of being one of so few rather than to claim the distinction of being first? To aspire to supremacy may be the mark of a great spirit, but to take umbrage at the mere presence of the supreme masters certainly looks like pride.

I have heard that our old man of Ravenna,[2] no mean judge in such matters, regularly assigns you the third place whenever the question comes up. If this revolts you, if you think I am keeping you out of the first place, as in fact I do not, I shall gladly yield to you, leaving the second place open. If you refuse this, I must think you are really outrageous. If only the first are glorious, how innumerable are the obscure! Upon how few does the bright light shine! Consider further that the second place is safer and sometimes stands actually higher. You have someone to bear the first attacks of envy, to point your course at the risk of his own reputation, to indicate pitfalls and the straight way by his steps astray. He will excite you, banish your sloth by stimulating our rivalry. You will long to pass him, in order not to see him forever ahead of you in the race. Such are the stimuli of noble minds; they have often produced admirable results. Surely he who can bear to be second may soon come to merit first place, while he who cannot bear it is already beginning to be unworthy of the place he is refusing. Certainly if you consult your memory you will hardly find a foremost general, philosopher, or poet who did not reach the heights under such goads.

While the first place awakens in nearly all its occupants an arrogant self-satisfaction, and in others envy, it may also produce idleness. Jealousy provokes both the lover and the scholar. Love without a rival, virtue without an emulator, grows dull. An industrious poor man is better than a rich idler. It is fitter to be fired with enthusiasm for Virgil and thus to struggle toward his eminence than to languish in torpid ease. It is better and safer to make an effort, with the aid of active virtue, than to repose in the commendations of idle fame.

Thus, I think, you have good reason not to refuse the second place. But what if you are put third? Or fourth? Will you be

2. Unidentified.

furious? Perhaps the passage has slipped your memory where Annaeus Seneca defends Fabianus Papirius against Lucilius. When the latter set Cicero above Papirius, Seneca remarked: "It is no small matter to be second only to the highest." Then he put Asinius Pollio next to Cicero, saying: "It is a great thing to follow those two." Then he gave Livy the next place, and said: "How many does he surpass who is surpassed by only three, and those three the noblest speakers of all men!" And you, my friend, think whether these words might not be said of you. Except that whatever place you occupy, and whomever you may see standing before you, it is surely not I who precede you. Therefore spare the bonfire, and have mercy on your poems.

If, however, either you or others are inwardly convinced that I outrank you, whether I wish it or not, need you grieve at being placed next to me, and need you regard it as a disgrace? Pardon my frankness; but if this is the case you have long deceived me, and your modesty of mind and your love for me are not what I had hoped. True friends naturally prefer the other's interest to their own; they wish to be surpassed, and when they are surpassed they feel a most particular pleasure. Thus no affectionate father will deny that his greatest joy is to be bested by his own son. I have hoped, I still hope, to be a lesser man than you—though I can hardly call myself your dear son, or allege that my reputation is dearer to you than your own. I remember that you once scolded me for this, with a show of kindly anger. If you were telling the truth, you should now rejoice to see me take precedence. You should not quit the race, but follow me the more resolutely, and make sure that no other competitor thrusts himself between us to usurp your place. A friend running beside a friend, or sitting with him in his chariot, does not ask their ranking; he wants only to be by his friend's side. There is nothing sweeter than this so longed-for intimacy. Between friends there is only love, without measurement. The last are first, the first last, for all are in fact one.

I have made my charge against you. Now let us hear your defense. Though I know your own confession, and though I have had the report of our good friend, I shall try to find some other and more elevated reason for your action than the one you give. For an identical act can be either laudable or blamable according to the motives of the actor.

I shall tell you what I think. It was not arrogance, so foreign to your gentle character, or jealousy of anyone, or resentment at your lot in life, that prompted you to destroy your own works, so unfairly to them and to yourself. It was a fine, noble indignation against our vain, futile times, which understand nothing, corrupt everything, and—what is intolerable—despise everything. You wanted to remove from them the products of your genius. As in the past Virginius stabbed his own daughter, so did you commit to the flames your lovely inventions, the children of your mind, to save them from shameful abuse.

How far, my dear friend, have I guessed right? What has inspired this conjecture is that I have sometimes thought of doing the same with my few poor works in Italian. Perhaps I should have done so, if they had not long since been scattered far beyond my power to recall them. On the other hand, I have sometimes been in a quite contrary mood, to give all my time to writing in the vernacular. Latin is of course the loftier language, but it has been so developed by ancient geniuses that neither we nor anyone else can add much of anything to it. The vulgar tongue however has only recently been formulated. It has been mishandled by many and tended by only a few; rough as it is, it could be much beautified and enriched, I am sure. Inspired by this hope and filled with youthful ardor, I once began a *magnum opus* in Italian. I laid the foundations, as of a building, and collected the lime, stone, and wood. And then I observed our age, the mother of pride and sloth, and I began to reflect sourly on the power of the smug critics and on their charming pronunciations, such that they mutilate whatever they read. Hearing their performances again and again, I thought it through and concluded that my structure would be swallowed in soft mud and quicksand; I should see myself and all my work mangled by the mob. Like one who meets a serpent in the middle of the road, I stopped short. I changed my mind and chose, I hope, a higher and a shorter way. My brief works in Italian are now so widely scattered, as I have said, that I no longer regard them as mine, but rather as the property of the general public. I shall take care that my major works shall not be similarly lacerated.

But why should I distress myself about the unlettered masses when I have a much juster and more serious quarrel with those who call themselves scholars? To all their absurdities they have added that most repulsive quality, a mighty arrogance based on ignorance. Thus they carp at the fame of those whose least words they once sought to understand piecemeal, applauding the author. O inglorious time! Do you spurn antiquity, your mother, the discoverer of all honest arts and crafts? Do you dare to proclaim yourself not merely the equal but the superior of antiquity? I say nothing of the dregs of men, the base mob, whose words and opinions deserve only our laughter, rather than our reproof. I say nothing of our soldiers, our generals, who do not blush to allege that in our time military art has reached its peak of perfection, whereas in fact it has certainly perished and totally collapsed in their hands. They possess no art and skill, but rely on their indolence and on happy chances. They go to war as if to a wedding, wearing their best clothes and dreaming of wine, good food, and lust. They confuse flight with victory. All their art and purpose is to hold out their hands to the adversary, not to smite him, and to gain sweet glances from their mistresses, not to terrify the enemy. But perhaps we should pardon their errors on the ground of their ignorance and total want of understanding.

Nor shall I mention kings, who act as if their rule consisted in wearing robes of purple and gold, in bearing scepter and diadem. Thinking themselves equal to their predecessors therein, they presume they are equal in virtue and glory. Raised to the throne only in order to rule (for *rex* comes from *regere,* to rule) they do not rule in fact; as their actions show, they are masters of the people, but they are mastered by their pleasures. Rulers of men, they are slaves of sleep and luxury. Ignorance of history, the dazzle of fortune's favor, vanity built on excessive prosperity, may possibly excuse them.

But what, pray, will excuse men of education? They can hardly be ignorant of the ancients; how then account for their dwelling in the same eclipse of vision? You recognize, my friend, that I am discharging my spleen and anger. Lately a school of dialecticians has arisen, not so much ignorant as mad. Like a black army of ants, they have emerged from the recesses of some old rotten oak, devastating all the fields of sound doctrine. They damn Plato and Aristotle, they laugh at Socrates and Pythagoras. Dear God, what things they say under the cover of their idiotic leaders! I don't want to give his school a name; they have done nothing to deserve one, though their nonsense has caused a great stir. I don't want to class as philosophers those I have seen among these insignificant thinkers. They have deserted sound authorities and glorify the names of men who displayed no vigor of thought, no knowledge, and no reputation for knowledge. They may have learned something after death; I don't know. What can I say of men who despise Marcus Tullius Cicero, the shining sun of eloquence? Who condemn Varro and Seneca? Who shudder at the style of Livy and Sallust, as rough and unpolished? Meanwhile they rely on the authority of new, obscure masters, of whom they ought rather to be ashamed.

I happened to be present at one of their gatherings, where they were picking to pieces Virgil's style, as is their wont. Amazed at this fantastic outburst, I asked a certain scholar what he had found so shocking in the work of the great author. His face put on a mighty sneer; and listen to his answer: "He uses too many conjunctions!" O Virgil, spend thy genius and toil on thy heaven-born verses, blessed by the Muses, file and polish them only that they may fall into such hands as these!

Let me speak now of another kind of monstrosity, dressed in

clerical garb but profane at heart and in habits. These call Ambrose, Augustine, Jerome merely long-winded, not deep-thinking. I don't know the origin of these new theologians, who do not now spare the great doctors, and who will not long spare the Apostles and the Gospel itself. They will soon launch their audacious shafts against Christ himself, unless he whose cause is at stake steps in and muzzles these wild animals. It has become common practice among this folk that whenever a reverend or sacred name is uttered, they mock at it either with a silent gesture or with some blasphemous remark. "Augustine," they say, "saw much, but he knew little." Nor do they speak more decently of others.

I was recently in my library when one of these fellows called. He was not a religious in costume, but he professed Christianity, and what is that if not religious? He is a modern-style philosopher, who thinks his time is wasted unless he can yelp something against Christ and Christ's celestial doctrine. I happened to quote something from the Scriptures. He foamed with rage; his face, ugly enough by nature, was distorted with anger and with his scowl of contempt.

"You can keep your miserable church doctors," said he. "I have my own leader; I know the one I have learned to trust."

Said I: "You have used the words of the Apostle. If only you would apply them to your faith!"

"That Apostle of yours was just a wordmonger, and what's more, he was crazy."

"Very good," said I. "You talk like a philosopher. Your first accusation was made by other philosophers; the second by Festus, Governor of Syria. Certainly Paul was a sower of words, and very profitable ones, for we can all see how this seed, cultivated with the salutary plow of his successors, irrigated by the sacred blood of the martyrs, has brought forth a mighty harvest of faith."

At this he laughed, as if nauseated. "You can be a good Christian if you like; I don't believe a word of their stories. Paul and your Augustine and all the others you prate about were so many drivelers. I wish you could take Averroes seriously; you would see how much greater he is than those jokers of yours."

I was enraged, I admit. I could hardly keep my hand from his foul, blasphemous mouth. "It's the same old quarrel I have with other heretics," said I. "Get out, you and your heresy, and never come back!" I took him by the gown, and with a rudeness more consistent with his habits than my own, I pushed him out of the house.

There are thousands of such cases. Against them nothing avails, not the majesty of the name of Christian, not reverence for Christ (whom wretched men insult while assembled angels worship him), not fear of punishment, not inquisitors armed against heresies, not prison and the stake. All fail to restrain the impudence of ignorance, the effrontery of heresy.

So these are the times, my friend, in which we live, into which our lot has cast us, wherein we are growing old. As I often angrily complain, we must bear with ignorant critics holding a mistaken opinion of their own merits. Not content with losing the books of the ancients, they must insult classic genius and classic remains. They parade their ignorance, as if whatever they do not know were not worth knowing. They indulge in the license of their fat, swollen heads, and introduce among us unheard-of authors and absurd, exotic studies.

So if, lacking any other deliverer, you have invoked the aid of fire to save your work from such critics, such tyrants, I cannot disapprove the deed, and I can sympathize with your reasons. I have done the same with many of my writings; I can almost wish that I had so disposed of all my works when I had the opportunity; for I see no hope of more enlightened judges while their numbers and their excesses increase from day to day. They are no longer confined to the schools; they spread through the cities, they block the streets and the public squares. I often reprove myself for deploring the recent destructive years, for bewailing the ravaged world. Perhaps indeed the world has been robbed of true men; but never, I think, was it more filled with wickedness and wicked men. In short, I think I should have acquitted the daughter of Appius Claudius, if I had lived then and felt as I do now.[3]

But now farewell, as I have said all I had on my mind.

[On Boccaccio's *Decameron* and the Story of Griselda] †

Your book, written in our mother tongue and published, I presume, during your early years, has fallen into my hands, I know not whence or how. If I told you that I had read it, I should deceive you. It is a very big volume, written in prose and for the

---

3. She was fined for excoriating the Roman people.

† This letter from Francesco Petrarca to Giovanni Boccaccio was written in 1373 and is found in the collecton entitled *Letters of Riper Years* (XVII, 3). Besides Petrarca's evaluation of *The Decameron*, an attitude rather typical of early humanist scholars who preferred works in a polished Latin to those in the vulgar languages, the original letter contained Petrarca's Latin translation of the last story of the last day in *The Decameron*, that of patient Griselda, which was later to be used by Chaucer in his *Canterbury Tales* ("The Clerk's Tale"). The translation is reprinted from James Harvey Robinson and Henry Winchester Rolfe, *Petrarch: The First Modern Scholar and Man of Letters* (New York: Greenwood Press, 1968), pp. 191–96. Used with the agreement of Greenwood Press, the reprint publisher, a division of Williamhouse-Regency Inc.

multitude. I have been, moreover, occupied with more serious business, and much pressed for time. You can easily imagine the unrest caused by the warlike stir about me, for, far as I have been from actual participation in the disturbances, I could not but be affected by the critical condition of the state. What I did was to run through your book, like a traveller who, while hastening forward, looks about him here and there, without pausing. I have heard somewhere that your volume was attacked by the teeth of certain hounds, but that you defended it valiantly with staff and voice. This did not surprise me, for not only do I well know your ability, but I have learned from experience of the existence of an insolent and cowardly class who attack in the work of others everything which they do not happen to fancy or be familiar with, or which they cannot themselves accomplish. Their insight and capabilities extend no farther; on all other themes they are silent.

My hasty perusal afforded me much pleasure. If the humour is a little too free at times, this may be excused in view of the age at which you wrote, the style and language which you employ, and the frivolity of the subjects, and of the persons who are likely to read such tales. It is important to know for whom we are writing, and a difference in the character of one's listeners justifies a difference in style. Along with much that was light and amusing, I discovered some serious and edifying things as well, but I can pass no definite judgment upon them, since I have not examined the work thoroughly.

As usual, when one looks hastily through a book, I read somewhat more carefully at the beginning and at the end. At the beginning you have, it seems to me, accurately described and eloquently lamented the condition of our country during that siege of pestilence which forms so dark and melancholy a period in our century. At the close you have placed a story which differs entirely from most that precede it, and which so delighted and fascinated me that, in spite of cares which made me almost oblivious of myself, I was seized with a desire to learn it by heart, so that I might have the pleasure of recalling it for my own benefit, and of relating it to my friends in conversation. When an opportunity for telling it offered itself shortly after, I found that my auditors were delighted. Later it suddenly occurred to me that others, perhaps, who were unacquainted with our tongue, might be pleased with so charming a story, as it had delighted me ever since I first heard it some years ago, and as you had not considered it unworthy of presentation in the mother tongue, and had placed it, moreover, at the end of your book, where, according to the principles of rhetoric, the most effective part of the composition belongs. So one fine day when, as usual, my mind was distracted by a variety of occupations, discontented with myself and my surroundings, I suddenly sent everything flying, and, snatching my pen, I attacked this story of yours. I sincerely trust that it will gratify you that I have of my own free-will undertaken to translate your work, something I should certainly never think of doing for anyone else, but which I was induced to do in this instance by my partiality for you and for the story. Not neglecting the precept of Horace in his *Art of Poetry*, that the careful translator should not attempt to render word for word, I have told your tale in my own language, in some places changing or even adding a few words, for I felt that you would not only permit, but would approve, such alterations.

Although many have admired and wished for my version, it seemed to me fitting that your work should be dedicated to you rather than to anyone else; and it is for you to judge whether I have, by this change of dress, injured or embellished the original. The story returns whence it came; it knows its judge, its home, and the way thither. As you and everyone who reads this knows, it is you and not I who must render account for what is essentially yours. If anyone asks me whether this is all true, whether it is a history or a story, I reply in the words of Sallust, "I refer you to the author"—to wit, my friend Giovanni. With so much of introduction I begin. . . .[1]

My object in thus re-writing your tale was not to induce the women of our time to imitate the patience of this wife, which seems to me almost beyond imitation, but to lead my readers to emulate the example of feminine constancy, and to submit themselves to God with the same courage as did this woman to her husband. Although, as the Apostle James tells us, "God cannot be tempted with evil, and he himself tempteth no man," he still may prove us, and often permits us to be beset with many and grievous trials, not that he may know our character, which he knew before we were created, but in order that our weakness should be made plain to ourselves by obvious and familiar proofs. Anyone, it seems to me, amply deserves to be reckoned among the heroes of mankind who suffers without a murmur for God, what this poor peasant woman bore for her mortal husband.

My affection for you has induced me to write at an advanced age what I should hardly have undertaken even as a young man. Whether what I have narrated be true or false I do not know, but the fact that you wrote it would seem sufficient to justify the inference that it is but a tale. Foreseeing this question, I have prefaced my translation with the statement that the responsibility for the story rests with the author; that is, with you. And now let me tell you my experiences with this narrative, or tale, as I prefer to call it.

1. Here, Petrarca's Latin translation of the Griselda story, entitled *De obedientia ac fide uxoria mythologia*, was inserted into the letter; it is not included in the translation by Robinson and Rolfe. [*Editors.*]

In the first place, I gave it to one of our mutual friends in Padua to read, a man of excellent parts and wide attainments. When scarcely half-way through the composition, he was suddenly arrested by a burst of tears. When again, after a short pause, he made a manful attempt to continue, he was again interrupted by a sob. He then realised that he could go no farther himself, and handed the story to one of his companions, a man of education, to finish. How others may view this occurrence I cannot, of course, say; for myself, I put a most favourable construction upon it, believing that I recognise the indications of a most compassionate disposition; a more kindly nature, indeed, I never remember to have met. As I saw him weep as he read, the words of the Satirist came back to me:

> "Nature, who gave us tears, by that alone
> Proclaims she made the feeling heart our own;
> And 't is our noblest sense." [2]

Some time after, another friend of ours, from Verona (for all is common between us, even our friends), having heard of the effect produced by the story in the first instance, wished to read it for himself. I readily complied, as he was not only a good friend, but a man of ability. He read the narrative from beginning to end without stopping once. Neither his face nor his voice betrayed the least emotion, not a tear or a sob escaped him. "I too," he said at the end, "would have wept, for the subject certainly excites pity, and the style is well adapted to call forth tears, and I am not hard-hearted; but I believed, and still believe, that this is all an invention. If it were true, what woman, whether of Rome or any other nation, could be compared with this Griselda? Where do we find the equal of this conjugal devotion, where such faith, such extraordinary patience and constancy?" I made no reply to this reasoning, for I did not wish to run the risk of a bitter debate in the midst of our good-humoured and friendly discussion. But I had a reply ready. There are some who think that whatever is difficult for them must be impossible for others; they must measure others by themselves, in order to maintain their superiority. Yet there have been many, and there may still be many, to whom acts are easy which are commonly held to be impossible. Who is there who would not, for example, regard a Curtius, a Mucius, or the Decii, among our own people, as pure fictions; or, among foreign nations, Codrus and the Philæni; or, since we are speaking of woman, Portia, or Hypsicratia, or Alcestis, and others like them? But these are actual historical persons. And indeed I do not see why one who can face death for another, should not be capable of encountering any trial or form of suffering.

2. Juvenal, XV, 131–33, as translated by William Gifford.

LEONARDO BRUNI

Note on Boccaccio †

I will not write Boccaccio's biography at this time, not because he does not deserve greatest praise, but because I do not know the particulars of his birth or his personal condition and life. Without knowledge of such things, one should not write. However, his works and books are well known to me, and it is clear to me that he had a great mind and was extremely cultured and hardworking. It is amazing that he wrote so many things. He learned grammar as an adult, and for this reason did not have a good command of the Latin language. But through what he wrote in the vernacular, it is apparent that he was by nature very eloquent and had a gift for oratory. Of his works written in Latin, *The Genealogy of the Gods* is the best.[1] He was greatly hindered by poverty, and was never content with his life; on the contrary he continually wrote complaints and moaned about himself. Sensitive and disdainful by nature, he had many problems because he could neither bear to be with his own peers, nor in the company of princes and lords.

FILIPPO VILLANI

[The Life of Giovanni Boccaccio] ‡

When the blacksmith's hammer strikes a piece of red-hot iron, flaming chips shoot out like rockets flashing on their course; just

---

† Leonardo Bruni (1369–1444) was an important Florentine humanist who served not only as apostolic secretary to several popes but also as chancellor of the Florentine Republic. He is perhaps best remembered for his twelve-volume *History of the Florentine People,* which analyzed the history of the city from its foundation in classical times until 1402, and for his *Life of Dante,* in which he attempted to correct some of the errors he felt he had found in the earlier biography of Dante by Boccaccio. This brief biographical sketch is all Bruni completed on the life of Boccaccio and is freshly translated for this critical edition by Hugh Skubikowski from Angelo Solerti, ed., *Le vite di Dante, Petrarca e Boccaccio scritte fino al secolo decimosesto* (Milan: Vallardi, 1904), p. 679. An evaluation of Boccaccio's Italian masterpiece is conspicuously absent, a testament to the common humanist belief that Latin was a superior language to the Italian vernacular.

1. This influential work of scholarship represented an encyclopedic collection of classical mythology in fifteen books. It was extremely popular as a source book for Renaissance poets and was used by such English writers as Chaucer, Spenser, Jonson, Milton, and many others. Besides a consideration of the various classical myths, Boccaccio includes in the work an important treatment of the nature of poetry and a discussion of the allegorical method of interpreting literature. For a partial translation of this section of the work, see Charles G. Osgood, ed., *Boccaccio On Poetry: Being the Preface and the Fourteenth and Fifteenth Books of Boccaccio's Genealogia Deorum Gentilium* (Indianapolis: Bobbs-Merrill, 1956). [*Editors.*]

‡ Filippo Villani (1325?–1405?) was the son of the Florentine historian Matteo Villani, and at one time chancellor of the city of Perugia (1376–81). His Latin work, *Liber de origine civitatis Florentiae et eiusdem famosis civibus,* con-

so, first Dante, then Petrarca—men of highest genius—struck at the antiquated poetry to free it from the rust of many centuries, rust which had attacked it so horribly as to consume it almost completely. Just as when a flintstone is struck, the glittering sparks grow into bright, blinding flames, so Zanobio,[1] whom we mentioned earlier, and Giovanni, whom we will discuss here, fortunately emerged, moved by the poetic spirit.

His father, Boccaccio, was a gentleman well known for his integrity. He was from Certaldo—a town in the Florentine countryside—but was living in Paris, attending to his commerce. Just as he was pleasant and generous, so he was cheerful, understanding, and had a ready inclination for love. Because of his pleasant character and manners, he fell in love with a young Parisian girl whose social status was between noble and bourgeois, and for whom he burned with passionate love. As those who examined Giovanni's works would have it, he took her for his wife, and she later gave birth to Giovanni. As a child he was unable, for financial reasons, to complete his study of grammar under Master Giovanni (the poet Zanobio's father). Instead, he was forced by his father to attend to the abacus and to travel about. He had traveled for a long time through many and various regions when, at the age of twenty, he stopped in Naples—in the Pergola—at his father's command. There one day, seeking diversion alone, he came by chance to the place where the ashes of Virgilius Maro are buried.[2] When Giovanni had thought admiringly about the grave and its contents for some time, he suddenly began to blame and lament his fortune, which forced him to devote himself to the hated commerce. Thus, seized by a sudden love for the Pierian Muses,[3] he returned home scorning all that was commerce, and gave himself to studying poetry ardently. Combining his great genius and ardent desire, he made great progress in a very short time. Upon perceiving this, his father concluded that a celestial inclination had greater power

tained evaluations of many of Florence's most illustrious citizens, including this biography of Boccaccio. Villani views Boccaccio as a source of Florentine civic pride and groups him together with Dante and Petrarca in a poetic trinity which, he believes, has created a poetic renaissance in Italy. Like Bruni, however, Villani values Boccaccio's Latin works more than those he wrote in Italian. This new translation by Hugh Skubikowski is taken from a fifteenth-century Italian version of the Latin original which enjoyed a wide circulation at the time and which is reprinted in Angelo Solerti, ed., *Le vite di Dante, Petrarca e Boccaccio scritte fino al secolo decimosesto* (Milan: Vallardi, 1904), pp. 671–76.

1. Zanobio da Strada, a contemporary of Petrarca, and fellow poet, who was crowned as poet laureate in 1353 by Emperor Charles IV in a ceremony which recalled the more important coronation of Petrarca in 1341. [*Editors.*]
2. The Latin poet Virgil (70 B.C.–19 B.C.), author of *The Aeneid. The Eclogues,* and *The Georgics.* Boccaccio and Petrarca both attempted to imitate Virgil in the writing of epic, pastoral, and bucolic poetry and their example was to be followed by many other important European Renaissance writers. [*Editors.*]
3. The Pierian spring, located in Macedonia, was traditionally associated with the Muses of poetry in Greek mythology. [*Editors.*]

than paternal authority, and finally consented to his studies. He did all in his power to help him.

Now that Giovanni felt free, he began carefully to investigate the requirements of poetry. Seeing that the principles and fundamentals of the poets, found in the fiction and in the tales, had been almost totally lost, he set out as if moved by destiny to learn what he could about the poets. Nor was he daunted in his endeavors by exhausting wandering; for he certainly traveled the length and breadth of many different provinces. Boccaccio also pursued Greek studies; and with laborious and persistent study sought to gain what he could. For his teacher he had the Greek Leontius, a great expert in Greek poetry.[4] Finally, what information he was able to gather he placed in one volume entitled The Genealogy of the Gods. In it he revived the commentaries of the ancient poets with admirable orderliness and elegant style, as well as what he understood to be the meaning of allegory. Certainly a pleasant and useful work, it is indispensable to those wishing to see through the poets' veils, for it would be difficult to understand poets and to study their discipline without it. With a surprisingly perceptive mind he restored to the public—indeed brought to their fingertips —all the mysteries of the poets and the meaning of the allegories, which concealed either historical fiction or fantastical compositions. The names of rivers, mountains, woods, lakes, ponds, and seas, occurring in volumes of poetry and history, had been altered either by the passing of many centuries or by various events. Thus they were called by different names; and these names altered or prevented understanding by the reader. So he wrote a book, On Rivers and Mountains,[5] and on other aforementioned things, in which he convincingly identified the names by which each had become known during the course of time. This book can free readers of ancient writings from many errors.

He wrote another book, The Lives of Famous Men,[6] and another, Of Noble Ladies;[7] in both he is brilliant for his ease and elegance with words, and for his seriousness. It can be said—and deservedly—that in these treatises he not only equals, but perhaps surpasses, the great minds of the ancients. In addition to the afore-

4. Leontius Pilatus or Leonzio Pilato (?–1365), a Calabrian scholar whom Boccaccio had invited to Florence as professor of Greek, on Petrarca's recommendation. Pilatus produced one of the earliest Latin translations of Homer's Iliad and Odyssey. [Editors.]

5. This Latin work, originally titled De montibus, silvis, fontibus, lacubus, fluminibus, stagnis seu paludibus et de nominibus maris liber, is a minor treatise listing all the geographical allusions found in classical writings Boccaccio knew. It is thus a kind of appendix to

the more important Genealogy of the Gods and was intended to be used as a reference work. [Editors.]

6. The De casibus virorum illustrium (the original Latin title) is a collection of almost one hundred accounts of the fates of various male historical or mythological figures. [Editors.]

7. The De claris mulieribus, the companion piece to De casibus and also written in Latin, describes the lives of approximately one hundred women taken from legend, history, and mythology. [Editors.]

mentioned works, he composed sixteen very beautiful eclogues, and many epistles in verse and in prose which are greatly esteemed by the learned. Certainly the volumes he wrote are dear to the worthiest men; this is proof of the greatness of his mind, even if I were to say no more.

Even Petrarca, who was his friend (so much so that they were considered one soul in two bodies) greatly praises him for his merits, and not only out of warm friendship. Zanobio the poet makes him the arbiter of choosing topics suitable for writing, as is evident in Boccaccio's own verses.

There are still other works Boccaccio wrote in the vernacular: some composed in rhyme, some reported in flowing prose. In these works, his mind quite plainly delights in the lustful joys of youth. Later, in old age, he considered destroying them; but he could not recall to his heart words he had already written, nor could he extinguish through his will the fire he had fed with the bellows of inspiration.

Such a worthy man certainly deserved to be crowned with poetic laurels. He was prevented from being so honored by his own poverty, and by the wretched misery of a time in which the lords of temporal affairs were involved with dishonest gains. However, the volumes he wrote were worthy of being crowned with laurel, and were as fitting a crown as myrtle or ivy for his forehead.

Tall and of rather stout build, Boccaccio had a round face with the nose slightly flat above the nostrils; rather large, but nonetheless attractive and well-defined lips; and a dimpled chin that was charming when he laughed. He was pleasant and considerate in conversation and he greatly enjoyed talking. He was engaging and acquired many friends, but no one who would aid him in his poverty.

Boccaccio ended his last day in the year of grace 1375 at age sixty-two, and was honorably buried in the rectory of Saint James in the town of Certaldo.

* * *

GIANNOZZO MANETTI

[The Life of Giovanni Boccaccio] †

Giovanni Boccaccio, an illustrious poet of his time, seemed to have succeeded Petrarca in poetry, just as Petrarca had earlier suc-

† Giannozzo Manetti (1396–1459) was a Florentine humanist, student of the Greek scholar Ambrogio Traversari, and frequent ambassador of the Florentine republic. His most famous work was his Latin treatise, *On the Dignity and Excellence of Man*, which may be favorably compared to the more influential treatise on the same subject by Pico della Mirandola. His Latin biographies of

ceeded Dante. For just as Petrarca was seventeen years old when Dante died, so he was born nine years before Boccaccio. Therefore, in the succession of these excellent poets, I think the almost simultaneous appearance of their great minds was the work of Nature itself, for it seemed mankind had not witnessed such an event in a thousand years: almost as if by intention, mankind was reassured after many centuries—for poetry would have probably vanished for the human race if it had lain in darkness any longer.

Giovanni was surnamed Boccaccio after his father, a merchant and a very honest man born in Certaldo, a town in the Florentine countryside, as is clearly apparent from many passages in his writings and from his epitaph, which he himself composed. As a boy, his parents indulged him until he became of an age capable of learning, at which time he was directed by his father to the study of letters, in accordance with an old family custom. Under the grammarian Giovanni (father of a certain Zanobi, a good poet of the time) he was educated in Florence until his father, because of his greed for money, withdrew him before he had learned much. Having so firmly changed his mind, almost at the most important time of his son's literary education, he scarcely allowed him to learn the rudiments of letters, in spite of Giovanni's perceptive mind. Thus, while Boccaccio was still a child his father withdrew him from the grammarian's school to a school of arithmetic—in accordance with Florentine custom. Hence, a few years afterward (he himself declares he had not yet entered adolescence) Boccaccio was entrusted to a certain great merchant of those times to be instructed in commerce. He stayed with the study of business and with this man for six years and did nothing else. As he himself assures us, he wasted precious time, for by nature he loathed the arts of making profit, and felt himself more inclined to the study of letters. Then, he was once again by his father's command directed against his will; and from the commercial house he went to a law school to learn canon law. The same thing happened to Petrarca with civil law, as I said in my account of his life. Destined, then, by his father to study the aforementioned skill, with great regrets he wasted nearly as many years as he had in commerce. For, as he says, he did not profit from such studies, because papal decrees with their long commentaries greatly bored him. There-

---

Dante, Petrarca, and Boccaccio continue Villani's theory that these three poets brought about a renaissance of poetry in the modern world. Manetti, however, is more aware of the role classical translations played in this new poetic activity than Villani was, and he presents an interesting comparative evaluation of the three Florentine writers which, never-

theless, continues to undervalue the importance of Boccaccio's Italian works. This new translation by Hugh Skubikowski is based on the Manetti essay as printed in Angelo Solerti, ed., *Le vite di Dante, Petrarca e Boccaccio scritte fino al secolo decimosesto* (Milan: Vallardi, 1904), pp. 680–93.

fore, once he became of an age to make his own decisions, he resolved to abandon such studies and to turn to poetry above everything else. This he then did, in spite of the opposition of his father, a certain renowned teacher of his, and some of his friends. No one should find it astonishing that neither respect for his father, nor his teacher's authority, nor the entreaties of his friends were able to keep him from leaving canon law and turning to poetry. And, since he had a strong inclination for poetry and disliked everything else, he seemed to have been created by God himself for poetry alone. To make this clearer, we shall cite some of his sayings as certain and faithful evidence of such an aptitude.

He himself, in the last book of the *Genealogies*, speaking about the whole course of his studies, mentions that for the sake of practicality, he was directed by his father first to arithmetic, afterwards to commerce, and then to canon law. Finally when he had almost reached maturity, as he declares in his writings, he left everything else and completely dedicated himself to poetry. He confirms that he had a great leaning toward poetry: he had not yet reached his seventh birthday and could not at the time understand the poets or the poems on his own or with the help of others (he had barely learned the rudiments of letters), when (wondrous to say) he composed some short tales. What's more, before he was able to understand poems, he was generally hailed by all as a poet because of his natural gift for invention. And he says: "Later on, having almost reached maturity, and making my own decisions, I was not the least bit hesitant to concentrate on the poets, without having consulted anyone or being persuaded by a teacher. However, my father was opposed to this and judged such studies to be frivolous and useless. I have no doubt that if I had cultivated the same studies in the flower of my youth, I would not have become such a distinguished poet so late in life." We know that such things were said by him to make clear to posterity that he was naturally disposed to poetry.

Interrupting the study of other arts, he applied himself so diligently to these long studies that although he liked many other things besides poems, he nevertheless dedicated himself to poetry alone, leaving all else aside. To be sure, he attended lessons in mathematics by the Genoese Andalone, at that time the man most expert in the mathematical arts. He read through all the sacred books of the Holy Scripture eagerly and with pleasure. Although he greatly enjoyed reading all these things, he neglected them all after dedicating himself solely to the study of poets.

Since in this way he devoted himself exceedingly late to becoming acquainted with the poets, in a brief time he labored physically and mentally, through the diligent reading of the ancient poets and the extensive transcription of Latin books, to attain more easily a full knowledge of the poetic mysteries. Since he lacked books and could not purchase them for want of a patrimony, he made his own, copying by hand many volumes not only of the ancient poets, but also of the orators and historians—almost every ancient Latin text he could find. Those who saw the great number of his transcriptions would marvel that a corpulent man such as he had copied so many volumes by himself. Indeed it was a great task, even for an indefatigable scribe who did nothing else in the course of his lifetime, not to say for a man so completely devoted to understanding things human and divine as to later commit his thoughts to writing—which, as will be evident below, was excellently done by our poet.

Not content with our abundance—or rather scarcity—of books in Latin, he had a great desire to learn Greek letters so that through such knowledge he could compensate as best he could for those elements he thought were defective in the Latin language. In this, I firmly believe, he imitated Petrarca; but Boccaccio made greater progress with the foreign language. Petrarca wanted to learn from Barlaamo,[1] a monk from San Basilio Cesariense who was very well educated in Greek letters, so that by reading the Greeks he could satisfy his insatiable desire to read, as he had not been able to do with the Latins. Boccaccio for three years listened to the public and private lectures of a certain Leontius Pilatus from Thessalonica, who had first been a very worthy disciple of the aforesaid monk, and had later become quite learned and well versed in all higher disciplines. And when Pilatus was setting out from Venice to go elsewhere, Boccaccio, by making him promises and giving advice, made him change his mind. Boccaccio called him to Florence, where he first received him respectfully in his own home, and later had him as a long-term guest, and saw to it that he was hired by the city to give public readings of Greek codices. It is said he was the first man in our city to lecture publicly in Greek. Not long afterwards, drawn by his eagerness for Greek letters, Boccaccio, at his own expense (although he was burdened by poverty), brought back to Etruria and to his native land from the center of Greece—so it is said—not only the books of Homer, but also other Greek codices. It was known that no one before him had carried Greek volumes back to Etruria. These first fruits of Greek letters, brought to us by two such distinguished poets, seem to have provided the seed which then found fertile earth here and gradually grew with time, so that, coming to flower in our day, they have produced a rich harvest. To make this more evident, I will take the present

1. Barlaam (1300–48), a Calabrian monk who gave Petrarca private lessons in Greek for a brief time. [Editors.]

opportunity to review briefly the reasons for progress in Greek studies.

Before Petrarca, after the Latin language slowly began to lose its early vigor, for many centuries almost no mention was made of Greek letters in Etruria. The men of the time, content with their learning, did not seek that of others. Petrarca, then, was the first of us who sought to come into contact with foreign letters, studying under Barlaamo—a monk of that time who, as we said, was the most learned of the Greeks. And had the untimely death of his teacher not hindered him as he was beginning to learn, Petrarca would certainly (not "maybe," as he modestly says of himself), have made great progress, because of the singular excellence of his genius and memory. In imitation of him, I think, Boccaccio was taught for three years by a certain Leontius from Thessaly, then a great expert in Greek letters. He came to learn many things, and would have had a better understanding (as he states) if his teacher, who was erratic, in the ancient way of his predecessors, had held to his purpose in teaching. Nevertheless, he gained much profit from this period of study and, among other things, he came to have a full knowledge of Homer's excellent poems, the *Iliad* and the *Odyssey*. He became acquainted with other poets through the explanations of his teacher, and made appropriate use of this acquaintance in his excellent book of *Genealogies*.

Not long after the death of Boccaccio there emerged at the same time many learned men who in their youth had ranged over the whole field of Latin and, following the recent example of Petrarca and Boccaccio, they did not hesitate to begin work in Greek letters. Motivated by their ardent desire to learn, they summoned to Florence from Constantinople, where he lived, not without great promises, a certain very learned man, Emmanuel. Once he was in Florence, they retained him at private and public expense until many had become more learned through their study. What more shall I say about Greek studies, since I seem to have expounded on their origin and progress at greater length than I had intended? This learned man was that Emmanuel Crisolora, who had many illustrious disciples.[2] They spread the alien language of the Greeks not only through Etruria, but also through some of the most renowned parts of Italy, as if it were the new seed of letters. Soon afterwards, growing gradually until our age, it seems to have sprouted wonderfully. But, someone will say, to what purpose is all this about Greek letters? To what purpose? Everything Greek we have with us, we received from Boccaccio, who, at his own

2. Emmanuel Crisolora (1350–1415), a Greek scholar whose presence in Florence helped to spread the knowledge of Greek language and literature in the late fourteenth century. [*Editors.*]

expense, brought back a teacher and Greek books which had been cut off from us by great expanses of land and sea.

Engaged unceasingly in humane studies of this sort until the end of his life, he left many literary monuments extant among us. These writings are of two sorts: some were produced in his mother tongue, some in Latin. The vernacular works are divided partly into poetry and partly into prose. And although we know he wrote these in his youth, we perceive in them such wit and such elegance that even those less knowledgeable in Latin letters, provided they have a modicum of intelligence, are greatly moved by the charm of his language. Thus it happens that, pervaded by his pleasant style of expression, his vernacular writings often seem elegant. The Latin writings are also of two kinds: some he composed in verse, others in prose. His bucolic poem is conveniently divided into sixteen eclogues, and he also composed some verse epistles. All the rest is in prose: he wrote nine books about the *Lives of Famous Men* addressed to Carlo Cavalcante, a man of the equestrian order and prefect of the Kingdom of Sicily; another work, concerning *Famous Women*, to Lady Andrea Acciacoli, countess of Altavilla; and finally the excellent work on the *Genealogies*, arranged in fifteen books and dedicated to Ugone, the renowned King of Jerusalem and Cyprus. It is unanimously agreed that this holds first place among all his works.[3]

Since I have thus far treated the beginning and progress of his studies, it remains for me to say something of his personal appearance and his way of living. He was said to have been of corpulent build and tall stature, round-faced and cheerful-looking; and so pleasant and affable in his speech that his great urbanity was evident if he said but a few words. Almost until maturity he seemed not to be too much interested in love. He was greatly vexed by poverty because it stood in the way of the smooth progress he had hoped for in his studies. Although this misfortune brought him down, he later managed to pull himself up. He knew from frequent experience the truth of that satirist's maxim, "Not easily does a man raise himself up, if his slender resources thwart his virtues." Unable to avoid poverty itself, he strove constantly, toiling day and night, to overcome as best he could, or at least to reduce, the many obstacles that poverty presented to him on his way to glory. Therefore, he copied many volumes by his own hand, partially satisfying the great desire for reading which burned in him. This is evidenced in the famous library which Niccolò Nic-

3. This value judgment, far removed from contemporary critical opinion which ranks *The Decameron* above all of Boccaccio's Latin and Italian works, demonstrates quite clearly the shift in critical perspective which has occurred since the early humanist period of the late fifteenth and early sixteenth centuries. [*Editors.*]

coli,[4] a man of great erudition, built at his own expense, it is said, in the Baslica of St. Augustine many years after Boccaccio's death. There they placed all the volumes of the poets he had copied, along with the excellent Latin works published by him, as an everlasting monument for posterity to Boccaccio's great and almost unbelievable diligence in transcribing codices. So proud was his nature that, although he was constrained by lack of an inheritance, he nevertheless could not bear to be the guest of a prince for even a short time: the cause, I believe, of his never being content with his own situation and ardently deploring his personal condition in many places in his writing.

He died in God's glory at age sixty-two, at the end of a lifetime of studies. He was buried with great honor at Certaldo, in the Basilica of St. James, beneath a square plaque with this epigram, which he composed himself:

> Giovanni's ashes lie sealed underneath;
> his liberated soul is now before God, rewarded
> for its merits in life.
> Boccaccio was his father, Certaldo
> was his fatherland. He was a poet.

Coluccio Salutati,[5] a very learned man, found these verses too humble for the singular excellence of the poet, and added twelve of his own to the original:

> Illustrious poet, why do you speak
> So humbly of yourself? You of renowned name
> Give accounts of woods, mountains, rivers,
> Pools, and lakes in your bucolic poem.
> You leave us the fruits of your toils in your own hand.
> You celebrate in lofty style the great men
> Who were struck by harsh fates, from Adam
> To our own times, as well as those noble women.
> You reveal the unknown origin of the gods
> In fifteen volumes; you are second to none
> Among the ancients; you are renowned
> In a thousand things; of you no ages will be silent.

Now that I have delineated as best I can the lives and ways of three outstanding poets, it remains to compare them with each

4. Niccolò Niccoli (1364–1437), Florentine humanist and bibliophile whose elaborate collection of manuscripts helped to form the nucleus of the first public library in Florence. After his death, his collection of over eight hundred codices was consigned to the care of Cosimo de' Medici. Although Niccoli wrote nothing of importance himself, his tireless efforts in assembling a vast collection of every known classical manuscript, at great personal expense, contributed much toward making Florence the cultural center of western Europe in subsequent years. [*Editors.*]

5. Coluccio Salutati (1331–1406), chancellor of Florence (1375–1406), humanist, and follower of Petrarca in his enthusiasm for the classics and in his attempts to revive Latin as a living literary language in the official correspondence of the Florentine republic. Largely because of his efforts, the Byzantine scholar Manuel Chrysoloras was brought to Florence as professor of Greek in 1397. [*Editors.*]

other in turn, as a brief conclusion to what has been said. And so, wishing to compare the excellent qualities they shared, I think it first necessary to assume what is granted by everyone: that the life which mankind leads is twofold, active and contemplative. With this as the presupposition for my comparison, I think it is not foolish to conclude that Dante is to be preferred to the other two in almost all aspects of each life, since he first did not hesitate to bear arms and fight bravely in defense of the fatherland, and then conducted himself very well during the time he was involved in the government of the republic. All this certainly pertains to the active life, and cannot be said about Petrarca or Boccaccio, since they spent most of their lives in peace, studying letters—which is commonly called the contemplative life. And so, since Petrarca and Boccaccio neglected all else, giving themselves to this alone, they certainly ought to have surpassed Dante: they had more time and led a more peaceful life. However, the case is quite different, for although Dante did not reach old age, nor (as was said) did he enjoy tranquillity in life· (rather he spent most of it drawn away from his studies by the constant business of the republic and was troubled by the difficulties of exile), on account of the almost divine excellence of his genius, he acquired in a short time a great knowledge of things human and divine. Thus in mathematics, the science which embraces numbers and dimensions, and the relationships, movements, and revolution of the stars; in both types of philosophy dealing with morals and natural things; and finally in the sacred Scriptures, which wholly comprehend all divinity, he made such progress that in knowledge of the aforesaid things he is rightfully set apart from the other two poets. As we have said, Dante without doubt excels Petrarca and Boccaccio in almost everything; but he is surpassed by Petrarca in a more comprehensive knowledge of Latin letters as well as a more accurate conception of ancient history—for Petrarca had a greater and clearer perception of both subjects. Likewise, Dante is outdone by Petrarca in Latin verse and prose: his poems are more harmonious and sublime, and his prose far more elegant. In their native language Dante and Petrarca are considered almost equal, for if Dante is superior to Petrarca in his poetry, he is surpassed by Petrarca in metrics. Thus in regard to their native tongue they are considered equal. For the rest, Dante so excels Boccaccio in nearly everything that he seems inferior in only a few things of little importance: in the knowledge of Greek letters, which, to be sure, Dante lacked entirely; and in Tuscan prose, of which he wrote little. These were the only two respects in which Boccaccio was superior to Petrarca; in all other things he was surpassed by Petrarca as the teacher excels his student.

LUDOVICO DOLCE

The Life of Messer Giovanni Boccaccio Described †

The illustrious Messer Giovanni Boccaccio was born—as we gather from reliable writers and as he himself shows in many places of *The Corbaccio* [1] and other works—in Certaldo, a small town located at the top of a very high hill, next to which runs the lovely river Elsa. According to what he writes, this town was once inhabited by the noble and well-to-do. He was born in the year 1313, at which time the emperor Henry V,[2] together with Frederick,[3] King of Sicily and the Genoese, declared war on King Robert,[4] who was killed near Benevento, in Puglia. His father, of humble birth and burdened by poverty, was named Boccaccio. Thus he first called himself Giovanni of Boccaccio and, like Petrarca of Petrarco, he later adopted Boccaccio as his surname. Boccaccio's father saw—as clearly as could be discerned in those first years of childhood—that his boy was of gentle disposition. But as he was constrained by his modest means, insufficient to support his family, he decided it would be in his best interest to give his son over to some rich merchant. He placed him in the care of a Florentine merchant, with whom Giovanni lived, and in a short time the boy became skilled in arithmetic. And so he was taken to Paris by his master, where he lived not without great boredom. Since his mind was inclined to greater things, he hated commerce—an occupation unworthy of his great intellect—and spent most of his time reading various books. But Boccaccio's master, seeing that he was of little use to him, sent him back to

---

† Ludovico Dolce (1508–68) was a Venetian scholar, art critic and editor whose edition of *The Decameron* (1552) included this biographical sketch as a preface. Unlike most of the other biographies of Boccaccio written before the sixteenth century, Dolce's study elevates Boccaccio's Italian works above his more scholarly Latin writings. It is therefore a reflection of the dramatic shift in literary tastes which had occurred since Boccaccio's times and a forerunner of the modern critical preference for Boccaccio's works in the vernacular. This biography has been newly translated for this edition by Hugh Skubikowski and is based on the Dolce essay as printed in Angelo Solerti, ed., *Le vite di Dante, Petrarca e Boccaccio scritte fino al secolo decimosesto* (Milan: Vallardi, 1904), pp. 720–22.
1. *The Corbaccio*, a satirical misogy-

nous work in Italian prose. [*Editors.*]
2. Henry VII (1269?–1313), Holy Roman emperor who hoped to restore imperial power in Italy. Crowned emperor in Rome (1312), he allied himself with Frederick III of Sicily against King Robert of Naples. On the march toward Naples, he fell ill and died near Siena. [*Editors.*]
3. Frederick III (1272–1337), king of Sicily and third son of King Peter of Aragon and Sicily. [*Editors.*]
4. Robert of Anjou (1275–1343), king of Naples who was appointed head of papal forces in the resistance against the invasion of Henry VII. He became the focal point of the papal faction in Italy, the Guelfs, in their long struggle against the partisans of the empire, the Ghibellines. During Boccaccio's stay in Naples, he was in close contact with Robert's court. [*Editors.*]

Florence. This greatly displeased his father; even more when he found the lad fully determined to begin studying letters. Rebuking him on many occasions and explaining to him that such studies were useless, that few men of letters were to be found who were not poor or beggars, his father begged him to learn some skill that would raise him from poverty. But, after seeing that reproaches as well as words of encouragement were in vain, his father was happy to grant him his wish. As he knew the study of law to be useful to those who pursued it, he placed his son under the tutelage of Messer Cino da Pistoia, who, in those days, in addition to his excellence in poetry, was outstanding in laws and was very knowledgeable in the humanities. Again, after a short time, Boccaccio became bored with his pursuits. He spent what time he could secretly reading the delightful works of the poets and the orators, in fear of his father, while also learning law and availing himself of the advice and wisdom of Messer Cino. Meanwhile (as happens with all things human) his father died, and, finding himself free, Boccaccio put aside the study of law and embraced Latin and Greek letters with all his soul.

And so, following the way of the ancient philosophers, he sold his few possessions and proceeded to Sicily to hear a certain Calabrian who in that time was renowned for his Greek. He profited greatly from his stay; from Sicily he went to Venice, attracted by the fame of a Greek named Leontius who was most outstanding in his use of language. Subsequently, Boccaccio brought him to Florence and supported him with what little money he had. Under Leontius's guidance he read Homer and translated him into Latin, although some hold that he had been translated by Petrarca, who was a great friend of Boccaccio. Such great affection developed between Petrarca and Boccaccio that each wore a ring engraved with the other's likeness as a symbol of their friendship. This relationship is said to have started when the Florentine Republic sent Boccaccio as an ambassador to Petrarca, granting the latter permission to return to Florence. Petrarca himself on many occasions helped him with money and books; and when Boccaccio, because of his poverty, almost wanted to abandon his studies, he wrote him that graceful sonnet: "La gola, il sonno e l'ociose piume" ("Gluttony, sleep, and the feathers of idleness").[5]

Boccaccio was a very haughty and proud person, and despised the friendship of princes. Nor did he like to receive anything as a reward, although he was often tempted to do so by his need. He preferred to enjoy his freedom quietly, without obligations, rather than to lose it in the pursuit of wealth and in the bother-

---

5. *Canzoniere*, 9. Contrary to Dolce's statement, Petrarca's sonnet was most likely not directed to Boccaccio. [*Editors.*]

some duties of the courts. It is true that because of civil strife, Boccaccio—a lover of peace—left Florence, and after roaming through most of Italy, ended up in Naples. As the city was in a pretty and extremely delightful location, he stayed for some time, to the great pleasure of King Robert—a prince of highest erudition and a great admirer of well-read and worthy men. In Naples Boccaccio fell deeply in love—for he was of lofty and generous heart—with the beautiful and remarkable Maria, a natural daughter of the king, whom he first saw in the church of San Lorenzo. This love caused him to write the *Filocolo* and *Fiammetta*.[6] To protect Maria, he dubbed his character "Fiammetta," just as Ovid had dubbed Augustus's daughter "Corinna." Some argue that with this lady his love was fulfilled, citing from the *Ameto* and from the beginning of the Proem to *The Decameron*. True or false as this may be, because of her Boccaccio lived in Naples for a long time. But as fate would have it, she was beheaded when she was old and sick, not long after Boccaccio's death. Because she used to call him *Caleone* (a Greek word denoting "toil") he nicknamed *The Decameron* "Prince Caleotto."[7] He had earlier loved a young Florentine girl named Lucia; but, as *The Corbaccio* clearly shows, he called her Lia and heaped insults on her. Because of these insults some believed that the incident of the Florentine scholar who almost died waiting in the snow refers to him.

Boccaccio was of average height, quite handsome, pleasant in speech and gesture, and very modest in dress. He wrote many works in the vernacular and in the Latin language. In Latin he wrote *Eclogues*,[8] *The Genealogy of the Gods*, a volume *On the Rivers and Springs*, and *The Lives of Famous Women*. In the vernacular he wrote the *Ninfale*, *Teseida*, *The Love of Arcita and Palemone*;[9] all books in *ottava rima*, a form which he appears to have invented.[1] He also composed a brief work in tercets entitled *Amorous Vision*. In prose he wrote a *Commentary* on various cantos of Dante's *Inferno* and a *Life* of Dante, as well as *Fiammetta*, the *Filocolo*, and the *Ameto* and, last of all, *The Decameron*. In the opinion shared by all those who are knowledgeable, it alone surpasses all his other works; it enabled Boccaccio to forge ahead of all the other prose writers who had written up to his

---

6. *Fiammetta*, an Italian prose romance depicting the love of Panfilo and Fiammetta. [*Editors*.]

7. Dolce's explanation substitutes the word "caleotto" for "galeotto," thereby obscuring the significance of the use of this term in Boccaccio's *Decameron* (see p. 1 for a discussion of the word). [*Editors*.]

8. Imitating his friend Petrarca and, ultimately the classical works of Virgil, Boccaccio attempted Latin pastoral poetry and helped to begin the Renais-

sance vogue for this learned, erudite literature that was continued by the period's most important writers. [*Editors*.]

9. *The Love of Arcita and Palemone* actually refers to two major characters from Boccaccio's Italian epic, the *Teseida*. [*Editors*.]

1. Although Boccaccio was the first major Italian poet to employ this verse form, its origins date back to thirteenth-century Sicily and fourteenth-century Tuscany in dialect folk songs. [*Editors*.]

time. He has a flowing and very direct style, abounding in beautiful images, and graced with discerning wit appropriate to the subject matter: the whole work reveals admirable genius, art, and eloquence.

Although he wrote very well in prose—and has never been equaled—he seemed quite awkward in poetry. And as hard as the esteemed Messer Francesco Sansovino [2] may try to demonstrate (with evidence from Petrarca) that Boccaccio was a great poet, I believe he does so to add to his praises—just as Navagero [3] did with Cicero in his preface to volume one of *De Oratione*, dedicated to Pope Leo X.[4] It is easy to understand why friends often cannot judge objectively, either out of modesty or because they are blinded by affection. However, Boccaccio came to the right decision when, upon seeing Petrarca's poems, he cursed his own and wanted to burn them immediately. But after thinking it over, he was dissuaded from doing so and decided not to destroy them.

He died in Certaldo at the age of sixty-two in the year 1375— one year after Petrarca's death. He was survived only by an illegitimate son, for he had no wife. Boccaccio was buried by his son, with all the honors befitting his standing, in the church of San Filippo Giacomo. On his grave he had the following verses inscribed, which he himself composed a short time before passing to a better life:

> Hac sub mole iacent cineres ac ossa Joannis;
> Mens sedet ante Deum meritis ornata laborum
> Mortalis vitae: genitor Boccatius illi,
> Patria Certaldum, studium fuit alma poesis.

2. Francesco Sansovino (1521–83), Venetian scholar and editor of an edition of *The Decameron* (1546) which contained a brief biography of Boccaccio, which Dolce probably consulted. [*Editors.*]

3. Andrea Navagero (1483–1529), Venetian humanist and diplomat who edited several important classical texts, served as official historian of Venice, and was ambassador to Emperor Charles V in Spain for four years. During that time, Navagero helped to popularize the Petrarchan sonnet form in Spain. [*Editors.*]

4. Leo X (1476–1521), born Giovanni de' Medici, the son of Lorenzo de' Medici, "Il Magnifico." Elected pope in 1513, Leo was a great patron of the arts and a worldly pontiff whose policies helped to spark the Protestant Reformation in Germany. [*Editors.*]

Modern
Criticism

UGO FOSCOLO

Boccaccio †

Considering the Novelle as a work of genius, their greatest merit consists in the variety of characters they contain. The author, with a skill and felicity truly wonderful, has adapted his style to princes, matrons, youths, maidens, friars, and thieves, without ever falling into exaggeration; and if his characters are deficient in force of expression, they always abound in fidelity and in grace; and the illusion is perfect, precisely because the author never appears to try to produce it. His most devoted commentators are however of opinion, that Boccaccio was a more dignified narrator than any ancient historian; that the discourses he puts into the mouths of his actors are more powerful than the orations of Cicero or Demosthenes; that his representations of strong minds struggling against passion or calamity, are more pathetic and touching than the tragedies of Aeschylus or any other writer; and that his wit and sarcasm are more pungent than those of Lucian. Admiration like this is mere fanaticism. Boccaccio, without being pre-eminent in any one of these various kinds of style, was felicitous in all; which can scarcely be said of any other writer whatever. Nevertheless, M. Ginguené, one of the most elegant and celebrated critics of our times, thinks that Boccaccio, having before his eyes the history of

† Ugo Foscolo (1778–1827) was one of Italy's greatest poets of the Romantic era; rather than swear allegiance to a government controlled by Austria, Foscolo chose voluntary exile from Italy and fled to Switzerland, and then to England in 1816, where he remained until his death. Although he ceased writing great poetry there, he became an important critic and a bridge between the cultures of Italy and England in an era of increased interest in Italian literature. The present essay appeared anonymously in *The London Magazine* 5 (June 1, 1826), pp. 146 and 148–57, and was occasioned by the publication of an English translation of *The Decameron* by William Pickering in 1825, with illustrations by William Stothard. Curiously enough, Foscolo himself wrote an introduction to this edition in Italian entitled *Discorso storico sul testo* and then, probably for financial reasons, provided the review of the same work. For a consideration of the critical view of Boccaccio in England at this time, see *Italian Poets and English Critics, 1755–1859*, ed. Beatrice Corrigan (Chicago: University of Chicago Press, 1969), especially pp. 1–30; or Herbert G. Wright, *Boccaccio in England from Chaucer to Tennyson* (London: Athlone Press, 1957).

Thucydides and the poem of Lucretius, aspired to the imitation of their respective merits so successfully, that he not only equalled, but surpassed them both; and described the plague like an historian, a philosopher, and a poet.[1]

It is not known whether Boccaccio had read both these writers; the Roman was however sufficient, since he follows precisely in the footsteps of Thucydides. Many passages in the Italian appear paraphrases, not only of the events which happened in Athens or in Florence respectively, in consequence of the same dreadful epidemy, but of reflexions and minute details in which it is improbable that writers should agree by mere accident. The merit of the description of the pestilence in the Decameron does not arise so much from the style—which, in comparison with those of Thucydides and Lucretius, is extremely cold—as from the contrast between the disease, the funerals, and the desolation of the city, and the tranquil pleasures, the dances and the banquets, the songs and tales of the villa. In this respect, Boccaccio, even if he were a copier of the main incident, copied it in the spirit of an inventor. But if we consider each description separately, we shall find that the words of the Greek historian excite powerful emotions either of sympathy or horror, which press with combined yet distinct force upon our hearts, because he follows the order marked out by nature in the beginning, progress, and consequences of such a calamity. He puts together twice as many circumstances as Boccaccio, and paints them forcibly in a few words, so that they combine to occupy every faculty of our minds. * * *

The black-letter scholars of Italy have ransacked every library and archive, to discover the ancient authors and anecdotes which furnished Boccaccio with the materials for his tales. But if genius consists rather in the invention of facts than in the novelty and skill with which they are related, Boccaccio has certainly no claim to originality. But for the same reason all tragic poets, not even excepting Shakespeare must be considered as copyists, since they founded the action of their drama on circumstances and characters described by historians. The first origin of dramas and of tales is of little importance to criticism. What is important is to observe the impulse given by every great writer to that department of literature in which he particularly excelled. In the middle ages storytellers (novellatori) were regularly salaried to amuse the tables and the idle hours of the great; in some cases they were even regarded as officers of the court. The telling of stories being then a regular vocation, rendered the writing of them more easy and common, even in those barbarous times when princes could scarcely read. The first rude and primitive specimens of the infant Italian lan-

1. Ginguené, *Hist. Litt. d'Italie*, Tom. III. p. 87, seq.

guage, in prose, are to be met with among compositions of this kind. The following tale was written more than a century before the time of Boccaccio:

"The damsel loved Lancelot so much that at length she lay dying, and commanded that when her soul should have departed from her body, a rich boat should be made ready, covered with a scarlet stuff, and having a rich bed therein, with rich and noble coverings of silk, adorned with rich precious stones; and that her body should be laid upon this bed, clad in her most noble garments, and with a beautiful crown on her head, rich with much gold, and with many rich precious stones; and with a rich girdle and purse, and in this purse there was a letter of the following tenor. But first let us tell concerning that which comes before the letter. The damsel died of the love sickness, and that was done which she had commanded, as to the boat without a sail and without oars, and without any one therein; and it was placed upon the sea. The sea guided it to Camelot, and it stopped at the shore. The cry of it went through all the court. The knights and barons came down from their palaces, and the noble King Arthur came thither, wondering very greatly that this boat had thus been brought thither without any steersman. The king entered therein; saw the damsel and the clothing. He caused the purse to be opened; they found this letter. He caused it to be read, and it said thus:—To all the Knights of the Round Table, this damsel of Scalot sends health, as to the best company of the world. And if you would know wherefore at my end I am come hither, it is for the best knight in the world, and the most cruel, that is, my Lord Sir Lancelot of the Lake, whom I knew not how so far to entreat for love, as that he should have pity upon me. And therefore, alas! I have died for living well, as you may see." [2]

If Boccaccio had chosen to amplify and embellish this story with the variety, the incidents, the passions, and characters, and the richness of style with which he adorned many others borrowed from old romances, he would certainly have made a wonderful use of the strange obsequies chosen by this damsel, and would have arranged and coloured the circumstances in such a manner as to give an air of rare similitude to so new an invention; unless, perhaps, by too great a desire to describe the damsel being dead, clad as for a marriage feast, and wandering over the deep without any certainty of finding burial, or by making her discourse in her last moments, comforting herself with the hope of showing the world that the knight by his cruelty had caused her death, he had chilled the fancy of the reader by his rhetoric, and dissipated all those images and emotions which arise spontaneously on the mere

2. Here, Foscolo's original essay cites the Italian version of this *novella* in a footnote. [*Editors.*]

relation of touching incidents in simple language. "The damsel died of the love sickness, and that was done which she had commanded, as to the boat without sail and without oars, and without any one therein; and it was placed upon the sea." The barrenness of almost all these early narrators is sometimes compensated by the liberty in which they leave the mind of the reader to think and feel for itself. Having now taken from the illustrations before us whatever has seemed to us necessary for appreciating the true value of the Novelle, as a literary work, we shall proceed to give an historical account of the causes which have led them to be regarded and adopted for so many ages, as the sole model of style, the sole grammatical authority of Italy. This phenomenon has never yet been explained.

The author died not only without the hope, but without the desire, that his Decameron should outlive him. His autograph copy has never been found, and from what we shall presently have occasion to observe about his hand-writing, we derive very strong presumptive evidence that he destroyed it himself.[3] A young friend of his, eight or ten years after his death, transcribed it with the most scrupulous exactness, frankly confessing that the copy he used was full of errors. After the introduction of printing, copies and editions were multiplied with mistakes, which, it was clear, were partly taken from the manuscripts of wretched copiers, and partly accumulated by the negligence of printers, while their art was yet in its infancy. But from the age of Boccaccio to that of Lorenzo de Medici, and the Pontificate of Leo X, the Italian language was so barbarized that it seemed lost to the learned men of Italy, and for more than a century they wrote in Latin which had fixed rules, and was common to all Europe. The critics of that illustrious epoch, strove by every means to form the language spoken by Italians into a literary language, well adapted for written composition, and for being understood by the whole nation, and in the penury of authors who could furnish observations, and examples, and principles, from which a right method might be derived, they had recourse, with common consent, to the tales of Boccaccio; they found words at once vernacular and perfectly elegant, distinct, and expressive, skilful construction, musical periods, and diversity of style; nor perhaps could any expedient at that time have been found better adapted for obviating numerous difficul-

---

3. Modern scholarship has proven Foscolo incorrect in his belief that no autograph manuscript of *The Decameron* exists; it is now commonly accepted that the manuscript referred to as the Hamilton 90, now located in the Staatsbibliothek in East Berlin, is an autograph manuscript. For information on this and other autograph manuscripts of Boccaccio's other works as well, see Evi Ianni, "Elenco dei manoscritti autografi di Giovanni Boccaccio," *MLN* 86 (1971), 99–113; or the new facsimile edition of the Hamilton 90 manuscript, Giovanni Boccaccio, *Decameron: Edizione diplomatico-interpretativa dell'autografo Hamilton 90*, ed. Charles S. Singleton (Baltimore: Johns Hopkins University Press, 1974), pp. ix–xii. [*Editors.*]

ties which presented themselves. But the maxims and the practice of the literary men of that age, consisted not so much in constructing rules from observations, as in imitating punctually, servilely, and childishly, the most admired writers. In poetry they were implicit copiers of Petrarch, and sang of pure and sacred love. In Latin they imitated Virgil and Cicero, and treated sacred things in profane words. Thus the system of restricting a whole dead language to the works of a few writers was still more absurdly applied to the living tongue of Italy, and critics were almost unanimous in decreeing that no example was to be adduced from any poem except the Canzoniere Amoroso of Petrarch.

From this circumstance, the Protestants took occasion to impute to the literary men of that time very small regard to manners, and no sense of religion. The first accusation is exaggerated, and was common to them with all orders of society in Europe; the other is most absurd, but has prevailed in Protestant universities from that day, and has been handed down by long tradition, on the testimony of the first religious reformers, who, in order to open every possible way for the reception of their doctrines, imputed infidelity to all the learned men of the court of Leo X. But most, if not all of these men, believed the faith they professed, and which was then attacked by hostile superstition. Some made a vow never to read a profane book, but being unable long to observe it, got absolution from the pope; others, that they might not contaminate Christian things with the impure latinity of monks and friars, tried to translate the Bible into the language of the age of Augustus. This system of servilely imitating excellent authors, did not prevent some men of genius, particularly historians, from attempting to relate in a style at once original, dignified, and energetic, the events of their country. But they were living writers, nor had long celebrity and prescriptive authority yet stamped them as models. To this reason, which holds good of every age and country, was added, that the liberty of the numerous republics of Italy which had sprung up in the barbarism of the middle ages, declined in the most fertile and splendid period of her literature, and the historians who were witnesses of the misfortunes and degradation of their country, wrote in a manner which was not agreeable to her tyrants. Hence Machiavelli, Guicciardini, Segni, and others who are now studied as masters of style, were not then read, except by a few; their works were hardly known in manuscript, and if published they were mutilated; nor were any complete editions of their histories printed until two centuries after they were written.[4]

4. Contrary to Foscolo's assertions here, many works by both Machiavelli and Guicciardini were widely distributed and read during this period, not only in the original Italian (both in manuscript and in print) but also in various European translations. For particulars on the history of the publication of these works, see Vicenzo Luciani, *Francesco Guicciardini e la fortuna' dell'opera sua*

Thus the Novelle of Boccaccio held the field and their popularity was greatly increased by the abhorrence and contempt which they inspired against the wickedness of the monks.

Certain young men of Florence conspired against Duke Alexander, bastard of Clement VII, with the design of driving him from their country, and reestablishing the republic. They held meetings under colour of amending the text of Boccaccio by the collation of manuscripts, and by critical examination. Such was the source, and such the authors, of the celebrated edition of Giunti, in 1527, now regarded as one of the rarest curiosities of bibliography, and preserved from that time as a record of the Florentine republic, almost all those young men having fought against the house of Medici, and died at the siege of Florence, or in exile. The work subsequently became more scarce, because it was constantly exposed to the danger of being mutilated or prohibited through the interest of the monks. Leo X made a jest of those things, and crowned the abbot of Gaeta, seated on an elephant, with laurel and cabbage-leaves. Adrian VI who succeeded him, had been immured in a cloister, and the cardinals of his school shortly after proposed that the Colloquies of Erasmus, and every popular book injurious to the clergy, should be prohibited. Paul III was of the opinion that the threat was sufficient, nor was it at that time put in execution; but when the Decameron, which had already been translated into several languages, was quoted by the Anti-Papists, the church ceased to confine herself to threats, and began actually to prohibit the reprinting and the reading of Boccaccio's tales; nor could any one have a copy in his possession without a licence from his confessor. The Protestant Reformation provoked a reform in the Catholic church, which though less apparent, was perhaps greater and more solid. The Protestants took as the basis of theirs, the liberty of interpreting the oracles of the Holy Spirit by the aid of human reason; while the Catholics admitted no interpretations but those inspired by God as represented by the popes. Which of these two was the most beneficial to the interest of religion, is a difficult question. Perhaps every religion which is much subjected to the scrutiny of reason, ceases to be faith; while every creed, inculcated without the concurrence of the reason, degenerates into blind superstition. But, as far as literature was concerned, liberty of conscience, in many countries, prepared the way for civil liberty, and for the free expression of thoughts and opinions; while in Italy, passive obedience to the religious power strengthened political tyranny, and increased the debasement and

---

(Florence: Olschki, 1949); Giuliano Procacci, *Studi sulla fortuna del Machiavelli* (Rome: Istituto storico italiano per l'età moderna e contemporanea, 1965); and Felix Raab, *The English Face of Machiavelli: A Changing Interpretation 1500–1700* (Toronto: University of Toronto Press, 1964). [*Editors.*]

long servitude of the public mind. The Protestant Reformation was principally confined to dogmas—the Catholic wholly to discipline; and, therefore, all speculations on the lives and manners of ecclesiastics were then repressed as leading to new heresies. The Council of Trent saw that the people of Germany did not stop short at complaining that the monks were traders in Indulgencies, but went on to deny the sacrament of confession, the celibacy of the clergy, and the infallibility and spiritual power of the pope. It therefore decreed, that any attack upon, or insinuations against, the clergy, should be followed by immediate registration of the book containing them in the index of prohibited works; and that the reading, or the possession of any such book, without licence from a bishop, should be regarded both as a sin and as an offence punishable in virtue of the anathema. These laws, of ecclesiastical origin, were thenceforth interpreted and administered by civil tribunals subjected to the presidency of inquisitors of the order of St. Dominick; who, moreover, by the consent of the Italian governments, were invested with authority to examine, alter, mutilate, and suppress every book, whether ancient or modern, previously to its being printed.

The Spanish domination in Italy, the long reign of Philip II (the most tyrannical of tyrants), and the Council of Trent, had imposed silence upon genius. Cosmo I Grand Duke of Tuscany kept in his pay one or two historians of the house of Medici; he caused all books of a less servile character to be collected together from every part and burnt. The Decameron was, therefore, by an absolute political necessity, resorted to by literary men as the sole rule and standard of the written prose language. To cancel every memorial of freedom, Cosmo I suppressed all the academies instituted in Tuscany during the republican government of its cities; the only indulgence he showed was towards an assembly of grammarians, who afterwards became rather famous than illustrious under the name of the Academy della Crusca; and then, when the indolence of slavery deadened and chilled the passions; when education, committed to the jesuits, had enfeebled all intellect; when men of letters became the furniture of courts, often of foreign courts; when universities were in the pay of kings, and under the direction of inquisitors;—then did the academy Della Crusca begin to claim supremacy over Italian literature, and to establish the tales of Boccaccio as the sole text and rule for every dictionary or grammar, and the basis of every philosophical theory regarding the language.

Nevertheless, the academicians found that the Decameron had never been printed in a genuine and correct form, fitted to serve as the ground-work of language. After many years spent in consulting, correcting, and collating manuscripts, they prepared an edition which they hoped to consecrate as an oracle in all grammatical questions; but the Holy Office interposed in the most furious manner, and did not allow it to be printed. They therefore consented, as they could do no better, to publish a mutilated edition. The grand dukes of Tuscany, in order to put an end to these difficulties, deputed certain learned men to negotiate with the Master of the Sacred Palace in the Vatican, one of whom was a bishop, and nearly all dignified ecclesiastics. The Master of the Sacred Palace, a Dominican friar and a Spaniard, attended their meetings in his own right. Writing his opinions in a bastard language, he gave his advice as an official grammarian: they did not, however, come to any conclusion.

At length an Italian Dominican, of a more facile character, was added to the council, and having been confessor to Pius V he prevailed on Gregory XIII to allow the Decameron to be printed without any other alteration than what was necessary for the good fame of the ecclesiastics. Thus, abbesses and nuns in love with their gardeners were transformed into matrons and young ladies; friars who got up impostures and miracles into necromancers; and priests who intrigued with their parishioners' wives into soldiers; and by dint of a hundred other inevitable transformations and mutilations, the academy, after four years' labour, succeeded in publishing the Decameron in Florence, illustrated by their researches. But Sextus V ordered that even this edition, though approved by his predecessor, should be infamized in the Index. It was therefore necessary to have recourse to fresh mangling and interpolation, and of texts so fabricated, therefore, the academicians of La Crusca weighed every word and every syllable of the Novelle, exaggerated every minute detail, and described every thing under the high-sounding names of the richness, propriety, grace, elegance, the figures, laws, and principles of language.[5]

These facts, which our limits compel us to condense and to strip of those circumstances which render them infinitely more diverting, would appear the inventions of a satirist, if the author of the Illustrations did not confirm his narrative, step by step, by authorities and documents. From the various reflections which he deduces from them, we shall select but one—that the literary language of Italy was founded on a collection of tales, not of the most edifying description, at the same period that the literary language of England was fixed by the translation of the Holy Scriptures.

This singular destiny of a work composed as a mere pastime, threw into comparative oblivion its other literary merits, which were more useful to the civilization of Europe, and stamped upon

5. For a more accurate and detailed description of the process of bowdlerizing The Decameron, see Peter M. Brown, Lionardo Salviati: A Critical Biography (London: Oxford University Press, 1974), pp. 160–82. [Editors.]

the name of its author an infamous celebrity, which has always hidden from the world the true character of his mind. The Illustrations before us are extremely interesting from the light they throw on the human heart. It is unquestionable, that if Petrarch had expended on writing Italian prose, the tenth part of the labour which he bestowed on his poetry, he would not have been able to write so much as he did. This reason, among many others, contributed to induce him to write in Latin: the chief motive, however, was the glory which then attached to the Latin poets, and which, in the universities and the courts of the princes, was scarcely granted to those who wrote in Italian. Few however, if any, had any real conception of the spirit and merits of the Latin tongue. Coluccio Salutato was a man of great learning, and enjoyed a high reputation among the scholars of that age; yet he pronounced that the pastoral poems of Boccaccio, written in Latin, were only inferior to Petrarch, and that Petrarch was superior to Virgil! [6] Erasmus, a critic of another age, and of a different turn of mind, when commenting on the literature of the fourteenth century, detracts a little from the praises bestowed upon Petrarch, and enhances those of Boccaccio, whose Latinity he esteems the less barbarous of the two.[7]

The injury which Petrarch did to his native tongue, by his ambition of writing in Latin, was compensated by his indefatigable and generous perseverance in restoring to Europe the most noble remains of human intellect. No monument of antiquity, no series of medals, or manuscript of Roman literature was neglected by him wherever he had the least hope of rescuing the one from oblivion, or of multiplying copies of the other. He acquired a claim to the gratitude of all Europe, and is still deservedly called the first restorer of classical literature. Boccaccio, however, is entitled not only to a share, but to an equal share, to say the least, of this honour. We are perfectly aware that our opinion on this subject will be at first regarded as a paradox put forth from a mere ambition of novelty; the proofs, however, which we shall briefly adduce, will convert the surprise of our readers at our temerity, into wonder at the scanty recompense which Boccaccio has hitherto received, in spite of his gigantic and successful endeavours to dispel the ignorance of the middle ages.

The allegorical mythology, together with the theology and metaphysics of the ancients, the events of the history of ages less remote, and even geography, were illustrated by Boccaccio in his voluminous Latin Treatises, now little read, but at that time studied by all as the chiefest and best works of solid learning. Petrarch knew nothing of Greek; and whatever acquaintance, in Tuscany or Italy,

6. *Colutius Salutatus Epist. ad Bocc.*   7. *Ciceronianus.*

they had with the writers of that language, they owed entirely to Boccaccio. He went to Sicily, where there were still some remains of a Greek dialect, and masters who taught the language, and put himself under two preceptors of the greatest merit, Barlaamus and Leontius. Under them he studied several years; he afterwards prevailed on the republic of Florence to establish a chair of Greek literature for Leontius. Had it not been for Boccaccio, the poems of Homer would have remained long undiscovered. The story of the Trojan War was read in the celebrated romance called the History of Guido delle Colonne, from which also were derived many wild inventions and apocryphal records of the Homeric times, and various dramas, like Shakespeare's Troilus and Cressida, containing not a single circumstance to be met with in the Iliad or Odyssey. Nor should it be forgotten, that undertakings like these demanded affluence, which Petrarch possessed; while Boccaccio's whole life was passed in the midst of difficulties and privations. He compensated for the want of pecuniary resources by indefatigable industry; he submitted to mechanical labours, wholly unsuited to the bent of his character and genius, and copied manuscripts with his own hand. Leonardo Bruni, who was born before the death of Boccaccio, was astonished when he saw the multitude of authors' copies transcribed by him.[8] Benvenuto da Imola, who was a disciple of Boccaccio, relates a curious anecdote on this subject, which as we do not recollect that is anywhere to be met with, except in the great collection of the writers of the middle ages, by Muratori, a work inaccessible to the greater number of our readers, we shall insert.[9]—Going once to the abbey of Monte Cassino, celebrated for the number of manuscripts which lay there, unknown and neglected, Boccaccio humbly requested to be shown into the library of the monastery. A monk dryly replied, "Go, it stands open," and pointed to a very high staircase. The good Boccaccio found every book he opened torn and mutilated; lamenting that all these fruits of the labours of the great men of antiquity had fallen into the hands of such masters, he went away weeping. Coming down the staircase he met another monk, and asked him "How those books could possibly have been so mutilated?"—"We make covers for little Prayer-books out of the parchment leaves of those volumes," said he, coolly, "and sell them for twopence, threepence, and sometimes fivepence each."—"And now go," concludes the pupil of Boccaccio, "go, you unfortunate author, and distract your brain in composing more books." Such were the obstacles opposed by the imperfect civilization of his age which this admirable man, together with Petrarch, had to surmount; and it is an act of tardy and religious justice to show that the tribute of grateful recollec-

8. Leonardo Aretino, *Vita del Petrarca in fine.*

9. *Benvenutus Imolensis apud Muratorium Script.* Rev. Ital.

tion to which they were both entitled to receive from posterity, was almost only awarded to his more fortunate contemporary. We cannot conclude our remarks, without paying another debt to the memory of Boccaccio. The indecency of the Novelle, and their immoral tendency, can neither be justified nor extenuated; but from the herd of writers in England, who confidently repeat this merited censure of Boccaccio, year after year, it appears but too much as if the study of the language and of the style had been made a pretext for feeding the imaginations of the readers with ideas which all are prone to indulge, but compelled to conceal; and that the tales of Boccaccio would not have predominated so much over all other literature, if they had been more chaste. The art of suggesting thoughts, at once desired and forbidden flatters while it irritates the passions, and is an efficacious instrument for governing the consciences of boys, and of the most discreet old men. The jesuits, therefore, no sooner made themselves masters of the schools of Italy, than they adopted this book, mutilated in the same manner as some of the licentious Latin poets, well knowing that the expunged passages are the most coveted, precisely because they *are* expunged, and that the imaginations of youth supply ideas worse than they would have formed had the books been left entire.

In order to excuse the use they made of the Decameron in their colleges, the jesuits succeeded in persuading Bellarmine to justify, in his controversies, the intentions of the author. Perhaps, indeed, they interpolated these arguments as they did soon many others, in the edition of Bellarmine, wherever the doctrines did not accord with the interests of their order.[1] It is, moreover, probable that they favoured a book famous for its invectives against the rules of the cloister, and written long before their order had arisen to acquire a jurisdiction over all. Bellarmine was much less indulgent than Boccaccio to the reputations of the old congregations; and although some writers who have undertaken their defence have called his Gemitus Columbae apocryphal, it was, at all events, printed among his works during his life. To return to Boccaccio. Before he died he had atoned for his want of respect for decorum; he felt that men thought him culpable, and he expiated his tales by a punishment heavier, perhaps, than the offence. There is some reason to believe that he wrote them when under the influence of a lady whom he abjured just before, and whom he defames in his Laberinto d'Amore. However this may be, he conjured fathers of families not to suffer the Decameron to go into the hands of any who had not already lost the modesty of youth.—"Do not let that book be read; and if it is true that you love me, and weep for my afflictions, have pity, were it only for my honour's sake."

1. Fuligatus, in *Vita Bellarmini.*

With remorse of conscience which does more honour to the excellence of his intentions than to the strength of his mind, he even tried to atone for the ridicule he had poured upon the priests and their infamous superstitions. No writer, perhaps, since Aristophanes, has so bitterly satirized the effrontery of ignorant preachers, and the credulity of their ignorant hearers, as Boccaccio in the Novelle, which are written in a spirit of implacable hostility to monks. In one of them he introduces one of these vagabonds boasting from the pulpit, that he had wandered through all countries in the terraqueous globe, and even beyond it, in search of relics of saints, and making the people in the church pay to adore them. And yet, in spite of this, he said, on his death-bed, that he had been long in search of holy relics through various parts of the world, and he left them, for the devotion of the people, to a convent of friars. This desire was found expressed in a will, written in Italian in his own hand; and in another in Latin, drawn up many years afterwards by a notary, and signed and approved by Boccaccio a short time before he died. In both these wills he bequeathed all his books and manuscripts to his confessor and to the convent of the Santo Spirito, in order that the monks might pray to God for his soul, and that his fellow-citizens might read and copy them for their instruction. It is therefore more than probable, that there was among these books no copy of the Decameron; and from the following anecdote, which being found in books which are read by very few is little known, it appears that the original manuscript of the Novelle was destroyed long before by the author; it is, in fact, as we have already mentioned, impossible to find it.

Towards the end of his life, poverty, which is rendered more grievous by old age, and the turbulent state of Florence, made social life a burden to him, so that he fled to solitude; but his generous and amiable soul was debased and depressed by religious terrors. There lived at that time two Sienese, who were afterwards canonized. One of them was a man of letters and a Carthusian monk, mentioned by Fabricius as Sanctus Petrus Petronus; the other was Giovanni Colombini, who founded another order of monks, and wrote the life of St. Pietro Petroni by divine inspiration. The Bollandists allege that the manuscript of the new saint, after having been lost for two centuries and a half, fell miraculously into the hands of a Carthusian, who translated it from Italian into Latin, and in 1619 dedicated it to a Cardinal de Medici. It is possible that Colombini never wrote, and that the biographer of the saints, who wrote in the seventeenth century, drew his descriptions of miracles from those recorded in the chronicles and other documents of the fourteenth century; and in order to exaggerate the miraculous conversion of Boccaccio, he perverted a letter of Petrarch, entitled De Vaticinio Morientium, which is to be found in his Latin works. The blessed Petroni, at his death, which happened about the year 1360, charged a monk to advise Boccaccio to desist from his studies and to prepare for death. Boccaccio wrote in terror to Petrarch, who replied: "My brother, your letter filled my mind with horrible fantasies, and I read it assailed by great wonder and great affliction. And how could I, without fearful eyes, behold you weeping and calling to mind your near-approaching death; whilst I, not well informed of the fact, most anxiously explored the meaning of your words? But now that I have discovered the cause of your terrors, and have reflected somewhat upon them, I have no longer either sadness or surprise. You write how that an—I know not what—Pietro di Siena, celebrated for his piety, and also for his miracles, predicted to us two, many future occurrences; and in the witness of the truth of them, sent to signify to us certain past things which you and I had kept secret from all men, and which he, who never knew us, nor was known by us, knew as if he had seen them with his mind's eye. This is a great thing, if indeed it be true. But the art of covering and adorning impostures with the veil of religion and of sanctity, is most common and old. Those who use it explore the age, the countenance, the eyes, the manners of the man; his daily customs, his motions, his standing, his sitting, his voice, his speech, and above all, his intentions and affections; and draw predictions which they ascribe to divine inspiration. Now if he, dying, foretold your death, so also did Hector in former times to Achilles; and Orodes to Mezentius, in Virgil; and Cheramenes to Eritia, in Cicero; and Calamus to Alexander; and Possidonius, the illustrious philosopher, when dying, named six of his contemporaries who were soon to follow him, and told who should die first, and who afterwards. It matters not to dispute now concerning the truth or the origin of such-like predictions; nor to you, if even this your alarmer (terrificator hic tuus) has told you the truth, would it avail any thing to afflict yourself. How then? If this man had not sent to let you know, would you have been ignorant that there remains not to you a long space of life? and even if you were young, is death any respecter of age?" But neither these, nor all the other arguments in Petrarch's letter, which is very long, nor the eloquence with which he combines the consolations of the Christian religion with the manly philosophy of the ancients, could deliver his friend from superstitious terrors.

Boccaccio survived the prediction more than twelve years, and the older he grew the more did he feel the seeds scattered in his mind by his grandmother and his nurse, spring up like thorns. He died in 1375, aged sixty-two, and not more than twelve or fourteen months after Petrarch. Nor did Petrarch himself always contemplate death with a stedfast eye. Such was the character of those times; and such, under varied appearances, will always be the nature of man.

FRANCESCO DE SANCTIS

[Boccaccio and the Human Comedy] †

Now, if we open *The Decameron*, we have hardly read the first story before we feel as though we are falling from the clouds and find ourselves asking with Petrarch: "How and when did I get here?" [1] What we have before us, then, is not an evolution, but a cataclysm, or at least a revolution—the kind that from one day to another shows us a changed world. Here the Middle Ages are not only denied, but ridiculed.

In Ser Cepperello, Boccaccio created a Tartuffe-like character several centuries ahead of Molière, with one essential difference: whereas Molière causes us to feel disgust for Tartuffe in order to arouse us against his hypocrisy, Boccaccio uses Cepperello not so much to provoke us against the hypocrite, but to amuse us and make us laugh at the expense of the good confessor, the credulous friars, and the people. Molière's weapon is sarcastic irony, while Boccaccio's is good-humored caricature. In order to reencounter these forms and intentions of Boccaccio, we must wait for Voltaire to come along; in a certain sense, Boccaccio is the Voltaire of the fourteenth century.

Many people blame Boccaccio, saying that he spoiled and corrupted the Italian spirit. He himself, in his old age, was overcome by remorse, became a religious clerk, and condemned his book.[2] But his book would not have been possible if the Italian spirit had not been well on its way to being spoiled—if spoiled is the correct word for it. If the things Boccaccio laughed about had been venerated (let us suppose that he could have laughed at them

---

† Francesco De Sanctis (1817–83), perhaps the greatest of modern literary historians, approached Boccaccio's *Decameron* as a moment in the history of an Italian national spirit. De Sanctis viewed the work as a reflection of a profound change in the Italian national character, a document demonstrating a shift from the theocentric world of Dante's "divine" *Comedy* to a more anthropocentric world view, Boccaccio's "human" comedy. This sometimes questionable but always thought-provoking philosophical interpretation of Boccaccio's masterpiece has influenced criticism of the book since it first appeared in the last century as part of his *Storia della letteratura italiana* (1870–71). The following selection is taken from the thirteenth edition of this work (Naples: Morano, 1910), I, 287–92, 302–3, 329–33, 338–41, 347–50, 355–57. It has been freshly translated for this edition by Lucio Bartolai. References to names not explained in the editors' notes are to characters in various *novelle* of *The Decameron* which De Sanctis mentions only in passing in his study.

1. Petrarca, *Canzoniere* 126, 1. 62. [*Editors*.]

2. For Petrarca's reactions to Boccaccio's religious crisis, which threatened his career as a writer, see the two letters he sent to Boccaccio reprinted in this edition, pp. 173–84. [*Editors*.]

then), his contemporaries would have felt indignation. But the opposite proved to be true. The book seemed to respond to something in people's souls which had been wanting to come out for a long time. It seemed to proclaim what everyone had been saying secretly, in the depths of their souls, and it was received with so much applause and success that the good Passavanti became frightened and set against it his *Specchio di penitenza* as an antidote.[3] Boccaccio was, then, the literary voice of a world about which men, in their consciousness, were already confusedly aware. A secret existed: Boccaccio guessed it and everyone applauded him. This fact, instead of being damned, deserves to be studied.

The essential quality of the Middle Ages was transcendence: a sort of ultrahuman and ultranatural "beyond" outside of nature and man, the genus and the species outside the individual, matter and form outside their unity, the intellect outside the soul, perfection and virtue outside life, the law outside consciousness, the spirit outside the body, and the purpose of life outside the world. The basis of this philosophical theology was the existence of universals. The world was populated with beings or intelligences, and their nature was discussed at length. Were they divine ideas? Were these genera or species real? Were they comprehensible species? This edifice was already quivering under the blows of the Nominalists, who denied the existence of the genera and the species. In fact, they called these terms meaningless and maintained that only the single, the individual, existed. Their banner carried the motto, which was to become very familiar afterwards: "Entities must not be multiplied unnecessarily." [4]

The natural product of this exaggerated, theocratic world was asceticism. Life here on earth was losing its seriousness and value, so that while man continued to dwell here, his spirit was in the next life. The culmination of perfection was sought in ecstasy, prayers, and contemplation. In this way theocratic literature, too, was born: legends, mysteries, visions, allegories, and the poem about the other life, *The Divine Comedy*.

Thought had no inwardness. Instead of descending and penetrating into man and nature, it stood outside of them, arguing about the nature and the qualities of the entities, which were the same human and natural forces freed from the individual and existing on their own. The abstractions of the spirit became living, viable beings. And because abstractions, the fruits of inexhaustible

3. Jacopo Passavanti (1302?–57), a Florentine Dominican monk who eventually became prior of the monastery of Santa Maria Novella, the Florentine church where Boccaccio's storytellers first gather and decide to leave Florence. Passavanti's *Lo Specchio di vera penitenza* ("The mirror of true penitence") is a work based upon Lenten sermons and is full of terrifying examples of the nature of human sin and its inevitable punishment. [*Editors.*]

4. Here, De Sanctis refers to a scholastic version of two of Aristotle's propositions found in *Metaphysics* (XII, 45) and *Physics* (I, 59). [*Editors.*]

intellects in their distinctions and subdistinctions, were of an infinite number, these beings multiplied within the acute minds of the scholastics. Thus the scholastic world was populated by abstract beings, in the same way that the poetic world was populated by allegorical beings, such as Man, the Soul, Woman, Virtues, and Vices. These were not persons, like the pagan divinities, but simple personifications.

Feeling, as the product of human or natural propensity, was always considered a sin. Passions were banned and poetry was considered the mother of lies. The theater was the food of the Devil and stories and romances were regarded as profane types of literature. All these things were called by one name: "the senses." And from the time of Fra Guittone [5] to that of Francesco Petrarca, the struggle between the senses and reason became the common meeting ground of this ascetic world. Feeling, torn from the human heart, spurned as sense, and forced to be reason, also became a universal. It became an exterior fact, now symbolic, now scholastic, or, as it was called then, "Platonic." Love, the father of feeling, became a philosophical fact, a unifying force for both the intellect and the act together. It was in this manner that the Platonic lyrics from Guinicelli [6] to Petrarca were born. The senses and the imagination rebelled against this Platonism, and in this rebellion, which was still little scrutinized and emphasized, can be found the greatness of Petrarca's verses. It was forbidden to describe the movements of the heart and of the imagination in their naturalness and intimacy. But Petrarca, more than anyone else, was the one who tasted and enjoyed these forbidden fruits.

The imagination was an instrument of the intellect, destined to create forms and symbols out of abstract concepts. And Dante, whose imagination was so tortured, knew this better than anyone. Symbolic and intellectual form arose, and the individual with his personality vanished in their generalities. These were typical forms, genera, and species rather than the individual. Even Woman, the queen of forms, was unable to retreat in time from this invasion of the universals, thereby remaining an ideal more divine than human. She had a beautiful face, but it was the face of wisdom, and she received more love than she gave, but often she was loved more as a ladder to heavenly things than as a woman. In this way Laura and Beatrice were born.

Certainly, no one has the right to speak with irreverence about this authoritarian world, which, after all, marks an important moment in the history of the human spirit and, moreover, is

5. Guittone d'Arezzo (1225?–93?), one of the first important lyric poets of Tuscany; he ended his life as a member of a religious order. [*Editors*.]

6. Guido Guinicelli (1230?–76?), a Bolognese jurist and lyric poet whose philosophical poetry was to influence Dante and subsequent love poets in Italy. [*Editors*.]

founded on life. Illuminism or mysticism, the ecstatic vision, or as it was called then, "living in abstraction," is a natural product of the spirit when it is separated from the body. It is a moment of excitement and enthusiasm, during which man seems to be more than man because a god or a demon seems to speak through his mouth. That enthusiasm was called "divine fury" or "rage" and it was considered the gift of prophets and poets, who for Dante were one and the same. This sublimation of the soul within itself, above the ordinary limits of real life, is the heroic side of humanity, the privilege of youth, the special quality of all primitive societies, the moment when material needs are satisfied and the spirit begins to awaken. Everything that leads us to scorn life, riches and pleasures deserves to be held in high esteem.

But a state of tension and imbalance like this cannot last. Art and culture, the knowledge and experience of life, work to modify it and transform it. Thus art, by seizing this world, had begun to humanize it, bringing it closer to man and nature; it mixed with other elements, allowing the passions and furies of the senses to invade it. Balance was still lacking; there was nothing that could be called life in its intimacy, paradise and hell in one. But at least paradise already had its opposite in hell, Beatrice in Francesca da Rimini,[7] Dante, the symbol of humanity, in Dante Alighieri, and the individual in his whole personality. In the *Canzoniere* of Petrarca that world divested itself even of its inherent theological, scholastic, and allegorical forms and took on a more human and natural aspect.

If this world had lasted longer in the consciousness, there is no doubt that art would have undergone a total development; and in the same way that vision and legend became *The Divine Comedy*, and Selvaggia [8] became Beatrice, and Beatrice Laura, from the bosom of the mysteries would have come the drama, and many other types of literature that are barely introduced and roughly sketched in *The Divine Comedy*—like the hymn and the satire—and they would have reached maturity. Already that world in the *Canzoniere* lacks the warmth and the enthusiasm of faith, and part of its substance disappeared in those elegant forms. The attrition of religious, moral, and political feelings left empty places in the poets' consciousness which were filled by art.

This enervation of the consciousness and this cult for beautiful form, amidst the increasing interest in Greco-Roman antiquity, were two of the most important characteristics of the generation that followed the virile, believing, and impassioned age of Dante. Men no longer conceived a passion for doctrines, nor did they

---

7. A key figure in Canto V of Dante's *Inferno*, condemned to eternal punishment for an illicit love affair. [*Editors*.]

8. A woman celebrated by the lyric poetry of Cino da Pistoia (1270–1336), a contemporary of Dante. [*Editors.*]

search for the truth underneath strange verses; beautiful appearances were sufficient to satisfy them. Their studies were not directed towards the investigation of truth, but erudition, and knowledge for knowledge's sake, like art for art's sake, were their goals. Collections of historical and scholarly material replaced the "flowers," "banquets," "gardens," and "treasures" where sacred and profane knowledge had been gathered and used for moral purposes. The Scholastics were still around to call Petrarca "silly," but their criticism was dispersed by the universally recognized belief that Petrarca was as great as Virgil. Virgil himself was no longer considered the magician, the precursor of Christianity, nor the "all-knowing" wise man, but only as the sweet and elegant poet. Dante crowned himself poet, prophet, and apostle in paradise; Petrarca was crowned by his contemporaries as the author of the new *Aeneid*, the *Africa*.[9] All in all, culture and art had become the new idols of the Italian spirit.

Yet, culture and art were not the natural flowering of an interior world. On the contrary, they were accompanied by a weakening of the consciousness while attempting to establish themselves, in their own right, as extrinsic factors which had intrinsic values, as means and ends in one. Culture and art were now of a "formal" nature but were not sufficiently warmed by their content. The same world as Dante's existed in them, but it existed as reason at war with feelings and the imagination, which resulted in a feeble and inconclusive struggle, since faith and the will had become languid. The unmistakable fact was that this world, which existed outside nature and man because of its exaggerated character, was completely out of touch with reality. It had already experienced its Golden Age, recalled by Dante with so much sadness, but in the long run it was bound to remain only a theory, tolerated by tradition and custom and contradicted by daily life.

* * *

This was called a time of transition. Two separate and distinct worlds existed in the heart of men—the past with its forms if not its spirit, and a new world, which affirmed itself as a reaction to the old world, founded on a reality taken from within itself, and void of ideal elements. Mysticism, with its forms reminiscent of the supernatural world, was still present, and there was pure naturalism. But mysticism, already in a state of atrophy, had become a mere commonplace and a tradition. In Petrarca it was commended as an artistic and literary thing rather than a sacred one.

9. A Latin epic poem concerning the life of Scipio Africanus and Rome's struggle with Carthage, which Petrarca intended to rival and to surpass Virgil's *Aeneid*. In spite of Petrarca's intentions, his fame today rests largely upon the Italian love lyrics of his *Canzoniere* rather than upon his Latin works. [*Editors.*]

In contrast, naturalism was arising in full harmony with daily life and the feelings of people, and possessed all the attractions of a novelty. This change of spirit was to completely overturn the foundations upon which literature had rested so far. The romance and the tale, which up to now had been considered vulgar literary forms to be ostracized, began gaining the upper hand. The lyrical world, with its ecstasies, visions, and legends, was replaced by the narrative or epical world, with its adventures, festivals, descriptions, pleasures and its malice. Contemplative life was transmuted into active life, and the other world disappeared from literature. Man no longer lived in spirit outside of the world, but he plunged into life feeling and enjoying it. The celestial and the divine were banished from the consciousness and replaced by human and natural elements. Life was no longer based on what *should be*, but on what *is*. Thus, Dante closed one world and Boccaccio opened up a new one.

* * *

The world represented by Boccaccio existed long before the writing of *The Decameron*. Romances, stories, Latin songs, and licentious songs abounded in Italy at this time. Women, as we have seen, secretly read, amongst themselves, these "profane" books, and the writers of tales kept on entertaining these happy groups with the continuous production of such materials. The common sources of the romances were the adventures of the Knights of the Round Table and of Charlemagne. In the *Amorosa Visione* [1] Boccaccio mentions a large number of these heroes and heroines: Arthur, Lancelot, Galahad, Iseult the Fair, Chedino, Palomides, Lionel, Tristan, Orlando, Rinaldo, Guttifre, Robert Guiscard, Frederick Barbarossa, and Frederick II. And like his fellow writers, Boccaccio wrote romances to please women. But after he had written a new version of the romance of Florio and Biancofiore, he began searching for a new arena of activity more closely related to his studies of the classics from the heroic and primitive times of Greek tradition. But of all the forms of literature prevalent in his time, the one that became most popular was the *novella*, the tale or short story, for it was in greatest harmony with the customs and the spirit of the age. All sorts of tales were created or renovated, some serious, others comic; some morally didactic, others obscene, but all revised and embellished to conform to the tastes of the reader. These short stories, left to the mercy of the imagination, developed into a living literary genre, despite the fact that learned men held them in contempt and disregarded them, considering their subject matter to be profane and frivolous. A direct rival of the short story was the legend,

1. An allegorical poem in Italian, written in *terza rima*. [*Editors.*]

encrusted with its miracles and visions. But these same learned men were indifferent to it as well and preferred to remain within their lofty spheres, leaving *The Little Flowers of Saint Francis* and *The Life of Saint Columbine* to the friars and the story of the simple Calandrino or the gallant adventures of Alatiel to the common people.

Boccaccio entered that profane and frivolous world with no other goal in mind than to write pleasant stories, gratifying to the women who commissioned them. He assembled and fashioned all that shapeless, rough material, dealt with by unlettered men, into the harmonious world of art.

Scholarly research has been done on the sources of Boccaccio's tales. And many have come to believe that a certain amount of glory is taken from Boccaccio by proving that most of the tales were not his own invention, as though the merit of the artist lies solely in inventing rather than shaping the material with which he works. As a matter of fact, the material of *The Decameron*, like that of *The Divine Comedy* or Petrarch's *Canzoniere*, was not the product of a single mind, but of a large number of people. This material passed through various stages until Boccaccio, with his genius, fixed it and made it eternal.

Tales, though called by different names, were the common heritage of all the Latin peoples, but *the* tale—and much less a collection of them where the single stories had been brought together in an organic whole by a storyteller—did not yet exist. This body of material inspired Boccaccio, who took various stories of different times, customs, and tendencies, and created a picture of the living world of his society with all its good and evil traits.

Boccaccio was not one of those haughty spirits who viewed society from above, discovering its good and bad qualities with a perfect and severe conscience. He is an artist who felt himself as one with the society in which he lived, depicting it with that semiconsciousness characteristic of men who are swayed by the shifting impressions of life without caring to analyze them. This quality distinguishes him substantially from Dante and Petrarca, who were withdrawn and ecstatic spirits. Instead, Boccaccio devoted himself to the pleasures, idlenesses, and vicissitudes of everyday life. He was so occupied and satisfied with them that he never felt the urge to bend inwardly or to lower his thoughtful head. The knitted brow never crossed his forehead nor did any shadow fall over his consciousness. It was no accident, then, that he was called "Giovanni the Tranquil." Through him intimacy, meditation, ecstasy, the unquiet depths of thought, the living in one's own spirit nourished by phantasms and mysteries, disappeared from Italian literature. Life rose to the surface, where it was smoothed down and embellished. The world of the spirit disappeared and was replaced by the world of nature.

This superficial world, superficial precisely because it was devoid of all internal and spiritual force, lacked seriousness of means and ends. It was not moved by God, science, or the unifying love of the intellect and act, the great basis of the Middle Ages, but by instinct or natural inclination; it was a true and violent reaction against mysticism. We see before us a happy group of people trying to forget the evils and boredom of life by passing the hot hours of the day listening to pleasing stories. It was the time of the plague, and men, confronted with death, felt the loosening of every bond and restraint, and they abandoned themselves to the carnivallike freedom of their imagination. The court, where Boccaccio had spent the happiest days of his life, was his image of this carnival, and he continued drawing his inspiration from that dungheap upon which the Muses and the Graces had strewn so many flowers. A similar gathering of people can already be found in the *Ameto*.[2] In this pastoral *Decameron*, the stories are allegorical and preordained to reach an abstract ending. They do not possess the spirit of *The Divine Comedy*, but the skeleton is there. In *The Decameron*, on the contrary, the sole purpose of the tales is to make time pass pleasantly. They are all real panders to pleasure and love, despite the fact that the real Italian title of the book, *Principe Galeotto*, was discreetly replaced with a Greek name. The characters evoked in the imagination by different peoples and times all belong to the same world, empty on the inside and corpulent on the outside. Characters, actors, spectators, and writers made up a unified world, characterized by the exterior expression of life in tranquil thoughtlessness.

This world was the theater of human events, abandoned to free will and guided by chance. God, or providence, existed only in name, as though by some sort of tacit accord, in the words of people who had fallen into the deepest religious, political, and moral indifference. Even the intimate force of things, which creates the logic of events and the necessity of their progress, was missing. In fact, the attraction of the work lies in just the opposite quality: in showing us how human actions arrive at a completely different outcome from the one we could have reasonably expected, due to the whims of Fortune. A new form of the marvelous was born, not from the intrusion into life of certain ultranatural forces, such as visions or miracles, but from the extraordinary confluence of events which could not be foreseen or controlled. Our final impression,

2. An Italian prose romance, wherein a number of stories and songs are told and sung in a form which anticipates the frame used to structure the *novelle* of *The Decameron*. [*Editors.*]

then, is that Fortune rules the world. And it is exactly in the varied play of human passions and inclinations, subjected to the changing events of life, that we find the *deus ex machina*, the god of this universe.

Because the machinery of the stories is made up of the marvelous, the fortuitous, and the extraordinary, their interest does not lie in the morality of their actions, but in the unusual qualities of their causes and effects. It is not that Boccaccio pretends to know nothing of morality or religion, or that he sets out to alter the common notions of right and wrong; these things simply do not interest him. It matters little to him whether an action be virtuous or corrupt; rather, he is interested in stimulating the curiosity of the reader by presenting unusual events and characters. Virtue, placed here to leave its impression on the imagination, lacks simplicity and moderation and becomes an instrument of the marvelous. Furthermore, it is exaggerated to such a degree that it shows the emptiness of the author's conscience and the defects of his sense of morality. A noteworthy example is Griselda, the most virtuous character in the book. To show what a good wife she is, she suffocates every natural and personal feeling, including her free will. And the author, in wanting to show an extraordinary example of virtue that will strike the imagination of his readers, falls into that very same mysticism against which he has rebelled and makes use of it by placing the ideal of feminine virtue in the abnegation of the self, just like the theologians who teach that the flesh is absorbed by the spirit and the spirit is absorbed by God. In a sense, it resembles Abraham's sacrifice, except that here it is the husband, instead of God, who so cruelly puts nature to the test.

* * *

Most evident in *The Decameron* is the reaction of the flesh against the excessive rigors imposed by the clergy, who had prohibited attending the theater and the reading of romances, while encouraging fasting and the wearing of sackcloth as the only means of winning paradise. Naturally, this reaction expressed itself through license and cynicism. The forbidden flesh avenged itself, calling "mechanistic" those people who had decided against it—meaning those who had judged stupidly or had followed vulgar opinions. The world of the spirit with all its excessiveness had become "vulgar."

In fact, it is easy to imagine the great joy with which the flesh, after such a long period of subjugation, exhibited itself. Or with what delight it unfolded its pleasures one by one, often choosing the most forbidden ways and expressions and even turning holy words and sayings into obscene ones. Clearly, this profane world was in open rebellion, had broken its bonds and ridiculed its master, who no longer was in control. Upon this comic ground-work Boccaccio interwove a great many chance events, whose heroes are the two immortal protagonists of all comedies: those who make fun and those who are made fun of, the clever man and the fool, and particularly among these the husbands, who are the most persecuted as well as the most innocent. A wealth of comic characters arose in the midst of so many events, and some developed into types, such as the naughty Calandrino or the revengeful scholar who knows where the Devil keeps his tail. On the other hand, the serious characters are rather unique and are not types, but individuals lost in the minuteness and exceptional character of their natures, like Griselda, Tito, the count of Anguersa, Madame Beritola, Ginevra, Salvestra, Isabetta, and Tancredi's daughter. But the real, intimate, living, and feeling characters of this world are the comic ones. These are universal types which we meet every day, like Compare Pietro, Maestro Simone, Fra Puccio, the ramlike priest, the silly judge, Monna Belcolore, Tofano, Gianni Lotteringhi, and all the others, for "the number of the stupid is infinite." And this thoughtless, jovial world begins to take shape, acquires an outline and a character, and becomes the "human comedy."

Thus, within a short amount of time are born the comedy and the anticomedy, *The Divine Comedy* and its parody, "the human comedy." In the same place and at the same time we have Passavanti, Cavalca, and Catherine of Siena—all three voices of the other world, overwhelmed by the loud and profane laughter of Boccaccio. * * * The troubadours and the storytellers, who had been silenced by the priests, returned to life, beginning their dances and merry songs anew in the Florence of the Guelfs. The tale and the romance, which had been forbidden till now, began to forbid in their turn, thus remaining the absolute masters of literature. Unlike an earthquake, this change did not take place suddenly. As we have seen, the lay spirit had been present throughout all of literature, maintaining an unbroken tradition, until in *The Divine Comedy* it took its place boldly, proclaiming itself to be sacred and of divine right, while Dante, the layman, assumed a sacerdotal and apostolic tone. But Dante does this with great skill, so that the edifice he has built will remain standing and its foundations sound. Dante's *Divine Comedy* is a reformation; Boccaccio's comedy is a revolution which causes the whole structure to collapse, and upon its ruins Boccaccio erects another.

The Divine Comedy ceased to be considered a living book. It was now interpreted as a classical work, and was little read, little understood, little enjoyed, but always admired. In this way, it came to be considered divine, but it was no longer a vital work, and as it sank into its tomb, it dragged down with it all of those types of literature whose germs appeared so alive and vigorous in its immortal sketches: tragedy, drama, the hymn, the laud, the legend, and the mystery. Simultaneously with them died the feeling for the family, nature, and the fatherland, the belief in a superior world, meditation, ecstasy, and intimacy, the joys of friendship and of love, and the ideal and the serious aspects of life. Only Malebolge,[3] the realm of malice, the seat of the "human comedy," remained of this immense world which collapsed before achieving maturity and coming to fruition: that Malebolge which Dante had cast into slime and where laughter is overcome by disgust and indignation. Here it is brought to earth with its infernal laughter, adorned by the Graces, and proclaims itself the true paradise, as Don Felice well understood, but not poor Fra Puccio. In effect, here the world is upside down, so that if for Dante *The Divine Comedy* was celestial bliss, "comedy" for Boccaccio was an earthly bliss which produced a number of pleasures, including that of driving away sadness by making jokes at the expense of heaven. The flesh entertains itself at the expense of the spirit.

* * *

The essence of Boccaccio's spirit lies more in the imagination than in the intellect, more in creating comic forms than in searching for distant, obscure relationships between things. He tries to incorporate what his predecessors had attempted to spiritualize. And he strives to create certain astonishing impressions—not in the individual parts, but in the whole work, in the amassing of supporting details into a compact and rigid scheme. Boccaccio writes descriptions where his predecessors wrote sketches. And instead of searching for impressions, Boccaccio entrenches himself in the object itself, investigating it carefully until he knows it inside out. As a result, we are most often left with the object rather than the impression, with the sensation instead of the feeling, with the imagination rather than the fantasy, and with sensuality instead of voluptuousness. His "flowers" are not scented and his light gives off no rays. His work is opaque due to its density and repetition. This kind of style is insupportable in works like the *Filocolo* [4] and the *Ameto*, because their interminable descriptions make us feel as though we have run aground and are unable to go on. Parts of *The Decameron* are just as irritating—for example, when the speeches of Tancredi's daughter and Tito adhere to all the rules of rhetoric and logic. But the comic form is

---

3. The name given by Dante to the Eighth Circle of Hell, a region consisting of ten stone ravines called *Malebólge* ("Evil Pockets"), each of which is crossed by an arching bridge. [*Editors.*]

4. An Italian prose romance, telling the familiar story of Fleur and Blanchefleur (Florio and Biancofiore). [*Editors.*]

one of the most natural in all of literature and was the first to appear after the initial explosion of mottoes and proverbs. The comic form is also the realm of the finite and the senses, and its first impressions are singularized in the minute folds of objects; whereas in serious literature, the first impressions give us allegories and personifications, both of which are forms generalized in the intellect. This first form of comedy is caricature.

Caricature consists in the *direct* representation of the object in order to make its defective and ridiculous side most evident. Certainly, it would be enough to show us the defects while allowing us to guess all the rest, since a single part of man's spirit would be sufficient to illuminate the whole body and show it to the imagination. But Boccaccio is not satisfied with this, and so, like the painter, he depicts the entire body, choosing and distributing colors and details to throw more light on the defective side than on the rest. Hence, the element of the ridiculous is not isolated but expands over the whole work, with each part contributing to the effect, finally producing a kind of crescendo in the comic scale. And because he has prepared us for this, and we ourselves are inclined to laugh, laughter rarely breaks out suddenly and irresistibly, as in those short passages which give us unexpected connections; instead of laughter, we feel a steady pleasure which keeps us peacefully satisfied. We feel appeased, not excited. Although we do not laugh, our faces are serene and happy; laughter is latently present, and we never feel that it is going to break out irresistibly in a contracted and convulsive way. And the reason is this: Boccaccio presents us with a series of forms made by his imagination, rather than a series of related thoughts, the product of his intellect. His forms are solid, fleshy, fully clothed, and minutely drawn. He seems to be sunk in that world of the imagination, and at the same time to be its creator; he has the air of adding nothing at all of his own. And we are thoroughly captivated and enchanted and cannot escape from it. The author is never distracted, he does not grimace to provoke laughter, nor does he treat his subject matter as something frivolous, laying it down and going back to it. He has a fixed idea which pursues him, catches hold of him, and keeps him there without giving him rest until it has been completely expressed. And we are not distracted but are rocked deliciously in our contemplation. And if laughter sometimes breaks out, interrupting our attention, we plunge right back into the subject and run at length with it; when the race is over, we are still running, gently exhausted. This is not the Eastern world, where the imagination, almost drugged by opium, springs trembling from the arms of love to fly away into the vast infinitude, allowing us to experience that feeling called voluptuousness, the infinitude of the senses—that vague, indefinite, and musical something which en-folds and reveals God to us. Boccaccio's world is purely sensual, completely enclosed by precise, round forms, and satisfied with itself; there is nothing here to detach us and carry us off into exalted regions. Exactly because these flowers have no scent and these lights emit no rays, we get sensations instead of feelings, imagination instead of fantasy, and sensuality instead of voluptuousness. We no longer hold our eyes fixed towards heaven in ecstasy; we have found our paradise in a full and attractive reality. The flesh, making its reappearance in the world, seems to be completely naked as it reveals all its pleasures and fills our paradise with deceiving allurements and flatteries. Therefore the form of this paradise is cynical, even more so where an ironical sense of modesty flirts to stir up the senses.

Because the essential form of Boccaccio's world is caricature, the product of a rich imagination capable of presenting things in detail, we are not shown just its peaks and higher projections, but the entire object with its most subtle gradations. Brief in his introduction and in the abstract depiction of his characters, Boccaccio immediately raises the curtain to reveal his characters in full action, moving and talking. The comic motifs spring forth from the very first, developing a little at the time, step by step, so that each new comic element is united to the rest with increasing effect. Boccaccio unfolds that special quality which the French call *verve* when they try to imitate his force and facility, and the Italians call *brio* when they aim at lively wit. Two marvelous examples of this quality are the tale of Alibech and that of Ciappelletto. To render the caricature more piquant Boccaccio employs irony, which here is not a primary but an accessory form. The narrator pretends to be scrupulous and modest with an apparent good nature and an air of ingenuity. Nonetheless, he says and believes in things even when he does not want to, and he makes the sign of the cross with a concealed sneer. This irony is like some kind of comic salt which makes laughter more savory, at the expense of the paternoster of Saint Julian and the miracles of Ser Ciappelletto.

* * *

When Latin authors wanted to express the comic, they usually discarded their heavy weapons and armed themselves lightly. Boccaccio conceives like Plautus and writes like Cicero. Yet his way of conceiving is so lively and true that his imagination transforms Cicero into an enticing and charming siren, who bends and moves her body alluringly. But often when he is totally involved in his subject, he disengages himself from all the tangles and contortions, and his style becomes slender, nimble, swift, direct, and incisive; he is a master of shortcuts and of vaulting over obstacles. When his imagination is warmed by feeling, it ranges masterfully between ancient and modern forms, fusing them together to create a world of his own, which he then brands with his personal mark. This world would be insupportable and deeply disgusting if art had not permeated it completely from the beginning, enveloping its nakedness with those ample Latin forms, as in a veil blown by lascivious winds. Boccaccio is only concerned seriously about art, only art makes him pensive even in the midst of the orgies of his imagination and knits his brow in thought even in his moments of greatest license—as happened to Petrarca and Dante in their highest and purest inspiration. Thus, the various men who lived within him are fused in Boccaccio's style: the literary man, the man of erudition, the artist, the courtier, and the man of the study and of the world. This style is so personal and in such complete harmony with his nature and his times that it is impossible to imitate it, and as such, it stands alone as a prodigious literary monument among many imitations.

What is missing from this world of Boccaccio's?

This world of nature and the senses lacks that feeling for nature and that voluptuous perfume which Poliziano [5] brought to it later on. This world of comedy lacks that high comic feeling with its humorous and capricious forms, which Ariosto [6] bestowed upon it later.

And what is this world?

It is the cynical, malicious world of the flesh, left in the lower regions of sensuality and of clownish caricature, gracefully enveloped in the graces and allurements of a form full of coquetry. It is a plebeian world which snaps its fingers at spiritual things, rough in its feelings, but refined and adorned by the imagination. And within it, the bourgeois world of the spirit moves elegantly, with reminiscences of chivalric life.

It is the new "comedy"—not the divine but the terrestrial one. Dante wraps his Florentine robe around him and vanishes. And the Middle Ages with their visions, legends, mysteries, terrors, shadows, and ecstasies are banished from the temple of art. Now Boccaccio noisily enters this temple, drawing all of Italy after him for many years to come.

* * *

5. Angelo Ambrogini (1454–94), called Poliziano (Politian, in English), one of the most important humanist poets at the court of Lorenzo de' Medici in Florence and the author of an important narrative poem in Italian entitled *Le Stanze per la giostra* ("Stanzas for the joust"). The exquisite descriptive passages in this poem may well have inspired several of Botticelli's paintings. [*Editors.*]

6. Ludovico Ariosto (1474–1533), one of the greatest poets of the Italian Renaissance and the author of several satires and comedies. His epic poem, *Orlando Furioso*, was greatly appreciated in Europe by other poets and critics and influenced both Spenser and Milton, among others. [*Editors.*]

ALDO D. SCAGLIONE

[Nature and Love in Boccaccio's *Decameron*] †

The first question about a book concerns its form, and the *Decameron* is, in form, an unusually systematic collection of no-vellas. A good deal of realistic literature had developed in the Middle Ages within the framework of the short story, from the Latin forms (variously called *exemplum, parabula, fabula, historia, legenda*), to the French *contes* and *fabliaux* (*fablel, fableau*) and the Italian *novella* (*conto*). Of the literature that lies at the formal origin of the *Decameron* one must distinguish two types: firstly, the parable or tale with a moral (*conte à queue*, as the French used to call it), closest to the ecclesiastical milieu, frequently used by priests in sermons; such paradigmatic stories could occasionally be gathered into allegedly edifying collections, with a general ethical or satirical purpose, such as the *Disciplina clericalis* and the *Novel of the Seven Sages* in the various languages. Secondly, the fabliau or *conte à rire*, pure divertissement without serious after-thought. A number of items of the first type derived from the Orient, a few from classical literature (for instance, from Aesop, from the ancient comedy and novel). What Boccaccio did to all this production was to treat the first type in the spirit of the sec-ond, and invest the second with the paradigmatic, 'symbolic' value of the first. In addition, the idea of a systematic collection produced with him for the first time a truly homogeneous and balanced ensemble.

At the outset, this imaginative representation of everyday experi-ences, in a spirit of close, keen observation of human nature, had explicitly shown a transcendent purpose, quite akin to the moral-istic *raison d'être* of the Indian narrative (regardless of the extent to which we are prepared to accept the derivation of the European novellas from Indian sources). The 'naturalism' of the Indian story, as well as of the early medieval European novella, is only one of method: in sharp contrast with the first appearance, inspiration and purpose lie in the ascetic refusal of worldly existence, whose basically evil nature is unmasked by the substance of the realistic incidents related by the narrator, amusing as such incidents are on the surface, ridiculous and disgusting in the last analysis. But

† Aldo D. Scaglione provides a discus-sion of *The Decameron*'s cultural con-text, with particular emphasis upon the problem of naturalism and its impact upon Boccaccio's ideas. The selection reprinted here is taken from *Nature and Love in the Late Middle Ages* (Berkeley: University of California Press, 1963), pp. 53–56, 60–65, 96–100, 101–108. Copy-right © 1963 by the Regents of the Uni-versity of California; reprinted by per-mission of the University of California Press. The author's footnotes are renum-bered and some have been omitted.

from this beginning the novella genre gradually evolved toward an expression of immanent wisdom: the acceptance of reality *as is*. When we think of what the genre was to become in later times at the hands of a La Fontaine, we clearly realize how thoroughly the cycle of this metamorphosis has been consummated. Most typical of the general process had been the novellas dealing with sexual adventures; the unmistakably misogynous aim of the Indian story-tellers was obvious in the exemplary treatment of lascivious aberrations intended to show the inner vulgarity of a life dominated by the senses, in a chaos of contradictions breaking all social and moral rules, at the mercy of the insatiable, basely corrupt instincts of womankind.

Prompted by a deeply pessimistic view of human nature, the ascetic-minded male had preferred to close his eyes to the impenetrable and unavoidable evils brought by womanhood into our lives. As Saint Bernard warned, "Should you have reason to suspect your women, you had better prófess ignorance of their doings. No physician could cure you once you found out the mischiefs of a bad wife." [1]

In fact, the medieval consciousness constantly swings like a pendulum between two opposed yet complementary views of womanhood: the religious-monastic (woman is sin, crime, error, folly, wickedness, in brief, the eternal Pandora) and the courtly (woman is the embodiment of all the best in life and the world). The one is the result of a realistic approach, the other of an idealistic one, but they are in actuality both abstractions. To put it differently, the realism of the former view is the way of looking at reality of one who searches for an ideal perfection irreconcilable with any given reality; while the 'idealism' of the latter view is the hypostasis of a good that one recognizes in reality but projects upon a screen of perfection without which that limited good would not seem satisfactory. Boccaccio's naturalism is, in its coherence, something different and new. He takes reality and woman as they are, in all their polyvalence. His women characters are both, and even simultaneously, interested and disinterested, loving in order to give and loving in order to take, safe and dangerous, self-centered and generous, in brief 'good' and 'bad.' They are *real* according to *nature*, not to a superimposed schema of man-made, mentally construed and idolized, supraworldly, suprahuman, and supranatural perfection. From them can come happiness, as for Federigo, or extreme suffering, as for the scholar, for they can behave, according to the situation, like Monna Giovanna or like the widow respectively. They are not all of one mold, and the same woman may vary according to circumstances. The absolutism of the Middle

---

1. Bernardus, *De cura rei familiaris*, ed., J. R. Lumby, Early English Texts Society, XLII (London, 1870), 6.

Ages, both in the positive and in the negative direction, is gone. Man is finally able to face the play of natural instincts and take them for what they are.

The two viewpoints could be occasionally found side by side in medieval literature: witness, above all, Jean de Meung's noted antifeminism at the same time that he was completing a poem-treatise on courtly procedure wherein the pursuit and conquest of the beloved lady was the way of all happiness. But in Jean the two attitudes are essentially juxtaposed, in a singularly medieval texture of unwitting and partly unconscious contradiction.[2] In the *Decameron* this juxtaposition gives way to harmonious and organic fusion. To be sure, we must not forget that the *Decameron* represents a unique moment of equilibrium in Boccaccio's career, standing as it does at an ideal middlepoint between the early attempts to follow the lead of the *stilnovisti* and the outburst of rampant misogyny in the *Corbaccio*.

Medieval naturalism is ordinarily disorganic; at times we encounter it, not without surprise, side by side with opposite elements, like the concern for the "figural," allegorical value of the event, or those sudden, arbitrary flights of fantasy so typical of the medieval mind but so charmingly conflicting with the occasional, though intense observation of reality. By contrast, the 'organic' coherence of the *Decameron* (not all of Boccaccio's fiction!) deserves to be emphatically stated, especially as it seems to extend to all aspects of the work. And even in the style the organic concentration of all traditional rhetorical devices contrasts with the typically 'centrifugal' construction of medieval prose, where the general impression is one of division, 'segmentation,' articulation into constitutive elements. This distinctive characteristic appears to have escaped V. Branca in his investigation of the medieval foundations of Boccaccio's work. And I should not hesitate to maintain that this 'organic composition' is as typical of Italy's Renaissance literature as it is of its Renaissance art, in contrast with the Northern art (including Flemish fifteenth-century painting).

* * *

There is an area of medieval culture in which philosophy, literature, and medicine are intimately intertwined. Official doctrine and science (specifically, medicine) agreed in condemning love as a sort of disease or madness. * * * In other words, medicine agreed in regarding sex as normality, passion as illness. Not the

---

2. This coexistence of distinct attitudes, not uncommon in the Middle Ages, may at times appear to us as a case of split personality. Aside from the conclusion of Capellaneus' treatise, belying all the courtly foundation after having extolled it, the English John Lydgate (1370?–1450?) offers one of the most telling cases of monastic mentality and courtly attitudes in the same person: he was a monk and a courtly poet consistently, but distinctly.

animal instinct or appetite was considered the enemy, but the psychic superstructure built on it by the imagination. Matter was healthier than the spirit.

In desperate cases, doctors were even advised to favor the meeting of the lover with the object of his passion, for this would end his infatuation and cure him. The obvious danger of incurring inflexible moral censure was lightly disposed of by formally recommending a restriction of these methods "within the legal and ecclesiastical rules" ("secundum modum permissionis fidei et legis")—which was obviously no more than a verbal palliative, since no such rules would admit of the sort of rendezvous that might cure an 'infatuation.'

This 'scientific' naïveté of curing the lover by pandering for him is, after all, not too surprising (though Boccaccio, himself no physician, simply by his psychological intuition could have easily perceived the alleged 'remedy' of intercourse as perhaps the most assured way to strengthen and perpetuate the disease). But aside from this, it will be even less surprising to find the same conception of passion in poets who spent their whole literary career singing the praises of this frightful 'disease.' The most pessimistic, even tragic note, was struck, in Italy, by Guido Cavalcanti, the best poet before Dante, who also stated his doctrine of love by "natural dimonstramento" in the obscure and much-discussed 'canzone' *Donna me prega*.[3] Here the erotic love of the courtly poets, sensual and 'fantastic,' was defined as passion issuing from the sensitive faculty, not the rational, causing an inevitable deviation of the judgment, feeding on the natural instincts but beyond the natural boundaries and the natural sense of measure. The fire of the senses is sparked by the ideal and fantastic elaboration the object of desire undergoes in the intellect of the lover. It is a physical phenomenon, but it feeds on the imagination. Its very excess (the angry Mars within us) guarantees its short duration, without hope of gaining any degree of wisdom by its experience. Because of opposition from the rational faculty, and because of the jeopardy in which it places the delicate and unstable balance of the faculties, the erotic experience is bound to end in unhappiness when not in tragedy. No obstacles can stop it, they can only make it all the more deadly if they are insurmountable. We are here confronted with a sharp dualism: the poet knows that there is no salvation outside the rational good and the control of reason over our passions ("Ma quanto che da buon perfetto tort'è / Per sorte, non pò dire om ch'aggia vita, / Ché stabilita non ha segnoria"), yet he sees love as an irrational but natural, hence irrevocable movement ("non perché oppost'a naturale sia").

3. J. E. Shaw, *G. Cavalcanti's Theory of Love* (Toronto, 1949), with the text and translation of the "canzone."

Another poet of the same school, Lapo Gianni, concluded his 'canzone' Amor, nova ed antica vanitade by sadly dismissing love as a mishap which darkens the mind and sickens the body. Some aspects of this 'doctrine' will be echoed as late as in Leo Hebraeus' Dialoghi d'Amore in the full bloom of the Renaissance, but certain particular motifs found an effective restatement in the philosophical naturalism of the Quaestio disputata de felicitate by Jacopo da Pistoia.[4] In this Aristotelian treatise with Averroistic overtones, the problem of sensuality is treated with apparent reference to Cavalcanti. First Jacopo admits that passions are the most natural result of inborn inclinations. Yet they are said to conflict with the balance of the faculties, since they are caused by a disproportionate development of the organs of the fantasy or imagination, thus hindering the operation of understanding. The conclusion is, not unexpectedly, that in order to attain the contemplation of the supreme intellectual objects, man will have to stifle the venereal passions, or at least regulate their process.

This relative parallelism between medical and literary language as well as basic attitudes extends, in the Decameron, beyond the specific treatment of love. We need read no further than the famous Introduction to be confronted with a first impressive case of general import.

The presence side by side of realism and flight from reality is notoriously characteristic of the 'primitive' psychology of the medieval man. But, in spite of our first impression, we must conclude that the striking contrast contained in the introduction to the Decameron is not really part of this dualistic attitude. The transition from the terrifying spectacle of the plague to the idyllic withdrawal for a lofty enjoyment of the best things of life sounds to us like an implicit, though conscious, reaction against a then current inference: namely that the evils of earthly existence should teach us that the world of nature is nothing but a valley of tears, and must be rejected or at least transcended for something radically different and superior. If, as L. Di Francia suggested, Jacopo Passavanti's stern warnings from the pulpit of Santa Maria Novella were occasioned by the Black Death of 1348, the striking contrast between the friar's and Boccaccio's lessons derived from that same experience is most enlightening.[5] But even more characteristic is Boccaccio's specific agreement with the instructions of the famous

---

4. P. O. Kristeller, "A philosophical Treatise from Bologna dedicated to G. Cavalcanti: Magister Jacobus de Pistoia and his Questio de Felicitate," in Medioevo e Rinascimento, Studi in onore di B. Nardi (Florence, 1955), 427–63 (with text).
5. Trattato dell'umiltà, Chap. IV. Quoted in L. Di Francia, La Novellistica (Milan, 1924), I, chap. 2, p. 107. This sermon,

delivered in the very church where the brigata of the Decameron gathered and decided to set forth on their pleasant holiday, was later incorporated in the Specchio di Vera Penitenza. For the complete text, in the absence of a critical edition, see the inadequate and incorrect I. Passavanti, Lo Specchio della Vera Penitenza, ed. F.-L. Polidori (Florence, 1856, 1863), p. 253.

physician Tommaso del Garbo—an agreement which appears to seal a sort of alliance between the author's pre-Renaissance mentality and the naturalistic orientation of Tommaso's science. Consider the baseness of our existence, let this ever-present spectacle of death lead you to forsake the lust and greed of earthly pleasures, says the eloquent preacher. Forget the death that surrounds you, do not let it contaminate your mind and body, flee all this sadness and give yourselves to gay entertainments and pleasant company, says the doctor. But, just as Boccaccio does, he adds the warning to do this with the measured restraint of good taste, orderliness, and moderation. Thus will health be preserved, in keeping with the remedy prescribed by science. Death is, accordingly, courageously challenged by Boccaccio's *brigata,* and toward the end of this adventurous vacation the author will have to exclaim, evidently pleased with his characters' performance, "Either they will not be vanquished by death, or they will meet it in a gay mood!" * * *

Humanism will speak in similar terms through L. B. Alberti's warnings not to endanger the life of a living man by the hopeless attempt to cure a dying one, no matter how dear to us.[6] The modern sensitivity, whereby we feel compelled to share the misfortunes of our fellow-humans and try to help them at any price, could not find room at times when the reasonable remedies in common disasters were so much more limited and risky.

The place itself chosen by the youthful *brigata* for their salvation —and for the very setting of the *Decameron*—must retain our attention briefly for another important consideration as to its specific function. The *villa* in the countryside was a middle point between sophisticated city life and the pastoral simplicity of the peasant's world. The peculiar way of life of Boccaccio's *brigata* during their retirement in the *villa* may appear to the present-day reader as a curious transposition of extraordinary rational discipline to a place where the senses and the imagination might be expected to have free play. We must, then, remember that in the Middle Ages the *villa,* the *locus amoenus,* or the garden are, indeed, an occasion for escape from the closed life of the walled city or the fortress-like house, but without quite plunging into the perturbing disorderliness, the 'wildness' of open nature. Places of this kind represent a compromise, a fusion of elements of city and wilderness, symbolical of a harmony between reason and the forces of the subconscious. A fitting climate, then, for naturalism as revaluation of instinctive life in a rational framework; or (to be more precise, if we deal with the *Decameron* in particular) an appropriate introduction for a gentle opening of the mind—without a direct, sudden, and drastic exposure—to those subterranean

6. *I Libri della Famiglia,* II, in L. B. Alberti, *Opere Volgari, I, I Libri della* *Famiglia, Cena Familiaris, Villa,* ed. C. Grayson (Bari, 1960), p. 122.

phenomena of life, those forces of matter and of the unconscious, which, in their full bloom, could but frighten and repel the medieval mind.[7] Besides, one ought not overlook the medieval fondness of enclosed gardens as allegorical settings wherein to stage the exclusive, aristocratic scene for actions of courtly love. To this effect the enclosed garden has been regarded as a symbolic place of refuge from the morality of the church.

* * *

I have shown how Boccaccio's intuition of nature evolves out of the world of courtly love, rather than being juxtaposed to it, as it appeared to De Sanctis, who, for this reason, felt obliged to assess the *courtois* tales as 'rhetoric.' * * * I have tried to do it in the name of 'naturalism,' which is, as I see it, not a historically new phenomenon in Boccaccio (as De Sanctis made it appear), but an old one in new form. Boccaccio sides, with unconditional sympathy, with all manifestations of the senses, against conventional morality (see VI, 7), with adulterers and sinning nuns and monks, and condemns only when hypocrisy attempts to hide nature (VII, 3; VIII, 4; IV, 2), or when venality contaminates the free choice guided by nature (VIII, 1), or finally when men stoop to "perversi piaceri contro natura" (V, 10, and the attacks in the Epilogue).

Petronio has appropriately warned against a 'romantic' misreading of the work: Boccaccio's, as he puts it, is not "the romantic world of passion unrestrained (*sbrigliata*), slave and, at the same time, proud of itself." [8] It is, rather, the world of 'sentiment' serenely fused with reason and the will. Love is, indeed, irrational, but reason follows and serves it, without being quite subjugated by it. Thus love and 'intelligence' appear not really distinct, but united in mutual coöperation, or more exactly love is accompanied by intelligence, a thriving force even by itself.

When seen in this light, it appears that such an attitude is already part of the Renaissance, no more of the Middle Ages, where love could well be pure romantic passion. But it is not the mature Renaissance, in which love will work more for the ends of reason, its rightful guide, than vice versa. Yet, the danger of Petronio's interpretation, as I see it, is in the extent to which one is ready to posit the control by reason over the senses and the heart. Serene coöperation there is between them, but we must never forget that it is a coöperation of opposites.

We may now feel ready to conclude that taken singularly, almost

---

7. On the psychological significance of gardens, landscapes, *loci amoeni* in the Middle Ages one can consult, among others, F. Crisp, *Medieval Gardens* (London, 1924); H. R. Patch, *The Other World, according to descriptions in* *medieval literature* (Cambridge, 1950); *passim;* E. R. Curtius, *European Literature and the Latin Middle Ages*, trans. W. R. Trask (New York, 1953), pp. 185, 193 ff.

8. *Il Decamerone*, p. 48.

every feature of the *Decameron*'s ethics of free love finds its antecedent in the courtly tradition, and particularly in its most significant codification, Andreas Capellanus' *De Amore*. The exalted praise of adultery and the consequent scorn for marriage were conspicuous pivots of Provençal poetry, and were embodied in the manual of Andreas. Andreas had singled out jealousy as the inevitable pest of marriage. He had also insisted on true nobility as an inner moral virtue (*probitas*) that found in love its 'fountain'; and such a principle had been developed in an original way by the School of the Sweet New Style, in the most favorable social environment. Some of the stories, and all of the conclusive Tenth Day, move in an explicit courtly environment. More particularly, Branca has likened the position of Capellanus to Boccaccio's principle whereby the plebeian may, even must, love a lady of nobility.[9] * * *

Yet, besides particular noncourtly elements, the general atmosphere, the spirit itself of the *Decameron* cannot be thought to have emanated from the courtly tradition. The feminine type that sweeps triumphantly through the work is eminently remote from the *midons* (= my lord) who had polarized the feudally conditioned idealism of Provençal society.[1] Above all, Boccaccio originally presents all precepts and attitudes, old and new, as willed and imposed by nature, far from the stylized and conventional ideology of the chivalric world. Furthermore, he surpasses the inflexibility of the courtly 'heresy' in its most consistent expression, as he significantly seems to forget a relevant corollary of Andreas' doctrine. The granting of favors by the lady, including the ultimate *guerdon*, was necessary and valuable inasmuch as it increased the lover's *probitas*, as a *free* reward for his true merits.[2] Hence true love could not be found in marriage, where favors are to be reciprocally returned as a *duty*. In such an atypical manner, on the contrary, marriage does end many of Boccaccio's love stories, because marriage by free choice and mutual consent is, for him, the logical crowning of love, whereas it is to be scorned as love's enemy when it comes about by social imposition. Wherever they conform with the natural order, Boccaccio is ready to accept social institutions.

9. V. Branca, *B. medievale*, pp. 154–155.
1. B.'s women are real, natural human beings, to be loved by "love as for a creature," not by "affectioun for holynesse," as the Provençal ladies so often were. As regards the specific term I have used, A. Viscardi, *Storia delle letterature d'oc e d'oil* (Milan, 1955) in dealing with Guillaume de Poitiers points out the singular and significant use of *midons* in Guillaume and Bernart de Ventadorn among others, in lieu of the customary *ma domna*. Also cf., on the feudal patterns in Provençal poetry, S. Pellegrini, "Intorno al vassallaggio d'amore nei primi trovatori," *Cultura neolatina* IV–V (1944–45), 21–36.
2. A minor, though striking example of love's virtuous effects is in IV, 10, the story of the lover stolen by thieves in a chest. The lady had wanted a lover, chooses a rascal, but tries to rehabilitate him by giving him money and advice to change his life for the sake of love.

Just though it may be to insist on Boccaccio's dependence on courtly ideology in the *Decameron* as a reaction to the neglect of this important element by Romantic criticism, I feel that enough has been made of this issue by recent critics. After all, to Boccaccio the appeal of the world of chivalry lay especially in its naturalistic substratum, on one hand, and, on the other, in its possibility of providing examples of magnanimity, that is, grandiose, heroic virtues—in other words, the sort of thing that indirectly served his humanistic cult of classic greatness. But he was uninterested in the more technical aspects of chivalry *per se*. One significant testimony 'by omission' may suffice here. The poignant story of Guiglielmo Guardastagno and Guiglielmo Rossiglione (IV, 9, the novella of the eaten heart), derives from the "Vida" of the troubadour Guillem de Cabestaing, but Boccaccio disregarded the very element which was most revealing of the courtly ethics of this story, that is the punishment of the revengeful husband by the king.

But in order to keep our notion of Boccaccio's naturalism in its proper focus, it is important to bear in mind that Boccaccio's true conception of love, like that of all great poets of love who preceded him (including the troubadours), must not be equated with eroticism. * * * This fine distinction, if I am not mistaken, amounts to the most effective defense against the possible charge of obscenity or pornography. In the *Decameron*, in spite of all appearances, the real accent is not on sense and sex. Boccaccio's message is naturalistic, not erotic.

On the other hand, the triumph of naturalism marked by the *Decameron* was premature: our author could not help reverting, sooner or later, to a medieval awareness of the incompatibility of a consistent naturalistic view and the superior rights of the pure spirit; and the result was the rejection of the *Decameron* as an error of his 'youth.' It was not before the sixteenth century that a coherent naturalism could inform the whole life of a man, without hesitation or crisis. Because he ushered in a new culture, in a somewhat dramatic way and at the price of his inner equilibrium, Boccaccio could not find, as an artist, that sublime though precarious harmony between spirituality and naturalism which had been the hallmark of certain medieval experiences, such as that of an Héloïse or, more fictionally, those of courtly literature at its best.

* * *

In one sense at least, Humanism, in the broadest philosophical implications of the term, can be said to have been restored by Boccaccio even more than by Petrarch: namely as an open, unprejudiced appreciation of all that is human inasmuch as it is part of human nature, however good or bad ethically, right or wrong rationally it might be. * * *

Even before the hundred stories were completed, Boccaccio had released parts of his *Decameron* for circulation among his friends. Thus he had early met with bitter opposition from certain quarters, as was to be expected. In the Proem to the Fourth Day, a piece of extraordinary directness, sincerity, and introspective power, the author replied to the book's critics in words addressed to his feminine public. Petrarch seems to have approvingly looked upon this eloquent 'apologia,' which he significantly singled out for an implicit mention when, in the last of his *Seniles* (1373), he complimented Boccaccio for having dealt with his literary detractors as they deserved: "This very book had been attacked by the teeth of vile dogs, but you defended it with the stick of your very effective words.[3]

As Boccaccio expounds them, four charges had been thrust upon him: immoderate attachment to the feminine sex ("che voi mi piacete troppo"); deviation from truly worthy literature ("farei più saviamente a starmi con le Muse in Parnaso"); inability to make a living by his frivolous literary activity ("farei più discretamente a pensare dond'io dovessi aver del pane"); and unfaithfulness to the originals of the stories ("in altra guisa essere state le cose da me raccontatevi"). He answers the objections in a very orderly manner, point by point, after having induced the right mood by one more novella, that of the women called *papere*, goslings ("devils" in *Barlaam*, Iacopo da Varazze, Jacques de Vitry, Vincent de Beauvais, the *Novellino*, and others). In this witty anecdote the departure from the medieval *exemplum* is quite drastic, and in such respect one can find here the best demonstration of the evolution which I have already discussed in general terms. For this purpose we must briefly retrace the background of the story in its essential lines.

Barlaam et Joasaf was the life of the Buddha turned Christian saint, in a spontaneous alliance between Buddhism and Christianity.[4] It contained an apologue (the tenth) wherein women were shown to be the best allies of the devil—rather devils themselves

3. "Librum ipsum canum dentibus lacessitum tuo tamen baculo egregie tuaque voce defensum." Cf. Branca, *B. medievale*, p. 214. When Petrarch wrote this (1373) he would no longer have subscribed to the "Proemio," and Petrarch himself had recanted his love in *Canzoniere*, 1. * * * As an example of the literary impact of B.'s self-defense on later authors, Straparola closely though poorly imitated it in the defense of his own work at the beginning of the second Book of his *Piacevoli Notti*

(1553).
4. Sérapie der Nersessian, ed., *L'Illustration du Roman de Barlaam et Joasaf* (Paris, 1937). The text is in *Patrologia Graeca*, XCVI, 875–1240 and in *Patrologia Latina*, LXXIII, 443–604 (Latin text from the sixteenth century). The Latin version of the twelfth century from the Greek original of John of Damascus (d. 749) or Euthymius (abbot of Mt. Athos, d. 1028), is in Br. Mus. Additional MS. 17, 299.

who deceive men. By this apologue a courtier had persuaded the king to send a wench to his young son (the prince Josaphat) as the surest of all temptations to turn him away from a life of religion. A young man, as the story has it, had been kept in the wilderness since his earliest years to ensure his dedication to a life of innocent asceticism away from all temptation. But at his first accidental glimpse of real women he suddenly and irrevocably grew so fond of them that, after learning of their being "devils," he decided he could no longer do without the devils' company.

The anecdote has a long story of popular derivations and transcriptions, through which one expediently notices the typical process whereby the originally moralistic, ascetic *exemplum* was irrevocably turned into a thoroughly immanent affair, naturalistic in inspiration and purpose. In retelling the story, Boccaccio followed the example of the English Odo of Cheriton and dropped the nickname "devils" for the women to call them "goslings." La Fontaine, the rightful heir of Boccaccio and Ariosto as a storyteller, in his turn completed the transformation by divesting the background of its medieval tone: in his "conte" *Les oies de frère Philipe* the ascetic atmosphere surrounding the hermit is obliterated in the constant, consistently sceptical smile of the narrator. We are not even aware, any longer, of any connection with a medieval environment. * * *

The dissolution of the medieval *exemplum*, outwardly naturalistic, inwardly ascetic, is one of the phenomena which mark the transition to the Renaissance, since, as a rule, the Renaissance novella does away with the 'moral,' that more or less consistent appendix to the short story which had officially justified its existence in the religiously inspired literature of the early Middle Ages (formal sermons or concealed ones as the case may have been). In this sense Boccaccio appears already immersed in the climate of the new culture. But his particular treatment of the "women-goslings" motif is indicative of something even more important. His naturalism is not the naïve, spontaneous, unconscious delight in detailed realistic representation which characterized so much of medieval realism. It is a conscious program, intellectually formulated and presented in a polemic, militant, aggressive tone, in explicit reaction to medieval prejudices. The attitude of conscious defense of the 'rights of nature' in a learned, intellectual art, must be placed into sharp focus and distinguished from the mere taste for the realistic, picturesque detail, the latter being characteristic of most late-medieval art. Erich Auerbach has rightfully recognized this polemic consciousness in Boccaccio's "un-Christian" (as he regarded it) doctrine of love and nature, and in his being so fully "certain of himself" in his views on earthly love.

To recapitulate, then, the traditional moral purpose of the

women-devils motif has been completely overturned: instead of a warning to avoid the all but irresistible temptation of 'Pandora'—since the only way to prevent the world from ensnaring us is asceticism, complete withdrawal from the world—the anecdote is treated as a demonstration of the ineradicability of man's attraction to woman, *therefore* of the goodness of the sexual instinct as part of nature's plans, and the unavoidable defeat of all attempts to stifle nature by escape. The antiascetic intention is made quite evident, though discreetly concealed in subtle irony, when the young hermit remarks to his father that the girls he has just seen for the first time "are fairer than the painted angels that you have so often shown me." Finally, the story is bodily subtracted from its traditional setting, as though to confirm even in the material details the rejection of its previous edifying character. In addition to what has been pointed out before, this is also achieved by the attribution of the incident to a well known Florentine merchant family, the Balducci (agents of the Bardi, like Boccaccio's own father), thus making it psychologically close to the reader's experience. This is particularly noteworthy in a context where the author is preparing to reject the charge of being untrue to his sources. He is obviously aware of the meaning of certain deliberate changes, and takes full responsibility for them. He does not deign to linger on lengthy and dialectical justifications of his behavior. He simply admits that his tastes and standards are not those of the past, nor those of his critics. For these latter, for instance, as for the Filippo Balducci of the anecdote, women are bad things, *mala cosa*, devils who should better be named after some insignificant thing or animal—like *papere*. * * * So this is the new moral: the hermit suddenly realized that *nature* was stronger than man's will to thwart it.[5]

Now to the particular censures. The one he takes more time to discuss is the first: Does he like women too much? Perhaps so; but he has no intention of retracting himself: * * * He and his adversaries belong to different worlds: they are scandalized by the very things which are for him the finest part of life. He will not even try to persuade them. If they are surprised that some people, like him, cannot help but be charmed by intercourse with women, by their kisses and embraces, by their "ornati costumi e la vega bellezza e l'ornata leggiadria," plus their "donnesca onestà"; if his adversaries are "persons who have neither feeling for, nor

5. Likewise, the tales of lust in monks and nuns had more than a role of attack on the clergy or sheer fun at their expense. They implicitly tended to prove the truth of the principle stated in the Proem. The medieval ascetic had not been unaware that the temptation is made fiercer by inhibition. But he had also believed that conventional seclusion would guarantee the suppression of desire by removing the occasion to fulfill it. B. apparently wanted to show the futility of this illusion, as prohibition, solitude, and constant introversion increase the temptation until it becomes unbearable.

notion of the honest pleasures of *natural* affections," his only reaction will be to leave them to their destiny. * * * At any rate, and leaving jokes aside, he is proud to "devote himself to those matters to which Guido Cavalcanti and Dante Alighieri, on the threshold of their old age, and Cino da Pistoia even in his advanced old age felt honored to minister." Of course, at least as far as Dante and Cino were concerned, Boccaccio knew full well that their ways of caring for the same objects were not quite the same as his; but we cannot really blame him for neglecting to underline it. In one way or another, Boccaccio seems to imply, all true poets are on the same level, they all must love life—and life's quintessence are love and women—, for poetry is 'aesthetic' activity, feeling for earthly, sensorial and sensual values. This Boccaccio knew, or at least felt intuitively, and he dared bring it to the open fore with a frankness unexpected at his time, and with a clarity of consciousness of which Dante would not have been capable, no matter how much greater he may have been as a poet and as a man.

As to the three remaining objections, the gist of his replies is the following: Muses are women too, and he reckons that precisely for the sake of women they have helped him to write the *Decameron*, contrarily to his enemies' scorn for this book; he is quite confident that he will find greater riches in literature than many a wealthy man does in his treasures, metaphorically and, a little, even literally; let them produce the originals and show him that he did not respect their integrity.[6] In conclusion, from now on he will be more determined than ever to tread his path, for all objections in the end amount to nothing more than charging him with operating *according to nature.* * * * Of course, some people have—or pretend to have—the strength to resist nature. Well, he doesn't. As a matter of fact, if he had it, he had rather lend it to someone else than use it for himself. Boccaccio then cuts his eloquent self-defense short by summarily rejecting any concern on his part for 'supernature,' and he rejects it with irony and sarcasm. He takes the goodness of life's pleasures for granted. Actually, everybody does so in practice, Boccaccio hints on the sly in closing. It is only a matter of choosing the good or the bad pleasures, the natural or the unnatural ones. * * *

But in the first two objections there lay hidden another, and most important question. Boccaccio's whole career had been placed under the aegis of 'feminine' muses. Both the form and the subject matter of his tales and romances had often, and avowedly, been conditioned by the needs, and directed to please the taste,

6. As to the association of Muses with femininity, L. Russo, *Letture critiche del Decameron* (Bari, 1956), pp. 1–8, contends that the women to whom B. addressed himself as his audience are the very symbol of the Muses, and extends this personal interpretation to point out how with B. art thus ceases to have a mystic purpose and object and at last takes a purely human direction.

of a feminine audience. Dante himself had already justified the use of the vernacular in literature addressed to women. Nor was the appeal to a feminine audience a mere rhetorical convention. Indeed, at the base of courtly love lay the hopes and aspirations of women, who had been the center of inspiration and the intended audience of most of that literature. We have seen how Chrétien de Troyes seemed to have some misgivings about his woman-centered *Lancelot*, so that he took pains to warn his readers that plot and treatment had been dictated to him by Marie de Champagne, his patroness. * * * Indeed, the historians of this genre well know how close women have been to the novel as readers, critics, and authors. But these historians have never gone, to my knowledge, farther back than the seventeenth-century French novel in this regard. The problem is, as we are now ready to see, much older. The role of the modern novel, this most 'democratic' and woman-oriented of all literary forms, was fulfilled in the Middle Ages by the 'romances' and various forms of 'tales' as well. * * * Similarly, in the seventeenth and eighteenth centuries, the literary enemies of the novel were often conservative moralists of anti-feminist sentiments, who were worried about the alleged corruption of tastes and mores brought about by the social tyranny of women and the authors' catering to their whims. Such were, undoubtedly, Boccaccio's critics, and we are therefore fully entitled to give this Proem a high place in the centuries-old *querelle des femmes*. Concurrently, from a more literary viewpoint, the critics of the novel, like those of the *Decameron* and of much of earlier narrative, turned up their noses at these Cinderellas of literature, popular but lowly, frivolous, unlearned, and, last but not least, such that on them an author could not even make a decent living.

* * *

WAYNE BOOTH

[Telling and Showing in Boccaccio's *Decameron*] †

* * *

Our task will be simpler if we begin with some stories written long before anyone worried very much about cleaning out the

† From Wayne Booth, *The Rhetoric of Fiction*, copyright © 1961 by The University of Chicago. Reprinted with permission of the University of Chicago Press. Recent narrative theory has sometimes tended to maintain that the presence of the narrator in a fictional work should be as unobtrusive as possible, following the examples of the styles of Gustave Flaubert or Henry James. But, as Wayne C. Booth demonstrates in a section of his very influential work, *The Rhetoric of Fiction* (Chicago: University of Chicago Press,

244 · Wayne Booth

rhetorical impurities from the house of fiction. The stories in Boccaccio's *Decameron*, for example, seem extremely simple—perhaps
even simple-minded and inept—if we ask of them the questions
which many modern stories invite us to ask. It is bad enough that
the characters are what we call two-dimensional, with no revealed
depths of any kind; what is much worse, the "point of view" of
the narrator shifts among them with a total disregard for the kind
of technical focus or consistency generally admired today. But if
we read these stories in their own terms, we soon discover a splendid and complex skill underlying the simplicity of the effect.

The material of the ninth story of the fifth day is in itself conventional and shallow indeed. There was once a young lover,
Federigo, who impoverished himself courting a chaste married
woman, Monna Giovanna. Rejected, he withdrew to a life of poverty, with only a beloved falcon remaining of all his former possessions. The woman's husband died. Her son, who had grown fond
of Federigo's falcon, became seriously ill and asked Monna to
obtain the falcon for his comfort. She reluctantly went to Federigo
to request the falcon. Federigo was overwhelmed with excitement
by her visit, and he was determined, in spite of his poverty, to
entertain her properly. But his cupboard was bare, so he killed the
falcon and served it to her. They discovered their misunderstand-
ing, and the mother returned empty-handed to her boy, who soon
died. But the childless widow, impressed by Federigo's generous
gesture in offering his falcon, chose him for her second husband.

Such a story, reduced in this way to a bare outline, could have
been made into any number of fully realized plots with radically
different effects. It could have been a farce, stressing Federigo's
foolish extravagance, his ridiculous antics in trying to think of
something to serve his beloved for breakfast, and the absurdity of
the surprise ending. It could have been a meditative or a comic
piece on the ironical twists of fate, emphasizing the transformation
in Monna from proud resistance to quick surrender—something on
the order of Christopher Fry's *A Phoenix Too Frequent* as derived
from Petronius. It could have been a sardonic tale written from the
point of view of the husband and son who, like the falcon, must
be killed off, as it were, to make the survivors happy. And so on.

As it is, every stroke is in a direction different from these. The
finished tale is designed to give the reader the greatest possible
pleasure in the sympathetic comedy of Monna's and Federigo's deserved good fortune, to make the reader delight in this instance of
the announced theme for all the tales told on the fifth day: "good

---

1967), such a modern view of the narrator's proper function is only a recent
development and would not permit a
proper appreciation of older works like

The Decameron. This consideration of
Boccaccio's narrative technique is taken
from pp. 9–16.

fortune befalling lovers after divers direful or disastrous adventures." [1] Though one never views these characters or their "direful or disastrous adventures" in anything like a tragic light, and though, in fact, one laughs at the excesses of Federigo's passion and at his willingness to pursue it even to poverty, our laughter must always be sympathetic. Much as Federigo deserves his disasters, in the finished tale he also deserves the supreme good fortune of winning Monna.

To insure our pleasure in such an outcome—a pleasure which might have been mild indeed considering that there are nine other tales attempting something like the same effect—the two main characters must be established with great precision. First the heroine, Monna Giovanna, must be felt to be thoroughly worthy of Federigo's "extravagant" love. In a longer, different kind of story, this might have been done by showing her in virtuous action; one could take whatever space were required for episodes dramatizing her as worthy of Federigo's fantastic devotion. But here economy is at least as important as precision. And the economical method of imposing her virtues on the reader is for the narrator to *tell* us about them, supporting his telling with some judiciously chosen, and by modern standards very brief and unrealistic, episodes. These can be of two kinds, either in the form of what James was later to call "going behind" to reveal the true workings of the heroine's mind and heart or in the form of overt action. Thus, the narrator begins by describing her as the "fairest" and "most elegant," and as "no less virtuous than fair." In a simple story of this kind, her beauty and elegance require for validation no more than Federigo's dramatized passion. Our belief in her virtue, however—certainly in Boccaccio a more unlikely gift than beauty and elegance—is supported both by her sustained chastity in the face of his courtship and, far more important, by the quality of what is revealed whenever we enter her thoughts.

> Whereupon the lady was silent a while, bethinking her what she should do. She knew that Federigo had long loved her, and had never had so much as a single kind look from her: wherefore she said to herself:—How can I send or go to beg of him this falcon, which by what I hear is the best that ever flew, and moreover is his sole comfort? And how could I be so unfeeling as to seek to deprive a gentleman of the one solace that is now left him? And so, albeit she very well knew that she might have the falcon for the asking, she was perplexed, and knew not what to say, and gave her son no answer. At length, however, the love she bore the boy carried the day, and she made up her mind, for his contentment . . . to go herself and fetch him the falcon.

1. Trans. J. M. Rigg (Everyman ed., 1930). All quotations are from this edition.

The interest in this passage lies of course in the moral choice that it presents and in the effect upon our sentiments that is implicit in that choice. Though the choice is in one respect a relatively trivial one, it is far more important than most choices faced by the characters who people Boccaccio's world. Dramatized at greater length, it could in fact have been made into the central episode for the story—though the story that resulted would be a far different one from what we now have. As it is treated here, the choice is given precisely the degree of importance it should have in the whole. Because we experience Monna's thoughts and feelings at first hand, we are forced to agree with the narrator's assessment of her great worth. She is not simply virtuous in conventional matters like chastity, but she is also capable of moral delicacy in more fundamental matters: unlike the majority of Boccaccio's women, she is above any casual manipulation of her lover for her own purposes. Even this delicacy, admirable in itself, can be overridden by a more important value, "the love she bore the boy." Yet all this is kept strictly serviceable to our greater interest in Federigo and the falcon; there is never any question of our becoming sidetracked into deep psychological or sentimental involvement with her as a person.

Because the narrator has *told* us what to think of her, and then *shown* her briefly in support of his claims, all the while keeping our sympathy and admiration carefully subordinated to the comic effect of the whole, we can move to the most important episode with our expectations clear and—in their own kind—intense. We can move to Monna's relatively long and wonderfully delicate speech to Federigo requesting the falcon, with our hopes centered clearly on the "good fortune" of their ultimate union.

If all this skilful presentation of the admirable Monna is to succeed, we must see Federigo himself as an equally admirable, though not really heroic, figure. Too much moral stature will spoil the comedy; too little will destroy our desire for his success. It is not enough to show his virtues through his actions; his only admirable act is the gift of the falcon and that might be easily interpreted in itself as a further bit of foolish extravagance. Unless the story is to be lengthened unduly with episodes showing that he is worthy, in spite of his extravagance, the narrator must give us briefly and directly the necessary information about his true character. He is therefore described, unobtrusively but in terms that only an omniscient narrator could use with success, as "gallant," "full of courtesy," "patient," and most important of all, as "more in love than ever before"; the world of *his* desires is thus set off distinctly from the world of many of the other tales, where love is reduced for comic purposes to lust.

These completely straightforward statements of the narrator's opinions are supported by what we see of Federigo's own mind. His comic distress over not having anything to feed his beloved visitor, and his unflinching sacrifice of the bird, are rendered in intimate detail, with frequent—though by modern standards certainly shallow—inside views; his poverty "was brought home to him," he was "distressed beyond measure," he "inwardly" cursed "his evil fortune." "Sorely he longed that the lady might not leave his house altogether unhonoured, and yet to crave help of his own husbandman was more than his pride could brook." All this insures that the wonderful comedy of the breakfast will be the comedy of sympathetic laughter: we are throughout completely in favor of Federigo's suit. And our favor is heightened by the method of presenting the scene of discovery. "No sooner had Federigo apprehended what the lady wanted, than, *for grief that 'twas not in his power to serve her* . . . he fell a-weeping. . . ." At first Monna supposed that " 'twas only because he was loath to part with the brave falcon that he wept." We might have made the same mistake but for the author's help provided in the clause I have italicized.

Once we have become assured of his character in this way, Federigo's speeches, like Monna Giovanna's, become the equivalent of inside views, because we know that everything he says is a trustworthy reflection of his true state of mind. His long speech of explanation about the falcon serves, as a result, to confirm all we have learned of him; when he concludes, "I doubt I shall never know peace of mind more," we believe in his sincerity, though of course we know with complete certainty, and have known from the beginning, that the story is to end with "good fortune."

Having seen this much, we need little more. To make Monna the heiress as provided in the will, her son must die in a passage only one or two lines longer than the one or two lines earlier given to the death of the husband. Her "inward commendation" of Federigo's "magnanimity" leads her to the decision to marry him rather than a wealthy suitor: "I had rather have a man without wealth than wealth without a man." Federigo *is* a man, as we know by now. Though his portrait is conventional, "flat," "two-dimensional," it includes everything we need. We can thus accept without irony the narrator's concluding judgment that married to such a wife he lived happily to the end of his days. Fiammetta's auditors all "praised God that He had worthily rewarded Federigo."

If we share in the pleasure of seeing the comic but worthy hero worthily rewarded, the reason is thus not to be found in any inherent quality of the materials but rather in the skilful construction of a living plot out of materials that might have been used in many different ways. The deaths of the husband and son, which in the finished version are merely conveniences for Federigo's exaltation, would in any truly impartial account occupy considerably more space than Federigo's anxiety over not having anything to serve his mistress. Treated impartially, the boy's death would certainly be dramatized as fully as the mother's hesitation about troubling Federigo for his falcon. But the demands of this plot are for a technique that wins us to Federigo's side.

Quite obviously this technique cannot be judged by modern standards of consistency; the story could not have been written from a consistent point of view without stretching it to three times its present length and thereby losing its taut comic force. To tell it entirely through Federigo's eyes would require a much longer introductory section, and the comedy of the visit to fetch the falcon would be partially lost if we did not see more of the preparation for it than Federigo can possibly be aware of. Yet since it is primarily Federigo's story, to see it through Monna's eyes would require a great deal of manipulation and extension. Such conjectural emendations are in a way absurd, since they almost certainly would never have occurred to Boccaccio. But they help to make emphatic the great gap that separates Boccaccio's technique from the more obviously rigorous methods we have come to look for. In this story there is no important revelation of truth, no intensity of illusion, no ironic complexity, no prophetic vision, no rich portrayal of moral ambiguities. There is some incidental irony, it is true, but the greatness of the whole resides in unequivocal intensity not of illusion but of comic delight produced in extraordinarily brief compass.

Any temptation we might have to attribute its success to unconscious or accidental primitivism can be dispelled by looking at the radically different experience offered by other tales. Since his different effects are based on different moral codes, Boccaccio can never assume that his readers will hold precisely the correct attitudes as they approach any one story. He certainly does not assume that his readers will approve of the license of his most licentious tales. Even Dioneo, the most lewd of all the ten narrators, must spend a good deal of energy manipulating us into the camp of those who can laugh with a clear conscience at his bawdy and often cruel stories. In the potentially distressing tale of how the holy man, Rustico, debauches the young and innocent Alibech by teaching her how to put the devil in hell (third day, tenth tale), great care is taken with the character and ultimate fate of the simple-minded girl in order to lead us to laugh at conduct that in most worlds, including the world in which Boccaccio lived, would be considered cruel and sacrilegious rather than comic.

If Dioneo, the lusty young courtier, must use care with his rhetoric in a bawdy tale, Fiammetta, the lovely lady, must use even more when she comes to praise infidelity. On the seventh day the subject is "the tricks which, either for love or for their deliverance from peril, ladies have heretofore played their husbands, and whether they were by the said husbands detected, or no." In "The Falcon" Fiammetta worked to build admiration for the virtue of Federigo and Monna Giovanna; she now (fifth tale) employs a different rhetoric. Since her task is to insure our delight in the punishment of a justifiably jealous husband, her commentary tells us directly what is borne out by our views of the husband's mind: he is "a poor creature, and of little sense" who deserves what he gets. More important, she prefaces the story with a little oration, about one-seventh of the length of the whole story, setting our values straight: "For which reason, to sum up, I say that a wife is rather to be commended than censured, if she take her revenge upon a husband that is jealous without cause."

In support of this general argument, the whole tale is manipulated in such a way as to make the reader desire the comic punishment of the husband. Most of it is seen through the eyes of the woman, with great stress on her comic suffering at the hands of the great bullying fool. The climax is his full punishment, in the form of a clever, lashing speech from his wife. Few readers can feel that he has received anything but what he deserves when Fiammetta concludes that the cuckold's wife has now earned her "charter of indulgence."

These extremes by no means exhaust the variety of norms that we are led to accept by the shifting rhetoric as we move through the *Decameron.* The standards of judgment change so radically, in fact, that it is difficult to discern any figure in Boccaccio's carpet.[2] I shall try later on to deal with some of the issues raised when an author heightens specific effects at the expense of his general notions of moral truth or reality. What is important here is to recognize the radical inadequacy of the telling-showing distinction in dealing with the practice of this one author. Boccaccio's artistry lies not in adherence to any one supreme manner of narration but rather in his ability to order various forms of telling in the service of various forms of showing.

* * *

2. Erich Auerbach, for example, complains that he can find no basic moral attitude and no clear approach to reality lying back of all the tales. So long as he considers what Boccaccio does "for the sake of comic effect," he has nothing but praise for his "critical sense" of the world, "firm yet elastic in perspective, which, without abstract moralizing, allots phenomena their specific, carefully nuanced moral value" (*Mimesis: The Representation of Reality in Western Literature* [Berne, 1946], trans. Willard Trask [Anchor Books ed., 1957], p. 193). It is only on the level of the most general qualities, common to all the stories despite the differing needs of the moment, that Auerbach encounters difficulties and complains of the "vagueness and uncertainty" of Boccaccio's "early humanism" (p. 202). Auerbach's account is invaluable in showing how Boccaccio's style, in so far as it is common to all of the tales, serves as a kind of rhetoric convincing the reader of the reality of his world.

TZVETAN TODOROV

Structural Analysis of Narrative †

The theme I propose to deal with is so vast that the few pages which follow will inevitably take the form of a resumé. My title, moreover, contains the word "structural," a word more misleading than enlightening today. To avoid misunderstandings as much as possible, I shall proceed in the following fashion. First, I shall give an abstract description of what I conceive to be the structural approach to literature. This approach will then be illustrated by a concrete problem, that of narrative, and more specifically, that of plot. The examples will all be taken from the *Decameron* of Boccaccio. Finally, I shall attempt to make several general conclusions about the nature of narrative and the principles of its analysis.

First of all, one can contrast two possible attitudes toward literature: a theoretical attitude and a descriptive attitude. The nature of structural analysis will be essentially theoretical and non-descriptive; in other words, the aim of such a study will never be the description of a concrete work. The work will be considered as the manifestation of an abstract structure, merely one of its possible realizations; an understanding of that structure will be the real goal of structural analysis. Thus, the term "structure" has, in this case, a logical rather than spatial significance.

Another opposition will enable us to focus more sharply on the critical position which concerns us. If we contrast the internal approach to a literary work with the external one, structural analysis would represent an internal approach. This opposition is well known to literary critics, and Wellek and Warren have used it as the basis for their *Theory of Literature*. It is necessary, however, to recall it here, because, in labeling all structural analysis "theoretical," I clearly come close to what is generally termed an "external" approach (in imprecise usage, "theoretical" and "external," on the one hand, and "descriptive" and "internal," on the other, are synonyms). For example, when Marxists or psychoanalysts deal with a work of literature, they are not interested in a knowledge of the work itself, but in the understanding of an abstract structure,

† One of the indications of Boccaccio's continuing relevance to modern culture is the variety of critical approaches contemporary critics employ to explain his style. Recently, the theory of narrative has been enriched by insights from two European schools of criticism—the Russian formalist group and the structuralists of France and, to a lesser extent, Italy. Tzvetan Todorov's work combines influences of both critical tendencies, and one of his most important works (originally published in French) is devoted entirely to a structural analysis of Boccaccio's prose masterpiece. This essay is a brief explanation of the structural method as applied to *The Decameron* and originally appeared in *Novel: A Forum for Fiction* 3 (1969), 70–76, as translated by Arnold Weinstein. Reprinted with permission.

social or psychic, which manifests itself through that work. This attitude is therefore both theoretical and external. On the other hand, a New Critic (imaginary) whose approach is obviously internal, will have no goal other than an understanding of the work itself; the result of his efforts will be a paraphrase of the work, which is supposed to reveal the meaning better than the work itself.

Structural analysis differs from both of these attitudes. Here we can be satisfied neither by a pure description of the work nor by its interpretation in terms that are psychological or sociological or, indeed, philosophical. In other words, structural analysis coincides (in its basic tenets) with theory, with poetics of literature. Its object is the literary discourse rather than works of literature, literature that is virtual rather than real. Such analysis seeks no longer to articulate a paraphrase, a rational resumé of the concrete work, but to propose a theory of the structure and operation of the literary discourse, to present a spectrum of literary possibilities, in such a manner that the existing works of literature appear as particular instances that have been realized.

It must immediately be added that, in practice, structural analysis will also refer to real works: the best stepping-stone toward theory is that of precise, empirical knowledge. But such analysis will discover in each work what it has in common with others (study of genres, of periods, for example), or even with all other works (theory of literature); it would be unable to state the individual specificity of each work. In practice, it is always a question of going continually back and forth, from abstract literary properties to individual works and vice versa. Poetics and description are in fact two complementary activities.

On the other hand, to affirm the internal nature of this approach does not mean a denial of the relation between literature and other homogeneous series, such as philosophy or social life. It is rather a question of establishing a hierarchy: literature must be understood in its specificity, as literature, before we seek to determine its relation with anything else.

It is easily seen that such a conception of literary analysis owes much to the modern notion of science. It can be said that structural analysis of literature is a kind of propaedeutic for a future science of literature. This term "science," used with regard to literature, usually raises a multitude of protests. It will therefore perhaps be fitting to try to answer some of those protests right now.

Let us first of all reread that page from Henry James's famous essay on "The Art of Fiction," which already contains several criticisms: "Nothing, for instance, is more possible than that he [the novelist] be of a turn of mind for which this odd, literal opposition of description and dialogue, incident and description, has little meaning and light. People often talk of these things as if they had a kind of internecine distinctness, instead of melting into each other at every breath, and being intimately associated parts of one general effort of expression. I cannot imagine composition existing in a series of blocks, nor conceive, in any novel worth discussing at all, of a passage of description that is not in its intention narrative, a passage of dialogue that is not in its intention descriptive, a touch of truth of any sort that does not partake of the nature of incident, or an incident that derives its interest from any other source than the general and only source of the success of a work of art—that of being illustrative. A novel is a living thing, all one and continuous, like any other organism, and in proportion as it lives will it be found, I think, that in each of the parts there is something of each of the other parts. The critic who over the close texture of a finished work shall pretend to trace a geography of items will mark some frontiers as artificial, I fear, as any that have been known to history."

In this excerpt, the critic who uses such terms as "description," "narration," "dialogue," is accused by Henry James of committing two sins. First, there will never be found, in a real text, a pure dialogue, a pure description, and so on. Secondly, the very use of these terms is unnecessary, even harmful, since the novel is "a living thing, all one and continuous."

The first objection loses all its weight as soon as we put ourselves in the perspective of structural analysis; although it does aim at an understanding of concepts like "description" or "action," there is no need to find them in a pure state. It seems rather natural that abstract concepts cannot be analyzed directly, at the level of empirical reality. In physics, for example, we speak of a property such as temperature although we are unable to isolate it by itself and are forced to observe it in bodies possessing many other qualities also, like resistance and volume. Temperature is a theoretical concept, and it does not need to exist in a pure state; such is also true for description.

The second objection is still more curious. Let us consider the already dubious comparison between a work and a living thing. We all know that any part of our body will contain blood, nerves, muscles—all at the same time; we nonetheless do not require the biologist to abandon these misleading abstractions, designated by the words: blood, nerves, muscles. The fact that we find them together does not prevent us from distinguishing them. If the first argument of James had a positive aspect (it indicated that our objective should be composed of abstract categories and not concrete works), the second represents an absolute refusal to recognize the existence of abstract categories, of whatever is not visible.

There is another very popular argument against the introduction of scientific principles in literary analysis. We are told in this instance that science must be objective, whereas the interpretation of literature is always subjective. In my opinion this crude opposition is untenable. The critic's work can have varying degrees of subjectivity; everything depends on the perspective he has chosen. This degree will be much lower if he tries to ascertain the properties of the work rather than seeking its significance for a given period or milieu. The degree of subjectivity will vary, moreover, when he is examining different strata of the same work. There will be very few discussions concerning the metrical or phonic scheme of a poem; slightly more concerning the nature of its images; still more with regard to the more complex semantic patterns.

On the other hand there is no social science (or science whatsoever) which is totally free of subjectivity. The very choice of one group of theoretical concepts instead of another presupposes a subjective decision; but if we do not make this choice, we achieve nothing at all. The economist, the anthropologist, and the linguist must be subjective also; the only difference is that they are aware of it and they try to limit this subjectivity, to make allowance for it within the theory. One can hardly attempt to repudiate the subjectivity of the social sciences at a time when even the natural sciences are affected by it.

It is now time to stop these theoretical speculations and to give an example of the structural approach to literature. This example will serve as illustration rather than proof: the theories which I have just exposed will not be necessarily contested if there are some imperfections in the concrete analysis based on them.

The abstract literary concept I would like to discuss is that of plot. Of course, that does not mean that literature, for me, is reduced to plot alone. I do think, however, that plot is a notion that critics undervalue and, hence, often disregard. The ordinary reader, however, reads a book above all as the narration of a plot; but this naive reader is uninterested in theoretical problems. My aim is to suggest a certain number of useful categories for examining and describing plots. These categories can thus implement the meager vocabulary at our command with regard to the analysis of narrative; it consists of such terms as action, character, recognition.

The literary examples that I shall use are taken from the *Decameron* of Boccaccio. I do not intend, however, to give an analysis of the *Decameron*: these stories will be used only to display an abstract literary structure, that is, plot. I shall begin by stating the plots of several of the tales.

A monk introduces a young girl into his cell and makes love to her. The abbot detects this misbehavior and plans to punish him severely. But the monk learns of the abbot's discovery and lays a trap for him by leaving his cell. The abbot goes in and succumbs to the charms of the girl, while the monk tries his turn at watching. At the end when the abbot intends to punish him, the monk points out that he has just committed the same sin. Result: the monk is not punished (I,4).

Isabetta, a young nun, is with her lover in her cell. Upon discovering this, the other nuns become jealous and go to wake up the abbess and have Isabetta punished. But the abbess was in bed with an abbot; because she has to come out quickly, she puts the under-shorts of the abbot on her head instead of her coif. Isabetta is led into the church; as the abbess begins to lecture her, Isabetta notices the garment on her head. She brings this evidence to everyone's attention and thus escapes punishment (IX,2).

Peronella receives her lover while her husband, a poor mason, is absent. But one day he comes home early. Peronella hides the lover in a cask; when the husband comes in, she tells him that somebody wanted to buy the cask and that this somebody is now in the process of examining it. The husband believes her and is delighted with the sale. The lover pays and leaves with the cask (VII,2).

A married woman meets her lover every night in the family's country house, where she is usually alone. But one night the husband returns from town; the lover has not come yet; he arrives a little later and knocks at the door. The wife asserts that this is a ghost who comes to annoy her every night and must be exorcised. The husband pronounces the formula which the wife has improvised; the lover figures out the situation and leaves, pleased with the ingenuity of his mistress (VII,1).

It is easy to recognize that these four plots (and there are many others like them in the *Decameron*) have something in common. In order to express that, I shall use a schematic formulation which retains only the common elements of these plots. The sign ➔ will indicate a relation of entailment between two actions.

X violates a law ➔ Y must punish X ➔ X tries to avoid being punished ➔

➔ $\left\{ \begin{array}{l} \text{Y violates a law} \\ \\ \text{Y believes that X is not violating the law} \end{array} \right.$ ➔ Y does not punish X

This schematic representation requires several explanations.

1. We first notice that the minimal schema of the plot can be shown naturally by a clause. Between the categories of language and those of narrative there is a profound analogy which must be explored.

2. Analysis of this narrative clause leads us to discover the

existence of two entities which correspond to the "parts of speech."
a) The agents, designated here by X and Y, correspond to proper
nouns. They serve as subject or object of the clause; moreover,
they permit identification of their reference without its being described. b) The predicate, which is always a verb here: violate,
punish, avoid. The verbs have a semantic characteristic in common: they denote an action which modifies the preceding situation. c) An analysis of other stories would have shown us a third
part of narrative speech, which corresponds to quality and does not
alter the situation in which it appears: the adjective. Thus in I,8:
at the beginning of the action Ermino is stingy, whereas Guillaume is generous. Guillaume finds a way to ridicule Ermino's
stinginess, and since then Ermino is "the most generous and
pleasant of gentlemen." The qualities of the two characters are
examples of adjectives.

3. Actions (violate, punish) can have a positive or a negative
form; thus, we shall also need the category of status, negation being
one possible status.

4. The category of modality is also relevant here. When we say
"X must punish Y," we denote thereby an action which has not
yet taken place (in the imaginary universe of the story) but which
is nonetheless present in a virtual state. André Jolles suggested
that entire genres could be characterized by their mood; legends
would be the genre of the imperative, to the extent that they offer
us an example to follow; the fairy tale is, as is often said, the genre
of the optative, of the fulfilled wish.

5. When we write "Y believes that X is not violating the law,"
we have an example of a verb ("believe") which differs from the
others. It is not a question of a different action here but of a
different perception of the same action. We could therefore speak
of a kind of "point of view" which refers not only to the relation
between reader and narrator, but also to the characters.

6. There are also relations between the clauses; in our example
this is always a causal relation; but a more extensive study would
distinguish at least between entailment and presupposition (for
example, the relation introducing modal punishment). Analysis of
other stories shows that there are also purely temporal relations
(succession) and purely spatial ones (parallelism).

7. An organized succession of clauses forms a new syntagmatic
pattern, sequence. Sequence is perceived by the reader as a finished story; it is the minimal narrative in a completed form. This
impression of completion is caused by a modified repetition of the
initial clause; the first and the last clause will be identical but they
will either have a different mood or status, for instance, or they
will be seen from different points of view. In our example it is
punishment which is repeated: first changed in modality, then

denied. In a sequence of temporal relations, repetition can be total.

8. We might also ask: is there a way back? How does one get from the abstract, schematic representation to the individual fate? Here, there are three answers:

a) The same kind of organization can be studied at a more concrete level: each clause of our sequence could be rewritten as an entire sequence itself. We would not thereby change the nature of the analysis, but rather the level of generality.

b) It is also possible to study the concrete actions that incorporate our abstract pattern. For instance, we may point out the different laws that become violated in the stories of the *Decameron* or the different punishments that are meted out. That would be a thematic study.

c) Finally, we can examine the verbal medium which composes our abstract patterns. The same action can be expressed by means of dialogue or description, figurative or literal discourse; moreover, each action can be seen from a different point of view. Here we are dealing with a rhetorical study.

These three directions correspond to the three major categories of narrative analysis: study of narrative syntax, study of theme, study of rhetoric.

At this point we may ask: what is the purpose of all this? Has this analysis taught us anything about the stories in question? But that would be a bad question. Our goal is not a knowledge of the *Decameron* (although such analysis will also serve that purpose), but rather an understanding of literature or, in this specific instance, of plot. The categories of plot mentioned here will permit a more extensive and precise description of other plots. The object of our study must be narrative mood, or point of view, or sequence, and not this or that story in and for itself.

From such categories we can move forward and inquire about the possibility of a typology of plots. For the moment it is difficult to offer a valid hypothesis; therefore I must be content to summarize the results of my research on the *Decameron*.

The minimal complete plot can be seen as the shift from one equilibrium to another. This term "equilibrium," which I am borrowing from genetic psychology, means the existence of a stable but not static relation between the members of a society; it is a social law, a rule of the game, a particular system of exchange. The two moments of equilibrium, similar and different, are separated by a period of imbalance, which is composed of a process of degeneration and a process of improvement.

All of the stories of the *Decameron* can be entered into this very broad schema. From that point, however, we can make a distinction between two kinds of stories. The first can be labeled "avoided punishment"; the four stories I mentioned at the beginning are examples of it. Here we follow a complete cycle: we begin with a state of equilibrium which is broken by a violation of the law. Punishment would have restored the initial balance; the fact that punishment is avoided establishes a new equilibrium.

The other type of story is illustrated by the tale about Ermino (I,8), which we may label "conversion." This story begins in the middle of a complete cycle, with a state of imbalance created by a flaw in one of the characters. The story is basically the description of an improvement process—until the flaw is no longer there.

The categories which help us to describe these types tell us much about the universe of a book. With Boccaccio, the two equilibriums symbolize (for the most part) culture and nature, the social and the individual; the story usually consists in illustrating the superiority of the second term over the first.

We could also seek even greater generalizations. It is possible to contrast a specific plot typology with a game typology and to see them as two variants of a common structure. So little has been done in this direction that we do not even know what kinds of questions to ask.[1]

I would like to return now to the beginning argument and to look at the initial question again: what is the object of structural analysis of literature (or, if you wish, of poetics)? At first glance, it is literature or, as Jakobson would have said, literariness. But let us look more closely. In our discussion of literary phenomena, we have had to introduce a certain number of notions and to create an image of literature; this image constitutes the constant preoccupation of all research on poetics. "Science is concerned not with things but with the system of signs it can substitute for things," wrote Ortega y Gasset. The virtualities which make up the object of poetics (as of all other sciences), these abstract qualities of literature exist only in the discourse of poetics itself. From this perspective, literature becomes only a mediator, a language, which poetics uses for dealing with itself.

We must not, however, conclude that literature is secondary for poetics or that it is not, in a certain sense, the object of poetics. Science is characterized precisely by this ambiguity concerning its object, an ambiguity that need not be resolved, but rather used as the basis for analysis. Poetics, like literature, consists of an uninterrupted movement back and forth between the two poles: the first is auto-reference, preoccupation with itself; the second is what we usually call its object.

---

1. A few bibliographical suggestions: I deal more at length with the same problems in the chapter "Poétique" of the collective work *Qu'est-ce que le structuralisme?* (Paris: Editions du Seuil, 1968); and in my book *Grammaire du* *Décaméron* (The Hague: Mouton, 1969). Several studies using a similar perspective have been published in the periodical *Communications* (Paris, Editions du Seuil), Nos. 4, 8, 11 (articles of Barthes, Bremond, Genette, etc.).

There is a practical conclusion to be drawn from these speculations. In poetics as elsewhere, discussions of methodology are not
a minor area of the larger field, a kind of accidental by-product:
they are rather its very center, its principal goal. As Freud said,
"The important thing in a scientific work is not the nature of the
facts with which it is concerned, but the rigor, the exactness of
the method which is prior to the establishment of these facts, and
the research of a synthesis as large as possible."

ROBERT J. CLEMENTS

Anatomy of the Novella †

In the informative introduction to his collection of Italianate
tales, entitled *The Palace of Pleasure*, Maurice Valency notes that
"the term *novella* has no great precision in Italian." After a discussion of the ambiguity of the term, he concludes, "Chiefly we
apply it to prose tales of the Renaissance, and we feel most secure
in its use when those stories are of Italian origin or of Italian cut."
After proceeding to enumerate *novella* collections from mediaeval
Italy to Elizabethan England, he leaves his reader with a general
idea of this narrative form: a tale strong on plot, humor, and satire
although weaker in psychological depth, character delineation, background description, or personal involvement of the author.

The term *novella* is indeed one of the most ill-defined and mis-
used in literary history. When Hemingway's *Old Man and the Sea*,
a narrative of 27,000 words, was twice reviewed in a single issue of
the *New York Times Book Review*, both reviewers referred to it
as a *novella*. Of the several cognates of this noun in the European
languages, including *nouvelle* and *novela*, only two non-English
forms have become a permanent part of our literary vocabulary.
These are *Novelle* (German) and *novella* (Italian). Whereas *Novelle* may by extension refer to a short story, it is traditionally the
novelette form which allowed such nineteenth-century figures as
Storm and Keller plenty of space to swell their tales with background atmosphere, nature feeling, sentimental evocation of a
Christmas marzipan or a boyhood kiss, and the eternal round of
the four seasons. If we borrow the German term *Novelle*, it can be
useful only in this special native acceptance. Indeed, it defines this
post-Romantic type of narrative with the greatest possible economy. The same holds true for our adopting the Italian form *no-*

† While the Italian *novella* may have
some characteristics in common with our
modern short story, it nevertheless differs from the short story in several important ways, as this analysis of the
novella's structure and literary history
underlines. The essay originally appeared
in *Comparative Literature Studies* 9
(1972), 3–16. Copyright © 1972 by The
Board of Trustees of the University of
Illinois. Reprinted with permission.

vella, the definition of which will emerge hopefully with greater precision after the following anatomy.

The *novella* structure which the Italians perfected (after a retrospective glance at several Oriental archetypes) spread over Western Europe and retained its identity until the seventeenth century. In addressing myself to this structure—or cut, as Valency puts it—of the *novella*, I shall comment in turn on four of its most characteristic elements: the cornice, the days-nights unity, the word-length, and its separable components of theme and subject matter. These few pages will then close with some generalities on the *novella* as an autonomous genre.

I. The Cornice

The cornice, framework, or binding situation goes back of course to such ancient tale-sequences as *The Seven Sages* and *The Thousand and One Nights*. The drama of the unjustly condemned prince Florentine, in the former work, rivals in interest the tales told by the king's counselors. Similarly, one's concern over the fate of Scheherezade in the clutches of the cruel, sadistic Shahriyar is just as suspenseful as any elicited by the tales themselves, including Ali Baba's perils with the thieves. It is natural for one to conclude from the vividness of these cornices that they themselves are popular tales—that, for example, *The Book of Sindibad* may be (as Clouston alleges) an episode out of the life of Osaka, the defender of Buddhism. With the exception of the *Decameron* and especially *The Canterbury Tales*, the cornice does not so firmly hold our attention in the derivative *novella* collections of the Middle Ages and the Renaissance. In Chaucer (who modified the *novella* tradition in several fundamental ways) the enmity of the Reeve and the Miller, like that of the Friar and the Summoner, not only holds our attention, but motivates the themes of the stories they are to tell.

Usually the contents of the Italianate *novella* are less conditioned by the circumstances surrounding their being told. Since the cornice is so often provided by an unhappy act of God or deed of man—plague, pilgrimage, sea voyage, siege or sack of a city, flood, or the like—it not only serves as *oscuro* to the *chiaro* of the tales, but minimizes the triviality of many of them at a time when literature was supposed to be a handmaid to theology; and Boccaccio is pleading its cause in the epilogue to the *Decameron*. It is worthy of note that whereas Boccaccio, Straparola, and several other *novellieri* were trying to shake off the censor by insisting that their tales were trivial creations to delight women and thus beneath the attention of serious churchmen and scholars, many of them suggested this indirectly by making half or more of their storytellers and listeners women (*Decameron, Heptaméron, Piacevoli notti, Il Pentamerone*, etc.). Basile's ten tales per day are told by ten women, reminding us of the tale-spinning of Leuconoe, Alcithoe, and the other daughters of Minyas in the cornice of Ovid's ever-popular *Metamorphoses* (as described in Book IV).

Ever since *El Conde Lucanor*, set down by Juan Manuel thirteen to twenty years before the appearance of the *Decameron*, the cornice furnished not only seriousness resulting from acts of God or man but supplied a moralizing element as well. The young Count Lucanor keeps consulting his old counselor Patronio on questions of morality and public policy, receiving in return tales and fables illustrative of the issues raised along with austere instruction. In Marguerite de Navarre's *Heptaméron* the storytellers hold the censor at bay by reasoning on the moral lessons to be drawn from the saucy tale which they have just heard.

The cornice is not always, however, of a serious mood, even when set in pestilence, siege, disaster, or pilgrimages. We remember from W. S. Davis's *Life on a Mediaeval Barony* that pilgrimages in the Middle Ages, especially when not imposed as a penance, were festive occasions.[1] The framework sometimes allows for songs, dances, poems, banquets, and even swimming (Boccaccio) as aftermaths or intervals in the story sessions. Straparola's noble company gathered on Murano opened their sessions with "amorose danze" and madrigals. In Basile's group the madrigal becomes an eclogue. The shipboard fugitives of Cinzio, after witnessing the cruel 1527 sack of Rome, are only too happy to welcome such entertainments as songs and dances while their ship moors at the various ports between Civitavecchia and Marseilles.

The cornice would seem an unconscious clue to the oral tradition behind the *novella*, for it usually involves people gathering together for companionship, comfort, commiseration, or entertainment. The apparently real, localized nature of the setting not only makes it more easily acceptable as fact, but also lends greater historicity or authenticity to the tales themselves. Such authenticity is lent as well by the occasional historic figures (there are several in the cornice of the *Piacevoli notti*) who put in an appearance in the framework. Not only may the three-dimensional characters in the cornice experience their autonomous dramas, but they sometimes intrude (like the self-willed personages of Pirandello and Unamuno) upon the fictions themselves. Thus the Franklin interrupts the Squire, and the host dismisses Chaucer's tale about Sir Thopas as so much worthless doggerel.

How reassuring to find ourselves witnesses right within the framework, the contemporary world bequeathing us these tales. Yet when we are denied the privilege of witnessing the social

1. William Stearns Davis, *Life on a Mediaeval Barony* (New York, 1923), pp. 296–300.

circumstances surrounding the telling of the tales, we can only resent the author's excluding us from being allowed to sit in. Thus, Bandello could have further enlivened his tales by recreating those three splendid salons of Ippolita Sforza, Imperia, and Elisabetta Gonzaga at which he had heard and collected them. How much more grateful we are to Straparola, who takes us within the villa of another Sforza—Ottaviano Maria Sforza, heir to the Duchy of Milano and bishop elect of Lodi—so that we may enjoy the scene as well as the licentious stories in his luxurious sanctuary on Murano. In the case of Bandello, we have only fleeting reminiscences of those three salons in the names of the noblemen to whom he dedicated his 230 tales.

When, on the other hand, Cervantes betrayed the epithet of "Spanish Boccaccio" given to him by Tirso and did away with the cornice in his *Novelas ejemplares*, we regretfully note that the framework collection of stories is now on the wane. By the eighteenth century it will be a thing of the past, except for such sporadic revivals as *Tales of a Wayside Inn*. The *Novelas ejemplares*, with their greater length, deeper psychology, and consciously artistic *costumbrismo*, were a resolute departure from Boccaccio and Boccaccio's way of collecting tales. Instead of reproving Cervantes for neglecting the cornice in his *Novelas*, we shall instead be grateful to him for the masterful framework he provided for his *novella* on the "Curioso impertinente."

II. *The Days-Nights Unity*

Along with the unity of place often supplied by the cornice, one usually finds in the *novella* collection a conscious unity of time. Ever since *The Thousand and One Nights* (Burton's title *The Arabian Nights' Entertainments* abandons a tradition), the *novellatori* have tended to incorporate such a time-span into their titles. Not that they always succeeded in writing or collecting enough tales to fill out the announced temporal framework. Typical titles are *Il Decameron, l'Heptaméron, Il Pentamerone* (not the author's original formulation), *Le cento notti*, etc. There is a curious tendency, apparently never studied, among these tale-spinners to relate their temporal strictures to the pre-Lenten or Lenten season. Lucrezia invites her guests in Straparola's *Piacevoli notti* to gather on the last thirteen evenings before Lent, when the licentious tales would coincide with the Carnival spirit. The tales in Il Lasca's *Cene* are narrated on the last three days of Carnival. Similarly María de Zayas is motivated in having her tales told during "the carefree days of the Carnestolendas," that is, the three Carnival days before Ash Wednesday. Yet she, or her editor, subsequently decided to follow the tradition of Boccaccio, and redistributed her ten stories from the original 4-4-2 pattern by assigning one each to ten separate nights.[2] Mariana de Carbajal's *Navidades de Madrid y Noches entretenidas* would seem to promise twelve *novelle* for the wintry Paschal season, although she composed only eight. The ten-day limitation of Boccaccio, as old as the Persian *Bachtiyar-Nama*, generally inspired his followers to imitate not only his time unity, but also his egregious total of stories. Thus the decimal time limit is suggested indirectly by such titles as *Les cent nouvelles nouvelles, Le cento novelle, The Hundred Mery Tales, The Hecatommithi.*

The actual number of days announced in the titles was dictated by several factors. A few authors conceivably wished to avoid the same total utilized by others. The requirement of verisimilitude was another factor, for the total had to correspond logically with the lapse of time for the situation prompting the telling to run its course. Thus ten days was a minimum time span for the black plague to subside in Boccaccio's Florence, but a maximum period, as the King in the last story explains, for the young people to absent themselves from the stricken city. In any case, when one includes the interruption of the holy days, the period of avoiding contagion turns out to be the more adequate fifteen days. Eight days was apparently considered by Chaucer as the minimum period of penance for his pilgrims (who never seem very penitent for that matter), and he planned to bulk out his collection by calling on each pilgrim to tell not two, but four stories:

> That each of you, beguiling the long day,
> Shall tell two stories as you wend your way
> To Canterbury Town; and each of you
> On coming home, shall tell another two.

Sercambi's fleeing peregrines had ample time to exchange 155 tales since they made a circular flight from the plague in Lucca to Naples, Brindisi, Venice, Genoa, and then back to Luni, northwest of Lucca. Similarly, Cinzio's fugitives allow themselves considerable time for their 110 stories on their long sea voyage to Marseilles. Knowing the swift-coursing rivers of the Pyrenees, Marguerite de Navarre knew that eight or ten days at Notre Dame de Serrance would be adequate for the swollen rivers from that watershed to return to normal levels. Even the local workmen focused unconsciously on the time limit of the *Decameron* by assuring the abbé that they could not bridge the local river in fewer than ten or twelve days. In Basile's *Pentamerone* the prince arranges for the lady storytellers to entertain his expectant wife until parturition, due within five days ("che ancora tarderà a sgonfiare la pancia"). The entertainments in Tirso's *Cigarrales de Toledo* were to last

2. Edwin B. Place, *María de Zayas, an Outstanding Woman Short Story Writer of Seventeenth Century Spain,* University of Colorado Studies, XIII (June, 1923), p. 6.

for twenty days of the canicular period, but do not correspond to the "dog days" limits *ab quo* and *ad quem*, 23 July to 2 September.

In general, then, the contemporary concern for verisimilitude made the *novellieri* seek a logical correspondence between the number of tales and the time inevitably elapsing during the cornice situation. Days of idleness, enforced time schedules, holidays, delayed labor pains, and such other exigencies could make the correspondence easier to achieve. We are not deceived, however. Most of the imaginative cornices adopted could have allowed for greater elasticity and more variable duration: plagues, floods, sieges, and most certainly the house party framing Il Lasca's *Cene* or Parabosco's *Diporti*, in which the participants are merely camping out and loafing, fowling, and fishing. These are not cornices of a fixed, predictable duration like a plague of locusts.

III. *The Word Length*

How does one assign an optimum word length to the *novella*? Poe, reviewing Hawthorne's *Twice-Told Tales*, showed how remote the *novella* had become by defining the short story as a prose narrative requiring a half-hour to an hour and a half for its perusal. Few of the earliest *novellatori* honor even this minimum length. The tales of *El Conde Lucanor*, with three exceptions, vary from two to six pages in length. Many of Sacchetti's *novelle*, like those of the *Cento novelle antiche*, *Les cent nouvelles nouvelles*, and *The Hundred Mery Tales*, are little more than anecdotes of fewer than 1000 words. Story eleven of the *Cent nouvelles nouvelles* is limited to 370 words. Story twenty-nine ("The Cow and the Calf") manages to fill out three pages, although its model in the *Cento novelle antiche* totals five short paragraphs. During the last nights, the tales of Straparola's *Piacevoli notti* become quite short, with the prolific Pietro Bembo ironically telling the shortest of all.

It is ironic as well that Cervantes, who was to increase so remarkably the length of the *novella* (even to the extent of padding his "La Gitanilla" with 351 verses of balladry), should have paid lip service to the brevity of his predecessors. For in the "Coloquio de los perros," Cipión urges Berganza, the narrator, not to go on babbling: "Sigue tu historia y no te desvíes del camino carretero con impertinentes digresiones; y así, por largo que sea, la acabarás presto." [3]

For two centuries most *novellieri* respected the word lengths they found in the *Decameron*. Boccaccio had encouraged simplicity of intrigue and brevity of composition by the quick plot summaries which preceded his tales, a curious counterpart to Dante's summary recapitulations of his *Vita Nuova* sonnets. Adapting the

3. Miguel de Cervantes, *Novelas ejemplares* (Barcelona: Editorial Juventud, 1958), p. 229.

novella to various media of narration, Chaucer of necessity varied the length of his well-paced stories. Despite the exceptional length of the Parson's Tale (eighty-three pages in the Nicolson version), that of the Miller with its 700 lines or so probably strikes the average. The length will vary with the verbosity of the teller. It is after Bandello (averaging eight pages) and Marguerite of Navarre (thirty-eight stories of 300-1000 words, one of 12,480 words) that the *novella* becomes extended. The longest story told by Marguerite's aptly-named alter ego Parlamente, on Floride and Amadour, is presented as abridged, "car mon compte seroit assez long pour employer toute une journée." [4] If Tirso in his *Cigarrales* observes conventional length as a rule, his "Don Juan de Salcedo" and "Los tres maridos burlados" attain that of a novelette.

As Caroline Bourland has written, by the time of Cervantes, characterization and psychological justifications of behavior increase wordage, as does the natural desire of an imitator to embroider on his plagiarized model. Cervantes's stories vary in a standard edition of 500 pages from fifteen to seventy. María de Zayas y Sotomayor (1590–1660?), who inspired two lengthy works of Scarron, shows the influence of Cervantes in her title *Novelas amorosas y ejemplares* and in her word lengths, which vary from thirty to forty pages, extensive enough to inspire Ángel Valbuena Prat to call them *novelitas* (here, novelettes).

In England, despite the moderate size of Pettie's stories (16-28 pages), Fenton and Painter expand and dilute the stories they pilfer. Whereas Bandello required 2,300 words to relate the fortunes of Giulia da Gazuolo, Fenton helps himself to 13,000. The French intermediaries had no comparable hand in this amplification. As C. S. Lewis has written, Fenton "loads or stuffs every rift with rhetorical, proverbial, and moral ore." [5] René Pruvost agrees, "Everywhere the situations indicated in a few lines by Bandello are developed at great length; everywhere the heroes launch into long speeches; everywhere an attempt is made at analyzing their feelings." [6] In a study on Belleforest, Frank S. Hook has given several amusing examples of Fenton's habit of expanding the original texts of the "French Bandello," as he calls him. Listen for example to Belleforest's translation of Bandello's description of a distressed heroine:

> c'estoit grand' pitié de veoir la belle Angélique se deschirer la face, & arracher les cheveulx, voyant qu'il estoit impossible d'oster ceste cruelle délibération de la teste de son frère . . .

4. Marguerite de Navarre, *L'Heptaméron*, I (Paris: Librarie des Bibliophiles, 1879), p. 110.
5. C. S. Lewis, *English Literature in the Sixteenth Century excluding Drama* (Oxford: Clarendon Press, 1954), p. 311.
6. René Pruvost, *Matteo Bandello and Elizabethan Fiction* (Paris, 1937), p. 158.

Fenton takes a deep breath and translates,

> who (Angelica), besides whole rivers of tears distilling from her watery eyes with dolorous cryes in dolefull voice, redoubled with an eccho of treble dule, entred into a mortall war wyth her garmentes and attyre on her head, neither forbearing to dischevel her crispy lockes and here exceeding the collor of amber, nor commit cruel execution upon the tender partes of her body. And giving free scope to the humour of her fury, she spared not to imprinte with her nayles upon the precious complexion of her oriente face, a pitiful remembrance of the tragical trouble of her desolate brother, whom she could not in any way persuade to a chaunge or alteration of purpose . . .[7]

After this example, it is difficult to accept the fact that it is William Painter who is the most long-winded. Since he admittedly composed his tales "as a relaxation against weighty duties of state," Painter displayed a sybaritic talent for relaxation. They remind one of the long-winded storyteller in the *Novellino* (recalled by Valency) who was accused by a bored listener,

> "The man who taught you that story didn't teach you all of it."
> "How is that?"
> "He didn't teach you the end."

As Maurice Valency has written in his introduction to his anthology, *The Palace of Pleasure*, "Unity was always a structural characteristic of the novella." Unity and verbosity are mortal enemies. Verbosity, moreover, would tempt an author to introduce moralizing and descriptive elements into his tale foreign to the Italianate tradition. Marguerite de Navarre and Cervantes both passed *obiter dicta* on the goal of brevity in the *novella,* even though neither practised such economy. If we recall the oral tradition behind the *novella,* we might define its length as long enough for a dry split birch log to be consumed by a blazing bivouac fire.

IV. *Thematic Division of Novelle*

As far back as the Sanskrit collection of tales, the *Panchatantra,* the stories and tales were classified under headings: discord among friends, winning friends, war and peace, loss of acquired wealth, consequences of hasty behavior. None of these corresponds exactly to any of the classifications within which Boccaccio grouped his *novelle.* The principal themes adopted by Boccaccio are: peril averted by wit, through vicissitudes to good fortune, patience and perseverance rewarded, unhappy issues of love, happy issues of love, quick wit averting disaster, treasonable stratagems of wives, war of the sexes, love's magnanimity. Tales which do not fit into such categories are sometimes accommodated by the device of *ad*

7. Frank S. Hook, ed., *The French Bandello: A Selection,* University of Missouri Studies, XXII (1948), p. 23.

libitem days. This would indicate that the *novellatori* were collectors, folklorists, who could not apportion their hoard of tales in hand in a balanced disposition.

* * *

Another *novelliere* who is most precise about the themes of his tales is Giraldi Cinzio, who declares them as follows: conjugal vs. free love, loves with happy or unhappy ending, marital infidelity, conjugal fidelity, evil intrigues punished, acts of chivalry, quick and witty answers, ingratitude, instability of fortune.

Not all the *novellieri,* of course, announced a thematic distribution of their tales. Thus, it has become a challenge to scholars to assume such a distribution and to sort out the dominant themes on behalf of the author. The challenge has proved irresistible to Cervantists and mildly intriguing to Chaucer scholars.

Among appropriate thematic groupings which have been assigned by scholars to *novella* collections, the following may be mentioned. The tales told by Lucrezia's merry company in the *Piacevoli notti* deal principally with family and matrimonial relationships, adultery, vendetta, luck of the fool, the trickster tricked, and the live-and-let-live theme. These themes are more easily conveyed by the *novelle* than the *fiabe*. As Letterio di Francia has pointed out, "the balance between *fiabe* and *novelle* in the two volumes, maintained carefully in the first five *Notti,* is soon broken in favor of the *novelle.*" [8] The tremendous variety of themes in the *Pentamerone* has been noted in Stith Thompson's *Motif-Index of Folk Literature*, specifying 400 identifiable motifs concerning supernatural beings, especially animals, tabus, magic objects and powers, the dead, marvels, tests, sex, and so on.

Returning to the thematic unity of Chaucer, one must recognize the "marriage group" emphasized by Robert Dudley French: "Nine-tenths of the stories of the world are built upon the themes of love and marriage, and it seems quite unnecessary to conjecture that Chaucer's pilgrims told so many tales of love and lust because the poet had determined to utilize this motif to unify his collection of stories." [9] A contrasting polarity between secular and religious sentiment is suggested by Ruggiers as the thematic preoccupation. Topical unities are sought outside as well as within the tales themselves. Thus Harson suggests of the stories of the Friar, Summoner, and Canon's Yeoman that they are united by the fact that they deal with religious persons who are hardly specimens of their profession.

Rotunda, Pinkerton, and Petrocchi have made dissonant classi-

---

8. Letterio di Francia, *Novellistica* (Milan, 1925), II, 730.
9. Robert Dudley French, *A Chaucer Handbook* (New York, 1947), pp. 200–201.

fications of Bandello's 214 *novelle*, the latter scholar reducing everything down to *amore* as Yvonne Rodax has noted. Robert Kramer has selected "seven areas of concern" among the *Gesta Romanorum:* battle of the sexes, family relationships, law and justice, ideals of heroic virtue, nature of the human condition, God and the problem of evil, and the supernatural, miraculous, and prodigious. Similar attempts have been made to isolate the chief motifs in the tales of Tirso, María de Zayas y Sotomayor, Fenton, and even the twelve tales of Pettie. Needless to say, the chief concern of all of them concerns the man-woman relationship. It now remains only to consider the case of Cervantes.

From the eighteenth century to the present scholars have tried to isolate the most meaningful motifs in the *Novelas ejemplares.* Agustín Amezúa y Mayo's study, *Cervantes creador de la novela corta española* (1956), lists the major classifications since 1797. Typical are these categories which vary from generic and tonal to subject matter:

1797: Heroic, comic, popular, and humorous (Pellicer)
1890: Ideal of perfection, social vices and prejudices, sheer satire (Orellana y Rincón)
1917: Tales from lived experience, invented tales, mixture of each (Rodríguez Marín)
1933: Everyday life, customs, sententious wisdom (Pfandl)
1946: Love, marriage, tales unrelated to these (Casalduero)

At least a dozen other literary historians have had a go at separating the categories of these tales, with the criterion of stylistics sometimes intruding upon their thinking. If one is to agree with Chandler and Schwartz in their history of Spanish literature that two divisions are sufficient, perhaps the happiest solution would be a separation into idealistic/romantic and realistic/satirical *costumbrista.*

Four structural characteristics of the Italianate *novella*, then, make of it a homogeneous genre distinct from other tales: the cornice, the time unity, the evolving length, and the thematic classification centering on the everyday dramas of men and women during the Middle Ages and Renaissance. Since the term anatomy implies the formal or structural nature of a work of literature, I am permitted here to omit other elements of the *novella* which will be present in a forthcoming study on this literary genre and which will complement this study by examining its style and speech, its subject matter, its religious and social impact, its sources and literary influences, its public, and its relationship to other genres, among other considerations.

It will suffice then to conclude these remarks with a brief defense of the *novella* as a literary genre, and an influential one.

Perhaps no one was less certain than Boccaccio himself that he was forming a durable genre. Recall his words in the proemium to the *Decameron*: "Intendo di raccontare cento novelle o favole o parabole o istorie, che dire vogliamo." Nor was he more certain later on when Petrarch attempted to give his *novelle* a firmer status by translating one of them, the Griselda story, into Latin.

Even to the critics of the Renaissance the *novella* was an unrecognized genre. It was thus to be relegated to that second-class citizenship in the republic of letters shared by the farce and the fabliau, with which it had so much in common, especially plots. Predictably the Aristotelians ignored it. It got caught up in the debate whether Aristotle's remarks on poetry had any applicability to prose. Minturno thought *novelle* could be evaluated by Aristotelian canons. Patrizi did not. Only Francesco Bonciani tried to discuss the *novella* seriously, before the Accademia degli Alterati, and if anything he vindicated Patrizi's stand by trying to impose on the *novella* katharsis, unity through complication and dénouement, and one or two other echoes of Aristotelian thought. We, too, could join him in this exercise. Thus, the insistence of the *novellieri* on plot-centered "man in action." The *cornice* principle coincides with the unity of place, and the days-nights strictures with the unity of time. One could even adduce here María de Zayas y Sotomayor's insistence on having no more than five people "on stage." Yet Doña María is hardly the person to call upon in our endeavor to isolate the *novella* as a serious genre, for almost alone she complained of the word itself in the *cornice* of one edition of the first part of her *novelas*. She claims that her storytellers will relate rather *"maravillas,* que con este nombre quiso desempalagar al vulgo del de novelas, título tan enfadoso que ya en todas partes le aborrecen." [1] Yet even she retains the abhorrent word in the title of her corpus of tales.

Welcome would be a transcript of the discussion during those months around 1615 when Basile was reading his *Cunti*, as Croce assumes, to the Neapolitan Academies.

If the critics were negligent of the novella as an established genre, the great authors after Boccaccio were not. They occasionally acknowledged in their prefaces that they were perpetuating a durable form. Tirso knew that although he had not "stolen" from them, he owed a debt to the "Tuscans" of which he wished to be free. Cervantes felt the same way about Boccaccio. Even as the academicians and theorists struggled with Procrustean insistence to fit the novella into their Aristotelian thinking, even as Francesco Bonciani proposed the *Decameron* as a Homeric archetype of a new genre, the great writers of the Renaissance, Rabelais, Bandello,

---

1. Dona María de Zayas y Sotomayor, *Novelas amorosas y ejemplares* (Madrid, 1948), p. 31.

Shakespeare, Tirso, and Cervantes knew that the *novella* collections were by their time an established genre and a source of inspiration.

In sum, the *novella* structure, as we observed at the outset, permeated Western Europe and retained its identity until the seventeenth century. As one of the most popular forms of literature, paying scant lip service to Church, feudalism, monarchy, or empire, it accepted content, form, and tone from Boccaccio. Riding the rest of the tidal Italian influence, the Italianate *novella* was most influential. One should not associate this influence with the unfortunate remark of the late C. S. Lewis, who saw the Italian tale as "compost" for the Elizabethan drama. One wonders how familiar Lewis was with this vast corpus of *novelle* whose weakest practitioners were Englishmen. (One recalls that when another authority on Elizabethan letters, George Lyman Kittredge, set out to summarize the plot of Cinzio's "Moor of Venice," he revealed an inaccurate reading of it.)

One must on the contrary accept the obvious fact that the Italianate *novella* was a strong influence on social, political, and religious developments in Western Europe between the age of Boccaccio and that of Cervantes and Painter. It was surely a factor in the growth of the Reformation, the modification of feudalism, the reform of the courts and professions, and the strengthening of the bourgeoisie and mercantile class who were, as Professor Branca has discovered, the first mass readers of the *Decameron*.

ERICH AUERBACH
Frate Alberto †

In a famous novella of the *Decameron* (4, 2), Boccaccio tells of a man from Imola whose vice and dishonesty had made him a social outcast in his native town, so that he preferred to leave it. He went to Venice, there became a Franciscan monk and even a priest, called himself Frate Alberto, and managed to attract so much attention by striking penances and pious acts and sermons that he was generally regarded as a godly and trustworthy man. Then one day he tells one of his penitents—a particularly stupid and con-

† Selection from "Frate Alberto" in Erich Auerbach, *Mimesis: The Representation of Reality in Western Literature,* translated by Willard R. Trask. (Copyright © 1953 by Princeton University Press; Princeton Paperback 1968) pp. 203–231. Reprinted by permission of Princeton University Press.

This study remains one of the most important works of twentieth-century criticism. Auerbach uses a series of close textual analyses of key passages in Western literature from Homer to the present, all firmly grounded upon an intimate acquaintance with the cultures involved and a profound knowledge of their languages, to consider the evolution of levels of style in Western literature and the intellectual implications of this phenomenon. His study of a passage from Boccaccio reprinted here is taken from pages 203–31.

ceited creature, the wife of a merchant away on a journey—that
the angel Gabriel has fallen in love with her beauty and would
like to visit her at night. He visits her himself as Gabriel and has
his fun with her. This goes on for a while, but in the end it turns
out badly. This is what happens:

Pure avenne un giorno che, essendo madonna Lisetta con una
sua comare, et insieme di bellezze quistionando, per porre la sua
innanzi ad ogni altra, si come colei che poco sale aveva in zucca,
disse: Se voi sapeste a cui la mia bellezza piace, in verità voi ta-
cereste dell'altre. La comare vaga d'udire, si come colei che ben
la conoscea, disse: Madonna, voi potreste dir vero, ma tuttavia
non sappiendo chi questo si sia, altri non si rivolgerebbe così di
leggiero. Allora la donna, che piccola levatura avea, disse: Comare, egli non si vuol dire, ma l'intendimento mio è l'agnolo Gabriello, il quale più che sè m'ama, si come la più bella donna,
per quello che egli mi dica, che sia nel mondo o in maremma. La
comare allora ebbe voglia di ridere, ma pur si tenne per farla
più avanti parlare, e disse: In fè di Dio, madonna, se l'agnolo
Gabriello è vostro intendimento, e dicevi questo, egli dee ben
esser così; ma io non credeva che gli agnoli facesson queste cose.
Disse la donna: Comare, voi siete errata; per le piaghe di Dio egli
il fa meglio che mio marido; e dicemi che egli si fa anche colassù;
ma perciocchè io gli paio più bella che niuna che ne sia in cielo,
s'è egli innamorato di me, e viensene a star meco ben spesso: mo
vedi vu? La comare partita da madonna Lisetta, le parve mille
anni che ella fosse in parte ove ella potesse queste cose ridire; e
ragunatasi ad una festa con una gran brigata di donne, loro ordinatamente raccontò la novella. Queste donne il dissero a' mariti
et ad altre donne; e quelle a quell' altre, e così in meno di due dì
ne fu tutta ripiena Vinegia. Ma tra gli altri, a' quali questa cosa
venne agli orecchi, furono i cognati di lei, li quali, senza alcuna
cosa dirle, si posero in cuore di trovare questo agnolo, e di sapere
se egli sapesse volare; e più notti stettero in posta. Avvenne che di
questo fatto alcuna novelluzza ne venne a frate Alberto agli orecchi, il quale, per riprender la donna, una notte andatovi, appena
spogliato s'era, che i cognati di lei, che veduto l'avean venire,
furono all'uscio della sua camera per aprirlo. Il che frate Alberto
sentendo, e avvisato ciò che era, levatosi, non avendo altro rifugio,
aperse una finestra, la qual sopra il maggior canal rispondea, e
quindi si gittò nell'aqua. Il fondo v'era grande, et egli sapeva ben
notare, si che male alcun non si fece: e notato dall'altra parte del
canale, in una casa, che aperta v'era, prestamente se n'entrò, pregando un buono uomo, che dentro v'era, che per l'amor di Dio
gli scampasse la vita, sue favole dicendo, perchè quivi a quella
ora et ignudo fosse. Il buono uomo mosso a pietà, convenen-
dogli andare a far sue bisogne, nel suo letto il mise, e dissegli che
quivi infino alla sua tornata si stesse; e dentro serratolo, andò a
fare i fatti suoi. I cognati della donna entrati nella camera trovarono che l'agnolo Gabriello, quivi avendo lasciate l'ali, se n'era

volato: di che quasi scornati, grandissima villania dissero alla donna, e lei ultimamente sconsolata lasciorono stare, et a casa lor tornarsi con gli arnesi dell'agnolo.

(However, it chanced one day that Madam Lisetta, being in dispute with a gossip of hers upon the question of female charms, to set her own above all others, said, like a woman who had little wit in her noddle, "An you but knew whom my beauty pleaseth, in truth you would hold your peace of other women." The other, longing to hear, said, as one who knew her well, "Madam, maybe you say sooth; but knowing not who this may be, one cannot turn about so lightly." Thereupon quoth Lisetta, who was eath enough to draw, "Gossip, it must go no farther; but he I mean is the angel Gabriel, who loveth me more than himself, as the fairest lady (for that which he telleth me) who is in the world or the Maremma." The other had a mind to laugh, but contained herself, so she might make Lisetta speak further, and said, "Faith, madam, an the angel Gabriel be your lover and tell you this, needs must it be so; but methought not the angels did these things." "Gossip," answered the lady, "you are mistaken; zounds, he doth what you wot of better than my husband and telleth me they do it also up yonder; but, for that I seem to him fairer than any she in heaven, he hath fallen in love with me and cometh full oft to lie with me; seestow now?" The gossip, to whom it seemed a thousand years till she would be whereas she might repeat these things, took her leave of Madam Lisetta and foregathering at an entertainment with a great company of ladies, orderly recounted to them the whole story. They told it again to their husbands and other ladies, and these to yet others, and so in less than two days Venice was all full of it. Among others to whose ears the thing came were Lisetta's brothers-in-law, who, without saying aught to her, bethought themselves to find the angel in question and see if he knew how to fly, and to this end they lay several nights in wait for him. As chance would have it, some inkling of the matter came to the ears of Fra Alberto, who accordingly repaired one night to the lady's house, to reprove her, but hardly had he put off his clothes ere her brothers-in-law, who had seen him come, were at the door of her chamber to open it. Fra Alberto, hearing this and guessing what was to do, started up and having no other resource, opened a window, which gave upon the Grand Canal, and cast himself thence into the water. The canal was deep there and he could swim well, so that he did himself no hurt, but made his way to the opposite bank and hastily entering a house that stood open there, besought a poor man whom he found within, to save his life for the love of God, telling him a tale of his own fashion, to explain how he came there at that hour and naked. The good man was moved to pity and it behoving him to go do his occasions, he put him in his own bed and bade him abide there against his return; then, locking him in, he went about his affairs. Meanwhile, the lady's brothers-in-law entered her chamber and found that the angel Gabriel had flown, leaving his wings there; whereupon, seeing themselves baffled, they gave her all manner hard words and ultimately made off to their own house with the angel's trappings, leaving her disconsolate.) *The De-cameron.* Giovanni Boccaccio. Translation by John Payne. The Macy Library edition.

As I have said, the story ends very badly for Frate Alberto. His host hears on the Rialto what happened that night at Madonna Lisetta's and infers who the man he took in is. He extorts a large sum of money from Frate Alberto and then betrays him nevertheless; and he does it in so disgusting a way that the frate becomes the object of a public scandal with moral and practical consequences from which he never recovers. We feel almost sorry for him, especially if we consider with what delight and indulgence Boccaccio relates the erotic escapades of other clerics no better than Frate Alberto (for instance 3, 4—the story of the monk Don Felice who induces his lady love's husband to perform a ridiculous penance which keeps him away from home nights; or 3, 8, the story of an abbot who takes the husband to Purgatory for a while and even makes him do penance there).

The passage reprinted above contains the crisis of the novella. It consists of Madonna Lisetta's conversation with her confidante and the consequences of their conversation: the strange rumor spreading through the town; the relatives hearing it and deciding to catch the angel; the nocturnal scene in which the frate escapes for the time being by boldly jumping into the canal. The conversation between the two women is psychologically and stylistically a masterly treatment of a vivid everyday scene. Both the confidante who, suppressing her laughter, voices some doubt with simulated politeness to get Lisetta to go on talking, as well as the heroine herself who, in her vaingloriousness, lets herself be lured even beyond the limits of her innate stupidity, impress us as true to life and natural. Yet the stylistic devices which Boccaccio employs are anything but purely popular. His prose, which has often been analyzed, reflects the schooling it received from antique models and the precepts of medieval rhetoric, and it displays all its arts. It summarizes complex situations in a single period and puts a shifting word order at the service of emphasizing what is important, of retarding or accelerating the tempo of the action, of rhythmic and melodic effect.

The introductory sentence itself is a rich period, and the two gerunds *essendo* and *quistionando*—one in initial, the other in final position, with a leisurely interval between them—are as well-calculated as the syntactic stress on *la sua* which concludes the first of two rhythmically quite similar cadences, the second of which ends with *ogni altra*. And when the actual conversation begins, our good Lisetta is so enthusiastic about herself that she

fairly bursts into song: *se voi sapeste a cui la mia bellezza piace.*
. . . Still more delightful is her second speech with its many
brief and almost equisyllabic units in which the so-called *cursus
velox* predominates. The most beautiful of them, *ma l'intendiménto mío / è l'ágnolo Gabriéllo,* is echoed in her confidante's
reply, *se l'ágnolo Gabriéllo / è vóstro intendiménto.* In this second speech we find the first colloquialisms: *intendimento,* presumably of social rather than local color, can hardly have been in
polite usage in this particular acceptation (roughly, *desiderium,*
English "sweetheart"), nor yet the expression *nel mondo o in
maremma* (which gives us another charming cadence). The more
excited she grows, the more numerous are the colloquial and now
even dialectical forms: the Venetian *marido* in the enchanting
sentence which stresses the praises of Gabriel's erotic prowess by
the adjurational formula, *per le piaghe di Dio,* and the climactic
effect (again Venetian), *mo vedi vu,* whose note of vulgar triumph
is the more humorous as, just before, she had again been singing
sweetly, . . . *ma perciocchè io gli paio più bella che niuna che
ne sia in cielo, s'è egli innamorato di me.* . . .

The next two periods comprise the spreading of the rumor
throughout the town, in two stages. The first leads from *la comare*
to the *brigata di donne,* the second from *queste donne* to *Vinegia.*
Each has its own source of motion: the first in the confidante's
impatience to unburden herself of her story, an impatience whose
urgency and subsequent appeasement come out remarkably well
in a corresponding movement of the verbs (*partita,. . . le parve
mille anni che ella fosse . . . dove potesse . . . e ragunatasi . . .
ordinatamente raccontò*); the second, in the progressive expansion,
paratactically expressed, of the field covered. From here on the
narration becomes more rapid and more dramatic. The very next
sentence reaches all the way from the moment when the relatives
hear the rumor to their nocturnal ambush, although there is room
in it for a few additional details of fact and psychological description. Yet it seems relatively empty and calm compared with the
two which follow and in which the entire night scene in Lisetta's
house, down to Frate Alberto's bold leap, takes its course in two
periods which, however, together constitute but a single movement. This is done by interlacing hypotactic forms, with participial constructions (generally a favorite device with Boccaccio)
playing the most important part. The first sentence begins quietly
enough with the principal verb *avenne* and the corresponding subject clause *che . . . venne . . . ;* but in the attached relative
clause, *il quale* (a secondary subordinate clause, that is), the catas-
trophe bursts: . . . *andatovi, appena spogliato s'era, che i cognati
. . . furono all' uscio.* And then comes a tempest of verb forms:
sentendo, e avvisato, levatosi, non avendo, aperse, e si gittò. If only

274 • Erich Auerbach

by reason of the brevity of the crowding units, the effect is one
of extraordinary speed and dramatic precipitation. And for the
same reason—despite the learned and classical origin of the stylistic devices employed—it is not at all literary; the tone is not that
of written language but of oral narrative, the more so because the
position of the verbs, and hence the length and tempo of the in-
tervening sections of greater calm, is constantly varied in an artisti-
cally spontaneous fashion: *sentendo* and *avvisato* are placed close
together, as are *levatosi* and *non avendo, aperse* soon follows, but
the concluding *si gittò* appears only after the relative clause referring to the window. I do not quite see, by the way, why Boccaccio
has the frate hear of the rumor which is going the rounds. So
shrewd a knave would hardly put his head in such a trap, in order
to give Lisetta a piece of his mind, if he were at all aware that
there was any risk. The whole thing, it seems to me, would be
more natural if he had no inkling that something was afoot. His
quick and bold escape requires no special motivation in the form
of a previously crystallized suspicion. Or did Boccaccio have some
other reason for making the statement? I see none.[1]

While the frate swims the canal, the narrative becomes momentarily quieter, more relaxed, slower: we have principal verbs, in an
imperfect of description, arranged paratactically. But no sooner has
he reached the other side than the verbs begin jostling each other
again, especially when he enters the strange house: *prestamente
se n'entrò, pregando . . . che per l'amor di Dio gli scampasse la
vita, sue favole dicendo, perchè . . . fosse.* The intervals between
verbs are likewise brief or urgent. Exceedingly condensed and hur-
ried is *quivi a quella ora e ignudo.* Then the tide begins to ebb.
The ensuing sentences are still packed full of factual information
and hence with participial hypotaxes, but at least they are gov-
erned by the progressively more leisurely pace of principal clauses
linked by "and": *mise, et dissegli, e andò. Entrati . . . trovarono
che . . . se n'era volato* is still quite dramatic; but then comes
the progressive relaxation of the paratactic series *dissero, e ultimamente lasciarono stare, e tornarsi.*

1. Franca Schettino, "Auerbach e la
novella di Frate Alberto," *Romanische
Forschungen* 71 (1959), 406–13, believes
Auerbach is mistaken here and that
Alberto was not aware of the rumor
(and therefore of the danger he ran)
as he went to "possess once again" the
lady. Oscar Budel, "Boccaccio ed Auerbach: A proposito di un'interpretazione
recente," *Romanische Forschungen* 73
(1961), 151–59, reads the passage as
Auerbach does and claims that Alberto
did know something of the rumor and
that he had gone to the lady's home to
reprove her; furthermore, Budel notes
that the verb *riprendere* can be translated as either "reprove" or "possess
once again," thus opening the passage
to a double interpretation. The section
at issue here demonstrates how necessary
a close linguistic analysis of the *novelle*
is to a clear understanding of the work's
meaning. In this case, the fact that
Brother Alberto returned to "reprove"
and or to "possess once again" the lady,
even when he knew something of the
rumor and that he might be in jeopardy,
is crucial to a determination of how
clever he really is and, therefore, to the
interpretation of both his character and
the significance of the *novella*'s plot.
[*Editors.*]

Of such artistry there is no trace in earlier narrative literature. First let us take a random example from the Old French genre of droll tales in verse, the greatest number of which were produced about a century before Boccaccio. I choose a passage from the fablel *Du prestre qui ot mere a force* (from Berlin Ms Hamilton 257, after the text by G. Rohlfs, *Sechs altfranzösische Fablels,* Halle, 1925, p. 12). The theme is a priest who has a very mean, ugly, and stingy mother whom he keeps away from his house while he spoils his mistress, especially in the matter of clothes. The cantankerous old woman complains of this, and the priest answers:

> "Tesiez", dist il, "vos estes sote;
> De quoi me menez vos dangier,   25
> Se du pein avez a mengier,
> De mon potage et de mes pois;
> Encor est ce desor mon pois,
> Car vos m'avez dit mainte honte."
> La vieille dit: "Rien ne vos monte   30
> Que ie vodre d'ore en avant
> Que vos me teigniez par covent
> A grant honor com vostre mere."
> Li prestre a dit: "Par seint pere,
> James du mien ne mengera,   35
> Or face au pis qu'ele porra
> Ou au mieus tant com il li loist!"
> "Si ferai, mes que bien vos poist",
> Fet cele, "car ie m'en irai
> A l'evesque et li conterai   40
> Vostre errement et vostre vie,
> Com vostre meschine est servie.
> A mengier a ases et robes,
> Et moi volez pestre de lobes;
> De vostre avoir n'ai bien ne part."   45
> A cest mot la vieille s'en part
> Tote dolente et tot irée.
> Droit a l'evesque en est allée.
> A li s'en vient et si se claime
> De son fiuz qui noient ne l'aime,   50
> Ne plus que il feroit un chien,
> Ne li veut il fere nul bien.
> "De tot en tot tient sa meschine
> Qu'il eime plus que sa cosine;
> Cele a des robes a plenté."   55
> Quant la vieille ot tot conté
> A l'evesque ce que li pot,
> Il li respont a un seul mot,
> A tant ne li vot plus respondre,
> Que il fera son fiz semondre,   60
> Qu'il vieigne a court le jour nommé.
> La vieille l'en a encliné,

Si s'en part sanz autre response.
Et l'evesque fist sa semonse
A son fil que il vieigne a court;   65
Il le voudra tenir si court,
S'il ne fet reson a sa mere.
Je criem trop que il le compere.
Quant le termes et le jor vint,
Que li evesques ses plet tint,   70
Mout i ot clers et autres genz,
Des proverres plus de deus cens.
La vieille ne s'est pas tue,
Droit a l'evesque en est venue
Si li reconte sa besoigne.   75
L'evesque dit qu'el ne s'esloigne,
Car tantost com ses fiz vendra,
Sache bien qu'il le soupendra
Et toudra tot son benefice. . . .

("Be still," he said, "you are silly! What are you complaining about, since you have bread to eat and my soup and my peas? And even that is a burden to me, for you keep saying nasty things to me." The old woman says: "That won't do you any good, for I want from now on that you bind yourself to honor me greatly as your mother." The priest said: "By the Holy Father, never again shall she eat of what I have. Let her do her worst, or her best, as she likes." "I shall, and more than will suit you," says the old woman, "for I am going to go to the bishop and tell him about your misdoing and your life, and how well your mistress is served. She has enough to eat and plenty of clothes, and me you want to feed on empty words. Of your wealth I have no part." With these words the old woman runs off, grieved and angry. Straight to the bishop she went. She gets to him and complains of her son who loves her no more than he would a dog and will do nothing for her. "He cares for his mistress above everything else and loves her more than his relatives. She has plenty of clothes." When the old woman has told the bishop everything she could, he answers her in a word. For the moment he will not say more than that he will have her son summoned and he must come to court on the appointed day. The old woman bowed, and leaves without further reply. And the bishop issued his summons to her son that he must come to court. He means to rein him in short if he does not do what is right by his mother. I am very much afraid he is going to pay dearly for it. When the time and the day came on which the bishop held his court, there were many clerks and other people and more than two hundred priests. The old woman did not keep quiet. She went straight up to the bishop and told him her business. The bishop tells her not to leave, because as soon as her son arrives she should know that he will suspend him and take away his whole benefice. . . .)

The old woman misunderstands the word *soupendra*. She thinks her son is to be hanged. Now she regrets having accused him, and in her anxiety she points out the first priest who comes in, and claims that he is her son. To this uncomprehending victim the bishop administers such a tongue-lashing that the poor fellow has no chance to get in a word. The bishop orders him to take his old mother with him and henceforth to treat her decently, as a priest should. And woe to him if there should be any more complaints about his conduct! The bewildered priest takes the old woman with him on his horse. On his way home he meets the old woman's real son and tells him about his adventure, while the old woman makes signs to her son not to give himself away. The other priest ends his story by saying that he would gladly give forty pounds to anyone who would rid him of his unwanted burden. Fine, says the son, it's a bargain; give me the money, and I will relieve you of your old woman. And it was done.

Here too the part of the story reprinted begins with a realistic conversation, an everyday scene, the quarrel between mother and son, and here too the course of the conversation is a very lively crescendo. Just as, in the other case, Lisetta's confidante, by replying with ostensible amiability, gets Lisetta to talk on and on until her secret is out, so here the old woman, by her cantankerous complaints, irritates her son until he flies into a rage and threatens to cut off the supply of food he has been giving her, whereupon the mother, also beside herself with rage, runs off to the bishop. Although the dialect of the piece is hard to identify (Rohlfs considers that of the Ile de France likely), the tone of the conversation is far less stylized and more directly popular than in Boccaccio. It is invariably the common speech of the people (and the people includes the lower clergy): thoroughly paratactic, with lively questions and exclamations, full, and indeed overfull, of popular turns of expression. The narrator's tone is not essentially different from that of his characters. He too tells his story in the same simple tone, with the same sensory vividness, giving a graphic picture of the situation through the most unpretentious means and the most everyday words. The only stylization he permits himself is the verse form, rhymed octosyllabic couplets, which favors extremely simple and brief sentence patterns and as yet knows nothing of the rhythmic multiplicity of later narrative verse forms, such as those of Ariosto and Lafontaine. Thus the arrangement of the narrative which follows upon the dialogue is wholly artless, even though its freshness makes it delightful. In paratactic single file, without any effort to complicate or to unravel, without any compression of what is of secondary importance, without any change of tempo, the story runs or stumbles on. In order to bring in the joke about *soupendre*, the scene between the old woman and the bishop has to be repeated, and the bishop himself has to state his views no less than three times. No doubt these things and, more generally,

the many details and lines of padding brought in to resolve difficulties of rhyme, give the narrative a pleasantly leisurely breadth.
But its composition is crude and its character is purely popular, in
the sense that the narrator himself belongs to the type of people
he describes, and of course also to the people he addresses. His
own horizon is socially and ethically as narrow as that of his personages and of the audience he wishes to set laughing by his story.
Narrator, narrative, and audience belong to the same world, which
is that of the common, uneducated people, without aesthetic or
moral pretensions. In keeping with this is the characterization of
the personages and of the way they act, a characterization which is
certainly lively and graphic but also relatively crude and mono-
chromatic. They are popular in the sense that they are characters
with which everybody was familiar at the time: a boorish priest
susceptible to every kind of worldly pleasure, and a cantankerous
old woman. The minor characters are not described as specific
individuals at all; we get only their behavior, which is determined
by the situation.

In the case of Frate Alberto, on the other hand, we are told his
previous history, which explains the very specific character of his
malicious and witty shrewdness. Madonna Lisetta's stupidity and
the silly pride she takes in her womanly charms are unique of their
kind in this particular mixture. And the same holds true of the
secondary characters. Lisetta's confidante, or the *buono uomo* in
whose house Frate Alberto takes refuge, have a life and a character
of their own which, to be sure, is only hastily indicated but which
is clearly recognizable. We even get an inkling of what sort of
people Madonna Lisetta's relatives are, for there is something
sharply characteristic in the grim joke, *si posero in cuore di trovare
questo agnolo e di sapere se egli sapesse volare.* The last few words
approach the form which German criticism has recently come to
call *erlebte Rede* (free indirect discourse). Then too the setting is
much more clearly specified than in the fablel. The events of the
latter may occur anywhere in rural France, and its dialectal pecu-
liarities, even if they could be more accurately identified, would
be quite accidental and devoid of importance. Boccaccio's tale is
pronouncedly Venetian. It must also be borne in mind that the
French fablel is quite generally restricted to a specific milieu of
peasants and small townspeople, and that the variations in this
milieu, insofar as they are observable at all, owe their existence
exclusively to the accidental place of origin of the piece in question,
whereas in Boccaccio's case we are dealing with an author who in
addition to this Venetian setting chose numerous others for his
tales: for example Naples in the novella about Andreuccio da
Perugia (2, 5), Palermo in the one about Sabaetto (8, 10), Florence
and its environs in a long series of droll tales. And what is true of

the settings is equally true of the social atmosphere. Boccaccio surveys and describes, in the most concrete manner, all the social strata, all the classes and professions, of his time. The gulf between the art of the fablel and the art of Boccaccio by no means reveals itself only in matters of style. The characterization of the personages, the local and social setting, are at once far more sharply individualized and more extensive. Here is a man whose conscious grasp of the principles of art enables him to stand above his subject matter and to submerge himself in it only so far as he chooses, a man who shapes his stories according to his own creative will.

As for Italian narrative literature before Boccaccio, the specimens known to us from that period have rather the character of moralizing or witty anecdotes. Their stylistic devices as well as the orbit of their views and concepts are much too limited for an individualized representation of characters and settings. They often exhibit a certain brittle refinement of expression but in direct appeal to the senses they are by far inferior to the fablels. Here is an example:

> Uno s'andò a confessare al prete suo, ed intra l'altre cose disse: Io ho una mia cognata, e'l mio fratello è lontano; e quando io ritorno a casa, per grande domistichezza, ella mi si pone a sedere in grembo. Come debbo fare? Rispose il prete: A me il facesse ella, ch'io la ne pagherei bene! (From the *Novellino*, ed. Letterio di Francia, Torino, 1930. Novella 87, p. 146.)

> (A man went to his priest to confess and said to him, among other things: I have a sister-in-law, and my brother is away; and when I get home, in her great familiarity, she comes and sits on my lap. What shall I do? The priest answered: If she did that to me, I'd show her!)

In this little piece the whole emphasis is on the priest's ambiguous answer; everything else is mere preparation and is told straight forwardly, in rather flat parataxes, without any sort of graphically sensory visualization. Many stories of the *Novellino* are similarly brief anecdotes, whose subject is a witty remark. One of the book's subtitles is, accordingly, *Libro di Novelle e di bel parlar gentile*. There are some longer pieces as well; most of these are not droll tales but moralizing and didactic narratives. But the style is the same throughout: flatly paratactic, with the events strung together as though on a thread, without palpable breadth and without an environment for the characters to breathe in. The undeniable artistic sense of the *Novellino* is chiefly concerned with brief and striking formulations of the principal facts of the event being narrated. In this it follows the model of medieval collections of moral examples in Latin, the so-called *exempla*, and it surpasses them in organization, elegance, and freshness of expression. With sensory visualization it is hardly concerned, but it is clear that here, as with its Italian contemporaries, this limitation is a result of the linguistic and intellectual situation which prevailed at the time. The Italian vernacular was as yet too poor and lacking in suppleness, the horizon of concepts and judgments was as yet too narrow and restricted, to make possible a relaxed command of factual data and a sensory representation of multiplex phenomena. The entire available power of sensory visualization is concentrated upon a single climactic witticism, as, in our example, upon the priest's reply. If it is permissible to base a judgment upon a single case, that of Fra Salimbene de Adam, a Franciscan and the extremely gifted author of a Latin chronicle, it would seem that, at the end of the thirteenth century, Latin, as soon as a writer heavily interspersed it with Italian vulgarisms, as Salimbene did, could yield a much greater sensory force than written Italian. Salimbene's chronicle is full of anecdotes. One of these—which has been repeatedly quoted by others as well as by myself—I will cite at this point. It tells the story of a Franciscan named Detesalve, and runs as follows:

> Cum autem quadam die tempore yemali per civitatem Florentie ambularet, contigit, ut ex lapsu glatiei totaliter caderet. Videntes hoc Florentini, qui trufatores maximi sunt, ridere ceperunt. Quorum unus quesivit a fratre qui ceciderat, utrum plus vellet habere sub se? Cui frater respondit quod sic, scilicet interrogantis uxorem. Audientes hoc Florentini non habuerunt malum exemplum, sed commendaverunt fratrem dicentes: Benedicatur ipse, quia de nostris est!—Aliqui dixerunt quod alius Florentinus fuit, qui dixit hoc verbum, qui vocabatur frater Paulus Millemusce ex ordine Minorum. (Chronica, ad annum 1233; Monumenta Germaniae historica, Scriptores 32, 79.)

> (One day in winter when he was walking about in the city of Florence, it happened that he fell flat on the frozen ground. Seeing this, the Florentines, who are great jokers, began to laugh. One of them asked the friar who was lying there if he would not like to have something put under him. To which the friar answered Yes, the wife of him who asked. When they heard this, the Florentines did not take it amiss but praised the friar, saying: Good for him, he is one of us!—Some say that he who said this was another Florentine, named Paul Thousandflies, of the Minorite Order.)

Here too the point is a witty rejoinder, a *bel parlare*. But at the same time we have a real scene: a winter landscape, the monk who has slipped and lies there on the ground, the Florentines standing about making fun of him. The characterization of the participants is much livelier, and in addition to the climactic jest (*interrogantis uxorem*) there are other witticisms and vulgarisms (*utrum plus vellet habere sub se; benedicatur ipse quia de nostris est; frater Paulus Millemusce*; and before that *trufatores*) which are doubly amusing and savory by reason of their transparent Latin disguise. Sensory visualization and freedom of expression are here more fully developed than in the *Novellino*.

Yet whatever we choose from among the products of the earlier period—be it the crude, boorish sensory breadth of the fabliaux, or the threadbare, sensorily poor refinement of the *Novellino*, or Salimbene's lively, vividly graphic wit—none of it is comparable to Boccaccio. It is in him that the world of sensory phenomena is first mastered, is organized in accordance with a conscious artistic plan, caught and held in words. For the first time since antiquity, his *Decameron* fixes a specific level of style, on which the relation of actual occurrences in contemporary life can become polite entertainment; narrative no longer serves as a moral exemplum, no longer caters to the common people's simple desire to laugh; it serves as a pleasant diversion for a circle of well-bred young people of the upper classes, of ladies and gentlemen who delight in the sensual play of life and who possess sensitivity, taste, and judgment. It was to announce this purpose of his narrative art that Boccaccio created the frame in which he set it. The stylistic level of the *Decameron* is strongly reminiscent of the corresponding antique genus, the antique novel of love, the *fabula milesiaca*. This is not surprising, since the attitude of the author to his subject matter, and the social stratum for which the work is intended, correspond quite closely in the two periods, and since for Boccaccio too the concept of the writer's art was closely associated with that of rhetoric. As in the novels of antiquity, Boccaccio's literary art is based upon a rhetorical treatment of prose; as in them, the style sometimes borders on the poetic; he too sometimes gives conversation the form of well-ordered oratory. And the general impression of an "intermediate" or mixed style, in which realism and eroticism are linked to elegant verbal formulations, is quite similar in the two cases. Yet while the antique novel is a late form cast in languages which had long since produced their best, Boccaccio's stylistic endeavor finds itself confronted by a newly-born and as yet almost amorphous literary language. The rhetorical tradition—which, rigidified in medieval practice into an almost spectrally senile mechanism, had, so recently as the age of Dante, been still timidly and stiffly tried out on the Italian *volgare* by the first translators of ancient authors—in Boccaccio's hands suddenly becomes a miraculous tool which brings Italian art prose, the first literary prose of postclassical Europe, into existence at a single stroke. It comes into existence in the decade between his first youthful work and the *Decameron*. His particular gift of richly and sweetly moving prose rhythms, although a heritage from antiquity, he possessed almost from the beginning. It is already to be found in his earliest prose work, the *Filocolo*, and seems to have been a latent talent in him, which his first contact with antique authors brought out. What he lacked at first was moderation and judgment in using stylistic devices and in determining the level of style; sound relationship between subject matter and level of style had still to be achieved and become an instinctive possession. A first contact with the concept of an elevated style as practiced by the ancients—especially since the concept was still influenced by medieval notions —very easily led to what might be termed a chronic exaggeration of the stylistic level and an inordinate use of erudite embellishment. This resulted in an almost continuously stilted language, which, for that very reason, could not come close to its object and which, in such a form, was fit for almost nothing but decorative and oratorical purposes. To grasp the sensory reality of passing life was completely impossible to a language so excessively elevated.

In Boccaccio's case, to be sure, the situation was different from the beginning. His innate disposition was more spontaneously sensory, inclined toward creating charmingly flowing and elegant forms imbued with sensuality. From the beginning he was made for the intermediate rather than the elevated style, and his natural bent was strongly furthered by the atmosphere of the Angevin court at Naples where he spent his youth and where the playfully elegant late forms of the chivalric culture of Northern France had taken stronger hold than elsewhere in Italy. His early works are *rifacimenti* of French romances of chivalric love and adventure in the late courtly style; and in their manner, it seems to me, one can sense something characteristically French: the broader realism of his descriptions, the naive refinement and the delicate nuances of the lovers' play, the late feudal mundaneness of his social pictures, and the malice of his wit. Yet the more mature he grows, the stronger become the competing bourgeois and humanist factors and especially his mastery of what is robust and popular. In any case, in his youthful works the tendency toward rhetorical exaggeration—which represented a danger in Boccaccio's case too—plays a role only in his representation of sensual love, as do the excess of mythological erudition and of conventional allegorizing which prevail in some of them. Thus we may assert that despite his occasional attempts (as in the *Teseida*) to reach out for something more, he remains within the limits of the intermediate style—of the style which, combining the idyllic and the realistic, is designated for the representation of sensual love. It is in the intermediate, idyllic style that he wrote the last and by far the most beautiful of his youthful works, the *Ninfale fiesolano*; and the intermediate style serves too for the great book of the hundred novelle. In the determination of stylistic level it is unimportant which of his youthful works were written partly or wholly in verse and which in prose. The atmosphere is the same in them all.

Within the realm of the intermediate style, to be sure, the nuances in the *Decameron* are most varied, the realm is no narrow one. Yet even when a story approaches the tragic, tone and atmosphere remain tenderly sensual and avoid the grave and sublime; and in stories which employ far more crudely farcical motifs than our example, both language and manner of presentation remain aristocratic, inasmuch as both narrator and audience unmistakably stand far above the subject matter, and, viewing it from above with a critical eye, derive pleasure from it in a light and elegant fashion. It is precisely in the more popularly realistic and even the crudely farcical subjects that the peculiarity of the intermediate elegant style is most clearly to be recognized; for the artistic treatment of such stories indicates that there is a social class which, though it stands above the humble milieu of everyday life, yet takes delight in its vivid representation, and indeed a delight whose end is the individually human and concrete, not the socially stratified type. All the Calandrinos, Cipollas, and Pietros, the Peronellas, Caterinas, and Belcolores are, like Frate Alberto and Lisetta, individualized and living human beings in a totally different way from the villein or the shepherdess who were occasionally allowed to enter courtly poetry. They are actually much more alive and, in their characteristic form, more precise than the personages of the popular farce, as may be apparent from what we have indicated above, and this although the public they are meant to please belongs to an entirely different class. Quite evidently there was in Boccaccio's time a social class—high in rank, though not feudal but belonging to the urban aristocracy—which derived a well-bred pleasure from life's colorful reality wherever it happened to be manifested. It is true, the separation of the two realms is maintained to the extent that realistic pieces are usually set among the lower classes, the more tender and more nearly tragic pieces usually among the upper. But even this is not a rigidly observed rule, for the bourgeois and the sentimentally idyllic are apt to constitute borderline cases; and elsewhere too the same sort of mixture is not infrequent (e.g., the novella of Griselda, 10, 10).

The social prerequisites for the establishment of an intermediate style in the antique sense were fulfilled in Italy from the first half of the fourteenth century. In the towns an elevated stratum of patrician burghers had come to the fore; their mores, it is true, were still in many respects linked to the forms and ideas of the feudal courtly culture, but, as a result of the entirely different social structure, as well as under the influence of early humanist trends, they soon received a new stamp, becoming less bound up with class, and more strongly personal and realistic. Inner and outer perception broadened, threw off the fetters of class restriction, even invaded the realm of learning, thitherto the prerogative of clerical specialists, and gradually gave it the pleasant and winning form of personal culture in the service of social intercourse. The language, so recently a clumsy and inelastic tool, became supple, rich, nuanced, flourishing, and showed that it could accommodate itself to the requirements of a discriminating social life of refined sensuality. The literature of society acquired what it had not previously possessed: a world of reality and of the present. Now there is no doubt that this gain is strictly connected with the much more important gain on a higher stylistic level, Dante's conquest of a world, made a generation before. This connection we shall now attempt to analyze, and for that purpose we return to our text.

Its most conspicuous distinguishing characteristics, if we compare it with earlier narratives, are the assurance with which, in both perception and syntactical structure, it handles complex factual data, and the subtle skill with which it adapts the narrative tempo and level of tone to the inner and outer movement of the narrated events. This we have tried to show in detail above. The conversation between the two women, the spreading of the rumor through the town, and the dramatic night scene at Lisetta's house are made a clearly surveyable, coherent whole within which each part has its own independent, rich, and free motion. That Dante possesses the same ability to command a real situation of any number of constituent parts and varied nuances, that he possesses it to a degree which no other medieval author known to us can even distantly approach, I tried to show in the preceding chapter, using as my example the occurrences at the beginning of the tenth canto of the *Inferno*. The coherence of the whole, the shift in tone and rhythmic pulse between let us say the introductory conversation and the appearance of Farinata, or upon Cavalcante's sudden emergence and in his speeches, the sovereign mastery of the syntactic devices of language, I there analyzed as carefully as I know how. Dante's command over phenomena impresses us as much less adaptable but also as much more significant than the corresponding ability in Boccaccio. In itself the heavy beat of the tercets, with their rigid rhyme pattern, does not permit him as free and light a movement as Boccaccio allowed himself, but he would have scorned it in any case. Yet there is no mistaking the fact that Dante's work was the first to lay open the panorama of the common and multiplex world of human reality. Here, for the first time since classical antiquity, that world can be seen freely and from all sides, without class restriction, without limitation of the field of vision, in a view which may turn everywhere without obstruction, in a spirit which places all phenomena in a living order, and in a language which does justice both to the sensory aspect of phenomena and to their multiple and ordered interpenetration. Without the *Commedia* the

Decameron could not have been written. No one will deny this, and it is also clear that Dante's rich world is transposed to a lower level of style in Boccaccio. This latter point is particularly striking if we compare two similar movements—for example, Lisetta's sentence, *Comare, egli non si vuol dire, ma l'intendimento mio è l'agnolo Gabriello,* in our text, and *Inferno* 18, 52, where Venedico Caccianimico says, *Mal volontier lo dico; / ma sforzami la tua chiara favella, / Che mi fa sovvenir del mondo antico.* It is of course not his gift of observation and his power of expression for which Boccaccio is indebted to Dante. These qualities he had by nature and they are very different from the corresponding qualities in Dante. Boccaccio's interest is centered on phenomena and emotions which Dante would not have deigned to touch. What he owes to Dante is the possibility of making such free use of his talent, of attaining the vantage point from which it is possible to survey the entire present world of phenomena, to grasp it in all its multiplicity, and to reproduce it in a pliable and expressive language. Dante's power, which could do justice to all the various human presences in his work, Farinata and Brunetto, Pia de' Tolomei and Sordello, Francis of Assisi and Cacciaguida, which could make them arise out of their own specific conditions and speak their own language—that power made it possible for Boccaccio to achieve the same results for Andreuccio and Frate Cipolla or his servant, for Ciappelletto and the baker Cisti, for Madonna Lisetta and Griselda. With this power of viewing the world synthetically there also goes a critical sense, firm yet elastic in perspective, which, without abstract moralizing, allots phenomena their specific, carefully nuanced moral value—a critical sense which, indeed, causes the moral value to shine out of the phenomena themselves. In our story, after the relatives reach home *con gli arnesi del agnolo,* Boccaccio continues as follows: *In questo mezzo, fattosi il dì chiaro, essendo il buono uomo in sul Rialto, udì dire come l'agnolo Gabriello era la notte andato a giacere con Madonna Lisetta, e da cognati trovatovi, s'era per paura gittato nel canale, nè si sapeva che divenuto se ne fosse.*

> (Broad day come, the good man with whom Fra Alberto had taken refuge, being on the Rialto, heard how the angel Gabriel had gone that night to lie with Madam Lisetta and being surprised by her kinsmen, had cast himself for fear into the canal, nor was it known what was come of him.) Trans. John Payne.

The tone of seeming seriousness, which never mentions the fact that the Venetians on the Rialto are bursting with laughter, insinuates, without a word of moral, aesthetic, or any other kind of criticism, exactly how the occurrence is to be evaluated and what mood the Venetians are in. If instead Boccaccio had said that

Frate Alberto's behavior was underhanded and Madonna Lisetta stupid and gullible, that the whole thing was ludicrous and absurd, and that the Venetians on the Rialto were greatly amused by it, this procedure would not only have been much clumsier but the moral atmosphere, which cannot be exhausted by any number of adjectives, would not have come out with anything like the force it now has. The stylistic device which Boccaccio employs was highly esteemed by the ancients, who called it "irony." Such a mediate and indirectly insinuating form of discourse presupposes a complex and multiple system of possible evaluations, as well as a sense of perspective which, together with the occurrence, suggests its effect. In comparison, Salimbene strikes us as decidedly naive when, in the anecdote quoted above, he inserts the sentence, *videntes hoc Florentini, qui trufatores maximi sunt, ridere ceperunt*. This note of malicious irony in our present passage from Boccaccio is his own. It does not occur in the *Commedia*. Dante is not malicious. But the breadth of view, the incisive rendering of a clearly defined, complex evaluation by means of indirect suggestion, the sense of perspective in binding up event with effect, are Dante's creation. He does not tell us who Cavalcante is, what he feels, and how his reactions are to be judged. He makes him appear and speak, and merely adds: *le sue parole e il modo de la pena m'avean di costui già letto il nome.* Long before we are given any details, Dante fixes the moral tone of the Brunetto episode (*Inf.*, 15):

> Così adocchiato da cotal famiglia
> fui conosciuto da un che mi prese
> per lo lembo e gridò: Qual maraviglia!
> E io, quando 'l suo braccio a me distese,
> ficcai li occhi per lo cotto aspetto,
> sì che 'l viso abbrucciato non difese
> la conoscenza sua al mio intelletto;
> e chinando la mia a la sua faccia
> rispuosi: Siete voi qui, ser Brunetto?
> E quelli: O figliuol mio. . . .

(Thus eyed by that family, I was recognized by one who took me by the skirt, and said: "What a wonder!" And I, when he stretched out his arm to me, fixed my eyes on his baked aspect, so that the scorching of his visage hindered not my mind from knowing him; and bending my face to his, I answered: "Are you here, Ser Brunetto?" And he: "O my son! . . .") Trans. Dr. J. A. Carlyle, "Temple Classics."

Without a single word of explanation he gives us the whole Pia de' Tolomei in her own words (*Purg.*, 5):

> Deh, quando tu sarai tornato al mondo
> e riposato de la lunga via,

(seguitò il terzo spirito al secondo),
ricorditi di me che son la Pia. . . .

("Pray, when thou shalt return to the world, and art rested
from thy long journey," followed the third spirit after the second, "remember me, who am La Pia. . . .")

And from among the abundance of instances in which Dante illustrates the effects of phenomena, or even phenomena through
their effects, I choose the famous simile of sheep coming out of
the pen, by which he describes the slow dispelling of the amazement which fell upon the crowd in the Antipurgatorio at the sight
of Virgil and Dante (*Purg.*, 3). Compared with such methods of
characterization, which operate with the most exact perception of
what is individual and the most varied and subtle means of expression, everything earlier seems narrow and crude and without any
real order as soon as it attempts to come close to phenomena. Take
for instance the lines in which the author of the previously quoted
fabel describes his priest's old mother:

> Qui avoit une vieille mere
> Mout felonnesse et mout avere;
> Bochue estoit, noire et hideuse
> Et de touz biens contralieuse.
> Tout li mont l'avoit contre cuer,
> Li prestres meisme a nul fuer
> Ne vosist pour sa descreson
> Qu'el entrast ja en sa meson;
> Trop ert parlant et de pute ere. . . .

(He had an old mother who was a horrible creature and very
avaricious. Hunch-backed she was, and black and hideous and
opposed to everything that was good. Everybody loathed her.
Even the priest, because of her unreasonableness, would under
no conditions let her come into his house. She was too much of
a gossip and too disgusting. . . .)

This is by no means devoid of graphic elements, and the transition from a general characterization to effect upon the surroundings, and then the *meisme*-climax giving the son's attitude,
represents a natural and vivid continuity. But everything is stated
in the coarsest and crudest manner possible; there is no personal
and no precise perception. The adjectives, on which, after all, the
principal work of characterization must fall, seem to be sprinkled
into the lines at random, as syllable count and rhyme happened to
permit, in a hotchpotch of moral and physical characteristics. And
of course the entire characterization is direct. To be sure, Dante
by no means scorns direct characterization through adjectives, at
times through adjectives of the widest content. But then the effect
is something like this:

La mia sorella che tra bella e buona
non so qual fosse più. . . .

(*Purg.*, 24, 13–14.)

(My sister, who, whether she were more fair or more good I
know not. . . .)

Nor does Boccaccio scorn the direct method of characterization.
At the very beginning of our text we find two popular phrases
which serve to set forth Lisetta's stupidity directly and graphically:
che poco sale avea in zucca and *che piccola levatura avea*. Reading
the beginning of the novella, we find a whole collection of things
similar in form and intent: *una giovane donna bamba e sciocca*;
sentiva dello scemo; *donna mestola*; *donna zucca al vento, la quale
era anzi che no un poco dolce di sale*; *madonna baderla*; *donna
poco fila*. This little collection looks like a merry game Boccaccio
is playing with his knowledge of amusing colloquial phrases and
perhaps it also serves to describe the vivacious mood of the teller
of the tale, Pampinea, whose purpose it is to divert the company,
who have just been touched to tears by the preceding story. In any
case, Boccaccio is very fond of this sort of play with a variety of
phrases drawn from the vigorous and imaginative language of the
common people. Consider for instance the way in which (in novella
10 of the sixth day) Frate Cipolla's servant, Guccio, is characterized, partly directly and partly by his master. It is a striking example of Boccaccio's characteristic mixture of popular elements and
subtle malice, ending in one of the most beautifully extended
periods that he ever wrote (*ma Guccio Imbratta il quale era*, etc.).
In it the stylistic level shifts from a most enchanting lyrical movement (*più vago di stare in cucina che sopra i verdi rami l'usignolo*)
through the coarsest realism (*grassa e grossa e piccola e mal fatta
e con un paio di poppe che parevan due ceston da letame*, etc.) to
something approaching horror (*non altramenti che si gitta l'avol-
toio alla carogna*), yet all the parts form a whole by virtue of the
author's malice, which glints through everywhere.

Without Dante such a wealth of nuances and perspectives would
hardly have been possible. But of the figural-Christian conception
which pervaded Dante's imitation of the earthly and human world
and which gave it power and depth, no trace is to be found in Boccaccio's book. Boccaccio's characters live on earth and only on
earth. He sees the abundance of phenomena directly as a rich world
of earthly forms. He was justified in so doing, because he had not
set out to compose a great, weighty, and sublime work. He has
much better reason than Dante to call the style of his book *umilis-
simo e rimesso* (introduction to the fourth day), for he really writes
for the entertainment of the unlearned, for the consolation and
amusement of the *nobilissime donne*, who do not go to study at

Rome or Athens or Bologna. With much wit and grace he defends himself in his conclusion against those who claim that it is unseemly for a weighty and serious man (*ad un uom pesato e grave*) to write a book with so many jests and fooleries:

> Io confesso d'essere pesato, e molte volte de' miei dì esser stato; e perciò, parlando a quelle che pesato non m'hanno, affermo che io non son grave, anzi son io si lieve che io sto a galla nell'acqua: e considerato che le prediche fatte da' frati, per rimorder delle lor colpe gli uomini, il più oggi piene di motti e di ciance e di scede si veggono, estimai che quegli medesimi non stesser male nelle mie novelle, scritte per cacciar la malinconia delle femmine.

> (I confess to being a man of weight and to have been often weighed in my time, wherefore, speaking to those ladies who have not weighed me, I declare that I am not heavy; nay, I am so light that I abide like a nutgall in water, and considering that the preachments made of friars, to rebuke men of their sins, are nowadays for the most part seen full of quips and cranks and jibes, I conceived that these latter would not sit amiss in my stories written to ease women of melancholy.) Trans. John Payne.

Boccaccio is probably on solid ground with his malicious little thrust at the preaching friars (to be found in almost exactly the same words, though on a quite different level of tone, in Dante, *Par.*, 29, 115). But he forgets or does not know that the vulgar and naive farcicality of the sermons is a form—already, it is true, a somewhat degenerate and disreputable form—of Christian-figural realism. Nothing of the sort applies in his case. And the very thing which justifies him from his point of view ("if even the preachers joke and jape, why cannot I do the same in a book designed to amuse?") puts his venture, from the Christian-medieval point of view, in a dubious light. What a sermon, under the aegis of Christian figuralism, has a perfect right to do (exaggerations may go to objectionable extremes, but the right as a matter of principle cannot be denied), a secular author may not do—all the more because his work is not in the last analysis quite as light in weight as he claims; it is simply not naive and devoid of basic attitudes, as the popular farces are. If it were, then, from the Christian-medieval point of view, it could be regarded as a venial irregularity of the kind occasioned by man's instincts and his need for entertainment, as proof of his imperfection and weakness. But such is not the case with the *Decameron*. Boccaccio's book is of the intermediate style, and for all its frivolity and grace, it represents a very definite attitude, and one which is by no means Christian. What I have in mind is not so much Boccaccio's way of making fun of superstition and relics, nor even such blasphemies as the phrase *la resurrezion della carne* for a man's sexual erection (3, 10). Such things are part and parcel of the medieval repertoire

of farce and need not necessarily be of fundamental importance—
although of course, once an anti-Christian or anti-ecclesiastical
movement was under way, they acquired great propagandistic ef-
fectiveness. Rabelais, for example, unmistakably uses them as a
weapon (a similarly blasphemous joke is to be found toward the
end of chapter 60 of *Gargantua*, where words from the 24th Psalm,
ad te levavi, are used in a corresponding sense, a fact which serves,
however, to show once again how traditional, how much a part of
the repertoire, this type of joke really was; for another example see
tiers livre, 31, toward the end). The really important characteristic
of the attitude reflected in the *Decameron*, the thing which is
diametrically opposed to medieval-Christian ethics, is the doctrine
of love and nature which, though it is usually presented in a light
tone, is nevertheless quite certain of itself. The reasons why the
modern revolt against Christian doctrines and forms of life could
prove its practical power and its propagandistic efficacy so successfully in the realm of sexual morality are grounded in the early
history and in the essential nature of Christianity. In that realm
the conflict between the worldly will to life and the Christian suf-
ferance of life became acute as soon as the former attained to self-
consciousness. Doctrines of nature which praised the instinctive
life of sex and demanded its emancipation had already played an
important role in connection with the theological crisis at Paris
in the seventies of the thirteenth century; they also found literary
expression in the second part of the *Roman de la Rose*, by Jean
de Meun. All this has no direct bearing on Boccaccio. He is not
concerned with these theological controversies of many decades
earlier. He is no half-scholastic pedagogue like Jean de Meun. His
ethics of love is a recasting of courtly love, tuned several degrees
lower in the scale of style, and concerned exclusively with the
sensual and the real. That it is now earthly love which is in question is unmistakable. There is still a reflection of the magic of
courtly love in some of the novelle in which Boccaccio expresses
his attitude most clearly. Thus the story of Cimone (5, 1)—which,
like the earlier *Ameto*, has education through love as its central
theme—clearly shows that it is descended from the courtly epic.
The doctrine that love is the mother of all virtues and of everything noble in man, that it imparts courage, self-reliance, and the
ability to make sacrifices, that it develops intelligence and social
accomplishments, is a heritage from courtly culture and the *stil
nuovo*. Here, however, it is presented as a practical code of morals,
valid for all classes. The beloved is no longer an inaccessible mistress or an incarnation of the divine idea, but the object of sexual
desires. Even in details (though not quite consistently) a sort of
ethics of love is discernible—for example, that it is permissible to
employ any kind of treachery and deceit against a third person

(the jealous rival, the parents, or whatever other powers hinder the designs of love) but not against the object of one's love. If Frate Alberto gets so little sympathy from Boccaccio, it is because he is a hypocrite and because he won Madonna Lisetta's love not honestly but by underhanded methods. The *Decameron* develops a distinct, thoroughly practical and secular ethical code rooted in the right to love, an ethics which in its very essence is anti-Christian. It is presented with much grace and without any strong claim to doctrinal validity. The book rarely abandons the stylistic level of light entertainment. Yet at times it does, when Boccaccio defends himself against attacks. This happens in the introduction to the fourth day when, addressing himself to the ladies, he writes:

> E, se mai con tutta la mia forza a dovervi in cosa alcuna compiacere mi disposi, ora più che mai mi vi disporrò; perciocchè io conosco che altra cosa dir non potrà alcun con ragione, se non che gli altri et io, che vi amiamo, naturalmente operiamo. Alle cui leggi, cioè della natura, voler contrastare, troppe gran forze bisognano, e spesse volte non solamente in vano, ma con grandissimo danno del faticante s'adoperano. Le quali forze io confesso che io non l'ho nè d'averle disidero in questo; e se io l'avessi, più tosto ad altrui le presterei, che io per me l'adoperassi. Per che tacciansi i morditori, e, se essi riscaldar non si possono, assiderati si vivano; e ne' lor diletti, anzi appetiti corrotti standosi, me nel mio, questa brieve vita, che posta n'è, lascino stare.

> (And if ever with all my might I vowed myself to seek to please you in aught, now more than ever shall I address myself thereto; for that I know none can with reason say otherwise than that I and others who love you do according to nature, whose laws to seek to gainstand demandeth overgreat strength, and oftentimes not only in vain, but to the exceeding hurt of whoso striveth to that end, is this strength employed. Such strength I confess I have not nor ever desired in this to have; and an I had it, I had liefer lend it to others than use it for myself. Wherefore, let the carpers be silent and an they avail not to warm themselves, let them live benumbed and abiding in their delights—or rather their corrupt appetites,—leave me to abide in mine for this brief life that is appointed me.) Trans. John Payne.

This, I believe, is one of the most aggressive and energetic passages Boccaccio ever wrote in defense of his ethics of love. The view he wishes to express cannot be misunderstood; yet one cannot fail to see that it is without weight. Such a battle cannot seriously be fought with a few words on the irresistibility of nature and a couple of malicious allusions to the private vices of one's adversaries. Nor, indeed, did Boccaccio have any such intention. We treat him unfairly and judge by a wrong standard if we measure the order of life which speaks from his work by Dante's standard or by the works of the later and fully developed Renaissance. The figural unity of the secular world falls apart at the very moment when it attains—in Dante—complete sovereignty over earthly reality. Sovereignty over reality in its sensory multiplicity remained as a permanent conquest, but the order in which it was comprehended was now lost, and for a time there was nothing to take its place. This, as we said, must not be made a reproach against Boccaccio, but it must be registered as a historical fact which goes beyond him as a person. Early humanism, that is, lacks constructive ethical force when it is confronted with the reality of life; it again lowers realism to the intermediate, unproblematic, and non-tragic level of style which, in classical antiquity, was assigned to it as an extreme upper limit, and, as in the same period, makes the erotic its principal, and almost exclusive, theme. Now, however, this theme contains—what in antiquity there could be no question of its containing—an extremely promising germ of problem and conflict, a practical starting point for the incipient movement against the culture of medieval Christianity. But at first, and merely in itself, the erotic is not yet strong enough to treat reality problematically or even tragically. When Boccaccio undertakes to depict all the multiplex reality of contemporary life, he abandons the unity of the whole: he writes a book of novelle in which a great many things stand side by side, held together only by the common purpose of well-bred entertainment. Political, social, and historical problems which Dante's figuralism penetrated completely and fused into the most everyday reality, fall entirely by the wayside. What happens to erotic and metaphysical problems, and what level of style and human depth they attain in Boccaccio's work, can easily be ascertained from comparisons with Dante.

There are in the *Inferno* several passages in which damned souls challenge or mock or curse God. Good examples are the important scene in canto 14 in which Capaneus, one of the seven against Thebes, challenges God from amid the rain of fire and exclaims: *Qual io fui vivo, tal son morto*—or the scornful gesture of the robber of churches Vanni Fucci in canto 25, upon his recovery from the dreadful metamorphosis caused by the serpent's bite. In both cases the revolt is conscious and is in keeping with the history, character, and condition of the two condemned sinners. In Capaneus' case it is the unvanquished defiance of Promethean rebellion, an enmity to God which is superhuman; in Vanni Fucci it is wickedness immeasurably exaggerated by despair. Boccaccio's first novella (1, 1) tells the story of the vicious and fraudulent notary Ser Ciappelletto who falls mortally ill away from home, in the house of two Florentine usurers. His hosts know the evil life he has led and fear the worst for themselves if he should die in their house without confession and absolution. That he will be refused absolution if he makes a true confession, they have no doubt. To extricate his hosts from this difficult situation, the mortally ill old man deceives a naive confessor with a false and absurdly overpious confession in which he represents himself as a virginal, almost faultless paragon of all virtues, who is yet beset by exaggerated scruples. In this fashion he not only obtains absolution, but after his death his confessor's testimony gains him the reverence due to a saint. This sneering contempt for confession in the hour of death would seem to be a theme which could hardly be treated without the assumption of a basically anti-Christian attitude on the part of the penitent nor without the author's taking a stand—be it Christian and hence condemnatory, or anti-Christian and hence approving—in regard to the problem involved; but here it is merely auxiliary to working out two farcically comic scenes: the grotesque confession and the solemn interment of the supposed saint. The problem is hardly posed. Ser Ciappelletto decides upon his course of action quite lightly, merely in order to free his hosts from imminent danger by a last sly trick which shall be worthy of his past; the justification he alleges for it is so stupid and frivolous that it proves that he has never given a serious thought to God or his own life ("in the course of my life I have offended God so much that in the hour of death a little more or less won't matter"); and equally frivolous and exclusively concerned with what is momentarily expedient are the two Florentine masters of the house who, as they listen to the confession, do, it is true, say to each other: "What sort of man is he, who even now when he is old and ill and about to appear before the throne of the heavenly judge will not desist from his evil tricks but wishes to die as he has lived"—but who then, when they see that the end of assuring him a Christian burial has been gained, do not give the matter another thought. Now it is certainly true and quite in accordance with common experience that many people undertake the most momentous acts with no full conviction commensurate with such acts, simply in consequence of a momentary situation, force of habit, a fleeting impulse. Yet from the author who relates a matter of this kind, we still expect a comparative evaluation. And in fact Boccaccio does allow the narrator Panfilo to take a position in a few concluding words. But they are lame words, indecisive and without weight; they are neither atheistic nor decisively Christian, as the subject demands. There is no doubt, Boccaccio reports the monstrous adventure only for the sake of the comic effect of the two scenes mentioned above, and avoids any serious evaluation or taking of position.

In the story of Francesca da Rimini, Dante had given grandeur and reality in accordance with his way of being and his stage of development. Here, for the first time in the Middle Ages, is no *avanture,* no tale of enchantment; it is free from the charmingly witty coquetry and the class ceremonial of love which were characteristic of courtly culture; it is not hidden behind a veil of secret meaning, as in the *stil nuovo*. Instead it is a truly present action on the highest level of tone, equally immediate and real in terms of memories of an earthly destiny as in terms of an encounter in the beyond. In the love stories which Boccaccio tries to present tragically or nobly (they are mostly to be found among the novelle of the fourth day), the preponderant ingredients are the adventurous and the sentimental. At the same time the adventure is no longer, as it was in the heyday of the courtly epic, the trial and test of the chosen few, which as a fully assimilated element in the ideal conception of class had become an inner necessity, but really only coincidence, the ever unexpected product of quickly and violently shifting events. The elaboration of the coincidental character of the adventure can even be demonstrated in novelle in which comparatively little occurs, as for instance the first of the fourth day, the story of Guiscardo and Ghismonda. Dante scorned to mention the conditions under which Francesca and Paolo were surprised by her husband; in treating such a theme he scorns every kind of finely wrought coincidence, and the scene which he describes—the lovers reading the book together—is the most ordinary thing in the world, of interest only through what it leads to. Boccaccio devotes a considerable portion of his text to the complicated and adventurous methods the lovers are forced to employ in order to meet undisturbed, and to the chance concatenation of events which leads to their discovery by the father, Tancredi. These are adventures like those in the courtly romance—for example the love story of Cligès and Fenice in Chrétien de Troyes' romance. But the fairy tale atmosphere of the courtly epic is gone, and the ethical concept of the knight's testing has become a general morality of nature and love, itself expressed in extremely sentimental forms. The sentimental, in turn, which is often bound up with physical objects (the heart of the beloved, the falcon), and to that extent is reminiscent of fairy tale motifs, is in the majority of cases tricked out with a superabundance of rhetoric—think, for example, of Ghismonda's long apology. All these novelle lack any decisive unity of style. They are too adventurous and too reminiscent of fairy tales to be real, too free from magic and too rhetorical to be fairy tales, and much too sentimental to be tragic. The novelle which aim at the tragic are not immediate and direct in the realm either of reality or of feeling. They are at best what is called touching.

It is precisely when Boccaccio tries to enter the realm of problem or tragedy that the vagueness and uncertainty of his early humanism becomes apparent. His realism—which is free, rich, and assured in its mastery of phenomena, which is completely natural within the limits of the intermediate style—becomes weak and superficial as soon as the problematic or the tragic is touched upon. In Dante's *Commedia* the Christian-figural interpretation had compassed human and tragic realism, and in the process had itself been destroyed. Yet that tragic realism had immediately been lost again. The worldliness of men like Boccaccio was still too insecure and unsupported to serve, after the fashion of Dante's figural interpretation, as a basis on which the world could be ordered, interpreted, and represented as a reality and as a whole.

MARGA COTTINO-JONES

Fabula vs. Figura: Another Interpretation of the Griselda Story †

Boccaccio's fascination with women, their beauty and love, is evident everywhere in the *Decameron* where it is expressed each day in different fictional modes and narrative tones. Some novellas, for instance, are harmoniously built around remarkable female characters who influence the development of the story towards a successful finale, such as the Marchesana del Monferrato (I, 5), Madonna Zinevra (II, 9), Giletta di Nerbona (III, 9), Gostanza (V, 2), and Madonna Filippa (VI, 7). Others are developed around fascinating love situations, as in the adventures of Paganino da Monaco (II, 10), Pietro Boccamazza and l'Agnolella (V, 3), Nastagio degli Onesti (V, 8), and Federigo degli Alberighi (V, 9). Sometimes women and love become the central themes of a whole group of novellas, as in at least six of the novellas of the Fourth Day, centered around heroines elevated by love to become either tragic or elegiac personifications of noble womanhood. On the other hand, the same topics are dealt with in a completely different narrative tone in the stories of the Seventh Day, where the comic interplay of wit and sensual frenzy is brilliantly effective in the sketching of merry, love-making heroines of doubtful morality, but undoubted charm. And, finally, many novellas which belong to the Tenth Day are centered around idealized women and love: these are the stories of women greatly admired and desired, like Madonna Catilina and her near-magic resurrection from the tomb (X, 4), Madonna Dianora and the bewitched fulfilment of her wish (X, 5), and Sofronia, the quasi-static pivot of an incredi-

† Boccaccio's Griselda story is one of the most interesting *novelle* in the entire collection and has influenced many other poets (particularly Chaucer) and often puzzled many critics. This analysis of the tale by Marga Cottino-Jones interprets the meaning of the narrative with reference to Boccaccio's own definition of the function of fiction. It is reprinted from *Italica* 50 (1973), 38–52, by permission of the author and the publisher.

ble intrigue of love and friendship (X, 8). The novella of Lisa, the frail and inexperienced girl in love with the King, also belongs to this group for its idealized magnification of love (X, 7), as does the novella of Griselda and her martyrdom for love (X, 10).[1]

Keeping in mind that in most of the novellas thematically centered around women and love, the main incentive for action is the personal gratification of the protagonist's love, the novella of Griselda presents a distinctive difference in motivation. Griselda's love is no desire to be fulfilled for her own personal benefit; it is an extension of love still in human terms, but replacing personal gratification with unselfishness and self-sacrifice. Griselda is not simply a woman in love; she is the embodiment of love on a sacrificial level.

In the story of Griselda, placed—it seems purposedly—at the very end of the *Decameron*, the two themes of women and love appear to reach the maximum of their human potential to create an idealized embodiment of perfection in the heroine herself. The novella seems to be moving on two different levels at the same time: (1) a purely fact-presenting level of narrative which unfolds the story of the fortunes and misfortunes of the patient Griselda; and (2) a figurative level which may be discovered by a closer scrutiny of hidden symbols and mythical patterns. In this novella especially, Boccaccio applied his own critical principles as stated in Book XIV of the *Genealogia Deorum Gentilium*, wherein poetry is described as "a sort of fervid and exquisite invention, with fervid expression, in speech or writing, of that which the mind has invented" and its main effects are seen as "strange and unheard-of creations of the mind; it arranges these meditations in a fixed order, adorns the whole composition with unusual interweaving of words and thoughts; and thus it veils truth in a fair and fitting garment of fiction." [2]

* * *

Since there have been many different scholarly attempts to find a satisfactory critical interpretation of the novella of Griselda, I feel motivated to add my own viewpoint which is basically inspired by Boccaccio's statement in *Genealogia Deorum*: "but what the poet calls fable or fiction our theologians have named figure." [3]

---

1. For an ample treatment of the origin of the Griselda story, see especially Dudley D. Griffith, *The Origin of the Griselda Story* (Seattle: University of Washington Press, 1931); and Wit A. Cate, "The Problem of the Origin of the Griselda Story," *Studies in Philology* 29 (1932), 389–405.

2. Giovanni Boccaccio, *Boccaccio on Poetry: Being the Preface and the Fourteenth and Fifteenth Books of Boccac-* cio's *Genealogia Deorum Gentilium*, ed. Charles G. Osgood (Indianapolis: Bobbs-Merrill, 1956), p. 39.

3. Ibid., p. 49. Elsewhere in the same work, Boccaccio gives the following definition of *fabula*: "Fiction is a form of discourse, which, under guise of invention, illustrates or proves an idea; and, as its superficial aspect is removed, the meaning of the author is clear" (p. 48).

By accepting this suggestion of Boccaccio's, whereby the poet's "fabula" equals the theologian's "figura," a new interpretative dimension may be applied to the novella of Griselda. As a "figura" Griselda stands out as a sacrificial character, a *pharmakos*, a *figura Christi* who is called on to offer herself as the innocent victim needed to restore her surrounding community to the harmony and happiness emblematic of a Golden Age condition of existence.[4]

One becomes even more inclined to accept the story of Griselda in this light, if in addition to accepting Boccaccio's own critical explanations and suggestions, one directly analyzes the work in literary terms, and realizes the actual presence in it of special archetypal patterns and mythical elements.

There is an underlying archetypal pattern on which the story moves: the Hell-Paradise pattern [5] which suggests a movement from a negative condition of life, composed of conflicts and dissatisfaction, towards the opposite pole of a virtuous and harmonious form of life. In addition, two central myths are also present and identifiable with the two main protagonists of the story, Gualtieri, the Marquis, typifying the Divine Father archetype,[6] and Griselda, symbolizing the Christ archetype.

Boccaccio takes advantage also of the patristic predilection for typological exegesis in the episode of the marriage between Gualtieri and Griselda, where Gualtieri may be seen as symbolizing wisdom and Griselda patience. A medieval Christian audience, in fact, would have promptly recognized in this scene a symbolic representation of the marriage of Isaac and Rebecca, wherein Isaac, a prefiguration of Christ in the Old Testament, stands for perfect inborn virtue and perfect wisdom, and Rebecca, a prefiguration of the Church, stands for *patientia*, the sovereign feminine virtue.[7] After hinting at this well-known typological representation, Boccaccio, with an ingenious move, introduces some new implications

4. Several references to a Golden Age condition of existence and to nostalgia derived from the loss of it may be found in the works of Boccaccio, as amply demonstrated by Attilio Hortis in *Studii sulle opere latine del Boccaccio* (Trieste: Julius Dase, 1879), pp. 323–27 and 357–61. The works where most references occur are *Filocolo, Elegia di Madonna Fiammetta, Ameto, Genealogia Deorum Gentilium, Egloghe* VI and XI, and especially in an interesting allegorical-mythological work which appears in a codex by Boccaccio's hand, the so-called Zibaldone Laurenziano. This composition is supposed to be Boccaccio's first work in Latin prose, a sort of paraphrase of the first two books of Ovid's *Metamorphoses*, as Vittore Branca suggests in *Tradizione delle Opere di Giovanni Boccaccio* (Roma: Edizioni di Storia e Letteratura, 1958),

pp. 203, 209, 223, 228.
5. See Maud Bodkin's *Archetypal Patterns in Poetry: Psychological Studies of the Imagination* (London: Oxford Univ. Press, 1963), especially chapter III, "The Archetype of Paradise-Hades, or of Heaven and Hell," pp. 90–152.
6. For a thorough discussion of the Divine King archetype, see John Weir Perry's *Lord of the Four Quartets: Myths of the Royal Father* (New York: George Braziller, 1966); and Geza Roheim's *Animism, Magic, and the Divine King* (London: Kegan Paul-Trench Trubner, 1930).
7. See Jean Daniélou's *From Shadows to Reality: Studies in the Biblical Typology of the Fathers* (London: Burns and Oates, 1960), especially Chapter III, "The Allegory of the Marriage of Isaac," pp. 131–49.

by which Griselda turns out to be associated with the Christ archetype, while Gualtieri grows into a Divine King or Divine Father figure.

Gualtieri's wisdom is stressed all through the introductory part of the novella, especially in his relations with his subjects who are pressuring him to marry. This conflict of interests between Gualtieri and the society over which he rules, creates a gloomy mood which starts off the archetypal pattern of Hell-Paradise by conveying a general condition of unhappiness and discord. This negative condition is acknowledged in Gualtieri's remarks on human, and especially feminine, wickedness and dishonesty:

> "And to say that you can judge the character of a daughter by examining those of her father and mother is ridiculous (which is the basis of your argument that you can find a wife to please me), for I do not believe that you can come to know all the secrets of the father or mother; and even if you did, a daughter is often unlike her father and mother." [8]

Rather than accepting binding ties with the wicked world of human enterprises, Gualtieri prefers to lead a free and active life in the world of nature outside the society of the court and persistently tries to ignore the social obligations of his person and office regarding matrimony and the production of an heir. However, after a long period of unyielding resistance to all pressures, the awareness of his obligations to the society he rules forces him to consent to marry. In his acceptance of the marriage imposition, he poses two requisites: he will choose his future wife by himself, and his subjects will have to accept his selection unconditionally. These two clauses reveal the Marquis's intentions. He will set himself in search of a special feminine being who will prove at one with his wisdom, and thus he further reminds us of Rebecca, representing superior virtue and chosen for the same reason for Isaac, a man born with every virtue and perfect wisdom. The distinctive qualities of introspection, recognition of evil, and foresight, which mark Gualtieri's personality, designate him as a superior figure in his own society, akin to a Divine King figure, who takes it upon himself to reenact the salvation of his community through the creation and introduction of a sacrificial victim with a purifying function. The objective of Gualtieri's scheme, however, just like that of Divine Providence, will be revealed to and understood by the human society for which it is intended, only later, at the moment of fulfilment. In this context, Gualtieri's words and actions become endowed with a quasi-divine character, as designs

8. All citations from Boccaccio's *Decameron* are taken from the Griselda story as translated for this edition. [*Editors.*]

and arts carefully and purposely planned by a superior being for the welfare of his society.

Gualtieri's first creative act concerns the shaping of the heroine, first by selecting a few distinctive elements related to her physical configuration and then by adding in the symbolic scene of the marriage a few finishing touches which help in creating the Christ archetype.

The heroine is at first seen as an anonymous creature connected with the world of nature as to dwelling, esthetically qualified by beauty, and morally identified by goodness and by the Franciscan virtue of poverty:

> For some time Gualtieri had been pleased by the manners of a poor young girl who lived in a village near his home, and since she seemed very beautiful to him, he thought that life with her could be quite pleasant; so, without looking any further, he decided to marry her . . .

Gualtieri selects the physical configuration of his future wife from the world of nature which he himself prefers, and it seems appropriate to point out here that nature is constantly associated not only with Christ, in his many personifications as village-dweller, shepherd, and fisherman, but also with most prefigurations of Christ, such as Adam, for instance, the nature-dweller and name-giver to all animals, and Isaac, the desert-dweller and goat-herd.[9]

Virginity is another important element which provides striking connections both for Gualtieri and his creature: in the same way as God the Father of the Old Testament created Adam out of the "virgin earth," and Christ out of a "virgin mother," Gualtieri chooses a virgin body for the physical configuration of his heroine. A virgin body is indeed recognized by the heroine herself as the only element, "la dote mia," that she contributed to her own creation and which will provide her with a "sola camiscia" to cover her naked body in the last dramatic moment of her sacrificial path:

> ". . . I beg you, in the name of my virginity which I brought here and which I cannot take with me, that you at least allow me to carry away with me a single shift in addition to my dowry."

Later on, the heroine is further described as "guardiana di pecore," and this connection with sheep, the sacrificial animal, and with the shepherd, a symbolic Christ figure, intensifies the allu-

9. For an exhaustive discussion of the symbolic associations between Nature, Christ, and his prefigurations, see F. W. Dillistone's *Christianity and Symbolism* (Philadelphia: Westminster Press, 1955); see also Daniélou's *From Shadows to Reality*.

sion to the Christ archetype. This new creature takes her first steps therefore as a Christ-like allusive image, through her implied associations with a virginal origin, with the world of nature, and with the shepherding symbolism which is an intimation of sacrificial functions.

The association with the Christ figure is further strengthened in the symbolic scene of the marriage:

> When the day set for the wedding arrived, Gualtieri mounted his horse at about the middle of tierce, and . . . he said: "My lords, it is time to fetch the new bride." Setting out on the road with the entire company, they came to the house of the girl's father and found her returning from the well in great haste . . . when Gualtieri saw her, he called her by name—that is, Griselda —and asked her where her father was; to this she replied bashfully: "My lord, he is in the house."

The myth of the birth of the hero is reenacted in this scene: [1] it is dawn, the time of day symbolic of the beginning of a new life, and the heroine appears suddenly on the scene carrying water. This appearance strikes one immediately as suggestive, since among other things, water symbolizes the condition of innocence and purity connected with birth [2] as well as with Baptism. The heroine in this way makes her first appearance on the stage of her new life in all the integrity and virginity of the first moment of spiritual life. Her christening promptly follows, with the specification of her name provided for the first time in the story by Gualtieri himself. * * * The name itself seems to strengthen and corroborate the suggestion of the presence of the Christ archetype: Griselda or "image of Christ" as I am inclined to interpret etymologically from $\chi\rho\iota\sigma\acute{o}\varsigma$ = the anointed—as for the name of Christ—and $\epsilon\iota\delta o\varsigma$ = figure, image.[3] Gualtieri in addressing himself to her directly, calling her by such a resounding and symbolic name, seems to bring her to life for the first time, and her very first words "Signor mio" reveal now, and from now on in every one of her speeches, her recognition and acceptance of Gualtieri's significant role in her creation.

1. See Otto Rank's *The Myth of the Birth of the Hero and Other Writings* (New York: Vintage, 1964).

2. Mircea Eliade has dealt with this topic in *Images and Symbols: Studies in Religious Symbolism* (New York: Sheed & Ward, 1961), especially in Chapter V, "Baptism, the Deluge, and Aquatic Symbolism," pp. 151–60. Another work of his discusses the same subject, *Patterns of Comparative Religion* (Cleveland: Meridian, 1967), Chapter V, "Waters and Water Symbolism," pp. 188–215.

3. For further information on Greek etymology for the purpose of Christian exegesis, consult *Theological Dictionary of the New Testament*, ed. by Gerhard Kitted and trans. by Geoffrey W. Bromiley (Grand Rapids: Eerdmans, 1964–65), 3 vols.; Edward Robinson, *Greek and English Lexicon of the New Testament* (New York: Harper, 1855); John Parkhurst, *A Greek and English Lexicon of the New Testament* (London: Davidson, 1829). An interesting study of the method used by Boccaccio in his manipulations of Greek words is offered by Agostino Pertusi in "Le etimologie greche nel Boccaccio," in *Studi sul Boccaccio* 1 (1963), 363–85.

The heroine has come to life, christened and aware of the stigma of her birth. As for any true Christian hero, for Griselda, too, the moment of spiritual initiation promptly follows with her call to trial: [4]

Then Gualtieri dismounted and ordered all his men to wait for him; alone, he entered that wretched house, and there he found Griselda's father, who was called Giannucolo, and he said to him: "I have come to marry Griselda, but before I do, I should like to ask her some things in your presence." And he asked her, if he were to marry her, would she always try to please him, and would she never become angry over anything he said or did, and if she would always be obedient, and many other similar questions—to all of these she replied that she would.

The entrance of Griselda with Gualtieri into the poor hut of Giannucolo corresponds to a private initiation scene. When a hero is called to trial, according to many interpretations of the mythical quests of the hero,[5] he must be prepared to renounce his former way of living and to accept the new conditions of life set before him. Griselda undergoes such a ritual of renunciation and acceptance, enacted with Gualtieri in the little hut in front of one single older witness, Giannucolo, her guardian father. Giannucolo's little hut becomes the enclosure or initiation chamber [6] where the ritual is performed. A spiritually flawless creature is initiated to trials; she will accept the role of victim with the tacit consent of a parental kin whose name is reminiscent of Christ's baptizer. It seems cogent to notice at this point that the heroine will return for a short time to the hut and to her guardian father after her symbolic death at the end of her sacrificial path, in a kind of Limbo-like, preresurrection moment of expectancy. On the other hand, during Griselda's initiation Giannucolo and the little hut seem also to be connected with the life which Griselda is renouncing in order to consent to the call to trial which Gualtieri is setting before her. All of his demands for complete obedience, humbleness, and silent patience, are accepted by Griselda without reservations. Griselda's *crisma* of initiation is drafted and it has only to be sealed in the public acceptance ritual which follows immediately.

Gualtieri takes Griselda outside into the light of full recognition and has her undressed completely in front of all:

Then Gualtieri took her by the hand, led her outside, and in the presence of his entire company and all others present, he had her stripped naked. . . .

4. A fascinating study of the myth of the quest in four Medieval romances is offered by Heinrich Zimmer in *The King and the Corpse: Tales of the Soul's Conquest of Evil* (New York: Pantheon, 1948).
5. See Joseph Campbell, *The Hero with a Thousand Faces* (Cleveland: Meridian, 1966).
6. For an exhaustive discussion of the myths of initiation, consult Mircea Eliade's *Birth and Rebirth: The Religious Meanings of Initiation in Human Culture* (New York: Harper, 1958).

The initiation ritual is here repeated, in so far as the undressing corresponds to the ritual of renunciation of her previous condition of existence and the dressing represents her outfitting for the new life to come. Besides, this ceremony also suggests an enactment of the Christian ritual of Baptism, where nakedness stands for humble recognition of one's sins and for removal of them through the sacramental ritual. In her public nakedness, Griselda seems to reenact the ritual of Christ's baptism, and like him she takes it on herself to efface the sins of all those present at the ceremony. In so doing, she is already fulfilling the expectations of her sire who directs the ritual of undressing to be followed by a ceremony where new magnificent clothes are placed on her naked virginal body and a crown is set on her disheveled hair:

> . . . he had her stripped naked and the garments he had had prepared for her brought forward; then he immediately had her dress and put on her shoes, and upon her hair—as disheveled as it was—he had a crown placed. . . .

While the new clothes stand for the new life that Griselda has accepted in her private and public consent to her initiation, the last token of the ritual, the undefined crown, "una corona," placed on her disheveled hair, seems to suggest an even more revealing connection. In the light of the interpretation of Griselda as a *figura Christi*, the apparently unrelated detail of her hair being disheveled, may offer a further parallel with Christ and his own disheveled hair after his initiation ritual of undressing and flagellation. This last analogy between Christ's initiation and Griselda's seems also to offer a possible clue to the kind of crown which is here signified. Indeed, if we continue this analysis of parallels to include the crown also, we might suggest that it is the same crown made of thorns set by the soldiers on Christ's head when they "clothed him with purple and plaited a crown of thorns and put it on his head, and began to salute him 'Hail, King of the Jews'." In this context, the new clothing as well as the crown hint more and more poignantly at the Christ-like crucifixion road which Griselda is ready to take after sealing her *crisma* of initiation with those three words of final acceptance and endurance " 'Signor mio, sì.' " And Griselda is off on her V*ia Crucis*.

Fourteen are the stations of Christ's way to Calvary, or V*ia Crucis*, and "more than thirteen" are the years that Griselda spends on her road of tribulations. Three are the nails that fastened Christ's hands and feet to the cross, and three are the trials which deeply wound and bring Griselda to destruction. As a feminine counterpart of Christ, Griselda undergoes trials that are intended to hurt a woman the most, in her vital roles of mother and wife. The first two trials wound Griselda in her mother role: first her daughter, and then her son are taken away from her and she is left to believe that both have been put to death. The third trial harms Griselda in her wife role: she is made to feel unwanted and rejected, and eventually she is repudiated and left to believe that another woman will take her place.

However harsh the trials are, Griselda still remains faithful to her initiation promises, and the words she pronounces at every time of tribulation are repetitions of the consent she gave at the sealing of the *crisma* of her acceptance:

"My lord, do with me what you believe is best for your honor and your happiness, and I shall be completely happy. . . ."

This she says at the beginning of the first trial. When the second trial is in sight, she reassures Gualtieri in these words:

"My lord, think only of making yourself happy and of satisfying your desires and do not worry about me at all, for nothing pleases me more than to see you contented."

Finally, when the time comes to face the third trial which requires from her an act of renunciation of her married life and the acceptance of a return to Giannucolo's little hut, her long speech begins on the same note:

"My lord, I have always realized that my lowly origins were not suitable to your nobility in any respect, and the position I have held with you, I always recognized as having come from God and yourself; I never made it mine or considered it given to me —I always kept it as if it were a loan; if you wish to have it back again, it must please me (as it does) to return it to you . . ."

With these words, Griselda restates her acceptance of the stigma of her birth and her consent to the call to trial of her initiation. She keeps her promises up to the point of complete renunciation of that very life for which she had been created by her sire, and she disappears without complant.

At the precise moment of Griselda's disappearance, the ritual of undressing and dressing, which had such an important function in the initial ceremony at the beginning of her trials, takes place again in reverse order. Griselda disrobes herself of her attire and receives in exchange of her virginity "una sola camiscia" to cover her naked body:

. . . and in her shift, without shoes or anything on her head, the lady commended him to God, left his house, and returned to her father, accompanied by the tears and the weeping of all those who witnessed her departure. Giannucolo, who had never believed that Gualtieri would keep his daughter as his wife, and who had been expecting this to happen any day, had kept the clothes that she had taken off that morning when Gualtieri had married her; he gave them back to her, and she put them on, and began doing the menial tasks in her father's house . . .

Clothed in one single "camiscia," like a dead body, Griselda disappears and hides away in a post-death condition, reminiscent especially in her sackcloth attire, of the ceremony of stripping down altars and images on Good Friday after Christ's death.[7]

The time of resurrection is, however, closing in. Gualtieri sends for Griselda and she returns to the castle still incognito and dressed in her sackcloth garments in order to perform some specific actions which are reminiscent of another important ceremony of the Church liturgy. The thorough cleaning of rooms and halls, the hanging of draperies and ornaments on walls and windows, the laying of precious covers and clothes on beds and tables, the whole apparatus of pre-festivity represents a symbolic ritual which parallels the Church ceremonial preparations for the resurrection of Christ on Easter Sundays.

The ritual function by which Griselda receives and introduces to Gualtieri—here more than ever representing a Divine King figure—all the guests attending the festivity, even the ones believed dead, points at a further analogy with the Christ myth and precisely with the episode of Christ's return to the Father in Heaven with the souls of all the wise and the just rescued from Limbo. The wounds which Griselda acknowledges as elements of her martyrdom accentuate the analogy between hers and Christ's death. Even the words of covert reproach which Griselda addresses to Gualtieri ("I beg you as strongly as I can not to inflict those wounds upon her which you inflicted upon the other woman who was once your wife") imply the recognition of her sufferings and constitute at the same time a significant indication of human weakness similar to the one shown by Christ on the cross in his cry to the Father, "My God, my God, why hast thou forsaken me?" In both cases, the human connotation of physical weakness admittedly revealed in the words uttered by the sacrificial hero, increases the impact of the scene on the reader who becomes fully aware of the cruelty and injustice of the hero's predicament and sufferings which he has been left alone to endure. It is a moment of high dramatic tension, which will be relieved by Gualtieri's revelation whereby Griselda's resurrection will be triumphantly achieved:

> "Griselda, it is time now for you to reap the fruit of your long patience, and it is time for those who have considered me cruel, unjust, and bestial to realize that what I have done was directed toward a pre-established goal, for I wanted to teach you how to

7. On the topic of Church Liturgy, see the enlightening work by Alan W. Watts, *Myth and Ritual in Christianity* (London: Thames & Hudson, 1954), especially Chapters V and VII, "The Passion," and "From Easter to Pentecost," pp. 138–205; also see Gilbert Cope, *Symbolism in the Bible and in the Church* (London: SCM Press, 1959).

be a wife, to show these people how to know such a wife and how to choose and keep one, and to acquire for myself lasting tranquillity for as long as I was to live with you . . ."

Threefold was the purpose of Gualtieri, the superior being, as it clearly results from the last part of the revelation speech quoted above: (1) to create a perfect creature as woman and wife through a purifying and sacrificial quest for perfection; (2) to regenerate a whole society of men and women through the sacrificial performance of the heroine-victim; (3) to establish himself securely within a perfected society which has reached the quintessence of human happiness and harmony.

On this apotheosis of human excellence, further magnified by a last vision of Griselda in shining apparel emblematic of triumphant royalty, the narrative world of the one hundred novellas closes. The *Decameron*, dedicated to women, narrated mostly by women, centered largely around women's actions and feelings, concludes with the apotheosis of the perfect woman, a feminine *figura Christi*, who stands diametrically opposite the *figura diaboli* which had opened the book, Ser Ciappelletto, the incarnation of a black saint in constant hedonistic pursuit of evil.[8] The internal movement of the narrative has developed from the negative mood of the novella of Ser Ciappelletto (I, 1), where moral confusion prevails and the protagonist's "ingegno" is conducive to social disintegration at the lowest step of the human ladder of ethical values; to the all positive vision of the novella of Griselda, where moral integrity prevails, and Gualtieri's "ingegno" is conducive to social harmony and to the acquisition of the highest level of human happiness and ethical values, an earthly paradise of matrimonial and social bliss.

At the close of his *Divine Comedy*, Dante achieves spiritual perfection in heavenly paradise with the enlightening guidance of Beatrice, the angel-woman. In the canzone "Alla Vergine" at the conclusion of his *Canzoniere*, Petrarch implores spiritual elevation and moral insight from the Virgin Mary, queen of Heaven. At the end of the *Decameron*, Boccaccio evokes a vision of earthly perfection through the introduction of Griselda, the heroine who is the creator of harmony and happiness in the closing scene of his "human comedy." In her earthly perfection, Griselda serves an important function in the world of the *Decameron*: she represents the liaison between reality and myth, the reality of the morally frail womanhood portrayed in most of the *Decameron*, and the myth of the cherished Christian ideal of perfection in women as signified and exalted by Dante and Petrarch.

8. This topic has been discussed in my monograph on Boccaccio, *An Anatomy of Boccaccio's Style* (Naples: Cymba, 1968), Chapter II, "Ser Ciappelletto or 'Le Saint Noir': A Comic Paradox," pp. 23–51.

BEN LAWTON

Boccaccio and Pasolini: A Contemporary
Reinterpretation of *The Decameron* †

Pier Paolo Pasolini's cinematographic interpretation of *The De-cameron* is, in its own way, as important as the many scholarly commentaries on Boccaccio's masterpiece. Murder, sexual adventures, and graphic scatology appear in both Boccaccio's text and in Pasolini's film, but while the former has been legitimized by the passage of time, the latter has been accused of being unfaithful to its literary source, to Pasolini's own cerebral style, and to the cinema itself.[1] These responses were predicated upon a justifiable admiration for Boccaccio's *Decameron*, and on the less comprehensible assumption that Pasolini was merely attempting a mechanical transcription of the text rather than a reinterpretation of the fourteenth-century masterpiece. Much of the criticism of Pasolini's works has been based on the political attitudes of his critics and on the controversy which constantly surrounded the director.[2] His earliest films, *Accattone* (1961) and *Mamma Roma* (1962), seemed to foreshadow a rebirth of Italian neorealism and were welcomed especially by nostalgic leftist critics. With *The Gospel According to St. Matthew* (1964), Pasolini's international reputation reached its zenith. Both Catholic and Marxist critics found much to praise in this work, which adhered strictly to the text of the Bible while revealing many of the contradictions in both the Gospel itself and in "two thousand years of storytelling about the life of Christ." [3] Pasolini's next film, *Hawks and Sparrows* (1966), which was intended as an "ideo-comic" view of the end of neorealism as seen by a Marxist intellectual, turned out to be a rather intellectual commentary on the passing of the grandiose Brechtian drama of social denunciation, and of the more humble neorealist indictment

---

† Pier Paolo Pasolini (1922–75) was one of Italy's most controversial writers and film directors. Between 1954 and 1962, while writing two critically acclaimed novels, *The Ragazzi* (1955), and, *A Violent Life* (1959), Pasolini worked on the scripts of fifteen films for such directors as Federico Fellini and Bernardo Bertolucci. He then turned his attention to direction and made nineteen films before he met a violent death in 1975. *The Decameron* (1971), his cinematic interpretation of Boccaccio's masterpiece, sparked a new debate on the meaning of the medieval classic for twentieth-century readers.

1. Among the many reviews and essays which attack Pasolini's *Decameron* on these grounds, see Goffredo Fofi, "Qualche film," *Quaderni Piacentini* 44–45 (1971), 258; Guy Allombert, "Contre *Décameron*," *Image et Son* 255 (1971), 108; and Marc Gervais, *Pier Paolo Pasolini* (Paris: Seghers, 1973).

2. For a more extensive treatment of the life and works of Pasolini, see Gervais, *Pier Paolo Pasolini*; Oswald Stack, ed., *Pasolini on Pasolini* (Bloomington: Indiana University Press, 1969); and Sandro Petraglia, *Pier Paolo Pasolini* (Florence; La Nuova Italia, 1974).

3. Stack, *Pasolini on Pasolini*, p. 83.

of social and political ills. The films which followed—*Oedipus Rex* (1967), *Teorema* (1968), and *Pigsty* and *Medea* (1969)—became increasingly complex. While the director received the plaudits of a number of avant-garde critics, he progressively alienated the general public.

This trend defeated the purpose of Pasolini's original decision to enter the cinema in order to reach a broader audience than had been possible with literature. In his transition from the novel and poetry to film, Pasolini had, at first, felt that the shift involved only a change in technique, but he came to realize that the cinema had a "language" of its own. As he studied the nature of this language, he also decided that the attempts of most filmmakers to try to force film into the structure of prose narrative through an emphasis upon plot were mistaken.[4] Film, he argued, is intrinsically poetic: "it is a nonconventional language [*linguaggio*] unlike the written or spoken language [*lingua*] and expresses reality not through symbols but via reality itself." [5] And precisely because film is a more immediate form of expression, Pasolini felt that it had a "dreamlike" quality (*oniricità*) and was, therefore, closer to "the mystery and ambiguity of reality." [6] However, Pasolini came to reject the increasingly hermetic tendencies characterizing his later films and renewed his commitment to reaching a broader public. At the same time, he believed that the only valid films were those which caused scandal and forced the viewer to reconsider his preestablished attitudes. Thus, he rejected not only conventional films but also avant-garde works, since these, too, catered to a public which could no longer be shocked.[7] With *The Decameron*, Pasolini returned to the firing line and alienated a significant number of those critics who had championed his earlier works; at the same time, he acquired a broader, more eclectic audience. While the change in style and subject matter from his previous films seemed considerable, the director was, in fact, attempting to attain a greater fidelity to his artistic and ideological beliefs by means of his tribute to Boccaccio's *Decameron*.

Pasolini did not attempt a literal reproduction of Boccaccio's original. Having made *The Gospel According to St. Matthew*, he came to realize that a film will always differ from its literary source, even when it attempts to reproduce faithfully both dialogue and narrative, because the power of the visual images alters the text

4. Many of Pasolini's essays on the language of cinema have been gathered in *Empirismo eretico* (Milan: Garzanti, 1972), pp. 171–301. Unfortunately, the bulk of this work is not yet available in English. Among his more important essays available, at least in partial translation into English, see "The Cinema of Poetry," *Cahiers du Cinema in English*

6 (1966), 34–43; and "Cinematic and Literary Stylistic Features," *Film Culture* 24 (1962), 42–43.
5. Stock, *Pasolini on Pasolini*, p. 29.
6. Ibid., p. 150.
7. These theories are discussed by Pasolini in "Il cinema impopolare," *Nuovi Argomenti* 20 (1970), 166–76.

to an extreme degree.[8] Recreating the past by analogy, he intended
it to be a metaphor for the present.[9] Nonetheless, his *Decameron*
is extremely faithful to the spirit and the structure of Boccaccio's
collection of *novelle*. On the most superficial level, he deviates
from Boccaccio's text no more than the latter deviated from his
own sources, which included not only popular tales but also well-
known classics. To cite only one example, Boccaccio's version of
Peronella's story (VII, 2) certainly modifies the original found in
Apuleius's *Golden Ass* far more than Pasolini alters that found in
The Decameron. Boccaccio's answer to his critics, in this context,
might well have been adopted by the filmmaker: "And as for those
who say that these things did not happen the way I have told
them here, I should be very happy if they would bring forward
the original versions, and if these should be different from what
I have written, I would call their reproach justified and would try
to correct myself; but until something more than words appears,
I shall leave them with their opinion and follow my own, saying
about them what they say about me" (Prologue to Day IV).[1]
Boccaccio suggests quite clearly in this passage that once such
sources are expressed in his own particular style and within his own
particular framework, they are his property alone. Although Pasolini's film does pay homage to its literary source, it must be
evaluated as an original cinematic work of art.

In an interview given in 1972, Pasolini discussed his film in relation to Boccaccio and compared the author's joyous celebration of
the birth of the bourgeoisie with his own depiction of the innocent
joy of the lower classes of southern Italy, a world "which is at the
limits of history, and, in a certain sense, outside history." [2] Several
of Pasolini's major deviations from Boccaccio's text immediately
reveal that the film is intended to be an evolution beyond the
original. Of the three social classes portrayed by the Florentine
writer, the filmmaker depicts only the bourgeoisie and the lower
classes, while he totally ignores the aristocracy, a class he considers
irrelevant today. Moreover, the director avoids a historical recon-
struction of Boccaccio's medieval Italy and, instead, creates a work
akin to the late Middle Ages by analogy, a technique used in *The
Gospel According to St. Matthew*.[3] The director tells us explicitly
that the film is a reinterpretation of Boccaccio's *Decameron* by
having the storyteller start to read the first convent story (X, 2)

8. See the discussion of *The Gospel According to St. Matthew* in Stack, *Pasolini on Pasolini*, pp. 73–97; and "Pier Paolo Pasolini: An Interview with James Blue," *Film Comment* 3 (1965), 25–32.

9. Pasolini outlines his theories in "An Epical-Religious View of the World," *Film Quarterly* 18 (1965), 31–45; and in "Il sentimento della storia," *Cinema*

Nuovo 205 (1970), 172–73.

1. See p. 78, this edition. [*Editors.*]

2. This interview is reprinted in part by Petraglia in *Pier Paolo Pasolini*, pp. 15–16.

3. This process is explained in detail for *The Gospel According to St. Matthew* in "Pier Paolo Pasolini: An Interview with James Blue."

from a printed edition of the work. This is a blatant anachronism, since Boccaccio's work was written well over one hundred years before the invention of the printing press. The storyteller then pauses and says: "Now I'll tell it to you in the Neapolitan way!" [4] In other words, Pasolini has taken the text reflecting the rising middle class of Boccaccio's world [5] and has rewritten it in terms of the subproletariat, the only class, in his opinion, which retains "mythical features." [6]

The film, nevertheless, reveals the director to be a perceptive, scholarly reader of *The Decameron*. The *novelle* in Boccaccio's work are placed within a general framework and are arranged according to topics determined by the king or queen of the given day of storytelling. The individual stories are introduced to some extent by their storytellers, and on several occasions, Boccaccio addresses his imaginary readers directly to explain his intentions and to counter possible objections. These devices tend to destroy the illusion of reality in the work, and they focus our attention on the text as literature, not on the events which are, at best, only a metaphor for something else. Similar devices found in Pasolini's film suggest that we should not look at the events portrayed as "real," nor should we demand an external logic of them. As one critic has put it, "Our perception of the narrative as real, that is as being really a narrative, must result in rendering the recited object unreal." [7] The absence of apparent coherence, logic, continuity, and credibility is significant in itself, and should draw attention to the film as film or as a work of art. That this interpretation of the film conforms with the intentions of the director is strongly suggested in a recent interview where Pasolini clearly outlines his rejection of his earlier *externally* ideological works. In *The Decameron*, he claims to have tried to conceal his ideology and to have focused upon the "ontology of narration," upon the "mysterious workings of artistic creation," upon the "sheer joy of telling and recounting, for the creation of narrative myths." [8]

Contrary to what several critics have suggested, Pasolini goes beyond the adoption of a title and a few random episodes from Boccaccio. Pasolini alludes to Boccaccio by emphasizing the number ten in several ways. Most importantly, his film contains ten episodes from Boccaccio's text and ten original episodes.[9] Divided

4. All translations of the script of Pasolini's *Decameron* are my own, in the absence on any published screenplay in English.

5. For a discussion of Boccaccio's work as the epic poem of the mercantile class, see Vittore Branca, *Boccaccio medievale* (Florence: Sansoni, 1964).

6. Stack, *Pasolini on Pasolini*, p. 48.

7. Christian Metz, *Film Language: A Semiotics of the Cinema* (New York: Oxford University Press, 1974), p. 21.

8. Gideon Bachmann, "Pasolini Today: The Interview," *Take One* 4 (1973), 18–21.

9. See the detailed chart explaining the structure of Pasolini's film and its relationship to Boccaccio's *Decameron* on pp. 319–22 of this edition.

into two parts, the film includes five of Boccaccio's *novelle* in each part. Pasolini, however, deliberately conceals this structure by the asymmetrical repartition of his episodes in each section of the film. We find three Pasolini episodes in Part I and seven Pasolini episodes in Part II, respectively the number of days of storytelling into which the two parts of Boccaccio's *Decameron* are divided by the author's appearance as narrator in the introduction to Day IV, and the number of male and female narrators in the original work. The total number of Pasolini episodes, like the total of those borrowed from Boccaccio, equals the number of days of storytelling in the original text. The film is further complicated by the irregular patterns of the succession of Boccaccio and Pasolini episodes (Part I: P, B, BP, B, B, BPB; Part II: B, P, B, P, B, P, BPBPB, P, BPB, P); by the fusion of original and derivative episodes (for example, Ciappelletto appears as thief and pederast while the storyteller narrates the first convent story); and by Pasolini's additions to Boccaccio's episodes (for example, the vision of Giotto's disciple appears abruptly in the middle of the episode of Meuccio and Tingoccio). Furthermore, the Pasolini episodes may be subdivided into discrete categories (Giotto's disciple at work in the church; Giotto's disciple in the market place), and the three appearances of Ciappelletto only seem to derive from Boccaccio's *novella* (I, 1). More specifically, Messer Muscià describes Ciappelletto in terms similar to those employed by Boccaccio (B5), but the actual events depicted in Pasolini's version (P1 and P2) do not appear in the literary text.

Like Boccaccio, Pasolini designs an elaborate framework for his film. The ten episodes from Boccaccio are framed by two of Pasolini's own invention (P1 and P10). The episodes in the film are arranged by topics which are determined by the "kings" or dominant figures in the two parts of the film, Ciappelletto and the artist, Giotto's pupil. Each of these characters frames one part of the film. Part I opens with Ciappelletto in the rather dark and confusing murder scene (P1) and closes on him as the peasants crowd around to worship his dead body as that of a saint (B5). The artist, played by Pasolini himself, opens and closes Part II. We first see him in B6 when he and some friends seek refuge from a storm in a peasant's hut, and the last shot of the film in P10 shows him as he looks at his painting. In P1, Ciappelletto's victim screams: "You have understood nothing!" And in P10, Giotto's pupil, having completed his painting, asks himself: "Why realize a work of art when it's so nice simply to dream it?" These remarks seem to suggest that the topics of the two parts concern an error or a failure to comprehend. However, paraphrasing both Pasolini and Boccaccio, we might say that under the rule of Ciappelletto in Part I, it is only with his death that an individual can express himself fully, and that under the rule of the artist in

Part II, it is only the finished work of art which can fully express itself.[1]

All the episodes of Part I, with the exception of the story of Ciappelletto and Messer Muscià (B5) are open ended and remain seemingly ambiguous. Pasolini, however, warns us rather explicitly that a more careful reading of the film is essential. The last Ciappelletto episode (B5) is abruptly interrupted by an insert which presents an odd juxtaposition of life and death, perhaps best illustrated by the shot of the clergymen who play a primitive form of volleyball with a human skull. Almost inevitably the viewer is disturbed by this painterly montage which initially seems to have no narrative function but which, in fact, is the key to the entire first part of the film. The director has deliberately fused two works of art, *The Combat of Lent and Carnival* and *The Triumph of Death*, by Peter Brueghel the Elder.[2] The closing shot of the skull, which replaces the Christian symbol of the fish in Brueghel's *Combat*, suggests that death is the only possible synthesis in the dialectical conflict between the primitive urges of Carnival and the repressive tendencies of Lent, and that it is from this perspective that all the episodes in the film must be viewed.

As B5 ends, Ciappelletto is dead and is, hence, defined forever. As Pasolini once remarked, "live and remain unexpressed, or express yourself and die." [3] In life or in film he argues, it is only with death that one can have a meaningful montage. He expresses this theory concretely through his own montage of the important episodes of the life/film of Ciappelletto. Ciappelletto is a victim of the bourgeoisie who, as his own victim warns him (P1), has understood nothing. In life, he is exploited first by Messer Muscià, and then by the usurers; in death, he is used by the church as a saint. During his death scene, Pasolini speaks directly to the spectators of his film by breaking one of the cardinal rules of traditional filmmaking. A usurer turns directly to the camera and tells us that Ciappelletto is "really a saint!" Pasolini considers him a saint because the montage of his life which culminates in and is defined

1. The recent death of Pasolini is a tragedy for all who are interested in literature and the cinema. And yet, as Michelangelo Antonioni remarked, "he was the victim of his own characters—a perfect tragedy foreseen in its different aspects—without knowing that one day it would end up overpowering him" (*New York Times*, November 3, 1975, p. 38). His self-confessed killer was a young, part-time male prostitute, similar to many of Pasolini's characters, including Ciappelletto in his *Decameron*. In "La paura del naturalismo (osservazioni sul piano-sequenza)," *Nuovi Argomenti* 6 (1967), 11–23, Pasolini argues that the "meaning" of a life can only

be determined after death, and that death resembles, in this regard, the montage of the cinema.
2. The first of the works was painted in 1559 and is located in the Kunsthistorishes Museum in Vienna; the second was completed in 1562 and is in the Prado in Madrid. I would like to thank Professor Fredi Chiappelli, director of the Center for Medieval and Renaissance Studies at the University of California at Los Angeles, for his help in identifying these and other paintings too numerous to mention in this context.
3. Pasolini, "La paura del naturalismo," p. 22.

by his death is a total indictment of the bourgeoisie and of the institutions which represent this class—the church, the family, and business. Even though Ciappelletto may appear to act independently when he appears as a murderer, a thief, and a pederast, his relationship with Messer Mus cià, the usurers, and the church reveals that he is, and has always been, only a pawn to be used to exploit others.

By making a film based on Boccaccio's *Decameron*, Pasolini pays tribute to the first major Italian writer to turn away from the medieval theocentric vision of the human condition, but the storyteller episode, the absence of the aristocracy, the visual anachronisms, and the indictment of the bourgeoisie suggest that the director also intended to present a more contemporary perception of the anthropocentric view. This is underlined by the appearance in Part II of the director himself as the best "disciple" of Giotto, the painter whose artistic style went beyond the Byzantine theocentric vision of the world in the plastic arts. Pasolini's explanations for his presence in the film have bothered numerous critics who have responded negatively to his role. While his statement that the first two choices for the part were unavailable is too facile to be accepted, the reactions of the critics themselves indirectly reveal the success of the device. Pasolini's presence is a clear manifestation of the process of unrealization in narrative. Because of the storm, Giotto's pupil supposedly becomes unrecognizable. But this is only the narrated event, and thus should cause us to perceive that the director is addressing himself to another issue. The very act of drawing attention to the unrecognizability of Giotto's pupil, if anything, makes Pasolini more recognizable. It is not Pasolini as Giotto's pupil who is potentially unrecognizable, but Pasolini's new style.

The indictment of the bourgeoisie which characterizes Part I of the film is reinforced by Part II, which is structured in such a manner that its Boccaccio episodes clarify the respective Boccaccio episodes in Part I. The segments in which the director appears as Giotto's disciple also reinforce this indictment. At the same time, the latter serve to undermine the apparent reality of the narrative by making it virtually impossible for the viewer to succumb to the illusion of reality normally proper to film. These segments urge the viewer to reflect not only on the director's hidden, but well-defined political ideology, but more importantly, on his artistic ideology which requires that a work of art, like the mural painting by Pasolini/Giotto's pupil be finished but not completed.

If we compare the episode in which the artist first appears (B6) to the Andreuccio episode (B1), we can see strong parallels in the process of unrealization. Ninetto Davoli, a well-known star of the

Italian cinema who, paradoxically, became famous as one of Paso-lini's favorite nonprofessional actors, plays Andreuccio, the charac-ter who supposedly becomes unrecognizable to the servants and to the "brother" of the "beautiful Sicilian woman" because of his fall into a cesspool. However, he is recognizable both to his new-found "family" as Andreuccio and to the literate spectator as Ninetto Davoli. This technique of challenging apparent reality should also lead us to question Andreuccio's nature as it is pre-sented to us. When the young servant invites him to visit the beautiful Sicilian lady, Andreuccio's less than chaste thoughts are visually rendered by his casting aside a yellow flower. The result of his "sin" seems to be his fall into the feces, a punishment which Tingoccio specifically mentions when he appears briefly to Meuccio after his death (B10). It is possible, however, that Pasolini, the apostle of sex as revolution, has come to consider sexual desire a sin? [4] If we reconsider the story of Andreuccio (B1) in the light of the first episode in which we see Pasolini (B6), we observe that the director presents a criticism of himself as a disciple of Giotto which might suggest one answer. Although the artist dislikes being called "Maestro" and is the only person to thank the peasant for loaning him his rags to protect himself from the rain, he neverthe-less is part of a class which exploits members of the proletariat such as this innocent, unwary peasant. Pasolini, writing about him-self, once remarked: "I too, like Moravia and Bertolucci, am a bourgeois, in fact a petit bourgeois, a turd, convinced that my stench is not only scented perfume, but is in fact the only perfume in the world." [5] Thus, we might argue that the condemnation of Andreuccio is predicated not upon his sexual desire, but rather, upon his condition as bourgeois. Andreuccio, having been told that the woman he had planned to seduce is his "sister," suddenly appears holding a red flower to his nose. His "original sin," in the Pasolinian order of things, is his unquestioning surrender to the repressive power of the family.

The Pasolini episodes which follow serve to explain the Boccaccio episodes in an ever-increasingly explicit manner, and at the same time, they are increasingly self-reflexive. In P4, Giotto's pupil ar-rives in Naples to paint Santa Chiara.[6] Giotto's disciple is a painter of murals, that art form then most accessible to the masses, much as film is today. In these scenes, Pasolini also demonstrates to us that mural painting, like filmmaking, is a collective effort which

4. In *Pasolini on Pasolini,* Stack writes: "In fact, rather than politics, it is sex which Pasolini now seems to see as the main threat to the bourgeoisie" (p. 9).
5. Pier Paolo Pasolini, *Oedipus Rex* (New York: Simon & Schuster, 1971), p. 7.

6. Giotto was in Naples between 1329 and 1333 in the service of Robert d'An-jou. He and his pupils are said to have painted Santa Chiara, but nothing re-mains of their work, since the walls of the church were covered with stucco in 1700.

requires the use of massive machinery.[7] We next see Pasolini/ Giotto's pupil in the market place, where he looks at different people and frames them with his fingers. The people he frames are individually framed by the film itself as the director/painter turns to the camera, lowers his hands, and smiles directly at us (and the camera) to underline this process. As the story of Riccardo and Caterina opens (B7), we discover the family which was framed at the market place by the artist (P4).

Pasolini's ideology and his reinterpretation of Boccaccio become clearer when we compare this story to that of Isabetta and Lorenzo (B8), and then both of these episodes in Part II to the two convent stories from Part I (B2 and B3). A consideration of the two superficially similar love stories reveals a major difference in ideological content. Because Riccardo was born a member of the bourgeoisie, his escapade ends happily. Although Caterina's father surprises him naked in her arms, he escapes harm because he is wealthy and a suitable match for the girl. Lorenzo, on the other hand, is murdered by Isabetta's brothers because he is a servant and a member of a despised, exploited class. Pasolini emphasizes this difference by changing Boccaccio's story significantly. Lorenzo (who in Boccaccio's *Decameron* comes from Pisa, a northern Italian city) becomes a Sicilian in Pasolini's film, and his death is thus a result of the antisouthern racism which Pasolini portrays as a characteristic of the Italian middle class.[8] The two love stories thus function as an indictment of the bourgeoisie and one of its most important institutions, the family.

The appearance of the dead Lorenzo to Isabetta in her sleep is the first of Pasolini's mysteries in the film, an element in the work which reflects the director's constant attempt to reconsecrate ancient myths and to remystify reality.[9] This "mystery" is followed by a last shot of Isabetta, gazing upon the pot of basil containing Lorenzo's head, in a position very much like that of various Renaissance adoration scenes. In opposition to the mystery of reality in this scene, we find several other adoration scenes connected with

7. Film criticism is also often a collective effort requiring the use of much machinery. I would like to thank Mr. Donald Krim of United Artists/16 for the use of a print of Pasolini's film for the preparation of this essay. With the assistance of students and faculty of the Interdisciplinary Film Studies Program at Purdue University (Colin Marshall, Blair Austin, Kathy Greaney, William Lafferty, Deborah Levin, Richard Schulte, Richard Shapiro, Loretta Vowter, and Professor Anna Lawton), it was possible to reconstruct a script from the print of the film. Since this essay was written, an Italian script has appeared. See Pier

Paolo Pasolini, *La trilogia della vita* (Bologna: Cappelli, 1975).
8. In discussing the prison sentence he received for the making of his film, *La Ricotta* (1962), Pasolini remarked: "The Italians are supposed not to be racist, but I think this is a big lie. . . . Public opinion rebelled against me because of some indefinable racist hatred, which like all racism was irrational. They couldn't take *Accattone* and all the subproletarian characters" (Stack, *Pasolini on Pasolini*, pp. 63–64).
9. Pasolini, "An Epical-Religious View of the World," pp. 31–45; or Stack, *Pasolini on Pasolini*, pp. 9, 83.

the clergy which are demystified. The first occurs when our view of the peasants' hands reaching up to touch Ciappelletto, now a dead "saint," is juxtaposed with the shot of the richly dressed clergyman flanked by the two usurers. The obvious suggestion is that even in death, Ciappelletto is being used to facilitate the exploitation of the poor. Thematically related are the two adoration scenes contained in the story of Masetto (B3). The first pictures two nuns gazing up at Masetto's sexual organs and is intended as a spontaneous reconsecration of the primitive, instinctive sexual drive. This first moment of worship, however, is immediately coupled with the typical bourgeois process of rationalization and leads inevitably to the exploitation of Masetto, pleasant though it may seem at first, which is revealed in the words of one of the nuns who addresses Masetto as "animal" ("bestia") just as he is about to lay with her. The second adoration scene in this episode, picturing the nuns crowding around Masetto after the Mother Superior has told him he will be able to pass for a "saint" because of the "miracle" which has restored his speech, is simply a culmination and an institutionalization of his sexual exploitation. The nuns have managed to channel his services in a direction which serves their purposes just as Caterina's father was able to use Riccardo's affair with his daughter to his advantage. In both instances, church and family reflect their bourgeois foundations, just as Ciappelletto's sainthood and the murder of Lorenzo bear witness to the darker side of this class relationship.

In P6, we return to the market place, and as Pasolini/Giotto's pupil observes the scene, two of the characters there (Don Gianni and Compare Pietro) move directly into a Boccaccio episode (B9) from the market place of P6; thus, the objects of the director/painter's interest appear directly in the film without the mediating fiction of the mural of the Santa Chiara church. The relationship of Don Gianni, Compare Pietro, and Gemmata is analogous to that existing between the church and the subproletariat. The story concerns the demystification of yet another false miracle performed by a clergyman which is revealed to be a deception and exploitation planned with malice aforethought. Just as the story of Masetto and the convent was prepared by the tale narrated orally by the Neapolitan storyteller (P2), so, too, here the episode is punctuated by the revelry of a peasant wedding (P7). At this wedding, an event which is not to be found in Boccaccio's text, the only dialogue to interrupt the picture of the bride dancing with a priest is a drunkard's remark that all present are cuckolds ("Tutti cornuti!"). There is, presumably, truth in wine, for this remark explains the outcome of Don Gianni's visit. As Don Gianni pins the "tail" on Gemmata, he is also pinning the cuckold's horns on Compare

Pietro. Ignorance, the belief in miracles (in this case, a false miracle contrived by a churchman to indulge his own illicit desires) and greed motivate Gemmata and her husband to submit themselves to Don Gianni's plan. A comparison with the Peronella episode (B4) reveals a similar theme, for there the cuckold motif is expressed in the familiar gesture of the fingers by one of her neighbors. Here, however, there is a significant difference. While it is the desperate poverty of the one couple which leads them to believe any ridiculous story in order to improve their economic status, Peronella manipulates the greed of her husband, on the one hand, and the sexual desire of her lover, on the other, for her own benefit. For Pasolini, she epitomizes the selfishness of the middle class much as Don Gianni typifies the church.

The Meuccio and Tingoccio episode (B10) becomes understandable if we recall the allusion to the two works by Brueghel which are included in the earlier story of Ciappelletto (B5). While Pasolini included an insert in the earlier story of Ciappelletto which was inspired by these two paintings (P5), in this case he refers to another famous work of art, Giotto's *Last Judgment*.[1] He makes a significant modification in this work, as he had done earlier with those of Brueghel, for he replaces the Christ-Judge figure with a Madonna. While Meuccio is very much caught up in the combat between Lent and Carnival, the subject of the first of the Brueghel paintings, Tingoccio passes to the side of Carnival with such enthusiasm that the result is the triumph of death, the subject of the second Brueghel work. Those who have not read Boccaccio will naturally assume that Tingoccio is placed among the damned for his excessive love-making, but, instead, we witness the second mystery of Pasolini's film as Tingoccio returns from the dead just as Lorenzo had returned earlier to Isabetta (B8). In response to Meuccio's anxious questions about his punishment in hell for his sex life, Tingoccio announces that he was told in the other world: "You turd! Forget it! Screwing your 'comare' is not a sin here!" [2] Upon hearing this revelation, Meuccio runs to his own "comare" and shouts: "It [sex] is not a sin!" Tingoccio's message from the realm of the dead expresses Pasolini's anthropocentric vision of the

---

1. Giotto's *Last Judgment* covers the entire entrance to the Arena chapel in Padua and confronts the viewer as he turns to leave. It was painted around 1306.

2. In *Opere di Giovanni Boccaccio*, Cesare Segre, ed. (Milan: Mursia, 1967), Maria Segre notes that "during Boccaccio's times the relationship between 'comare' (the woman whose child one has held during the baptism) and 'compare' (godfather) was considered particularly close, to such an extent that sexual relations between the two were considered incestuous" (p. 979). The more casual use of the expressions "compare" and "comare" in Pasolini's film would seem to suggest that he intended a more general meaning of the words, a form of familiar address which Boccaccio himself uses in the story of Don Gianni, Compare Pietro, and Gemmata (IX, 10).

world. After criticizing other directors for not committing themselves to an idea and expressing it in a finished form, for not "dying enough in their films," [3] Pasolini does just this in *The Decameron*. Tingoccio's death serves to give concrete form to Pasolini's point of view, here thinly disguised as that of Giotto's pupil. By replacing Christ the Judge in Giotto's original with the Madonna-like figure played by Silvana Mangano, who portrayed Pasolini's mother in *Oedipus Rex*, the director is suggesting that this film too is a "kind of completely metaphoric—and therefore mythicized—autobiography." [4] Pasolini in this manner reveals that he has rejected the "super-ego represented by the father repressing the child." [5] And while the triumph of death may inevitably follow the combat of Carnival and Lent, in Pasolini's own version of the Last Judgment, one is no longer punished for sexual transgressions. The oppression and the exploitation of the poor will now be considered as the cardinal sins in his anthropocentric cinematic universe.

Pasolini's controversial ideological statements in his *Decameron* do not ignore the humanist heritage of Boccaccio's *Decameron* but seek to preserve this heritage in the contemporary world. After a period of didactic films, Pasolini came to reject film as a tool for mass communication and remarked that, for him, "the only hope is a cultural one, to be an intellectual . . . for the rest I am consistently pessimistic." [6] Pasolini had not lost all faith in the potential of the cinema, however, and he believed that there still existed a "small space for culture of a humanist tendency" as there was "still a possibility of some sort of relationship of a personal nature, since the film *I* make is seen by *you*." [7] Within the film, Pasolini clearly outlines the limitations of his ideology. Tingoccio's last speech to Meuccio is deeply rooted in an ancient culture and tradition which have changed little from Boccaccio's times in spite of its revolutionary rejection of sexual repression: "Have masses said, and prayers. Be charitable. That helps us a lot." These limits are, furthermore, underlined by the mural painted by the director/artist in the church. It is an incomplete triptych, composed of a Gothic, heaven-directed arch in the first panel, an anthropocentric rectangle whose top line is perfectly horizontal in the second panel, and a third panel which is completely blank. Pasolini, the descendant of Boccaccio and Giotto, has taken a step forward through an imaginative retrieval of the past. He moves back in time to the medieval world which was their point of departure and then, using

3. Pasolini, "La paura del naturalismo," p. 21.
4. Stack, *Pasolini on Pasolini*, p. 120.
5. Ibid.
6. Ibid., p. 124.
7. Bachmann, "Pasolini Today: The Interview," pp. 19–21.

them as a springboard, he vaults into the contemporary world, completely bypassing the implicitly desperate Renaissance opposition of life and death which in the film is synthesized by the montage of Brueghel's works. He presumes to have done no more than this, and has no simplistic answers for the future; thus, the absence of a third panel.

Pasolini's *Decameron* is not without a structure; Boccaccio, Giotto, and Brueghel are not merely occasional sources, nor is the director's choice of episodes random. The film has a discernible ideological posture with both political and psychological dimensions.[8] The magic of Pasolini's film multiplies with each successive viewing as a number of tantalizing possible structures, apparently contradictory ideologies, and different potential films are discovered hidden beneath the surface. Two phrases frame the film: "You have understood nothing!" and "Why realize a work of art when it's so nice simply to dream it?" The first is a description of the great majority of the work's characters and is a warning to the spectators. The second reveals the internal contradiction which, according to Pasolini, is proper to both life and art. Neither Ciappelletto's life nor Pasolini's *Decameron* can express itself fully until it is completed. At the same time, the joy of creativity and of narration exists most intensely for the author during the process of creation preceding the work's final form. This awareness has driven the director to force the spectator to participate in his narration, to become not merely the user or the consumer of the work but the author of yet another work of his own creation. Pasolini defines this effort as a sadomasochistic process: sadistic for those spectators who do not understand and who wish to be spoon-fed; masochistic because these same spectators (and, in particular, critics) will heap abuse on the director. For those who *do* understand, for the liberated spectator, there remains the joy of witnessing the freedom of another human being, the director, who carries forward his revolution by breaking the laws of the "language" of cinema.[9]

Pasolini has rejected the limitations of traditional and of avant-garde cinema; he says that these types of film have already been analyzed, and that whether they are produced in Paris, Prague, Brazil, or Italy, their structures are identical and have been revealed, and their respective publics treat them as consumer products.[1] Their conventions are obvious and they have lost their oneiric, dreamlike qualities. Pasolini's *Decameron* avoids such es-

8. For a discussion of Pasolini's ideology, see Francesco Dorigo, "Pasolini da Marx a Freud," *Rivista del Cinematografo* 4 (1970), 135–41; and Franco Prono, "La religione del suo tempo in Pier Paolo Pasolini," *Cinema Nuovo* 215 (1972), 42–45.

9. Pasolini, "Il cinema impopolare," pp. 166–76.

1. Pasolini, "Il cinema di poesia," in *Uccellacci e uccellini* (Milan: Garzanti, 1966), p. 41.

tablished structures by remaining a process rather than becoming a completed form and is such not only for the director while he is making the work but also for the individual spectator while he views it. Pasolini tantalizes us by playing with a number of well-known structures from literature (Boccaccio's *Decameron*) and art (works by Brueghel and Giotto). Following a procedure anologous to Boccaccio's mixture of stylistic levels in *The Decameron*,[2] Pasolini confuses and delights us by altering slightly these artistic masterpieces and by mixing them with a parade of earthy faces, gestures, dialects, and actions which seem typically Italian and proletarian in origin. The structure of Pasolini's *Decameron* thus captures the essence of the mystery and the magic of Boccaccio's text. Pasolini, the reader of Boccaccio and the interpreter of both Giotto and Brueghel, becomes the author of a new masterpiece through his personal reading of them and, thus, gives them a new life. At the same time, he refuses to give us a work which we can merely consume. The rectangular shape of the second panel of the artist's triptych, representing the present, does not accidentally reproduce the shape of a single frame of film, nor is it accidental that it is virtually impossible to determine its contents. The dreamlike, memorylike nature of Pasolini's *Decameron* keeps it from ever being merely a consumer product. It is a dream which we as readers/authors must rewrite with every viewing.

2. For a consideration of the levels of style in Boccaccio, see the selection from Erich Auerbach's *Mimesis* reprinted in this edition on pp. 269–95.

ANALYTICAL TABLE [1]

Part I

Pasolini's *Decameron*	Boccaccio's *Decameron*
P1: Ciappelletto commits a murder; his victim screams: "You have understood nothing!"	
B1: Andreuccio da Perugia.	II, 5: Andreuccio from Perugia, having gone to Naples to buy horses, is caught up in three unfortunate adventures in one night; escaping from them all, he returns home with a ruby.

1. The episodes inspired by Boccaccio's *Decameron* are indicated with the letter B; the Pasolini episodes are indicated with the letter P. All of Boccaccio's *novelle* listed here and included in Pasolini's film are present in this edition of *The Decameron*.

Pasolini's *Decameron*	Boccaccio's *Decameron*
P2: The Neapolitan storyteller and Ciappelletto as a thief.	
B2: The first convent story, as told by the Neapolitan storyteller.	IX, 2: An abbess quickly gets up from her bed in the dark to surprise one of her nuns accused of being in bed with her lover. The abbess herself is with a priest in bed, and she puts his pants on her head, thinking that she is putting on her veil. When the accused nun sees the pants and points them out to the abbess, she is set free and is allowed to be with her lover.
P2: The Neapolitan storyteller and Ciappelletto as a pederast.	
B3: Masetto da Lamporecchio and the second convent story.	III, 1: Masetto from Lamporecchio pretends to be a deaf-mute and becomes the gardener for a convent of nuns, who all compete to lie with him.
B4: Peronella.	VII, 2: When her husband returns home, Peronella puts her lover inside a barrel which the husband has sold; she says she has already sold it to someone who is inside checking to see if it is sound. When her lover jumps out of the barrel, he has her husband scrape it and carry it off to his home for him.
B5: Ciappelletto and Messer Muscià.	I, 1: Ser Cepperello tricks a holy friar with a false confession and dies; although he was a most evil man during his lifetime, he is after death reputed to be a saint and is called Saint Ciappelletto.
P3: Pasolini's tribute to Brueghel's *The Combat of Carnival and Lent* and *The Triumph of Death*.	
B5: Ciappelletto's confession, death and sanctification.	

Part II

B6: Pasolini, the northern artist, is not recognizable as "Giotto's best disciple."	VI, 5: Messer Forese from Rabatta and Maestro Giotto, the painter, make fun of each other's poor appearance as they return from Mugello.

Pasolini's *Decameron*	Boccaccio's *Decameron*
P4: The artist arrives in Naples and the mural is produced as a collective effort; the view of Caterina's family in the marketplace; the painting of Santa Chiara.	
B7: Riccardo and Caterina.	V, 4: Ricciardo Manardi is found by Messer Lizio of Valbona with his daughter; Ricciardo marries her and remains on good terms with her father.
P5: The artist eats rapidly with the friars and returns to his work.	
B8: Isabetta, Lorenzo's decapitation, and the pot of basil.	IV, 5: Isabetta's brothers kill her lover. He appears to her in a dream and tells her where he is buried. She secretly digs up his head and places it in a pot of basil, over which she weeps every day for a long time. Her brothers take it away from her, and, shortly afterwards, she dies of grief.
P6: The artist sees Don Gianni and Compare Pietro in the marketplace.	
B9: Don Gianni goes to Compare Pietro's home and meets Gemmata, his wife.	IX, 10: At Compare Pietro's request, Father Gianni casts a spell in order to turn his wife into a mare; but when it comes time to stick the tail on, Pietro spoils the spell by saying that he doesn't want the tail.
P7: A view of the revelry at the peasant wedding.	
B9: Don Gianni at the home of Compare Pietro and Gemmata.	
P7: The wedding of Zita Carapresa ("all cuckolds").	
B9: Don Gianni puts the tail on Gemmata.	
P8: The artist paints while his assistants whistle.	

Pasolini's *Decameron*	Boccaccio's *Decameron*
B10: Meuccio and Tingoccio, the problem of the sinfulness of sex, and the death of Tingoccio.	VII, 10: Two Sienese are in love with the same woman, and one of them is the godfather of her child; when he dies and returns to his friend, according to a promise he had made to him, he describes how people live in the next world.
P9: Pasolini's tribute to Giotto's *Last Judgment* in a vision of the artist in which the Madonna replaces Christ.	
B10: Tingoccio returns from the dead to tell Meuccio: "It [sex] is not a sin!"	
P10: The painting is finished and a celebration ensues; Pasolini, the artist figure, asks: "Why realize a work of art when it's so nice simply to dream it?"	

MARK MUSA and PETER BONDANELLA

The Meaning of *The Decameron*

The meaning of Boccaccio's *Decameron* has been a hotly debated critical issue, seemingly incapable of any definitive solution since the moment the first manuscripts of the work began to circulate in public. And yet, the formal structure of this collection of *novelle* is deceptively simple. The tales number one hundred and are told by ten young people (seven of whom are women) on ten successive days of storytelling. Each day, one of the group is chosen to rule the activities of the day and to determine the topic of the tales to be told on that day. These storytellers are introduced in an author's prologue where Boccaccio speaks directly to the reader, explaining how the plague of 1348 has caused the ten men and women to flee their homes in Florence and to seek shelter in the countryside. When three days of storytelling have passed, Boccaccio again interrupts the narrative and speaks directly to his reader in a prologue to the tales of the fourth day. Again, after the final tale of the tenth day is related, the narrator concludes with a defense of his work.

This, then, is the basic form of the collection. But the narrative's complexity arises from a combination of several separate but integrally related fictional worlds: the world within the tales themselves; the world of the storytellers (the "bella brigata," as Boccaccio calls them); and finally, the world of the omniscient narrator who stands above the other worlds and functions as a mediator between the reader and the literary universe he has created around the collection's framework. Because studies of *The Decameron* too often limit themselves to considerations of only one aspect of this multifaceted work, no general agreement among scholars as to the work's meaning has yet been reached. The present essay will suggest an approach to *The Decameron* which may aid the reader in viewing the totality of Boccaccio's masterpiece without necessarily overlooking the importance of any single aspect of his creation.

Much of the criticism of *The Decameron* which is devoted to the world within the *novelle* concludes that the work reflects the ethos of a particular class or historical period. Thus, De Sanctis's influential treatment of Boccaccio shows him to be representative of a new secular era in the development of the Italian spirit.[1] Another important study speaks of the work as a "mercantile epic" and underlines how the book's main themes correspond to the interests of a new merchant class which first appeared in the Italy of Boccaccio's day.[2] A more aesthetic approach to the *novelle*, most characteristic of recent criticism, concentrates upon the form of the *novelle* rather than their content. This formalistic approach to the structure of individual *novelle* or to various categories of *novelle* within the collection leads quite naturally to an interest in Boccaccio's narrative style.[3] A final element is the imaginary world of the storytellers. Here, in a rustic but highly civilized Arcadia set apart from the workaday world of economic necessity, songs, dancing, and storytelling instead of work occupy the time of the merry company whose affluence allows a freedom not enjoyed by ordinary mortals. One controversial reading of *The Decameron*, concentrating upon this aspect of the book, attempted to explain the work's purpose by assigning to each storyteller an abstract, allegorical quality associated with Boccaccio's philosophical or literary interests.[4] An unfortunate by-product of this argu-

1. See the selection from De Sanctis's *History of Italian Literature* reprinted in this edition.
2. See Vittore Branca, *Boccaccio medievale* (Florence: Sansoni, 1964).
3. Analyses of *The Decameron* illustrating this approach to varying degrees can be found in the selections by Wayne Booth, Tzvetan Todorov, Marga Cottino-Jones, and Erich Auerbach which are reprinted in this edition.
4. See Angelo Lipari, "The Structure and Real Significance of *The Decameron*," in *Essays in Honor of Albert Feuillerat*, ed. Henri M. Peyre (New Haven: Yale University Press, 1943),

pp. 43–83. Lipari views the entire *Decameron* as replete with hidden meanings: "Panfilo represents the innate 'gentilezza' of the humanist poet; Filostrato his 'passione amorosa'; Dioneo the principle of 'docere delectando.' These three male figures constitute, as it were, the main pillars of the structure. The female figures, on the other hand, embody the chief characteristics or qualities of humanistic Renaissance art in general and of Boccaccio's art in particular. . . . This, then, is the structure and real significance of the *Decameron*" (p. 83).

ment was a counterargument which rejected not only any allegorical approach to the work but also any attempt to discover a serious purpose in the collection whatsoever. Far from defining the work as one wherein the purpose was hidden beneath an elaborate system of allegory, this interpretation defined *The Decameron* as "an art of escape . . . an art completely bare and defenseless, for it could not claim to teach." [5]

Since Boccaccio fashions his literary masterpiece out of these three fictional worlds, any view of the work's purpose must take them all into account, without unduly stressing any single element comprising the whole. Furthermore, the refusal to see any serious purpose in *The Decameron* is a position which cannot be substantiated after a careful examination of the work's structure or the narrator's own remarks in the work itself. In the last analysis, it is the skillful artifice of Boccaccio's literary creation which guarantees the serious purpose of *The Decameron*, for as Boccaccio himself noted in *The Genealogy of the Gods* (XIV, 9):

> Fiction is a form of discourse, which, under guise of invention, illustrates or proves an idea; and, as its superficial aspect is removed, the meaning of the author is clear. If, then, sense is revealed from under the veil of fiction, the composition is not idle nonsense. [6]

Any serious literature will, therefore, possess a significance accessible only to the careful reader. But no elaborate system of erudite allegory or mysterious symbolism is needed here. Rather, a thoughtful analysis of the poet's work and the ability to sort out the superficial aspects of it from those which contribute more directly to its meaning are required in order to assess the author's intentions.

We noted earlier that the ten days of storytelling each had a particular topic around which the stories were organized, and that at the end of each day in the collection, the topic for the following day is announced. No significant reason for choosing one topic or another is ever given, but the arrangement of the ten days according to the topics discussed in the day's *novelle* is carefully set out by Boccaccio in the following manner:

DAY   TOPIC TO BE DISCUSSED.
I   Subjects freely chosen.
II   Stories about those who attain a state of unexpected happiness after a period of misfortune.
III   Stories about people who have attained difficult goals or who have recovered something previously lost.

5. Charles S. Singletòn, "On Meaning in *The Decameron*," *Italica* 21 (1944), 118.
6. *Boccaccio On Poetry: Being the Preface and the Fourteenth and Fifteenth Books of Boccaccio's Genealogia Deorum Gentilium*, ed. Charles G. Osgood (Indianapolis: Bobbs-Merrill, 1956), p. 48.

The most striking characteristic of this arrangement is that within the frame of the ten days themselves, there is a second and more important frame established within the limits of the first and ninth days. By making the subject matter of these two different days the same, the only time such parallelism occurs in the work, Boccaccio underlines clearly the fact that the first nine days are to be set off by the reader from the final day. At the end of the ninth day, Panfilo announces the subject matter for the coming day, but in this particular instance, the topic of the following day has a significance which extends beyond the fictional world of Boccaccio's storytellers and reveals something of the narrator's intentions in creating his work of art while clarifying the motivation behind his careful arrangement of the collection's framework:

> Tomorrow I wish for each of you to be ready to tell a story on a subject concerning those who have acted freely or magnificently in affairs of the heart or other matters. Telling these stories and hearing them will, without a doubt, kindle your spirits to adopt a lofty course of action (your spirits, in fact, are already well disposed in that direction), and in so doing, our lives which cannot be anything but brief within our mortal bodies, will be perpetuated through our praiseworthy fame, which anyone who thinks beyond his belly should not only desire but strive for with every bit of his strength. (IX, 10)

Here, for the first time in the entire work, Boccaccio uses Panfilo's suggestion to point toward a goal to which both his storytellers and his readers might aspire. This goal is a very human one, and the medieval reader of Boccaccio's day might have been somewhat surprised at even the notion of such a goal. In contrast to Dante, Boccaccio does not take his reader beyond the sphere of the moon. Instead, he investigates every phase of human activity in this restricted sphere he knows so well. And Boccaccio does this during the first nine days of storytelling. At the end of the ninth day, after Panfilo's announcement of the topic for the concluding day, Boccaccio then tells his reader where his goal or happiness should rest, and in so doing, he underlines here, belatedly, what must have been his main purpose in writing *The Decameron* as a whole—to find man's goal on earth.

It is not by accident that the opening words in this work are "Umana cosa è . . ." ("Human it is . . ."). And in the first nine days of his masterpiece, Boccaccio deals with the topic of man's goal on earth by presenting ninety different views of the human condition, ninety human dramas or "umane cose." To find man's goal, Boccaccio first investigates man. He observes how man reacts in various situations. Boccaccio, the artist, paints these many miniatures of humanity struggling with Fortune and surviving with its intelligence. All the while, he has a definite end or purpose in mind—the final presentation to his reader of a tangible, attainable, and completely human goal following a thorough investigation of "umane cose" which seem to possess no direction or purpose in sight. And the investigation which precedes the presentation of the goal itself proves the need for such a purpose.

If there is really a serious purpose motivating this work, one may well ask why, in several places in the frame, Boccaccio tells the reader that the book is not for students or learned men but is aimed rather at "donne oziose," or "idle ladies." Surely, no "serious" work could be directed only to this kind of audience if it intended to impart as important a human goal as the achievement of fame in this world. But how serious is Boccaccio when he claims that his book is addressed only to these "idle ladies"? Is it not more likely that these women serve him as an excellent excuse for the writing of the work, since they assist the narrator in creating within the frame of the *novelle* the idle-moment atmosphere so necessary to the art of storytelling? So then, with the appropriate excuse of wanting to please these idle listeners, Boccaccio grants his creative fantasy complete freedom to interpret and comment upon the state of society in his times and upon the human condition in general. This work, then, is no mere escapist literature; on the contrary, Boccaccio directs his society to a definite end, an attainable human goal.

It is true, of course, that on the most literal level, the collection of tales can be considered as entertainment without the need to search for any further intent. But this literal level only begins to exhaust the work's possibilities. Even the simplest elements in it often reveal themselves to have a double-edged meaning. Take, for instance, Boccaccio's reference to the title of his work in the opening sentence: "Here begins the book called Decameron, also known as Prince Galeotto," a subtitle which he repeats again at the end of the collection to underline its significance. While this opening may puzzle the contemporary reader who is poorly acquainted with Italian literary history, an attentive reader of the fourteenth century would probably not have failed to catch Boccaccio's pointed reference to a famous line in Dante's *Inferno* (Canto V, line 137) in which he mentions Galeotto, the Italian form for Gallehault. In the Old French prose romance *Lancelot*, Dante and his contemporaries had learned to picture Galeotto as the go-between in the love affair of Lancelot and Queen Guinevere. In Canto V, Francesca informs Dante the pilgrim that "The book and its author was our galehot" ("Galeotto fu il libro e chi lo scrisse"), falsely implying that her love affair was caused by reading a romance with Paolo, her lover.[7] Does Boccaccio mean to imply that *The Decameron* can or should function, in like manner, as a work which will serve as a go-between for his "idle ladies"? And does he intend for his tales to spur his audience on to experience the same sensual indulgence he so frequently describes in his stories?

Fortunately, the answer to this question is supplied by the author himself in his Conclusion. There, Boccaccio admits that some of his readers will think he has exceeded the normal limits of propriety, but he affirms that the stories he presents are, in themselves, morally neutral:

> Whoever wishes to derive wicked counsel from them or use them for bad ends will not be prohibited from doing so by the tales themselves if, by chance, they contain such things and are twisted and distorted in order to achieve this end; and whoever wishes to derive useful advice and profit from them will not be prevented from doing so, nor will these stories ever be described or regarded as anything but useful and proper if they are read at those times and to those people for whom they have been written.

Moreover, he claims that everything, and this includes any and all of his *novelle*, "is, in itself, good for some determined goal, but badly used it can also be harmful to many."

Most of the *novelle* in *The Decameron* resist a simplistic interpretation and reveal, upon closer examination, a secondary and more significant meaning. The story of Andreuccio of Perugia (II, 5) seems simple enough; on a first reading, it appears to be an account of a country bumpkin who is deceived by several clever city slickers. But a deeper analysis of the story uncovers a purposeful pattern underlying the three mishaps that befall the protagonist which turns the tale into a profound prepicaresque journey from colossal ignorance to a clearer understanding of the nature of worldly affairs or "umane cose." Again, the story of Ser Ciappelletto (I, 1) at first glance seems to be an uncomplicated anticlerical story about a man who, while on his deathbed, tells lies and tricks a gullible priest, so that his sinful life is forgotten and

7. For a discussion of this problem in Dante, see Anna Granville Hatcher and Mark Musa, "The Kiss: *Inferno* V and the Old French Prose *Lancelot*," *Comparative Literature* 20 (1968), 97–109; or Mark Musa, *Advent at the Gates* (Bloomington: Indiana University Press, 1974), pp. 19–35.

he is made a saint on the strength of his amazing confession alone. Yet, without ignoring the humor in the text, the tale can also be read as a serious discussion of the nature of sainthood and the relationship between human affairs and divine grace. Finally, as a counterpart to Ser Ciappelletto, the perfect sinner, the hero of virtuoso villainy who attains sainthood, we have another extraordinary figure, patient Griselda in the concluding tale of the tenth day. Boccaccio, no doubt, meant to present Griselda's patience and fortitude as a virtuous source of admiration and deserved fame, and in enduring her trials, she becomes a kind of modern Job and a symbol of innocent and suffering femininity. Yet her fame is insufficient to make either the narrator or the reader forget that the cruelty involved in her trials and her husband's heartlessness are a product of a feudal system which, for all its obvious faults, Boccaccio may elsewhere present as admirable in certain respects (particularly in the story of Federigo and his noble falcon: V, 9).

The ambivalence Boccaccio creates in his *novelle* reflects his underlying belief that the nature of reality itself is not simple, one-sided, or limited in meaning; the search for the essence of "umana cosa" in his work uncovers the fact that human nature is capable of seeking a number of goals. We said earlier that the tenth day is set apart from the other days in order to put into relief the moral purpose towards which Boccaccio hopes his readers will strive. The distance between these nine days and the concluding day is, however, not a great one; no impassible chasm, this distance is just enough to inform the reader that the tenth is a special day. Even though the parallel between the ninth day and the first would seem to separate the first ninety stories from the last ten, there is a curious link between the last story of the ninth day and the final story of the tenth day. One of the elements of this link is to be expected: the storyteller must be the same. Not surprisingly, it is Dioneo who tells the story which concludes the ninth day, for he is the narrator who usually spices his tales with sexual escapades and passages which have often enraged the same prudish censors Boccaccio attacks in his prologue to the fourth day and in his conclusion. In this *novella*, we see Father Gianni "transform" Gemmata into a mare by a sexual act. It is true that, if read frivolously, this story might seem to be merely a comic indictment of an ignorant man's gullibility. Compare Pietro is taken in by one more clever than he and is cuckolded before his very eyes by a tall story about the magic transformation of a woman into a mare. But, if read seriously, it surely offers us a picture of a debased humanity delivered over to its animalistic instincts by a wily priest and with no hope of a redeeming and morally uplifting social purpose on this earth. It is that animal nature dormant in man which most humanists of Boccaccio's day and afterwards had hoped to discipline, educate, civilize, and finally eradicate.

Set apart by the framing device of the first and ninth days, the picture of "umana cosa" that Boccaccio presents to his reader in the first ninety *novelle* thus concludes with a sorry account of struggling humanity given over to its baser instincts. It is most likely that Boccaccio placed this tale in the tenth story of the ninth day of his collection to underline his departure from the theocentric view of man held by many of his contemporaries, since the number ten is achieved by the sum of the number nine—the square of three, symbol of the Holy Trinity—plus the number one—symbol of the divine unity of this tripartite God. It is typical of Boccaccio's turn of mind that he would employ numerical symbolism traditionally associated with religious themes for an entirely different purpose. But Boccaccio never indicates that the all-too-human qualities illustrated by Father Gianni and his victims do not have their proper place in his picture of the human condition. And the fact that the same storyteller, Dioneo, tells both the tale of Father Gianni and that of patient Griselda suggests that he and Boccaccio were warning us not to forget that human nature is an intricate and mysterious blend of saintliness and sin, of sex and sacrifice. In *The Decameron,* Boccaccio never expects man to rise above his nature through a religious conversion or a denial of his essential character. Instead, he only hopes that man's inherent variety can be channeled into some praiseworthy direction, that which he suggests and illustrates in the final day of storytelling. Although many critics have agonized over the proper interpretation of this mysterious tale of Griselda, a woman so patient as to cause some readers to doubt her intelligence, or even her humanity and her sanity, Boccaccio offers her to us as an example of fame acquired in this world. It is clear that his sympathies are with Griselda, but the narrator never completely ignores the other, less noble aspects of the human condition, and his picture of humanity at the end of the ninth day returns to us once again for a brief moment as the narrator adds his own comment to the conclusion of Griselda's story: "It might have served Gualtieri right if he had run into the kind of woman who, once driven out of her home in nothing but a shift, would have allowed another man to shake her up to the point of getting herself a nice-looking dress out of the affair!"

Boccaccio attains an essential unity in his collection by using the same basic forces in this final day which were at work throughout *The Decameron:* Love, Intelligence, and Fortune. In the tenth day, however, the reader sees these fundamental forces in operation for the greater glory of mankind. These forces, viewed at different times from different levels in the first ninety-nine stories, are now seen in operation at the highest possible level in the tale of Griselda which concludes the entire collection. In Griselda's story, Fortune makes a poor peasant girl a lady of the court; Love changes Gualtieri and makes Griselda a heroine; and Intelligence suggests a means of testing Griselda to Gualtieri.[8] The concluding *novella* in the work thus sums up the three forces that have been seen in operation throughout the book and puts them through a magnificent workout.

Critics of Boccaccio's *Decameron* have often searched for a unifying element in the work. If there is *one* unifying factor in this complex masterpiece, one which is suggested by the forward progression of the tales as they move towards the illustration of a new terrestrial purpose for mankind defined in the final day of storytelling, it is love. In Boccaccio's fictional universe, every man or woman is what his or her love is. No matter what type of love it may be—love of oneself or of others, a good or an evil form of love—it is always love which puts the psyche into motion and spurs it to its end. It is love of self which moves the ten young people out of Florence and into the countryside to tell their stories. Every character they describe in the course of their hundred *novelle* is what his or her love is. Various kinds of love have set them into motion during the first nine days and have brought them to various ends. It is not until the tenth and last day that Boccaccio gives this moving force an ennobling end towards which it may aspire. And that end is "fama," or earthly glory. For Boccaccio, the achievement of fame through the performance of magnificent deeds represents the attainment of a kind of earthly immortality. The search for such a completely human goal is an implicit denial of Christian principles, yet Boccaccio offers this as a worthy goal, one which will ennoble the human spirit and which is fitting for great minds. In so doing, he reveals himself as the true precursor of the later and fuller expression of the attitude reflected in the works of men like Leon Battista Alberti, Leonardo da Vinci, Niccolò Machiavelli, and Benvenuto Cellini, individuals for whom no price was too high nor any sacrifice too great in the pursuit of earthly fame. In his classic definition of the essence of Italian civilization in the Renaissance, Jacob Burckhardt spoke of the idea of earthly fame as the outward manifestation of the development of a new individualism in Italy.[9] Boccaccio's vivid portrait of a complex humanity in action, of countless individual illustrations of "umane cose" thus serves to underline the diversity of the human being as he searches in an infinite number of ways to

8. Branca, *Boccaccio medievale*, p. 14.
9. *The Civilization of the Renaissance* *in Italy*, Irene Gordon, ed. (New York: New American Library, 1961), p. 128.

achieve an earthly fame which will compensate for the mutability of the human condition and act as a bastion against the ravages of time and death. It is just such an example of earthly mutability, unforgettably set before us in Boccaccio's opening description of the plague in Florence, which ultimately occasions the telling of the *novelle* by the ten storytellers. And it is as a purely human response to this terrifying state of affairs that Boccaccio offers his new ideal of fame—fame achieved by noble deeds—as a means of perpetuating one's memory.

Selected Bibliography

ENGLISH TRANSLATIONS OF BOCCACCIO'S WORKS

Amorous Fiammetta. Translated by Bartolomew Young. Westport, Conn.: The Greenwood Press, 1970.
Boccaccio on Poetry, Being the Preface and the Fourteenth and Fifteenth Books of Boccaccio's Genealogia Deorum Gentilium. Edited and translated by Charles G. Osgood. Indianapolis: Bobbs-Merrill, 1956.
The Book of Theseus: Teseida delle Nozze d'Emilia. Translated by Bernadette Marie McCoy. New York: Medieval Text Association, 1974.
Concerning Famous Women. Translated by Guido Guarino. New Brunswick: Rutgers University Press, 1963.
The Corbaccio. Translated by Anthony Cassell. Urbana: Illinois University Press, 1975.
The Decameron. Translated by Richard Aldington. New York: Dell, 1930.
The Decameron. Translated by G. A. McWilliams. Baltimore: Penguin, 1972.
The Decameron. Translated by Frances Winwar. New York: Modern Library, 1955.
The Fates of Illustrious Men. Translated by Louis Brewster Hall. New York: Ungar, 1965.
The Filostrato of Giovanni Boccaccio: A Translation with Parallel Text. Translated by N. E. Griffin and A. B. Myrick. New York: Biblo and Tannen, 1967.
The Nymph of Fiesole. Translated by Daniel J. Donno. New York: Columbia University Press, 1960.
Nymphs of Fiesole. Translated by Joseph Tusiani. Rutherford, N.J.: Fairleigh Dickinson University Press, 1971.
The Story of Troilus. Translated by R. K. Gordon. New York: Dutton, 1964. (Contains a translation of *Il Filostrato*.)

SELECTED STUDIES OF BOCCACCIO'S SOURCES AND HIS INFLUENCE

Beidler, Peter G. "Chaucer's *Merchant's Tale* and the *Decameron*." *Italica* 50 (1973), 266–84.
Deligiorgis, Stravros. "Boccaccio and the Greek Romances." *Comparative Literature* 19 (1967), 97–113.
Gathercole, Patricia M. "Boccaccio in French." *Studi sul Boccaccio* 5 (1968), 275–316.
———. "The French Translators of Boccaccio." *Italica* 46 (1969), 300–309.
Galgani, Giuseppe, ed. *Il Boccaccio nella cultura inglese e anglo-americana*. Florence: Olschki, 1974.
Lee, A. C. *The Decameron: Its Sources and Analogues*. New York: Haskell House, 1972.
Ricapito, Joseph V. "From Boccaccio to Mateo Alemán: An Essay on Literary Sources and Adaptations." *Romanic Review* 60 (1969), 83–95.
Wright, Herbert G. *Boccaccio in England from Chaucer to Tennyson*. London: The Athlone Press, 1957.

CRITICAL STUDIES OF BOCCACCIO'S *DECAMERON*

Almansi, Guido. *The Writer as Liar: Narrative Technique in The Decameron*. London: Routledge and Kegan Paul, 1975.
Bonadeo, Alfredo. "Some Aspects of Love and Nobility in the Society of *The Decameron*." *Philological Quarterly* 47 (1968), 513–25.
Branca, Vittore. *Boccaccio: The Man and His Works*, trans. Richard Monges (New York: New York University Press, 1976).
———. *Boccaccio medievale*. Florence: Sansoni, 1956.

————. "The Myth of the Hero in Boccaccio." In Norman T. Burns and Christopher Reagan, eds., *Concepts of the Hero in the Middle Ages and the Renaissance*. Albany: State University of New York Press, 1975.

Carswell, Catherine. *The Tranquil Heart: A Portrait of Giovanni Boccaccio*. London: Lawrence & Wishart, 1937.

Cerreta, Florindo. "La novella di Andreuccio: problemi di unità e d'interpretazione." *Italica* 47 (1970), 255–64.

Chubb, Thomas Caldecott. *The Life of Giovanni Boccaccio*. London: Cassell, 1930.

Clubb, Louise G. "Boccaccio and the Boundaries of Love." *Italica* 37 (1960), 188–96.

Corrigan, Beatrice, ed. *Italian Poets and English Critics, 1755–1859: A Collection of Critical Essays*. Chicago: University of Chicago Press, 1969.

Cottino-Jones, Marga. *An Anatomy of Boccaccio's Style*. Naples: Cymba, 1968.

————. "Magic and Superstition in Boccaccio's *Decameron*." *Italian Quarterly* 18 (1975), 5–32.

Deligiorgis, Stavros. *Narrative Intellection in the Decameron*. Iowa City: University of Iowa Press, 1975.

Dombroski, Robert S., ed. *Critical Perspectives on The Decameron*. New York: Barnes and Noble, 1976.

Getto, Giovanni. *Vita di forme e forme di vita nel Decameron*. Turin: Petrini, 1958.

Gibaldi, Joseph. "Towards a Definition of the Novella." *Studies in Short Fiction* 12 (1975), 91–98.

Greene, Thomas M. "Forms of Accommodation in the *Decameron*." *Italica* 45 (1968), 297–313.

Hastings, R. *Nature and Reason in The Decameron*. Manchester: Manchester University Press, 1975.

Hauvette, Henri. *Boccace, étude biographique et littéraire*. Paris: Colin, 1914.

Kern, Edith. "The Gardens in the *Decameron* Cornice." *PMLA* 66 (1951), 505–23.

Krutch, Joseph Wood. *Five Masters: A Study in the Mutations of the Novel*. New York: Cape and Smith, 1930.

Layman, B. J. "Boccaccio's Paradigm of the Artist and His Art." *Italian Quarterly* 13 (1970), 19–36.

————. "Eloquence of Pattern in Boccaccio's Tale of the Falcon." *Italica* 46 (1969), 3–16.

Lepschy, Anna Laura. "Boccaccio Studies in English 1945–1969." *Studi sul Boccaccio* 6 (1971), 211–30.

Lipari, Angelo. "The Structure and Real Significance of the *Decameron*." In Henri Peyre, ed., *Essays in Honor of Albert Feuillerat*. New Haven: Yale University Press, 1943.

MacManus, Francis. *Boccaccio*. New York: Sheed & Ward, 1947.

Mazzotta, Giuseppe. "The *Decameron*: The Literal and the Allegorical." *Italian Quarterly* 18 (1975), 53–73.

————. "The *Decameron*: The Marginality of Literature." *University of Toronto Quarterly* 42 (1972), 64–81.

Moravia, Alberto. "Boccaccio." In *Man as an End: A Defense of Humanism*. New York: Farrar, Straus & Giroux, 1966.

Rotunda, Dominic P. *Motif-Index of the Italian Novella in Prose*. Bloomington: Indiana University Folklore Series, No. 2, 1942.

Russo, Luigi, *Letture critiche del Decameron*. Bari: Laterza, 1973.

Schilling, Bernard N. *The Comic Spirit: Boccaccio to Thomas Mann*. Detroit: Wayne State University Press, 1965.

Singleton, Charles S. "On Meaning in The *Decameron*." *Italica* 21 (1944), 117–24.

Sklovskij, Victor. *Lettura del Decameron*. Milan: Il Mulino, 1969.

Studi sul Boccaccio. Florence: 1963–.

Todorov, Tzvetan. *Grammaire du Décameron*. The Hague: Mouton, 1969.

NORTON CRITICAL EDITIONS